make the world
a stylish place
SEAGRAM'S
BLENDERS
PRIDE
Fashion Tour
Music CDs.

DANCE
EAT
PARTY
LIVE
Orbits is the largest and most happening discotheque in the central suburbs of Mumbai. It offers the latest audio & lightning system with the in-house DJ playing mind blowing mixes that suit every mood.
The beverage list features a selection of wines, cocktails and premium spirits and liqueurs. Do not miss out on the various events at Orbits.
PANORAMIC GROUP
UNITED-21
4-star hotel and lifestyle club
THANE
Orbits
DISCOTHEQUE
29, LBS Marg, Gokul Nagar, Thane (W) - 400 601 | Tel.: 022 4157 9999
Email: info@united21.in | orbits@united21.in

SOMEONE HAD TO BREW
SOMETHING ABOUT IT!
SO WE WENT FORWARD AND OPENED
THE FIRST MICRO BREWERY IN MUMBAI!
IMPOSSIBLE HAPPENS
AT THE BARKING DEER BREWPUB
BARKING DEER

TIMES NIGHTLIFE GUIDE

Bars . Nightclubs . Party Halls . Cocktails . The Great Bar Guide . Night Eatabouts

Mumbai

2014

RASHMI UDAY SINGH

timescity.com

Editorial team
Abhilasha Aggarwal

Design team
Subhasish Munshi
Balkishan Verma
Jitender Kumar

Project editor
Madhulita Mohanty

Production
Neeraj Bharti

Advertising enquiries
mumbai@timescity.com

Times Nightlife Guide: Mumbai

Ninth Edition 2014

Published by
Bennett, Coleman & Co. Ltd.,
New Delhi

Times Group Books

Times Group Books
(A division of Bennett, Coleman and Company Limited)
Times Annexe, 9-10, Bahadur Shah Zafar Marg, New Delhi-110002

Printed at: Paras Offset Pvt. Ltd.

Price: ₹100

CONTENTS

Author's Note 4
How to Use This Guide 5
Acknowledgements 7
Pick of the Guide 8

Mumbai by Night

Bars and Nightclubs 15
Ice Cream & Juice Parlours 114
Party Makers 132
Party Halls 156

The Great Bar Guide

A Beginner's Guide to Champagne 180
Wine? Cheers! My Introduction to Wine 183
A Beginner's Guide to Beer 185
A Beginner's Guide to Single Malt 190
A Beginner's Guide to Cognac 193
A Beginner's Guide to Sake 195
A to Z of Wine Terms 198
Setting up a Bar at Home 201
Cocktail Recipes, Tips and Guidelines 203
Eric Lobo's Cocktail Recipes 205
Shatbhi Basu's Cocktail Recipes 207
A Mix of Recipes from Mumbai's Bars 214
Wine-based Cocktails 220
Shooters 221
Pairing Indian Food with Wine 223
Fine Wines for Profit & Pleasure — Wine as an Investment 229
Music 233

Night Eatabouts — Street Eatabouts 238
Open 24 Hours 244
Late-night Eatabouts 246
Indices 272

Maps

About the Author

AUTHOR'S NOTE

Come get drunk with me. And that too without a drop of alcohol. Excuse me if I'm bleary-eyed, it's because in order to be updated, I've been on my all-night final weekend rounds (completely unannounced). I do this every year for this Times Nightlife Guide Mumbai. Each year, it's my young companions (who know the night scene really well) who guide me. I also hang about with strangers and get their views. Read on and you'll find yourself doing just that.

Let's raise a toast to the eternal temptress... she's Mumbai by Night. She lures with her *mujra* of glamour and poverty. She seduces with her throbbing and insistent continuous theatre of nightlife... be it the grotty Dadar station where Babban's peddles his steaming hot chocolate-chai in a short, clunky glass or the *garma garam* kebabs at the streetside Ayub's. The nightclubs are swanky, the babes slinky, the state-of-the-art lights and music enter your soul. Poverty and glamour do a macabre Mumbai *mujra* which is even more visible at night. But what a night!

Here's a quick peek into what follows in the book:

Bars & Nightclubs: Mega-wattage energy pumps up Mumbai's nightscape. Great news! After last years "thanda" scene, I am happy to report that Mumbai's nightlife has started rocking and is on steroids. The even better news is that both North and South Mumbai have begun to rock.

They're notoriously fickle... they close and they reopen, and they even reinvent themselves. All are alphabetically listed and rated on the "Buzz" and "Décor" factor.

Chicken Sanju Baba and Late Night Eating: Here's the rescue remedy for late-night hunger pangs. *Rasta ka stalls*. These are surprisingly popular even with the well-to-do (Amlait Bhurji, Kebabiyas, etc). I have covered them area-wise (please forgive me if they've been carried off by the municipality van). Food tastes very different when it's cooked and served on the streets at night. Check out Chicken Sanju Baba in Bhendi Bazaar (Sanju Dutt's favourite, hence, the name). From street-side eateries to the 16,000sq ft restaurant in Bhendi Bazaar, I've included them all here, for you.

A listing of 24-hour coffee shops and restaurants open till late is also included.

The Ultimate Party Kit: From live musicians to ventriloquists, bar managers, fireworks, customized balloons, home-delivered ice... *et al.*

Cheers! The Great Bar Guide: Here's a guide for the home-bartender. Making cocktails at home can add a real zing to your evening. I have included guidelines that I have picked up from bartenders and from two of our city's most respected bar-managers: Eric Lobo and Shatbhi Basu. There are cocktail recipes from the landmark bartenders of the city too.

The Beginner's Guide To: Everything you always wanted to know but were too busy (or did not know who) to ask. From how to store wine to tasting notes on sake, to what's house music. Snappy chapters on The Beginner's Guides... to champagne, sake, beer, wine, and cognac.

Note: You've got to be an insider to be a part of the night, my friend. And that's where the book steps in. Sure, the official closing hour of stand-alone bars and nightclubs is 1.30am and many law-abiding places do down their shutters, still others stay open, behind those shutters. Turn the pages for details and information to help you navigate the night.

Enjoy! Have a good night (in every single way)!

Keep smiling
Rashmi ☺

Rashmi Uday Singh

PS: Do share with me your favourite night places. Looking forward to hearing from you. Should you want to accompany me (provided you're a regular bar and nightclubber), please mail to me at *rashmiudaysingh2014@gmail.com*, or connet at #rashmiudaysingh.

HOW TO USE THIS GUIDE

Come enjoy the night... here are my tips and guidelines to do so...

1 Bars & Nightclubs
2 It's Party Time, folks... Party Halls & Party Makers
3 The Great Bar Guide
4 Where to eat after the party? Late-night Eatabouts

Hit the one which suits you most. And then all of them.

1 You can use this book to navigate the city's bars and nightlife (details follow, below).
2 It's party time folks... where to party? How to organize on your own? In these pages, you will find very useful information on party halls, party makers and wine shops.
3 The great bar guide: Make your party a heady success! You can learn to set up your bar at home, to shake your own cocktails and even get beginner's tips on wine, champagne and more (please see the chapters).
4 Late-night eatabouts to hit after the party.

Bars & Nightclubs: An alphabetical listing of bars, lounge bars, and discotheques, accompanied by reviews... an attempt to recreate the experience for you. These point out the drinks, cocktails, snacks, Happy Hours, and DJs too.

The addresses and telephone numbers appear right below the review, as also the Map Reference, where applicable. For example, this would mean that at Café Oval, which is a Resto-Bar, the buzz has been rated as 3.50 and the décor at 1.50. The cost of a Nightout for Two is ₹1,000 and the map reference would be map 1 number 3 on that map. You will find the maps at the back of the book.

Name | Category | Ratings | Review | Timings | Icons

Café Oval
RESTO-BAR
Buzz-3.50 | Décor-1.50 | Nightout for 2-₹500

AC
9am to 11pm

Cheap and cheerful! A boon for the serious beer drinker. This no-frills bar (centrally located opposite Oval) serves only beer and cheap eats: omelettes and chana. Transformed from an Irani joint to a beer shop when the government relaxed the prohibition laws, it still retains that functional look. It serves quite a few beer varieties such as Golden Eagle, London Pilsner, Foster's, good ol Kingfisher and others. And yes, it serves only beer. Its snacks include Cheese Sandwich, Omelettes and others. Check out their Bhurji Bread, Chana Dal, Moong Dal and sandwiches. It has a great location and since its food and drinks are pretty affordable, regulars continue to throng this place.

■ **Kambatta Bldg., Near Eros Cinema, Maharishi Karve Marg, Churchgate, Mumbai, Ph: 66345721, M1-3**

Address | Phone No. | Map Ref.

Rating: The Buzz index has been created to rate these: it indicates the current popularity of the place, while the décor ratings help you decide whether or not you'd like to visit the place and with whom.

1	POOR
1.50	Average –
2	AVERAGE
2.50	Average +
3	GOOD
3.50	Good +
4	VERY GOOD
4.50	V.Good +
5	EXCELLENT

Rating Scale: Each Buzz and Décor rating has been given on a maximum scale of 5. We have gone to great lengths to devise a rating system that fine-tunes the structure as accurately as possible. Every number between 1 and 5 has two variables to it. These would find reflection in the buzz index as well as the décor. The first grid explains this rating system in detail. The parameters are listed in the panel above the reviews, through the guide.

Other Info: Details of how much a nightout for two would cost you and a map reference are also included. In order to help you navigate these places better, they have been divided under "Bars", "Resto-bar" (Bar with restaurant), "Bar with Live Music" and "Discotheque/Nightclub". The icons that appear along with this information indicate whether or not the place has an AC and whether credit cards are accepted. The icons are:

Air-conditioned: [AC]

Credit Card Accepted:

Liquor Served:

Nightout for Two: This figure could be wildly inaccurate and hinge on your choice of alcohol. It's an educated guesstimate at best. Please allow for a variation. A bit tough to calculate the cost of two averagepriced drinks and a couple of snacks. At least, we have tried...

Pick of the Guide: Turn to the Pick of the Guide for a quick look at the top in each category.

Indices: The back of the book lists exhaustive cross indices of all the above chapters. These comprehensive cross-references have been made to enable you to use this guide more effectively and accurately, in order to access the information you require immediately. Exhaustive indices help you navigate the guide faster. Area-wise, zone-wise, and category-wise, too. So what are you waiting for? Enjoy!

ACKNOWLEDGEMENTS

I dedicate this three-volume set (triplets) to the universe's most fantastically creative gourmet... to God, who tempts us with appetite and then rewards us with pleasure. He protects, guides and makes my life a delicious miracle!

Impossible to produce the triplets without guidance, hard work, dedication and perseverance... and giving all those invaluable inputs were...

- Vineet Jain and Trishla Jain
- Sidhant Khosla, Sanjay Bhatnagar and Madhulita Mohanty
- **Editorial:** Abhilasha Aggarwal
- **Design:** Balkishan Verma & Jitender Kumar

How do I find the words to thank...
Sunayan Shahani, Sameer Malkani, Shanti Padukone, Prachi Joshi, Prachi Patange, Kumar Jhuremalani, Devika Manjrekar, Divisha, Pallavi & Gaurav, Fantara Roy, Anuja Deora, Samina Patel, Gitanjali Diwan, Roxanne, Nishant Gauli, Delnavaz, Kalyan, and Vishal and Apeksha.

Thanks to my wonderful family for bearing with my workaholic ways and for cheering me on. And to Vikas Bhatkar for working tirelessly.

Finally, I end with my wish for all of you who helped cook up all three books... "May God make your life (like He has mine) a series of miracles punctuated by great lunches and dinners."

Keep smiling
Rashmi ☺

Rashmi Uday Singh

BEST OF MUMBAI

PICK OF THE GUIDE

BEST BARS

Aer .19
The Beachcomber .25
China House .36
The Daily .39
Dome .41
Elbo Room .44
Harry's .58
Ivy Bar & Bistro .63
The Lazy Dog .67
Li Bai .68
Three Wise Men .103
Tote Bar .104
Wink .111

BEST BARS WITH DANCING

The Big Nasty .26
The Blue Frog Club .27
Bonobo .29
China House .36
Copa .38
D'Bell .43
The Eau Bar .43
Escobar .46
The Ghetto .53
Hard Rock Café .57
The Local .71
Loca Loca .70
Or-G .81
3 Wise Monkeys .103
Toto's Garage .104

BEST NIGHTCLUBS

Club Alibi .37
F Bar .46
Fever – The Night Club .47
Kino 108 .65
Liv .69
Or-G .81
Ren by China Garden .89
Rock Bottom .89
Royalty .90
Trilogy .106
Tryst .106

BEST RESTO-BARS

Amadeus .20
Big Bang café .26
Cheval .36
Hakkasan .56
Irish House .62
Olive Bar & Kitchen .79
Shiro .94
Yauatcha .113

BEST BAR WITH A VIEW

Aer .19
Arola .21
Aurus .23
Dome .41
The Eau Bar .43
Gallops .51
Li Bai .68

BEST AMBIANCE — RESTO-BAR

Aurus .23
Cheval .36
The Local .71
Hakkasan .56
Olive RWITC .79
Shiro .94

BEST AMBIANCE — NIGHTCLUB

China House .36
Club Alibii .37
Liv .69
Or-G .81
Rock Bottom .89
Trilogy .106
Tryst .106

BEST AMBIANCE — BAR

6 Degrees .17
Aer .19
The Beachcomber .25
Champagne Lounge .35
Geoffrey's .52
Tote Bar .104
Wink .111

BEST FOR LIVE BANDS

A Bar .18
The Blue Frog Club .27
Bombay High .28
Hard Rock Café .57
Merlin's .74

NOTEWORTHY NEWCOMERS

Cheval .36
Club Alibii .37
Copa .38
D'Bell .43
The Daily .39
Harry's .58
The Lazy Dog .67
Li Bai .68
The Local .71
Loca Loca .70

BEST FOR CELEBWATCHING

Aurus .23
China House .36
Indigo .61
Olive Bar & Kitchen .79
Ren by China Garden .89
Royalty .90

Tote Bar 104
Yauatcha 113

BARS FOR ENTERTAINING BUSINESS ASSOCIATES

Aer 19
The Daily 39
Dublin .42
Geoffrey's 52
Harbour Bar 57
Indigo .61
Jewel of India 64
The Lazy Dog 67
Lounge Bar 72
Olive Bar & Kitchen 79
Olive RWITC 79
Opium Den 81

PICK OF THE GUIDE: DELHI/NCR (2014)

BEST BARS

7° Brauhaus
blueFROG
Cocktails & Dreams
Easy
Flying Saucer Café, The
Fork You
Hard Rock Café
Library, The
Megu Bar
Mix Lounge and Bar
Nom Nom
Olive Bar & Kitchen
PCO
Piano Bar
Polo Lounge
Rick's
Rubicon Bar
S Bar & Restaurant — Shalom
Shiro
Striker Pub & Brewery
Striker Pub & Kitchen
Tease
T.G.I. Friday's
Threesixty°
Underdoggs Sports Bar & Grill
Warehouse Café

BEST LOUNGE BARS

@ Links
Aqua
B Bar
Easy
Piano Bar
Polo Lounge
S Bar & Restaurant — Shalom
Sky Bar

BARS WITH BEST AMBIENCE

Amour
Aqua
B Bar
Blue Bar, The
Dirty Martini, The
Enoteca Wine Bar
Fio — Cookhouse & Bar
Keya
Library, The
Magique
Mix Lounge and Bar
Nom Nom
Piano Bar
Polo Lounge
Rubicon Bar
Sevilla
Shiro
Sky Bar

MOST ROMANTIC BARS

Aqua
Chéri One Qutub
Lodi — The Garden Restaurant
Magique
Sevilla
Sky Bar

BEST THEME BARS

Golf Bar
Hard Rock Café
Howzatt
Ice Lounge
Orient Express
Polo Lounge
Revv Café
Striker Pub & Brewery
Underdoggs Sports Bar & Grill

BEST OUTDOOR BARS

1911
Amour
Aqua
Blue Bar, The
Keya
Lodi — The Garden Restaurant
Magique
Olive Bar and Kitchen
Olive Beach
Sevilla
Sky Bar

BEST BARS WITH DANCING

Agni
Barrique
blueFROG
Hard Rock Café
Mojo's
Shiro
Urban Knights

BEST DISCOTHEQUE/ NIGHTCLUB

blueFROG
G Bar
Kitty Su
LAP
Quantum — The Leap
Skooter

BEST BEER BARS

7° Brauhaus
Beer Café, The
Howzatt
Lemp Brewpub & Kitchen
Manhattan — The Craft Brewery
Pint Room, The
Striker Pub & Brewery
Soi 7
Underdoggs Sports Bar & Grill

BEST BARS FOR SINGLES

1911
B Bar
Keya
Polo Lounge
PCO
Shiro
Sky Bar
Smoke House Deli

BEST BARS FOR QUIET CONVERSATION

1911
Club Bar
Golf Bar
Kylin
Polo Lounge
Pomodoro
Sartoria
Savannah Bar
Threesixty°

BEST FOR ROCK MUSIC

100% Rock
Café Morisson
Hard Rock Café
Striker Pub & Brewery
Turquoise Cottage

NOTEWORTHY NEWCOMERS

Cocktails & Dreams
Flying Saucer Café, The
Fork You
Manhattan — The Craft Brewery
Skooter
Striker Pub & Kitchen
Soi 7
Tease
Warehouse Café

PICK OF THE GUIDE: BANGALORE (2014)

BEST ALFRESCO BARS

13th Floor Lounge Bar, The
Skyye

BEST BARS/PUBS

Blue Bar
Dublin
Durbar
Highland Nectar
Library Bar
Monkey Bar

BEST BREWPUBS

Arbor Brewing Company
Barleyz
Biere Club, The
Prost
Windmills Craftworks

BEST LOUNGE BARS

Liquid Lounge and Bar
M Bar
Sutra — The Lounge

BEST RESTO-BARS

Geoffrey's
Hard Rock Café
Shiro
Tavern Inn

PICK OF THE GUIDE: CHENNAI (2014)

BEST BARS

365 AS
Blend
Cheroot Malt and Cigar Lounge, The
Durrant's Bar
Elevate
Leather Bar
Library Blu
Madera
Q Bar
Vintage Bank
Westminister, The

BEST RESTO-BAR

10 Downing Street
Bike and Barrel
Fusion 9
Illusions -The Madras Pub
Zara

BEST BAR WITH A VIEW

High Sky Lounge
Library Blu
Q Bar

BEST BAR FOR BUSINESS ASSOCIATES

Cheroot Malt and Cigar Lounge, The
Dome, The
Durrant's Bar
Gallop
Vintage Bank
Westminister, The

BEST NIGHTCLUBS

Dublin
Elevate
Flying Elephant, The
Havana — The Club
High Time
Pasha

PICK OF THE GUIDE: GOA (2014)

BEST BAR: NORTH

Café Mambo's
Café Mojo
Cape Town Café
Capiz Bar
Cavala
Down The Road
High Tide Bar
Hype
Malts & Wines
Taverna
Tease

BEST BAR: SOUTH

Adega Cameoes
Edge Bar
Jazz Inn
Leda
Pentagon
Fins & Rambooze
Sagres
Sun Downer Bar

BEST LOUNGE BAR: NORTH

A Reverie
Az u r
Cantare
Chili n Spice
Club Cubana
Drift
LPK Waterfront
Marbela Beach
Mekong
Peace — The Bar
Sfx
SinQ

BEST LOUNGE BAR: SOUTH

Boat Quay Grill
Boomerang — The Down Under Bar
Edge Bar
Joecon's Garden Restaurant
Praia de Luz
Sagres
Tangerine

BEST NIGHTCLUBS/ DISCOTHEQUE: NORTH

Café Mambo's
Cape Town Café
Club Cubana
Club Tito's
Curlies Bar & Restaurant
Hilltop
Hype
Kamaki
LPK Waterfront
Nine Bar
SinQ

BEST NIGHTCLUBS/ DISCOTHEQUE: SOUTH

Café del Mar
Club Margarita
Titos@Radisson

BEST NIGHTLIFE WITH LIVE MUSIC: NORTH

Cavala

Down the Road
L'Orange
Malts & Wines
Marbela Beach
Peace — The Bar
Souza Lobo
Sofala, The
Taverna

BEST NIGHTLIFE WITH LIVE MUSIC: SOUTH

Joecon's Garden Restaurant
Leda
Nostalgia
Pentagon

BEST SHACK BAR: NORTH

Calamari
Curlies Bar & Restaurant
Flying Dolphin
Zanzibar

BEST SHACK BAR: SOUTH

Café del Mar
Lobster Shack
Palms
Susegado

PICK OF THE GUIDE: KOLKATA (2014)

BEST BARS/ PUBS

The Bar
The Chowringhee Bar
The Junction (Taj Bengal)
West View Bar & Grill (ITC Sonar)

BEST NIGHTCLUB

9F
Nocturne
Tantra
Underground

BEST LOUNGE BAR

Nirvana
Plush
Shisha Reincarnated

BARS WITH BEST COCKTAILS

Roxy
The Tapas Bar
Venom

BEST ALFRESCO BAR

Afraa Lounge
Aqua
Splash

BARS WITH BEST LIVE ENTERTAINMENT

The Basement
Backstage
Someplace Else

BARS/PUBS WITH BEST AMBIENCE

The Junction
Roxy
Someplace Else
Westview Bar & Grill

PICK OF THE GUIDE: JAIPUR (2014)

ALFRESCO BARS

3D — De-Mount/Déjàvu
Jharokha
Latitude
Nostradamus
Palki Bar
Tablu

BARS WITH BEST AMBIENCE

Amigo
Angara
Aza
B2B
Chukkar Bar & Lounge
Madeira Bar
Mansagar Bar
Marigold
Palki Bar
Shikarbadi Bar
Tablu
100% Rock
TFB

BARS/PUB WITH DANCING

Amigo
Angara
B2B
100% Rock
TFB

BEST BARS/PUBS

Bar Bar
Hardy's Pub

Henry's Pub
Liquid Ice
Madeira Bar
Marigold
Salsa
Shikarbadi Bar
Sunset Bar
Tablu

BEST LOUNGE BARS

Deck, The
Den, The
Grunge
Kasbah
Lounge 18
Nostradamus
Riva

LOBBY BARS

Hightz Bar
Madhushala
Mansagar Bar
Scarlet
Aza

PICK OF THE GUIDE: CHANDIGARH (2013)

BEST BARS/PUBS

Brio
Down Under
Hops n' Grains
Tao
Whisky 111

BEST RESTO-BARS

Crystal
Dak Bungalow
Orchid Lounge
Peddlars

BEST LOUNGE BARS

10 Downing Street
Black Magic
Blue Blazer
Kava
Lounge, The
S Lounge
Satva
Tao

BAR WITH DANCING

Aerizzona
S Lounge
Tao

BEST COCKTAILS

Hops n' Grains
Kava
Lounge, The
Tao
Whisky 111

PICK OF THE GUIDE: HYDERABAD (2013)

BEST RESTOBAR

10 Lounge & Night Club
1857
Aqua
Coco's
N — A Modern Grill
Syn Asian Grill & Bar

BEST PUBS

10 Downing Street
Bottles & Chimney
Cuba Libre
Dublin
Firangi Paani

BEST LOUNGE BAR

Altitude
The Bar, The
The Bar, The
Johnnie Walker Lounge
Marco Polo
Mix
Tease

BEST NIGHTCLUB

Club, The
Kismet
Rain

PICK OF THE GUIDE: PUNE (2013)

BEST BAR

Entresol
Fishbowl, The
Hard Rock Café
High Spirits
Kue Bar
Mix@36
Paasha
Single Malt & Co
Swig

BEST RESTO BAR

1000 Oaks
High Spirits
Terrtulia
Trikaya

BEST LOUNGE BARS

1 – The Lounge
Curve
Fish Bowl
Mix@36
Oakwood Lounge
Paasha
Single Malt & Co.
Trikaya

NIGHT CLUB

Area 51
Kue Bar
Mi-a- mi
Scream

BEST OPEN-AIR BAR

1000 Oaks
Fishbowl, The
High Spirits
Paasha
Penthouze
Trikaya

BEST AMBIENCE

1000 Oaks
Fishbowl, The
High Spirits
Kue Bar
Mi-a-Mi
Paasha
Shisha Café

BEST BAR WITH LIVE MUSIC

Hard Rock Café
High Sprits
Shisha Café

BEST BAR FOR YOUNG PEOPLE

1 – The Lounge
1000 Oaks
Area 51
Hard Rock Café
High Spirits

MUMBAI BY NIGHT

- Bars & Nightclubs
- Ice Cream & Juice Parlours
- Party Makers
- Party Halls

Fun-times ahead! Calling all night owls and party birds... come join me as I whizz you through North and South Mumbai's latest (and not-so-latest) bars and nightclubs. In order to be updated, I do these final weekend rounds (completely unannounced) every year for this Times Nightlife Guide Mumbai. *Each year, it's my young companions (who know the night scene really well), who guide me. I also hang about with strangers and get their views. Great news! After last year's "thanda" scene, I am happy to report that Mumbai's nightlife has started rocking and is on steroids.*

The even better news is that both North and South Mumbai have begun to rock. From the setting up of the highest bar ever (Li Bai on the 37th floor of Palladium Hotel) to the Cuban-themed Loca Loca and the Spanish-themed Copa (with alfresco swings and bar tables) open up. Old favourites like Trilogy reopen and Royalty rocks.

In dagger-shaped Mumbai's southern most tip, Club Alibi opens (replacing Ghost which replaced Privé) and revs up the scene. Kala Ghoda's Liv continues to throb to packed houses and right next to it, Cheval sets up with its bar scene. Injecting South Mumbai with a deliberately grungy look is The Local, a small, dimly lit, split-level room with industrial unfinished wood, exposed water pipes and Banksy's street art splattered all over. It's casual and relaxed and even has Sunday jam sessions. The Lazy Dog and Bottle Bar set up in the Fort business district.

Suddenly, the Lower Parel area starts buzzing with life... White Owl, and the latest, most publicized opening of D'Bell takes place as the book goes to press.

Tryst continues to rock the Phoenix Mills while Li Bai raises the bar (literally) by perching itself on the 37th floor. Trader Vic's Mai Tai opens in the mall right next to it. Andheri's resto bar Levo sprawls in 20,000sq ft restaurant. Andheri's casual Jam Jar Diner, Bandra's 3 Wise Monkeys rock as do Or-G.

But then bars and nightclubs are known to be notoriously fickle... they close and they reopen, and they even reinvent themselves. They're all here! All alphabetically listed and rated on the "buzz" and "décor" factor. This chapter bristles with the really small, serious boozy joints too where I hangout with taxi drivers and learn all about the "quarter" and the "paoli" system. Go on! Check out this heady section and you'll find that it's not just alcohol which gives that high!

PS: As the book goes to press, many new bars and nightclubs are about to open, Exo in the Palladium, Long and Short – A Gastro Bar in The InterContinental while Hype downs its shutters. Bandra's Shockk, shocks with its desolate spaces.

Note: Just so that you get the point about how far North the action has shifted... Powaii is where Singapore-based pub chain, Harry's, sets up as the book goes to press.

3 Wise Monkeys

Bar with Dancing Noon to 1.30am

Buzz-3.50 | Décor-3.00 | Nightout for 2-₹3000

I go past cows in the middle of the desolate Khar side streets and walk right into the rocking, noisy and air-conditioned year-and-a-half old bar of the UniContinental hotel. It has mastered the time-tested formula of a casual and relaxed vibe with cheap booze. Wooden wall panels, furniture and even the ceiling is clad in wood. Waiters buzz around wearing colourful, large hats and even share them with us as the music tempo builds up. Guests start dancing and swaying as "Papa Americano" blares. Beer barrels (mini 2.5 and 5litre beer barrels; ₹675 and ₹1,600) are in huge demand. Indian and international spirits at super reasonable prices (small Teacher's for ₹150, Grey Goose for ₹200). There's also a list of international beer, mix of *chatpata* snacks do the rounds, portion of Crispy Chilli Potato and refried fries, Jalapeño Poppers and the like. Kebabs, fries and tikkas along with mains of Chinese and pasta too. Food is obviously not the focal point in this open-through-the-day, popular hotspot with its mix of age-groups here.

SPECIAL NIGHTS: Karaoke Nights: Sunday and Wednesday, Live Band Night: Thursday (9pm onwards)

■ **The UniContinental, 3rd Road, Off SV Road, Khar (W), Mumbai, Ph: 65610325-26, M3** 37

6 Degrees

Bar 5pm to 1.30am

Buzz-2.50 | Décor-3.50 | Nightout for 2-₹6000

It maybe named after the perfect temperature for champagne, but there is nothing scientific or cut and dried about this glamorous venue at The Leela hotel. Champange-and-vodka walls, mysterious lighting and sheers in the relaxed wooden interiors. Add to this a lit-up fountain, waterfall, palm trees and gazebo kitchen dazzling the outdoors. Champagne cocktails and Vodka Martinis are the stars at this stylish venue. With a whopping 32 varieties, the Vodka Caipiroska with Raspberry thrills. Scotch, malt whiskies and wines by the glass too. The favourite martinis here include Tamarind, Apple and Watermelon. Try the Choco or Lemondrop for a difference. Black Russian, Kamakaze, Suzy Wong and Masquerade are popular too. Other speciality drinks include Long Island Ice Tea and Lemon Grass Martini. Nibble on the complementary Salty or Masala Peanuts, or choose from popular Indian starters (Chicken Tikka, Murgh Seekh Kebab), Continental (live barbecue counter between Sept and May) or Chinese (Crab Meat Dim Sum, Crystal Veg Dumplings). DJ Vineet Dave will keep you entertained with his unique blend of house and lounge music. With the introduction of Poolside Barbecue recently, it has added a new dimension to Six Degrees.

HAPPY HOURS: 6pm to 9pm; Buy one, get one free!

■ **The Leela Mumbai, Andheri-Kurla Road, Andheri (E), Sahar, Mumbai, Ph: 66911333, M4** 1

72

SPORTS & LOUNGE BAR 6pm to 1am

Buzz-3.50 | Décor-3.50 | Nightout for 2-₹5000

A coffee bar by day and a cocktail bar by night... that's 72 for you! Either way, both are great! A live band playing Jazz, Rock, Pop and other compositions will keep you spell bound in Holiday Inn's cosy bar just off its gleaming lobby. On game nights, tune in to the LCD and plonk yourself on a barstool or settle in a comfortable king-sized sofa chair. Order anything from wine (a varied global collection), champagne, aperitifs, or Single Malts (Glemorangie and Oban, 14 years are popular) in this bar with casual, brown couches with velvet touches, and warm wooden tones. Its exclusive cocktails and mocktails with the choicest range of brews, blends, concoctions will make the good times even better!! Espressotini or Paan Masala with Eristoff Vodka? For those who like the mainstays, there is B52 and Irish Coffee too. Check out their signature drink, Mojito Royale, which has ginger topped off with sparkling wine. Other favourites here include Twisted Mai Tai and the Red Corvette (Red Wine Cosmopolitan). Even their signature special rum-based cocktail B72 is good. One pint of beer here costs ₹299, and wine by the glass starts at ₹499. If you're in a snacky mood, choose from Saptami's street food menu, which has everything from Dahi Batata Puri to Pao Bhaji (live counter on alternate days). More substantial options include Cajun-spiced Buffalo Fries, Chilli-blasted Baby Corn, Tawa-fried Fish, Crispy Lamb with Honey Chilli Sauce and Mandarin Hot Garlic Chicken.

SPECIAL NIGHTS: Karaoke Nights: Thursdays, 8pm to midnight

■ **Holiday Inn, Saki Naka Junction, Andheri-Kurla Road, Andheri (E), Mumbai, Ph: 40851800, 40851894, M4** 2

A Bar

LOBBY BAR 11am to 1am

Buzz-2.50 | Décor-3.00 | Nightout for 2-₹5000

Instrumental music lilts in the background complimenting the serene backdrop of Powai Lake making this lobby bar a perfect place for business meetings. Single malts, cognacs and cocktails (try their Tikka Peru, a vodka-based twist of Bloody Mary) make the rounds. Drinks are served with cashew nuts, peanuts, almonds and Bingo chips. There are 20 options in all on the menu. Some of the dishes on the menu are Calamari Tempura, Buffalo Chicken Wings, Seekh Kebab, Murgh Tikka and Paneer Tikka! The well-stocked bar offers a wide range of international and domestic choices for hard liquor and cool cocktails like Bull Frog, Shade Aide and Knockout. Their signature drinks include Bombay Martini or Paantini. Teetotalers, Prince Charming and Berry Sweetheart, all mocktails!

■ **Renaissance Hotel & Convention Centre, 2&3-B, Powai, Mumbai, Ph: 66927570/8888, M4** 3

Adarsh Bar & Restaurant

RESTO-BAR Noon to 4pm, 7pm to Midnight

Buzz-1.00 | Décor-1.00 | Nightout for 2-₹1000

You have tubelight and television for company, but no windows or air-conditioning. It's all about liquor at rock-bottom prices at Adarsh, Chembur's cheap and cheerful watering hole. Be prepared for plastic crockery, brown rexine upholstery and sunmica tabletops. Fish Tawa Fry Green Masala, were told was good here. There's the same masala with surmai, pomfret or bangra. No imported alcohol but a fair variety in domestic. Pair with Masala Peanuts or papad, Chicken Satay, Prawns Koliwada, Crabs/Prawns in Butter Garlic or Fish Hariyali. This Chembur watering hole also holds live musical events once in a while, which is not bad.

■ Balkrishna Centre, NG Acharya Marg, Near Chembur Railway Station, Chembur (E), Mumbai, Ph: 25214441

Aer

ROOFTOP BAR, LOUNGE BAR 5.30pm to 12.30am

Buzz-4.50 | Décor-4.50 | Nightout for 2-₹8000

Oooh la la... what energy and buzz here. I zoom up to the 34th floor of the Four Seasons Hotel on a saturday night, just as the book goes to press. Star-spangled (sometimes smoggy) sky above and a glittering 360-degree city view below. Both the sections (the sea view and the city view side are packed). I pop in here at 2.30am and the tempo of the music has already built up. This is as close as you get to heaven in our city of high rises and crammed spaces! Go to this bar and enjoy high stratospheres (with prices to match). Multi-coloured scanners and laser beams colour as the large sign of the Four Seasons Hotel gleams above, reminding you of where you are. Contemporary, low-level, white sofas (made of weatherproof material), raised areas (a few steps above the main lounge offer additional privacy) buzz with nightbirds. DJ Ishan, Dino Moses play lounge, upbeat and commercial and keep the tempo pumping. The white, egg-shaped bar is manned by professionally trained barmen. Mixoligists mix winners, be it the vodka-based 114 or Lady Boy. Champagne and champagne cocktails (Bellini, Kir Royale, Black Pearl) are hugely popular too. Classic cocktails and mocktails too. The snacky menu is being changed to include pastas, salads and the rectangular long pizzas will be retained. A well-stocked bar but the grouse is that it has only premium liquor and, therefore, highly priced. The swish champagne set (literally and otherwise) raises a toast to Aer.

Note: A cover charge of ₹2,500 per head on weekends.

HAPPY HOURS: 5.30pm to 8pm

■ Four Seasons Hotel, 114, Dr E Moses Road, Worli, Mumbai, Ph: 24818000, M2 1

Alfredo's

Resto-Bar Noon to 12.30am

Buzz-2.50 | Décor-2.50 | Nightout for 2-₹2000

This cosy, air-conditioned and mirrored bar is a popular hangout for many, including groups of students from neighbouring colleges. While stone-arched gates greet you outside, cool granite stools and tables greet you inside. Beer is guzzled by the pitcher (₹665), drinks (brandy, vodka, tequila, rum, gin, scotch) by the several glasses. They even have champagne on hand for that extra special occasion. Electric Jolt, Dirty Dancing and Long Island cocktails make the rounds in this loud and bustling space. Chilli Cheese Toast, Spicy Chicken, Bruschetta and Veg Nachos are the munchies of choice. Pizzas, pastas and sizzlers for those looking for something more satisfying.

HAPPY HOURS: Noon to 7pm

■ **Hotel King's International, 5, Juhu Tara Road, Mumbai, Ph: 26178860, 26184381-82, 66922222**

Alfresco Nights

Discotheque/Nightclub

About to Open

As the book goes to press, Goregaon's Westin is all set to flag off Alfresco Nights at Prego. Guest DJs and live bands are getting ready to serve up Saturday nights.

■ **The Westin Mumbai Garden City, International Business Park, Oberoi Garden City, Goregaon (E), Mumbai, Ph: 61470000**

Amadeus

Resto-Bar 12.30pm to 3.30pm, 7.30pm to 1.30am

Buzz-3.50 | Décor-4.00 | Nightout for 2-₹5000

The walls of this resto-bar will draw your attention as soon as you enter it with the pictures of music legends donning the walls. If those don't, the live band performance certainly will. Sitting at the heart of Nariman Point this beautiful and funky place has a acoustically treated ceiling with digital prints of swirling flamenco dancers, Dali-inspired bar top (of pressed glass bottles) and bar stools and tables (sculpted by the famous Arzan Khambatta) set the mood right for the evening. Monday through Thursdays are reserved for background music, and live events are slotted for Fridays and Saturdays. House DJ and Guest DJ on most nights. An array of tapas and small plates to eat while you drink sangria and cocktails (Earl Grey Martini and Hibiscus Bellini recommended). A great and affordable wine list of Spanish, Chilean, Argentinean, World wines with traditional high-end wines and bubblies from France. They have a great selection of Single Malts, whiskies and vodkas too. To top it all, Dom Perignon has a special bottle label printed for Amadeus. Perfect place for a perfect evening.

■ **NCPA, Nariman Point, Mumbai, Ph: 22821212, M1 1**

Apicius

LOUNGE BAR — Noon to 3.30pm and 7pm to 1.30am

Buzz-3.50 | Décor-3.50 | Nightout for-₹4000

Zoom up to the eighth floor of a nondescript, Andheri office building to be pleasantly surprised by the sprawling, grey slate-walled space, chandeliers, alfresco lounge and large bar... all tastefully done. Never mind that though its name, Apicius, is derived from fifth-century Rome, yet it serves the predictable falafel, pasta and pizza. Except for the above-par John Dory enlivened with capers and mellow with parsley butter, the rest of the fare is strictly average. See the restaurant guide for more details. Apicius still ranks amongst the most tasteful of Andheri's restaurants and the buzz in its bar (with sprawling alfresco terraces) has been steadily picking up.

■ 8th Floor, Blue Wave Bldg., Off Link Road, Andheri (W), Mumbai, Ph: 26734337

The Ark Bar

BAR — 11.30am to 3pm, 6.30pm to 1.30am

Buzz-1.50 | Décor-2.50 | Nightout for 2-₹4000

A quiet and tucked away bar. Unwind at The Sea Princess hotel's bar after a hectic day. This place's most popular drink is the liquor-based Chocolate Milkshake (made from Kahlua, Dark Rum, Chocolate Ice Cream and Milk). Other specialities are The Sea Princess (a Vodka based Cocktail), P.S. I Love You and Caipiroska. And you thought Death by Chocolate can only be a dessert! Chocolate Syrup... milk and cream laced with liquor is another cocktail that you may try. You may also sit in this tranquil wooden-floored Ark Bar and just spend the evening watching your favourite sport on their LCD screens. They have a wide variety of spirits, as well as classic cocktails and mocktails (flavoured ones too). Try these... Magician Fruit Cup, Orange Tulip (with 3-coloured layers) and Forever End (with 4-coloured layers), in addition to the usual Virgin Colada and Litchi Passion. Enjoy the complementary salad, wafers and peanuts with your drinks (vegetarian samosas too with hard liquor and cocktails). They have quite a variety of finger-licking Indian, Chinese and European starters to go with your drinks.

HAPPY HOURS: 11.30am to 6pm

■ Hotel Sea Princess, Juhu Tara Road, Juhu, Mumbai, Ph: 26611111

Arola

LOUNGE BAR — 5pm to 1am

Buzz-3.50 | Décor-4.00 | Nightout for 2-₹7000

The good news: Arola has found its identity. No! don't go expecting leisurely fine dining. Go if you're looking for a high-energy bar and lounge with Spanish tapas. Sergi Arola (famed for his *Michelin*-starred restaurants around the world) debuted last year in Mumbai's JW Marriot. There was a clear identity crisis. Wasn't it more of a tapas lounge? And less of a gastronomique three *Michelin*-

starred restaurant that it was being marketed as in its high-profile glitzy launches? We were disappointed. Now, the crescent-shaped luminous bar takes centre stage, the DJ pumps up the music as the creative cocktails and bite-sized tapas do the rounds. Over 31 labels of gin, Arola's Dry Martini (Creole Bitters, Passion Fruit Bitters), Sangria Sergi made to his secret recipe. Sprawling spaces, textured wooden floors, geometric, latticework screens and a terrace with fabulous views of the sea here. The focus remains the glowing moon-shaped bar. Along with the announcement of its lounge bar concept comes new dishes. Still in the tapas style... served for all to share, presented on small beautiful ceramic, glass and stone plates. In the newly introduced dishes are many a (what I call) flavour-building assembly kits. Onto a Potato Egg Tortilla you scoop some of the Garlicky Aioli, add a dollop of Paprika Tomato Purée followed by crunchy fried onions. The deconstructed Chicken Caeser Salad, the Chicken Three Ways are all delightful variations. Recently introduced Cocas (including a vegetarian one) Spanish version of pizzas are crisp and topped with flavourful toppings. Ask for the traditional Patatas Bravas (fierce potatoes) rendered as small cylinders topped with cloudy tufts of creamy mayonnaise. Sous vide Chicken Stuffed with Salsify, tender Terrine of Suckling Pig in delectable cubes is superb. See the restaurant guide for more details. Small portions and high prices, but still there is nothing like this stylish, edgy, high energy lounge with so many seating options, a fantastic range of music and cocktails. There is contemporary, upscale Spanish Tapas that is not uniformly excellent. Arola has found its identity.

■ **JW Marriott, Lobby Level, Juhu Tara Road, Juhu, Mumbai, Ph: 66933000/3624**

Asia 7

RESTO-BAR Noon to 4pm, 7pm to Midnight

Buzz-2.50 | Décor-3.50 | Nightout for 2-₹4000

This Palladium (High Street Phoenix) resto-bar has a well-stocked bar but it's visited more for its quick and well-priced lunch (especially for the office goers nearby) and dinner. It does have a small crowd popping in here for an evening drink! Contemporary and pleasing, complete with a large backlit bar, it has comfy seating. Should you be here, check out the Watermelon Wonder and Red Wine Sangria.

■ **3rd Floor, Palladium Mall, High Street Phoenix, Mumbai, Ph: 43473901-02**

Asilo

ROOFTOP BAR

About to Open

As the book goes to press, Asilo is all set to open on the 40th floor of the Palladium Hotel. A glamorous, alfresco bar and grill restaurant from the Shiro and Hard Rock Café team promises to provide the the perfect sanctuary (asilo).

■ **Rooftop, Palladium Hotel, 462, Senapati Bapat Marg, Lower Parel, Mumbai, Ph: ??**

Atrium Lounge

LOUNGE BAR — 8am to 1am

Buzz-2.50 | Décor-3.00 | Nightout for 2-₹5000

Many a surprise in this Taj Lands End bar plonked in the lobby. The handsome, high-ceilinged space is a great place to nurse a drink and watch the world go by. This spacious and relaxing lounge is open through the day for light breakfast, snacks and pastries and offers the finest single estate teas, coffees, Single Malts and cognacs. A pianist performs during the early hours of the evening, setting the mood for the live jazz band that plays a repertoire of classic jazz and pop throughout the week. Try their fusion drinks like Paan Martini or the Kala Khatta Caipiroska. Lots of new additions at Atrium Lounge! Iced Espressos like Guellermo, Pesco (with peach), Hot Chocolate (made with authentic Belgian Calibaut Chocolate) — flavours such as Aztec Chilli and Australian Orange all new! Among the food menu, Maki Rolls, Manchego Cheese and Tomato Quesadillas, Kathi Wrap and Saigon Chicken too! They even have a Live Forever cocktail touted for its medicinal values (ginger and curry leaves added). Spice it up the Chaat Platter which combines five different *chaats*. Delightful old favourites includes the atrium-style burgers (three mini burgers with French fries). Also try the unique dessert cocktails afters like — Tiramusu, Choco Marnier and CWC (cognac, whisky and cointreau).

■ **Taj Lands End, Band Stand, Bandra (W), Mumbai, Ph: 66681234, M3** 1

Aurus

RESTO-BAR — 7.30pm to 1.30am

Buzz-2.50 | Décor-4.00 | Nightout for 2-₹5000

As the book goes to press, I pop in to this eight-year-old Juhu restaurant with its sexily glamourous open-air ambience by the sea. Sadly, it is not mobbed as it used to be. It continues to draw some regulars who dine under the monsoon air-conditioned shed (still intact and ready to be dismantled for the winter). The setting remains sensational and dining alfresco (especially in the cooler months) is magical. The languorous ocean laps and the elegantly seductive lighting infuses the tables and palm trees (a four poster bed too) with a magical glow. A large indoor section (formal tables, chandeliers, unisex loo, *et al.*). The hugely talented chef, Vicky Ratnani, is as comfortable whipping up ethereal foams as he is delivering home-style flavours. He not only balances textures and colours, uses sous vide and spherification techniques to perfection. In the new menu he keeps the flavour profiles simple, but the plate colourful and graphic. Please see the Restaurant Guide for more details. Sadly they've discontinued the Dessert Martinis.

■ **Nichani Kutir, 12th Juhu Tara Road, Mumbai, Ph: 67106666-67, M3** 2

The Bar & Verandah

LOUNGE BAR — 11.30am to 1.30am

Buzz-2.00 | Décor-2.50 | Nightout for 2-₹5000

A special trip to this bar is not recommended, even though it sure is a skilful use of the lobby space in the

Four Seasons Hotel. A well-stocked bar and a multi-cuisine menu: it doubles up as a 24-hour coffee shop. Relax on the verandah with your drinks (Sunset Worli, U R Kamakaze, mojitos) later in the evening, served with cashew nuts and peanuts. The Bar & Verandah also offers Mumbai street food like *garma garam* Vada Pao, Kachori, Bhel Puri and Cutting Chai. They have an exquisite collection of signature aged Single Malts (all the Glens), Vintage Armagnacs, Italian aperitifs and Bordeaux Wines (from ₹4,500–1,75,000). They also serve wine by glass such as White Sula Wine (Indian) for ₹400, Casa Matta (Italian) for ₹700, Chateaux Dori Red (Indian) for ₹450 and the Laughing Magpie (Australian) for ₹800. Thin-crust pizzas, sandwiches and Indian Kathi Rolls pile up on tables along with the new sizzling Chocolate Brownie (₹450+). Tiramisu, Apple Pie and cheesecakes make the rounds too. Catching up on work? They have Wi-Fi here, but you'll have to shell out ₹500/hour for that privilege.

■ **Four Seasons Hotel, 114, Dr E Moses Road, Worli, Mumbai, Ph: 24818000**

The Bar

Y ▬ AC

LOUNGE BAR — 3pm to 1.15am

Buzz-2.00 | Décor-3.50 | Nightout for 2-₹4000

Not for you if you are looking for a quiet hideaway! Set in the midst of the gleaming lobby of the Grand Hyatt, this sexily, dim-lit bar is an ideal place for pre- and post-dinner drinks. It pays impeccable attention to detail... temperature-controlled, bookshelf-style glass cabinets with separate sections for whisky, Red and White wines; cigar and cigarette Ritznhorf ashtrays and even a special ice-cube machine. An impressive drinks menu with 40 martinis, popular cocktails (Cosmopolitan, Journalist, Hot 'n' Dirty), Single Malts (hot sellers) and exquisite wine (Bentley Australian Shiraz, Oxford Landing Shiraz and Santa). The usual quick bites on the menu (bruschetta, nachos, samosas, chicken wings, calamari), but the service is fantastic. A rare collection of Single Malts at 'The Bar' like Glen Fiddich, 50 years old and Lady Purn.

■ **Grand Hyatt Mumbai, Off Western Express Highway, Santacruz (E), Mumbai, Ph: 66761234**

The Barking Deer

Y ▬ AC

RESTO-BAR — 11.30am to 1.30am

Buzz-3.50 | Décor-3.50 | Nightout for 2-₹3000

As the book goes to press, I am informed that the microbrewery license of this new arrival in Lower Parel, has been obtained. Barking Deer is definitely worth a visit for beer-buffs looking for variety (which comes for a steep price). All-purpose crowd pleaser dishes here, hearty gut busters too and desserts that go for gooey abandon. Dimly lit, exposed brick walls and ducts and wooden tables make up the décor of this large 4,000sq ft space with its elaborate brewing rig and bar at the far end. Thankfully, the music volume allows conversation. I do a beer tasting of the stouts, ales and more. Murphys Irish stout is too bitter for us, the Belgian Liefman fruity beer poured in a champagne flute delights with it's whispers of sweetness, the Mexican SOL and the Leff Belgian Blonde Wheat Beer pairs well with the robust starters. For details on the Global food, please turn to the Restaurant Guide.

■ **Todi Mills, Mathuradas Mill Compound, Plot No. 242, NM Joshi Marg, Lower Parel, Mumbai, M2 2**

Bayview Café

RESTO-BAR
7am to 12.30am
Buzz-3.00 | Décor-3.00 | Nightout for 2-₹1500

No frills, functional, perched on the terrace of one of Colaba's tiny seafront hotels, it's an ideal spot on cool nights especially. It's one of those few places in the city where you'll be able to order a beer as early as 8am(!). Pair that with one of their Indian, Continental or English breakfasts (7am to 10am). It has great views of the sea and the Gateway of India. Only Indian wine here, still definitely worth a visit. Try their specialities — non-veg platters, croquettes, kebabs and seafood. The food here is well tuned to the Indian-palate. Enjoy it with your choice of drinks.

■ **Hotel Harbour View, 25, PJ Ramchandani Marg, Apollo Bunder, Colaba, Mumbai, Ph: 22821089**

The Beachcomber Cocktail Lounge & Bar

BAR
4pm to 1am
Buzz-3.50 | Décor-3.50 | Nightout for 2-₹5000

As the book goes to press, Sun n Sand's recently renovated The Beachcomber Cocktail Lounge & Bar opens. The lobby-level bar with a striking view of the swimming pool and the Juhu beach stocks cocktails, imported wines and liquors. You can even walk onto the poolside and lounge in the open air on the beachfront. Check out its completely new cocktail menu designed by world renowned mixologist, "DréMasso" (who has been working and running bars across London and San Francisco).

Note: Call and check about its "Sunday Sundowners".

■ **Sun-n-Sand Hotel, 39, Juhu Beach, Mumbai, Ph: 66938888**

Beluga – The Bar

BAR
Noon to Midnight
Buzz-2.00 | Décor-3.50 | Nightout for 2-₹5000

Passionate about cognac, cigars, or aromatic White Wine? Exclusivity drips from every corner of the The Lalit's comfortable, wood-lined Beluga Bar. Also on offer are Single Malts, martinis, and beer (Tiger, Kingfisher and draught). Cosmos and B52's popularly make the rounds. Snack menu has been spruced up too. Oriental, Lebanese, Japanese and Continental cuisine is on offer. No buzz or crowd in this exclusive bar.

■ **The Lalit, Sahar Airport Road, Andheri (E), Mumbai, Ph: 66992222 (Extn. 3131)**

The Beryl Club

[Y] [card] [AC]

BAR

11.30am to 11.30pm

Buzz-2.00 | Décor-3.00 | Nightout for 2-₹3000

The wicker chairs, wooden flooring and the lighting of the place will instantly remind you of an English pub. Add to that live sporting events on LCD screens while you guzzle down the drinks on offer. The after-work crowd pours in for Margarita, Screwdriver and Bloody Mary which all are served with complementary wafers and peanuts. Draught Beer and Grey Goose Vodka are available here too. Try their Chicken Tikka, Spring Rolls, Fried Fish and kebabs. They have Veg and Non-veg Platters too. The food is not out of the world, but there isn't much to complain either. It's more of an after work place than a night time party one.

HAPPY HOURS: 3pm to 8pm

■ **Hotel Kohinoor Continental, Andheri-Kurla Road, Andheri (E), Mumbai, Ph: 28209999, 66919000**

Big Bang Café

[Y] [card] [AC]

BAR

6pm to 1.30am

Buzz-3.50 | Décor-3.00 | Nightout for 2-₹3000

This third-floored Big Bang Café is certainly "big"... but it ain't "bang" or "café". It opens only in the evening, is littered with fairy lights, has a large terrace section (overlooking hoardings and construction work) and very slow service. The multi-cuisine food menu (Indian, Italian, Mexican and Thai) is obviously not its strong point. Hard nachos, soggy French Fries, American Corn Cheese Balls, Prawn on Toast and the like. Cocktails like Roby Spice (whisky, ginger, chilli and lime juice), Sex on the Beach, Long Island Iced Tea and more here. Very average declare my companions.

■ **Kenilworth Bldg., 3rd Floor, Linking Road, Bandra (W), Mumbai, Ph: 26008833/77, M3** 3

The Big Nasty

[Y] [card] [AC]

BAR

7pm to 1am

Buzz-3.50 | Décor-3.50 | Nightout for 2-₹4000

As the book goes to press, we pop in for a quick check out of this Bandra nightspot (on top of Shatranj Napoli) and find it as packed as ever. We go up a somewhat smelly lift and into the second-floored large space. Everything here is rugged and has an unfinished bumpy undergo, including the metal corrugated flooring. Sprawling and done up with old grungy industrial walls and the innovative art installations of metallic craggy birds. Industrial objects for the street walls, windows, doors and loud music from the dynamic videos of class bands being played on the gigantic screen bounces off the walls. The Big Nasty, as expected, is all about being nasty complete with danger signs for radioactive, explosive and the bang! Well-stocked bar and Guava Chilli Mary, Pink Lemonade Mojito, Daiquiri are worth trying. Apart from the endless choice of Wiches (Paneer Akori and beef) and palate-teasing starters (Fish 'n' Chips, Roast Beef Chilli, spicy Cocktail Sausages) burgers and falafal are the stars of the menu. Not gourmet fare, but filling and tasty. Raise a toast with Nasty Mary, of course.

■ **2nd Floor, Shatranj Napoli Bldg., Union Park, Carter Road, Bandra (W), Mumbai, Ph: 9821524563, M3** 4

Blend N Brew

[Y] [card] [AC]

SPORTS LOUNGE BAR

Noon to Midnight

Buzz-1.50 | Décor-2.50 | Nightout for 2-₹2000

Chembur's bar doubles as a sports-bar showing Live Sports Action on a large projector screen. You can sit back in its leather chairs and recliners and just enjoy whatever you'd like to do with a glass of Single Malts, a cocktails, vodkas, wine or anything else. As for drinks, from flaming shots to cocktails like Caribbean Romance, BahaMama, Dancing Belly, Yummy Bikini, Spiced Up and 360 Degree (barman's special) and mocktails like Trans & Fusion, The Bond (007... ooh!) and Cool Cucumber to name a few, everything's available here. Some other drinks include Tequila Sunrise, Sex on the Beach, mojitos, Zombies and Long Island Iced Tea. Enjoy candle-light dinners on weekends (Fri–Sun), or watch your favourite sport or dance through the night with the DJ (except Tuesdays) who plays guest requests.

■ **70 (O), Central Avenue Road, Behind Geeta Bhavan, Chembur, Mumbai, Ph: 25280014**

The Blu Balcony

[Y] [card] [AC]

RESTO-BAR

4pm to 12.30am

Buzz-3.00 | Décor-3.00 | Nightout for 2-₹4000

Andheri's Blu Balcony is a great place to go for a casual drink and chat. It's their mocktail menu which is worth checking out... both the classics as well as new fruit and fizzy drink combinations. Have a go at their 'Blue Yonder' or the 'Blue Sea', both of which are very refreshing. They also offer alcoholic beverages like a cloying Coco Loco, Long Beach Iced Tea, Boston Tea Party and white wine sangrias. Okayish multi-cuisine mains and appetizers, Chilli Cheese Garlic Toast oversweet Chef's Special Prawns and Dry Barbecue Chicken Salad. Pizzas too.

■ **26, Ground Floor, Link Plaza, Next to Pratap da Dhaba, Oshiwara, Link Road, Andheri (W), Mumbai, Ph: 26327744, M5** 17

The Blue Frog Club

[Y] [card] [AC]

RESTO-BAR

Tue–Sun: 6.30pm to 1.30am

Buzz-4.00 | Décor-4.00 | Nightout for 2-₹4000

Live music fans hop over to the Blue Frog, at this opera house-meets-warehouse set in 6,000sq ft high-ceilinged, good-looking space with pod seating and stage, an open kitchen, and a bar. Dedicated to live music, this restaurant and bar houses four state-of-the-art music recording studios, a music production house, an independent record label and an artist management service. It also features live music six nights a week in every genre with international artists appearing regularly. High prices but standards to match. Premium wines, champagnes, Single Malts, and spirits (including a wide assortment of vodkas and Single Malts) at this well-stocked bar. Scarlet (vodka-based), Green Apply Mojito (rum-based), Blue Frog, Thai Mojito, Bamboo Glow, Wasabi Bloody Mary and Mango Blue Bellini are a few of the specialities too. The cuisine here is Modern European with a few Indian touches, but the focus is on the music.

HAPPY HOURS: 6.30pm to 9pm

■ **Mathuradas Mills Compound, Lower Parel, Tulsi Pipe Road, Mumbai, Ph: 40332300, 65251716/18, 61586158,** www.bluefrog.co.in, **M2** 3

Blue Waters

RESTO-BAR — Noon to 3.30pm, 7pm to 12.30am

Buzz-1.50 | Décor-2.50 | Nightout for 2-₹3000

The resto-bar reminds me of a squat Delhi bungalow with a garden in front, by which you can enjoy a Blue Waters cocktail. A small fountain trickles into a haze of blue light amidst stone benches and stone tables, making it an ideal outdoor seating during the cool Mumbai winters. An interesting menu of cocktalls and a decently stocked bar. Kebabs do a good *jugalbandi* with the drinks here. Good place to unwind with interesting cocktail menu (barman's special mocktail and cocktail with vodka) and decently stocked bar plus complementary nibbles of cheeselings, papads and peanuts. The bar is always open, but drinks are served inside only during happy hours.

PS: Mondays, Wednesdays and Fridays are the ghazal nights while Tuesdays and Thursdays are serenading nights with guitarists playing and entertaining the guests.

HAPPY HOURS: 6pm to 8.30pm

■ **Opp. Tata Power House, Andheri New Link Road, Andheri (W), Mumbai, Ph: 26743615/4805**

Bombay High

BAR — 11am to 1am

Buzz-3.50 | Décor-3.50 | Nightout for 2-₹5000

Open through the day, term it a bar at noon and you'd be wrong, term it a lounge at sunset and you'd be wrong again and if you dare term it as a disco at night, you'd be way off the mark! Multi-dimensional, Bombay High effortlessly blends the preceding three definitions into each other as the day goes by. Also enjoy a live band playing while you sip on your drinks (except Mondays). They also entertain you on your Sunday Brunch (12.30pm to 3.30pm). At all times of the day, this relaxed, glamorous, spacious, high-ceilinged bar is for you if you're looking for an extensive and premium wine list, Single Malts, cocktails and the works. Try their Floribunda cocktail which is a mix of scotch and gin with pineapple juice, rose syrup and lemon juice. For something stronger, savour any of the 17 Single Malt whiskies on offer. In fact,

Glenn Fiddich is bottling a whole oak barrel especially for ITC as its private vintage label. The wine list includes everything from Australia's Jacob's Creek to our very own Sula Brut. You can even find ITC's very own hand-rolled cigar brand Armenteros over here.

■ **ITC Maratha, Sahar Road, Andheri (E), Mumbai, Ph: 28303030,** www.itchotels.com**, M4** 4

Bonobo

Bar with Dancing Noon to 1am

Buzz-4.00 | Décor-3.50 | Nightout for 2-₹3000

Duck your way past Bandra's street-side clothes stalls, up into the lift to Bonobo. As the book goes to press, on a Friday night, we pop in here to find it buzzing and the dance floor packed. It's a jungle out there, but this Bandra hangout is dancing to the beat of its own drum. Bonobo (Bar.Love.Food.), named after an endangered ape living in the heart of the Congo, is popular and packed. Soft lighting, an outdoor terrace with Bandra's high-rises for a backdrop, a funky bar and drinks menu seem to be reeling in Mumbai's suburban crowd by the dozens. With live bands and various different events, Bonobo also has a new drinks menu that includes a sparkling wine Sangria Pitcher (₹1,370+), Fresh Fruit Margaritas, and Bonobo special cocktails like Mojito Nico, Vanilla Ice, Whats Up Doc (a dark rum-based cocktail with fresh carrot juice and ginger), and Funky Monk (dark rum, cola and coffee). With Monterey Jack, Gruyere, Mozarella, Grilled Chicken and 3-cheese Beef Quesadillas as starters, as well as Root Vegetable Seekh Kebabs, Lamb Seekh Kebabs, Mini Lamb Pitas, and the interestingly named Angry Birds (Chicken Meat balls with Scarmoza cheese). Try the Wild Mushroom & Truffled Mascarpone Risotto and pair Mezze Platters, Crostini, and Jalapeño Cheddar Poppers (finger foods) with a pitcher of beer or a cheeky Chardonnay. So get into the groove and do the funky monkey!

PS: Live band on every alternate Wednesday and DJ Night every Friday.

■ **Kenilworth Mall, Phase 2, 2nd Floor, Off Linking Road, Bandra (W), Mumbai, Ph: 26055050/5353, M3** 5

Bora Bora

Pub Noon to 1am

Buzz-2.50 | Décor-3.00 | Nightout for-₹3000

Bora Bora is setting up all over! As the book goes to press, I pop into the Juhu branch (desolate on a Friday night), Open during the day, this China Gate group's nautical-themed pub is decorated with models of ships between booths, a captain's wheel placed near the bar and barrel-shaped tablestands and menus. The theme is carried through thoroughly, while the space promises a "first-of-its-kind ecstatic journey in time". Some of their special drinks include cocktails like Woo Woo, Bull Frog, Long Island Beach Party and Alygony, mocktails like Tropical Storm, Loving Cup and Punk Lady. With 14 television sets, one six-panel LED screen and an additional projector this is a perfect place to head to for game nights (seats 80). Much like Hometown Café, the nautical-themed pub has a confused *avatar* (sports bar or pub?), service that needs to pick up and nothing on the menu thus far that is memorable.

■ Above Hometown Café, Opp. Juhu Beach, Juhu Tara Road, Juhu, Mumbai, Ph: 26112212, 26112211

■ Royal Plaza, Next to City Mall, New Link Road, Andheri (W), Mumbai, Ph: 26748700

■ 155, Opp. Saka Salon, Waterfield Road, Bandra (W), Mumbai, Ph: 42636000, 9167666713

Botticino

RESTO-BAR — Noon to 3pm, 7pm to 11.45pm

Buzz-3.00 | Décor-4.00 | Nightout for 2-₹5000

Botticino finds a place in this book only because it houses the city's only grappa bar. It is a fine-dine Italian restaurant and not a nightlife place at all. If you're a dinner guest, take full advantage of the complementary tutored wine-tasting in the enoteca. This elegant restaurant seems to 'float' over the hotel's coffee shop below, thanks to its glass floor. Begin the dining experience at the grappa lounge (only one in Mumbai). Three savoury choices of that rare, artisinal luxury await: Grappa di Moscato, Grappa di Cabernet Firuli Venezia Giulia or Alambieco Grappa di Prosecco — all in beautifully designed Venetian glass bottles from Grappa Alexander by Distilleria Bottega in Italy. A sampling of grappa sprays, grappa cocktails and frozen Grapparitas make for an interesting evening. A glass of Danzante' Pinot Grigio, anyone? You can pair your wine andd drinks with dishes such as Caramelised Goat Cheese and Rucola Salad with Fig Compote, honey and asparagus and many others.

■ Trident Bandra-Kurla, C-56, G-Block, Bandra-Kurla Complex, Mumbai, Ph: 66727640/44, M4 5

Bottle Bar

BAR — Noon to 1.30am

Buzz-2.50 | Décor-3.00 | Nightout for 2-₹3000

One of the longest Happy Hours in the city... a one-on-one-free offer on any drink from 4pm to 10pm. As the book goes to press, I walk down the desolate pedestrian street (near the Bombay Stock Exchange) where this fairly new bar is located. Walk up to the first floor and into the neon-lit, bathed in blue light, TV screen dotted bar. It obviously takes its name seriously, as empty glass bottles are lined in the front and bathed in ever-changing hues of coloured light. Sofas in the dark, tables with bar stool-style chairs and more tables and couches too. Tiger Ramp (their vodka-based in-house special), Long Island Iced Tea to flaming shots. Looking for a real stiff one? Go for the Blood on the Rooftop (tequila, rum, vodka, gin). Okayish fare (pure veggie, please note). Must ask for the Open Cheese Roomali (a crisp large, *kadak* rumali... standing like a large bowl and sprinkled with tangy chopped onion, tomato, coriander). Okayish Paneer Satay and Cheese Corn. Morrocan Paneer and Sizzling Pasta. Priced on the expensive side and located off the beaten track, the bar still has to pick up popularity.

SPECIAL NIGHTS: Tuesdays are Ladies Night, Wednesdays are Karaoke Night, Thursdays are Comedy Nights, Fridays are Bollywood and Saturdays are DJ Nights.

■ **Rajabahadur Mansion, 1st Floor, Near Bombay Stock Exchange, Ambalal Doshi Marg, Fort, Mumbai, Ph: 22100100, 22100200, M1** 2

Boveda

BAR
Just Opened

6.30pm to 1am

As the book goes to press, the multi-cuisine Spanish-named Boveda lounge and resto-bar opens in Andheri. There is a classic dining area, clad in wood and exposed brick walls and is alive with DJ music. Boveda is all set to serve Spiced Paprika Chicken Nachos, Goan Sausage in Refried Beans, Tossed Spiced Mushrooms and the like. A fully stocked bar, cocktails and mocktails are on offer too.

■ **G-04, Morya Landmark One, Off New Link Road, Oshiwara Village, Andheri (W), Mumbai, Ph: 67080859, M5** 1

Brass Monkey

LOUNGE BAR
Buzz-3.50 | Décor-3.50 | Nightout for 2-₹3000

Noon to Midnight

Goregaon's Brass Monkey offers many a choice: free (select) drinks for women on Mondays (until 9pm) and with identification, people in specific industries can enjoy 40 per cent off on their bills. IT & BPO Night on Tuesdays, Finance & Bank Night on Wednesdays, Jabardast Film Night on Thursdays (includes anyone in the media and film industry) and Airlines Night on Sundays. This is a plush lounge bar which is done up with red velvet sofas and music is quite good in this dimly lit and place sparkling with laser beams. DJ Cyrus spins hip-hop and house music and later into the night pumps up Bollywood music. And yes, it has a well-stocked with many house specials. They have different set of Happy Hours every day of the week. Check before heading here.

■ **Level 2, Off Western Express Highway, Goregaon, Mumbai, Ph: 26866867**

Busaba

RESTO-BAR
Buzz-4.00 | Décor-3.50 | Nightout for 2-₹3000

12.30pm to 3pm, 6.30pm to 1am

Go to investment-banker-turned-restaurateur Nikhil Chib's Busabas for a cosy drink in a cosy space. The tiny bungalow tucked behind the Taj (and just next to Indigo) continues to draw regulars. Push open the glass door and walk into a wooden-floored waiting area, a handsome lounge area alive with house and lounge music. Famous cocktails include Aja (Absolut Citron, Lemon Grass and Fresh Pineapple Juice) and Good Morning Vietnam

(Absolut Citron, fresh cucumber juice, mint leaves and lime juice). The larger twin-levelled Parel Busaba is slowly catching up. Knock back their famous Caipiroska.

HAPPY HOURS: 6.30pm to 8.30pm

■ **4, Mandlik Road, Colaba, Mumbai, Ph: 22043769/72/79**

■ **Mathura Das Mill Compound, NN Joshi Marg, Opp. Blue Frog, Lower Parel, Mumbai, Ph: 67478971-74**

Café Ideal

RESTO-BAR

8am to 11pm

Buzz-1.50 | Décor-2.50 | Nightout for 2-₹1000

Not a night time drinking joint as much as a beer during the day one. Head over to Café Ideal for: a chilled glass of beer, view of the Chowpatty Seaface and VFM prices. This café is a quintessential Irani joint established by Farooq in 1935 and has seen many avatars since then. What remains constant here is their famous Chilli Cheese Toast and a jukebox to listen to old faves while you enjoy the different flavoured breezers, Red Wine or even fruit juices, ice teas or fruit lemonade. A new addition to their list is mocktails — Getaway Sunrise, Purple Blaze, Spice Girl and April Lady. Also on their menu are hot appetizers like Paneer Chilli, Chana Masala, Schezwan Chilli with Egg, *chaats* and the new Veggie Sizzler Paneer Steak, Veg Tex-Mex and Veg Mexicano.

■ **5, Fulchand Nivas, Chowpatty Seaface, Mumbai, Ph: 23630943**

Café Mangii

RESTO-BAR

Mon–Fri: 11.30am to 12.30am, Sat-Sun: 9.30am to 12.30am

Buzz-3.00 | Décor-3.50 | Nightout for 2-₹3000

Though its bar is popular, it is mainly the casual Italian fare that draws the regulars here. Café Mangii's fresh fruit cocktails (₹550–700+taxes), Fresh Fruit Margaritas, flavoured caipiroskas and frozen margaritas make them different. It all started off with a mango tree... when Mangii Ferra set up in Vile Parle several years ago. It was one of the first to serve wood-fired pizzas this side of the town, which, by now, are their USP (try the Pepperoni 'n' Cajun Chicken Pizzas). Ever since then, Mangii's tribe has been increasing. First Khar and more recently, Powai. Perch yourself at the full-fledged bar and order their exotic caipiroskas (ask the bartender about their "twists" like the Muddy Mojito which is very popular) or fire up with the Spicy Lady (basil, cointreau, vodka, and jalapeño) or Currant Affair (black currants, cranberry juice and vodka with exotic garnish served in a chilled glass) to keep the action fresh and exciting. Old ad posters, wooden tones and cushioned furniture give the place a homely feel. More sedate wine cocktails (order the special sangria) and straight options like beer, whisky, vodka are available. The friendly and courteous staff is always happy to suggest wines (from dense to fruity they have them all — Pinot Noir, Hardy, Yellowtail and Bohemia — Red, White and Sizzling) that go well with whatever you've ordered.

■ **14th Road, Off Linking Road, Khar (W), Mumbai, Ph: 26498100, 26498200, 65268100**

■ **Ground Floor, 3, Transocean Garden, Hiranandani Garden Lane, Opp. Powai Lake, Powai, Mumbai, Ph: 25705136-39**

■ **Premises No. 28, Aram Nagar 1, Versova, Andheri (W), Mumbai, Ph: 26316100-02**

Café Oval

[Y] [card] [AC]

RESTO-BAR — 9am to 11pm

Buzz-3.50 | Décor-1.50 | Nightout for 2-₹1000

Cheap and cheerful! A boon for the serious beer drinker. This no-frills bar (centrally located opposite Oval) serves only beer and cheap eats: omelettes and chana. Transformed from an Irani joint to a beer shop when the government relaxed the prohibition laws, it still retains that functional look. It serves quite a few beer varieties such as Golden Eagle, London Pilsner, Foster's, good ol Kingfisher and others. And yes, it serves only beer. Its snacks include Cheese Sandwich, Omelettes and others. Check out their Bhurji Bread, Chana Dal, Moong Dal and sandwiches. It has a great location and since its food and drinks are pretty affordable, regulars continue to throng this place.

■ **Kambatta Bldg., Near Eros Cinema, Maharishi Karve Marg, Churchgate, Mumbai, Ph: 66345721, M1** 3

Café Sundance

[Y] [card] [AC]

RESTO-BAR — 8am to Midnight

Buzz 3.00 | Décor-3.50 | Night out for 2-₹3000

Go to this unpretentious, moderately priced, centrally located resto-bar for a casual drink through the day, pre or post dinner. It has a well-stocked bar and serves affordably priced comfort food, has a cheery newspaper menu and the bill is presented in a Jughead comic. But, its not about fussy gimmicks... the kitchen is the focal point and Café Sundance is ultimately about eating more than drinking. The two levels of this small 55-seater are spruced up, bright cream walls, glassed show kitchen, wooden tables and chairs, a giant backlit wall rack stacked with vintage odds and ends and comic books complete the charm. Knock back drinks with burgers, dogs and sliders here. Plenty of other café staples, such as sandwiches, pastas, pizzas and salads. Please see the restaurant guide for more details.

■ **Ground Floor, Eros Bldg., Churchgate, Mumbai, Ph: 22026212**

Café Universal

[Y] [card] [AC]

RESTO-BAR — Mon–Sat: 9am to 11pm, Sundays: 4pm to 11pm

Buzz-2.00 | Décor-3.00 | Nightout for 2-₹800

An all day place to pop in for a casual drink. Not a night time bar at all. Right across the GPO (Fort area) since 1921 this quaint gem is one of the places in Mumbai where you'll find personal dispensers of beer (3lt most popular) on the tables as well as B52 and Kamakaze shots and Long Island Iced Tea. This bright and airy place also has an interesting collection of framed paintings and posters that adorn the walls along with a wide display of alcohol bottles. Whisky and vodka (domestic: ₹250 for large and ₹175 for small peg, imported: ₹600 for large and ₹350 for small) along with Sula wines at great VFM (₹800 per bottle). Munch on complementary lacquered nuts as you relax and lay back and enjoy a chilled beer (a dozen options available; ₹200–250 for a bottle of domestic) and a good meal. Mini Meals for ₹200–275. Soft rock hums in the background as tourists and professionals working around the area visit. Ever-smiling and friendly waiters are always happy to offer suggestions with efficient service.

■ **299, Shaheed Bhagat Singh Road, Fort, Mumbai, Ph: 22613985, 22694893**

Canvas

NIGHTCLUB

7pm to 1.30am

Buzz-3.00 | Décor-3.50 | Nightout for-₹6000

Though the buzz still has to take off here, this 8,000sq ft sprawling Canvas is best for partying more than serious eating. On the top floor of the Palladium, it's a dizzyingly lit twin-levelled space. The semi-circle-shaped restaurant looks down at its lounge/bar/alfresco/smoking and cigar room and surreal projection screens. There is live music too, three bars and all through, there is lush red velvet, deep black tones and dancing, flickering screens and lighting. The multi-cuisine meandering menu, served on the noisy restaurant level, plonked on top of a noisier lounge, is a downside worth pointing out. And it is worth pointing out because Canvas also has virtues and because there's hope. If it's a relaxed night out fuelled with well-made cocktails and alcohol that you're looking for, then head to this opulent lounge complete with plush red velvet curtains, cushy couches and dancing red strobe lights. The bartenders shake, build and stir many a good fruity cocktail Pineapple-Pepper, Lemongrass-Litchi, Strawberry-Mint and Watermelon-Rosemary martinis to name a few. Canvas is right on top of my favourite Comedy Club (same owners) and after laughing your guts out, it's great to come for a smoke and drink.

■ **Palladium Mall, 4th Floor, Senapati Bapat Marg, Lower Parel, Mumbai, Ph: 43485050**

Captain's Bar

BAR

7.30pm to 11.30pm

Buzz-1.50 | Décor-2.00 | Nightout for 2-₹3000

Not buzzing at all. If you happen to be around Bandra Reclamation and need a quiet little drink then this place is just ideal for you. On the third floor of Hotel Rang Sharda nestled amongst a multi-cuisine coffee shop, a restaurant (Westerlies) and an open-air terrace lies Captain's Bar. The regular patrons enjoy a drink from this well-stocked bar. Champagne, brandy, vodka, rum, gin, scotch, tequila, liqueurs, and aperitifs. Cocktails (Pina Colada, Rang De Bar, Bloody Mary) and mocktails (Fruit Punch, Mickey Mouse, Strawberry Delite) too! Cocktails like Jombi, Orange Blossom, Planter Punch also do the rounds here. All these go well with the snacks available, especially the Indian kebabs while the complementary peanuts, wafers and poppadums do the rounds here.

■ **Hotel Rang Sharda, Bandra Reclamation, Opp. Lilavati Hospital, Bandra (W), Mumbai, Ph: 26401919, 26438120**

Cerveza

BEER BAR

3pm to 1am

Buzz-3.00 | Décor-3.00 | Nightout for-₹4000

Beer buffs head to this tiny Kala Ghoda beer bar. It may not be rocking but with nearly 40 types of beer including two wheat beers (Hoegaarden and Schneider Weisse) and one type of fruit beer (Liefman's), dry beer (Asahi) and farmhouse beer (Saison Dupont), beer fans will not go back unhappy. This Bollywood actor Sameer Dattani's South Mumbai beer bar is rather tiny, but one with a big heart. An orange mural of a world map that has facts about beer and quotes about drinking written across it, adorns a wall. Brace yourself for loud music here. Some varieties here include Four ales, two stouts (Guinness and Murphy's Irish), the most expensive being Chimay (₹850 + taxes for a 330ml) from Belgium, and the second most expensive is the Duvel (₹800 + taxes). The menu is quite impressive for this small dimly lit space. There are beer cocktails too... try Snakebite. Straight drinks like rum, whiskey and vodka are available too. Their new addition is Wine stepner. You can have Chinese and Pan-Asian snacks from Silk Route which is just below this place.

■ **38, K Dubash Marg, 1st Floor, In Silk Route, Near Rhythm House, Kala Ghoda, Fort, Mumbai, Ph: 22818572**

Champagne Lounge

LOUNGE BAR

8am to 11.30pm

Buzz-2.50 | Décor-4.00 | Nightout for 2-₹6000

Premium champagne by the glass? Okay, so this one is not exactly a rocking night place, but boy! Is it perfect for that quiet nightout? It's open through the day till 11.30pm and takes on the hues of the nightsky. Get high on champagne and soak in the view of this high-ceilinged, beautiful, glass-walled lobby area of the swanky, gleaming bar at Oberoi. Refreshing daylight and a stunning view of the sea and palm trees soothe in this lounge which serves a choice alcohol. Enjoy champagne by the sunset, between 6pm and 8pm which includes four varieties of champagnes by the glass. They also have Bollinger, Moet Chandon, Louis Roederer (₹1,000–1,500) by the glass, Louis Cristal 2002 which is served by the bottle now. They also have wines at ₹575. International and Indian beers in six varieties are listed, but the specialities, in addition to champagne, are the wines (Sula, Pinot Grigio, Merlot, Cabernet, and more from Australia, Italy, France, Chile, and other regions; ₹550/glass) and cognacs. Get high on the high tea here (20 varieties of tea served with pastries and scones for ₹775). Request the talented lobby pianist to dedicate your favourite song to your beloved.

■ **The Oberoi, Nariman Point, Mumbai, Ph: 66326209, M1 4**

Cheval Bar & Restaurant

Resto-Bar — Noon to 1am

Buzz-4.00 | Décor-3.50 | Nightout for 2-₹4000

Magnetizing a night-crowd that is looking for a bar-lounge, a relaxed space, conversation without ear-deafening music, is Kala Ghoda's fairly new Cheval. Located on the first floor (right across the landing from the frenetic and loud nightclub LIV) .this all-day eatery has the same owner (also of Khyber). Cheval (horse in French) pays tribute, in name at least, to the statue of King Edward VII on his steed that stood in Kala Ghoda's central plaza until 1965. Cheval sprawls in a bar, lounge and dining areas in two high-ceilinged large rooms, its textured pastel walls, exposed ceiling beams and circular light fittings infuse it with a rustic feel. Take your pick... there's the dining room with a mural of a black horse and chandeliers, and the other has a well-stocked bar. Many an interesting munchy, from Truffle Chips to Sliders and Liver Pâté and cocktail too. Cheval endears itself with its relaxed vibe, wait staff wearing T-shirts, fun descriptions (with equally yummy tasting) and innovative cocktails. It's open through the day, so you can pop in anytime for a drink. Raise many a toast with Whisky Sour and Green Asian Coolers!

■ **145, Near Rhythm House, Next to LIV, VB Gandhi Road, Kala Ghoda, Fort, Mumbai, Ph: 40396638**

Cheznous

Resto-Bar — 11.30am to 11.30pm

Buzz-1.50 | Décor-2.50 | Nightout for 2-₹2000

So what if it's not buzzing late at night? It's a quiet, down to earth bar in the Marine Lines' Hotel Westend. You can, at any point in time, spot doctors from the nearby Bombay Hospital enjoying their drinks here along with other office-goers and shoppers. Decently stocked bar and usual snacks here. What's popular here are cocktails like Tom Collins, Pina Colada, Gimlet, Bloody Mary, Screwdriver and Daiquiri and mocktails like Fruit Punch and Virgin Mary. Whisky (Teachers, Black Label, Black Dog) too! All served with complementary snacks like papad, chutney, peanuts, salad and wafers. A silent bar which seats 60 people also offers snacks including Reshmi Kebab, Chicken Tikka, Chilli Cheese Toast, cocktail samosas and pakodas.

■ **West End Hotel, 45, Near Bombay Hospital, New Marine Lines, Mumbai, Ph: 22039121**

China House Lounge

Bar, Discotheque — Wed–Sat: 10pm to 3am

Buzz-4.00 | Décor-4.50 | Nightout for 2-₹7000

China House Lounge at this luxury hotel in Mumbai adds a unique paradigm to stylish Mumbai lounges. This multi-level lounge is the perfect setting for intimate lounging and conversations over pre-dinner drinks or late night cocktails.The main feature of the China House Lounge at the Grand Hyatt Mumbai is the centre, island-style LED light bar, with an array of bottles and unconventional glassware that appear suspended on large glass shelves overhead. Avant-garde interiors form a part of the single private room, while semi-private booths with plush oversized armchairs and open spaces add to the space as the music lingers in the air. The in-house signature beverages, from the classics to the unique post-dinner cocktails, enhance the feel of the lounge Mumbai even further. Located on the mezzanine level is "I deck", the private area which is minimally lit and akin in décor to a private lounge. This relaxing retreat offers the perfect setting to linger after dinner over fine Single Malts, signature cocktails or celebrate an occasion with a few near and dear ones. Multi-faceted in spirit, the stylish China House Lounge area serves as a versatile retreat located within our 5-star luxury Mumbai hotel and the ideal place to party to the high energy music spun by the in-house DJ.

■ **Grand Hyatt Mumbai, Off Western Express Highway, Santacruz (E) Mumbai, Ph: 66761234, M3** 6

Clove Bar

BAR

6pm to 12.45am

Buzz-3.00 | Décor-3.00 | Nightout for 2-₹3000

Tucked into Powaii's Hotel Saffron Spice, this 50-seater watering hole is the right place to relax and unwind with their selection of wines and spirits from around the world. Try their popular cocktails, Black Russian, Blue Lagoon, Caipiroska, Bloody Mary, Sex on the Beach, Mai Tai, as well as their mocktails like Hawaiian Punch, Mango Bloom, White Cloud and Ryder Passion. Also try their shooters, Flaming Lambour, B52, BMW and Test Tube Baby. They also give peanuts and cheeselings complementary with all their drinks. You can enjoy all this with Bollywood music. Clove Bar serves flaming shots as the DJ Ganesh spins the night away with some good Bollywood and Hollywood tracks on all days except Sundays. Drinks menu... cocktails (₹385–485), domestic whisky, rum, gin, brandy, vodka and VFM snacks too! Take your pick from Chilli Garlic Chicken, Onion Rings, Fries, Veg Chilli, Manchurian or Kebabs.

HAPPY HOURS: 6pm to Midnight

■ **Hotel Saffron Spice, Above Pizza Hut, Sentinel Bldg., Opp. Powai Plaza, Central Avenue, Hiranandani Gardens, Powai, Mumbai, Ph: 25705858, 66990088**

Club Alibii

DISCOTHEQUE/NIGHTCLUB

7pm to 1.30am

Buzz-4.50 | Décor-3.50 | Nightout for 2-₹5000

The southernmost tip of dagger-shaped Mumbai begins to rock again. Club Alibii pulls out all the stops and dedicates itself to the seven sins (Greed, Pride, Indulge, Chill, Vanity, Lust, and Passion). It replaces the short-lived Ghost (which had replaced Privé). As the book goes to press, I pop in here for a final checkout round and Whoa! Find myself in a long queue. Since I am a single woman I am allowed to go in. I go past the double doors and am engulfed in a large 4,000sq ft space pulsating with music and light. The flooring sparkles with textured tiles with textured ceiling and design panelling on the bar. Everybody here is swaying to the music and the entire sprawling space seems to be a dance floor. I'm focused on the heartbeat of the club... a centerpiece spiral chandelier with over 500 crystals tubes appearing to pour down onto the intimate dance floor in an array of colours. Right there too, is a floating round stage DJ booth, where the DJs spin music and drama. There are cage tables (₹30,000 and above) and private booths designed around seven sins. The three 31-year-old partners Suved Lohia, Ankit Rawat and Gaurav Parikh ensure that a young, 25-and-above crowd rocks the lounge area, community tables and a VIP Exclusive Lounge (private butlers, *et al.*). Shots are doing the rounds and the well-stocked long bar is packed. Plenty of action pumps up this brand new nightclub. Let's hope it lasts longer than its predecessors.

SPECIAL NIGHTS: Wednesdays are Bollywood Night; Fridays are International Nights; Saturdays are Commercial Night; Cover charge: ₹3,000 for stags.

■ **Mon Repos Bldg., Radio House, Colaba, Mumbai, Ph: 9819300772**

Club Escape

DISCOTHEQUE/NIGHTCLUB — 6pm to 1.30am, Mondays Closed

Buzz-3.50 | Décor-3.50 | Nightout for 2-₹5000

Andheri's Club Escape serves up interesting drinks, great music in a dimly lit ambiance. Boogie all night long (1.30am) at Club Escape with DJ Swaps and DJ Sachin. Enjoy house, hip-hop and Bollywood music with special themed nights. They boast of the best sound system too. B52, Blue Lagoon and Sex on the Beach are the popular cocktails, while Banana Colada enjoys popularity among mocktails. You can also choose from their range of finger foods and starters and burgers and sandwiches, which are accompanied by wafers and fries to munch along with your drinks. Don't be surprised if you bump into celebrities in this popular place. Couple entry is free on all days except Wenesday (₹1,000 for a couple with unlimited food and starters) while stags have to dish out ₹1,500 cover charge.

HAPPY HOURS: 7.30pm to 9.30pm; 50 per cent discount on domestic liqupr and 20 per cent on foreign liquor

■ **3/A, Crystal Plaza, Opp. Fame Adlabs, New Link Road, Andheri (W), Mumbai, Ph: 67021691,** www.clubescape.com, **M5 2**

Copa

BAR — Noon to 1.30am

Buzz-4.50 | Décor-4.00 | Nightout for 2-₹3000

Sorry for the cheap pun, but, on a Friday night, when we pop in to this brand-new Copa (Juhu) it is "swinging". Literally, of course, with swing-seater tables, *et al.* and it's packed. The well-located Copa, sprawls into three sections... an indoor, outdoor and an alfresco bar zone (wooden swings, *et al.*). We check out the indoor, air-conditioned space throbbing with DJ music, but prefer to hang around outside. Here, both in the drinks and the food, the unusual is highlighted in the familiar... for instance, in the robustly spiced Panko-crusted Keema Pao, the chicken is spiced with molagapodi and the burger has a Tandoori Paneer with jalapeño stuffing. These combinations work and sometimes fall short of the mark. It's the unusual cocktails (off the street Kala Khatta Gola), Apple Pie-infused Tea, to a Ginger-spiked Apple and Pear Muddle, the Bailey's Kulfi and the Mumbai-inspired Maximum City Seven Spirits (one for each of Mumbai's islands) that come up tops. But above all, it is the buzz and the excitement that is the winner here at Copa.

■ Anna Bldg., 13th Road, Opp. Juhu Gymkhana, Juhu, Mumbai, Ph: 26708383, M3 7

The Daily

BAR — 7pm to 1.30am

Buzz-4.00 | Décor-3.50 | Nightout for 2-₹3000

Who says no news is good news? This handsome, six-month-old, popular Bandra bar is plastered with framed newspaper clippings (ceiling and everywhere) giving only good news. I walk past the candlit, alfresco area into a chilled, dimly lit, wood-clad bar. Packed. They have a well-stocked bar (no imported wines) and specialize in molecular cocktails (smoking them with hickory and cherry wood), pre-prohibition era cocktails, signature, tiki (Mai Tai, Yellow Bird) ones too.. I quiz several people here and come across Praveen Kumar and his investment banker friends who are not at all happy with the food. On offer are pizzas, pastas and likes. Cajun Chicken and (not to forget) the Pasta of Love (vegetarian pasta in a pink sauce).

■ Ground Floor, Suburbia Bldg., Behind Shoppers' Stop, Linking Road, Bandra (W), Mumbai, Ph: 26418409, M3 35

Dara's Dhaba

RESTO-BAR — 11am to 12.30am

Buzz-1.50 | Décor-3.00 | Nightout for 2-₹3000

Why on earth would a *dhaba* on the highway figure in this Nightlife guide? No! It does not have rocking buzzing bar. But it is just the place to take a break from the highway drive and recline on a charpoy while you down a B52 or a BMW shot. Yes! This *dhaba* does have cocktails and wines too. Charpoys, robust flavours from Punjab and beer make your heart go *balle balle* on the Western Express Highway! Munch on Bhindi Kurmuri, Makkai Tokri, Corn Tikka, Corn Pakoda and Corn Cheese Balls and sip on your chilled beer. Soak in the open-air ambience of this sprawling *dhaba* (indoor seating too) and listen to some Bollywood music. Choose from cocktails (Bloody Mary, Blue Lagoon, Margarita) or mocktails (Virgin Pina Colada or Virgin Mary), or an energy drink (Red Bull) in case you are a teetotaller. On offer are Punjabi and Chinese cuisines. The AC section is closed between 4pm and 7pm but the non-AC section is open throughout the day and one can order drinks anytime of the day. No complementary snacks with drinks here.

■ Western Express Highway, Post Mira, Thane, Ph: 28456119, 32970818, www.darasdhaba.com

Deccan Bar

Bar 11.30 am to 3.30pm, 6pm to 11.30pm

Buzz-1.50 | Décor-2.50 | Nightout for 2-₹3000

Relaxed, casual and tucked away in Byculla's Hotel Heritage. Deccan Bar is a quiet watering hole and not a nightbird's buzzing *adda*. The rich, wood-finished interiors and deep chairs are very welcoming. You can either sit with friends or sit at the counter and chat with the bartender at this bar located in the Heritage Hotel. Their most popular drinks are their Special Pina Colada and Mojito, which they make in their own style. Cocktails like Zombie, Old Fashion, and mocktails like Virgin Mary, Fruit Punch, Pink Chiller, and Virgin Pina Colada are all here. Munch on complementary peanuts, potato wafers, mixed farsaan or bar salad (chargeable), with your drink. You can order food from Nizam, the hotel's in-house restaurant. Only Indian wine and champagne here, along with beer of brands like Kingfisher, Foster's and Budweiser. They are now offering great discounts on imported and domestic liquor. No happy hours though.

HAPPY HOURS: Noon to 3pm, 7pm to 9pm

Hotel Heritage, Sant Savta Marg, Byculla (E), Mumbal, Ph: 23714891, 23734901

The Den

Wine & Lounge Bar Mon–Fri: 6.30pm to 1am, Sat-Sun: 12.30pm to 3.30pm

Buzz-2.50 | Décor-3.00 | Nightout for 2-₹2000

This is a small cosy, little place just off Linking Road and right next to the popular Elbo Room Previously Café Goa, it changed its name last year and now The Den has caught the fancy of the nightbird. Soft music sets the right mood. It has dull golden walls, barrels, wooden chairs and low sofa-seating that recreates the spirit of an English dining den. From wine to beers and everything in between, they have quite a few varieties. As for the music, they have different events every day and Wednesdays are reserved for well known DJ Rahul. They offer one for one on IMFL between 6 to 9. Their wine-based cocktails are trendy and are priced aptly between ₹200-250. Try the Red Wine-based Black Sangria, Red Devil, and Fusion. They have a huge wine menu here... over seventy, I am told... Chardonnay, Red Merlot, Gabriel Meffre and Italian Ruffino... to name a few brought from France, Italy, Spain and Chile. Top of the line champagne and sparkling wines. Wine-infused snacks, Goan food with the likes of Chicken Xacuti, Cafreal and Goan Red Curry with Steamed Rice here. But it's their burgers (beef mainly) and pizzas for a quick bite that come up tops. Their select choice of continental and Italian dishes are quite elaborate and good.

Shop Nos. 3&4, Prabhat Kunj, Road No. 24, Behind KFC, Linking Road, Khar (W), Mumbai, Ph: 26483136

Dhanraj

RESTO-BAR Noon to 3.30pm, 6.30pm to Midnight

Buzz-1.50 | Décor-2.50 | Nightout for 2-₹2000

Bandra's Dhanraj is a pure-vegetarian no-frills restaurant with a separate bar. Must try their starters Jalapeño Poppers and Moong Dal Pakoda. Paneer Pudina Tikka and Mushroom Nazakat along with their other popular options make for good snacky options with the drinks. They serve complementary peanuts, green salad and Batata Wada with your drinks (except Saturdays and Sundays). They have cocktails (Margarita, Martini, Long Island Iced Tea, Long Peach Iced Tea, 20-20, Bull Frog, Lady Killer and High Voltage) and mocktails (Virgin Pina Colada, Funky Toffee, Berry Blush). They serve Punjabi fare and pure Jain food, as well as some Chinese and Continental dishes, although, their regulars are mostly Gujarati and Marwari clients.

231, Link Corner Bldg., Linking Road, Bandra (W), Mumbai, Ph: 26423501, 26403081

Divyasagar Bar & Rest.

RESTO-BAR 10am to 12.30am

Buzz-1.50 | Décor-2.50 | Nightout for 2-₹1500

No fancy cocktails or mocktails here, it's just plain vanilla brandy, rum, vodka, whisky, beer and cheap booze that attracts people to this very basic resto-bar. You'll always find a mix of corporate, office-goers and a few youngsters (serious drinkers) in this three-sectioned (AC, non-AC & family) resto-bar. Food menu is limited too but nice spicy kebabs, rawas, pomfret and Tandoori Chicken are some of the famous eats here. They have Chicken Crispy, Chicken 90, Schezwan Chicken along with Murgh Masala, Banjara Kebab, Malai Kebab, Chicken Maharaja and Lahsuni Kebab to go with your Blender's Pride, Royal Challenge and Black Dog. No happy hours here! The service is quick and its not very heavy on the pocket either.

■ NS Phadke Marg, Saiwadi, Opp. Parsi Colony, Andheri (E), Mumbai, Ph: 26822222/3333/2277

Diwine

Sahara Star's bar, Diwine, is now only a 16-seater smoking lounge dedicated to smokers.

■ Sahara Star, Opp. Domestic Airport, Vile Parle, Mumbai, Ph: 39895000, M3 8

Dome

RESTO-BAR 5pm to 1.30am

Buzz-3.50 | Décor-3.50 | Nightout for 2-₹6000

Take in a spectacular sunset, watch the stars start to sparkle into the Mumbai sky. Perched on the eighth floor of Marine Drive's InterContinental hotel is the only space to soak in the glittering sweep of the Marine Drive. This sensuous rooftop bar started off as a romantic's dream come true but over the past many years has become quite the scene of action. Here, candles in glass jars flicker to music, potted-palms glow mysteriously and an elegant dome houses a small, indoor bar. While the alfresco lounge sets 72, the more exclusive Pool Deck seats 26 and the glassed-in Rouge Bar. Their everyday DJ is from Akhtar's house and Tuesday to Thursday lounge music is played here followed by saxophone and flute by Mr. Woody in the evenings. Ask for their signature cocktails... Margarita, Bellini, Kir Royale, Bull Frog, Long Island Iced Tea, Sex on the Beach, Cosmopolitan, and Black Russian along with Black Mojito and Chamomile Martini. Check out the menu of live grills (Sea Bass and Lamb Chops) and a sushi bar; Kebab Korner specialities too. Plenty for vegetarians... from Kapa Maki to Corn Mozzarella Tempura and Marwari Aloo. The Rouge Bar at the Dome is an ideal place for small parties and functions. You can book the pool deck too.

Note: Is it any wonder that Times UK Online, *Forbes Traveler* and *Telegraph* (UK) have voted Dome one of the top twenty open-air bars in the world!

■ **InterContinental Marine Drive, 135, Marine Drive, Mumbai, Ph: 39879999, M1** 5

Dublin

BAR — 12.30pm to 2.45pm, 6pm to 1.30am

Buzz-3.00 | Décor-3.50 | Nightout for 2-₹5000

Go to this quiet, good-looking, round and cosy room (with an Irish-pub feel) at the ITC Grand Central if you are looking for some privacy. It's an Irish bar and its ambience represents the core of Ireland captured by the three clover shamrock — symbol of Ireland. Dublin's interiors are done in green, with soft leather sofas, stained glass panels and an inviting bar. It is crowded on Monday, Wednesday and Thursday nights. Knock down a few beers or cognacs, Single Malts and martinis to name a few. You can nurse that exquisite Single Malt, Dalmore (12 year old) and 15-year-old Grand Reserve, while watching your favourite sports event on their big screen. Do try their Tall Story (Old Monk and orange juice), Pernod, Malibu and Lagavulin and beers like Amstel Light, Millers Light. Snack on Garlic Potato and Crispy Chilli Chicken. And since you are in Dublin, don't forget the Irish Coffee (well made too, with Jameson Irish Whisky). The snack menu offers the best from Kebabs & Kurries and Shanghai Club. Friendly waiters assist you here. Soft soothing music fills the air after 10pm as you enjoy your drinks (served till closing time 1.30am, food served till 11.45pm).

■ **ITC Grand Central, 287, Dr Babasaheb Ambedkar Road, Parel, Mumbai, Ph: 24101010, M2** 4

Dusk

LOUNGE BAR — 6pm to 12.30am

Buzz-2.50 | Décor-3.50 | Nightout for 2-₹5000

Open till half past midnight, Navi Mumbai's Dusk is more of a relaxed watering hole than a frantic, late night out. It's a contemporary space with walls dressed in a random series of vertical teak slats interspersed with mirror, formal leather sofas and armchairs. On offer are classic cocktails like rum-based Mojito, Rusty Nail and other house specials and shooters like Fruit Kick and the most stylish of all, the BMW. Flaming cocktails (Bend Me Over) and shooters served here too. Also on offer are wines and Single Malts (Oba Glenfiddich) and champagne (five varieties). Celebrity DJ Akhtar plays here. Munch on veg and non-veg starters like Blasted Chicken, Jamaican Jolt and Murgh Tikka. Jive in to their Carnival parties, which they have recently started. Changes will be made to their menu in a few months.

■ **The Park, No. 1, Sector-10, CBD Belapur, Navi Mumbai, Ph: 27589000, M6** 1

D'Bell

Lounge Bar

Buzz.3.00 | Décor-3.50 | Nightout for-₹4000

7am to 1.30am

As the book goes to press, I pop in to the most advertised and hyped D'Bell (café and lounge bar) on its opening night. Three bands played in the large, high-ceilinged space of One India Bulls centre. It was packed, but it was day one and it's too early to tell how this lounge bar will take off. It's been publicized as "A musical nirvana. A liquor connoisseur's delight. A multi-cuisine mania". Indulge in a musical affair to remember with frequent performances by maestros that include popular and established bands, DJs and other artistes.

■ **One Indiabulls Centre, Senapati Bapat Marg, Lower Parel, Mumbai, Ph: 61983100**

The Eau Bar

Bar With Live Music

Buzz-2.50 | Décor-3.00 | Nightout for 2-₹6000

Noon to 1am

If you miss the live bands of yesteryears with their romantic retro songs, then this bar of the Oberoi is your mecca. Here, the band belts out the most memorable numbers (and take requests too). It offers stunning views of the Arabian Sea by day, framed by large picture windows that inspire the name and theme of The Eau Bar at the Oberoi. Elegant white-marbled floors are offset by charcoal carpets. The bar's back-lit wall and marble-topped tables add to the enchantment. Interestingly, the coloured glass table-tops (and on the servers' trays) keep changing colour. Here, the emphasis is on champagne and creative cocktails, served in vibrant, hand crafted glassware. Cocktails are inspired by seasonal ingredients and latest trends. An extensive wine list, selection of Single Malts and other liquors are also available. Ask for the hotsellers, the Oberoi Gimlet, Brandy Alexander and the Spritzers. Mocktails like Virgin Mary and Mint and Ginger Mojito are well-made. Many champagne-based cocktails and contemporary cocktails like their signature Eau Martini (raspberry, vodka and pineapple). Saffron Martini (saffron-infused gin with martini bianco flavoured with smoky Single Malt) is famous too. Premium spirits and liquors (including Single Malts and whiskies) are all on the beverage menu. Complementary snacks like Rice Bites (lemon 'n' pepper flavour) and mixed nuts are served here. Spicy bruschettas, Barbecue Duck Rolls, Reshmi Kebab, Pan-fried Dumplings are the snacks of choice here. No reservations needed.

LIVE MUSIC: 8pm to Midnight (band plays from Monday through Saturday)

■ **The Oberoi, Nariman Point, Mumbai, Ph: 66326220, M1** 6

Eighteen Lounge & Bar

Lounge Bar — 4pm to 1am

Buzz-3.00 | Décor-3.00 | Nightout for 2-₹4000

Open through the evening, Goregaon's Westin Hotel's Eighteen (perched on the eighteenth floor) is a popular lounge bar. Teak wooden floors, raw stone-finish light-walled space with red couches and soothing music will attract you at this chic lounge. Enjoy your drinks while watching matches on their projector screen, which is on everyday! Go to unwind after a hard day at work with their famous cocktail Flirtini — their signature cocktail with vodka, triple sec and pineapple juice topped off with champagne. Do you happen to be in the pursuit of rare vintage Single Malt say a Ladyburn 1973 or a Balvenie 1978? you'll get it here. Cocktails here include Martinis and Long Island Tea. Mocktails here are herbal flavoured and there are also drinks like Berry Berry and Smooth 'n' Nuttie. Murgh Malai Tikka, Tandoori Gobhi and Paneer, Smoked Salmon, Chips 'n' Salsa, sandwiches and burgers are some of the snacks that you can have with your drinks. They also have a selection of premium teas and coffees.

HAPPY HOURS: 5pm to 8pm (on select alcohol)

■ **The Westin Mumbai Garden City, International Business Park, Oberoi Garden City, Goregaon (E), Mumbai, Ph: 61470000, 67361021, 67361830, M5** 3

Elbo Room

Bar — Noon to 12.30am

Buzz-4.00 | Décor-3.50 | Nightout for 2-₹4000

Packed and rocking. This charming little bar lies in the busy bylane of Khar Linking Road, right behind the Levis showroom. It has two sections — a colourful stamp-sized garden with an alfresco seating and a modern vintage pub-like atmosphere complete with bar stools and wooden table inside. A coat of arms with corkscrew and wine opener with the words "In Vino Veritas" adds to the décor. Actor Chunkey Panday's and Nicollo Morrea's aptly named joint venture bills itself as a singles' bar as you're bound to bump into someone interesting as you bustle about in the matchbox-sized bar area inside. Try their newly introduced cocktails like Elbo Kiss and Elbo Delight, also sip on their famous fruit-based cocktails (Margarita, Daiquiri or Martini in Watermelon, Litchi or Kiwi flavour) while you stomp your feet to the thumping music played by in-house DJs. They introduce new cocktails every week starting Wednesday. Catch up with your favourite sport on their TV screens. In their menu, order appetizers like Potato Skins, (Veg/Chicken), Quesidilla (Veg/Chicken) and Dragon Chicken Wings. In salads, order Green Salad, Seafood Salad, Bangkok, Express (Veg/Chicken). They also have burgers of

Grilled Chicken and Elbo Special (Chicken/Lamb). The Chef's Special is Shepard's Pie in Lamb and Beef.

HAPPY HOURS: Noon to 9pm (Sundays through Thursdays). Buy 1 get 1 free on liquor

■ **Plot No. 500, Sant Kutir Apts., Khar Linking Road, Khar (W), Mumbai, Ph: 26483316, M3** 9

Ellipsis

BAR — Tue–Sun: Noon to 3pm; 6pm to 1am

Buzz-3.00 | Décor-4.00 | Nightout for 2-₹5000

Weekends rock at this Colaba restaurant's edgy bar. Internationally renowned Thomas Schoos's décor works especially well at the bar downstairs which is like a stylish living room with its gorgeous tweed couch, statement chairs and large leather rug. American progressive food created by Chef Kelvin and bar consultants Alex Day and David Kaplan of New York's Death & Co. (celebrated cocktail lounge), have put together a unique beverage program. The dynamic young owner, Rohan Talwar, ensures that not only is Ellipsis the only restaurant to sell Pinot Grigio and on tap, but it also holds exclusive serving rights on more than 14 spirits and six beers. Guests can enjoy a healthy selection ranging from "Buzzfree" cocktails, housemade seltzers, syrups, garnishes and infusions, speciality cocktails and shots, the classics, fresh juices and international beers. Only premium spirits and double pours are used in cocktails. Bar bites from Executive Chef Kelvin make the perfect complement with house favourites including Garlic Prawns, Pork Buns, Fish Tacos, Flatbreads and Calamari.

HAPPY HOURS: 7pm to 9pm (only on alcohol). Buy 1 get 1 free

■ **1, Amarchand Mansion, 16, Madame Cama Road, Next to the YWCA, Colaba, Mumbai, Ph: 66213333**

Enigma

As the book goes to press, I am informed that the once rocking Enigma of the JW Marriott has been shut down and is used only for parties and private functions.

■ **JW Marriott, Juhu Tara Road, Mumbai, Ph: 66933288/3000**

Enigma – The Lounge

LOUNGE BAR — Mon, Tues & Thurs: 6pm to 1am, Weekends: Noon to 1am

Buzz-2.50 | Décor-3.00 | Nightout for 2-₹2000

Patrons swear by the music played at Andheri's rather small lounge bar. Two levelled and dimly lit, this place has quite a few cocktail options including the popular Sunset and Alexander. For teetotallers, they have Fruit Punch, Litchi Punch and Pink Lady. They serve these with complementary nachos, which are quite good. A selection of Chinese starters are available from Legacy of China. Enjoy the music by DJ Rahul.

HAPPY HOURS: 6pm to 12am (Mon–Thurs), 6pm to 8.30pm (Fri–Sun)

■ **Legacy of China, Tirupati Towers, JP Road, Versova, Andheri (W), Mumbai, Ph: 26312061/1332, 26368223**

Escobar

Lounge Bar — 7pm to 1.30am

Buzz-4.00 | Décor-3.50 | Nightout for 2-₹4000

As the book goes to press, we pop in here on a Friday night for a quick check out to find it rocking. The country's longest bar at a whopping 77ft that runs at the centre of this 6,000sq ft sprawling space with warm, wooden tanned interiors and white wooden French sofas has many a bar fly hanging on. The open deck as well the indoors are as busy. The menu here has wide variety of cocktails, spirits and bar food (a wide range of Tapas). The absolute must-tries are the Sangria, Long Island Ice Tea, Caipiroska, Mojito and Margarita de la Cartagena. Mocktail choices are many but do go for the Virgin Mojito and the Flavoured Minted Lemonade. Above average and well-made multi-cuisine fare here. From Thai Black Pepper Mushroom, Clay-oven roasted Creamy Garlic Paneer to Clay-oven roasted Chicken and Char-cooked Cilantro Pesto Prawns too. Pizzas and main courses too. So if hunger strikes after many a drink, go for their popular Fresh Herb Spiked Lasagne, Herb-scented Mushroom Crespelm even the Burnt Garlic and Thyme-rubbed BBQ Chicken and the Char-grilled Salmon with gremolata and lemon butter sauce are recommended.

Note: Check out Great Retro music every Wednesday with happy hours (buy one get one free) all through the night on both imported and domestic alcohol.

■ **199, VN Sphere Mall, 4th Floor, Linking Road, Bandra (W), Mumbai, Ph: 42760000**

Exo

Bar

About to Open

As the book goes to press, we are informed that Rishi Acharya is all set to team up with the Palladium Hotel to open their ultra-swish bar and club.

■ **Palladium Hotel, 462, Senapati Bapat Marg, Lower Parel, Mumbai, Ph: 61628000, M2** 5

F Bar

Lounge Bar — Noon to 1.30am

Buzz-2.50 | Décor-4.00 | Nightout for 2-₹6000

Last year, Mumbai's very own F Bar sashayed in (of all places) into the city's latest high-rise in a business district. However, it hasn't managed to rock the city, inspite of its Fashion TV, 10,000sq ft sprawling into restaurant, dance floor, terrace (*Michelin*-starred Vineet Bhatia's food was served here but he has since stopped). F Bar locates itself in the somewhat inaccessible location on the third floor of the One Indiabulls Centre (Lower Parel). At the ground floor, high-ceilinged lobby itself you will be stopped for the cover charge of ₹3,000 per couple. Be prepared for a long walk through the gleaming lobby and corridors of One IBC and into a dark, twin-levelled space with mesmerizing images of the FTV channel on four large walls. Both the bar and restaurant share a theatrical black ceiling upper wooden ceiling that rolls like a wave. God help women with heels who go up the steep stairwell (to the restaurant). No matter which table you sit at in the square-shaped restaurant area, the Fashion TV images are visible. As the book goes to press, I pop in here only to find it desolate.

■ One Indiabulls Centre, 3rd Floor, Next to Gold's Gym, Senapati Bapat Marg, Lower Parel, Mumbai, Ph: 66505820

Fever – The Night Club

PUB — 6pm to 1am

Buzz-3.50 | Décor-3.00 | Nightout for 2-₹3000

There's no cover charge for couples. That's the best thing about this Malad nightclub where the black-and-white décor matches the steward's attire. The music is fairly good with DJ Nishant keeping the crowd interested. Patrons generally agree that alcohol here is not as expensive other night clubs. Try their special cocktails, Tequila Sunrise, Sex on the Beach, Jager Bomb, Bull Frog, Flush Back and Island Affair, as well as their mocktails including Virgin Pina Colada, Virgin Mary, Summer Cooler, Monk Mix and Fantasy Night, among others. Enjoy their speciality exotic drinks, coolers, wines and champagnes. Knock back Karya Chow, Torch, Caipiroska, daiquiris, flavoured Margaritas and Carlabere. The popular kitchens of Jughead and Northern Tadka offer a mix variety of starters such as Mutton Seekh Kebab, Chilli Milli Kebab, Thai Chicken Sauté, Paneer in Oyster Chilli Sauce, Stir-fried Thai Veg and Veg and Non-veg platters. A mix of Indian and Chinese and European food is on the menu here.

HAPPY HOURS: 6pm to Midnight (Monday to Thursday) 6pm to 11pm (Friday to Sunday)

■ 1st Floor, Jagdamba Complex, Behind Movietime Cinema, Malad (W), Mumbai, Ph: 28808883-84

Finger Cross

PUB — Noon to 1am

Buzz-2.50 | Décor-2.50 | Nightout for 2-₹2000

Located off Andheri's Link Road, Finger Cross draws regulars to its indoor and outdoor sections. It draws a mixed crowd and is reasonably packed over weekends. Cocktails here include Pitcher Mojito, Blue Lagoon, Bloody Mary, Long Island Iced Tea, Kamakaze and mocktails like Virgin Pina Colada, Italian Smooch, Mickey Donald, Sun Rise Surprize, or Midnite Blue to choose from. How about a shot of tequila while you munch on the platters available here. Starters aplenty... Paneer Dry Chilli, Chicken Reshmi Kebab and Chicken Kampao. The DJ spins the usual mixes. We are told that their Wood-fired Chicken, Jamaican Spicy Chicken, Roast Lamb Chilli and Grill Lamb Squirts are popular here on their multi-cuisine menu. Service is quite prompt in this VFM place. No happy hours here.

HAPPY HOURS: Noon to 7pm, Midnight to 1am

■ 9, Raheja Classique, Off New Link Road, Lokhandwala, Andheri (W), Mumbai, Ph: 26339997

Firangi Paani

RESTO-BAR WITH LIVE MUSIC

Weekdays: 12.30pm to 3pm, 6pm to 1am, Weekends: Noon to 1am

Buzz-3.50 | Décor-3.50 | Nightout for 2-₹3000

Firangi Paani or FP, as its regulars call it, has a British pub feel... rich interiors, deep-pile carpets, leather-upholstered chairs with a rich, dark polish, a sumptuous fabric and mirror panelling, a flashy mural and a dance floor complete the décor. You can boogie the night away and knock down an Electric Lemonade while the DJ brings the house down everyday (11pm to 1am; except Sundays). This place is over the top but in a good way. They have everything right from cigars, a well-stocked bar, cocktails (Caipiroska, Tom Collins, Bloody Mary) and mocktails (Tropicano Oasis, Summer Cyclist). More of a multi-cuisine restaurant, than a night place, its bar and dance floor does get packed over the weekends. A good à la carte menu with a hearty mix of Mexican, Italian, sandwiches, pizzas and pastas and even the good ol' British Fish 'n' Chips. Platters (Veg, Non-veg and Seafood ₹500 onwards) too. Sizzlers are the speciality here... Kung Pao Chicken, Jack Daniel's Double Barrel Chicken and Steak Combo, Prawn Shashlik, Flaming Veggies with dumplings and Crisp Rolls. This place is over the top but in a good way.

PS: South Mumbaikars, please note, this Firangi Paani is not even remotely related to Frangipani, though both are hugely popular in their own way.

HAPPY HOURS: 6 pm to 10pm (Buy one, get one free on Indian and some imported liquor)

SPECIAL NIGHTS: DJ Nights (Fridays & Saturdays), Ladies' Nights (Mondays and Wednesdays)

■ **Fun Republic, Level 3, Link Road, Andheri (W), Mumbai, Ph: 26744144, 26734730-31, M5** 4

Flamboyante

WINE BAR, BAR WITH LIVE MUSIC 12.30pm to 3.30pm, 7pm to 1.30am

Buzz-3.50 | Décor-3.50 | Nightout for 2-₹4000

As the book goes to press, Flamboyante celebrates its seventh birthday by incarnating in a new *avatar*. It's air conditioned, it's brighter and has added on a lounge bar with coffees. It's 60-ft high ceiling gives it an enchanted airy look. Plants greenery and whites with splashes of colour is what it's all about. The bar also gets a shot of new energy. Not exactly a buzzing nightspot, it is still a place to get a pre- and post-dinner drink. With a guitarist that comes in every Sunday, request for a love song to serenade your date at Flamboyante. Enjoy your drink under the starlit skies while being seduced by the seductive courtyard lighting and the music from the live band. A well-stocked wine tasting room too. Sweet Melon Caipiroska and Kiwi Daiquiri are the signature cocktails here along with cocktails like Margarita, Sex on the Beach and mocktails like Virgin Margarita and Virgin Caipiroska. The menu here is a mix of Oriental and Lucknavi fare with barbecued delicacies and pizzas. Must-tries here include

Smoked Chicken, Cascade Chicken, Barbecued Spare Ribs, Prawns with Burnished Garlic and Kakori Kebabs. The pizzas are popular too.

■ **Shop No. 7, World Trade Centre, Cuffe Parade, Mumbai, Ph: 22180433-34, 40647700, M1** 7

Flute – Champagne Lounge

CHAMPAGNE LOUNGE — Tues–Sun: 8pm to 12.30am

Buzz-2.50 | Décor-3.00 | Nightout for 2-₹4000

With Fahrenheit, the live band playing on Tuesday, Wednesday, Saturday and Sunday, and a change of bar display, Flute – Champagne Lounge at the Sahara Star is a celebration of space, situated on the first floor. Under the world's largest pillarless dome, Flute has the finest view of the courtyard and offers a dozen champagnes to choose from. Complementary snacks like cashew nuts, multi-cuisine snacks (Labneh Chicken, Tandoori Jhinga, Fish 'n' Chips, Onion Rings, Paneer Tikka) served here along with cocktails (Margaritas, Bloody Mary, Mojito, Screw Driver and Martini), wines and other alcohols.

HAPPY HOURS: 7pm to 10pm

■ **Sahara Star, Near Domestic Airport, Vile Parle (E), Mumbai, Ph: 39895000, M3** 10

Frederick's Lounge

LOUNGE BAR — 9am to 10pm

Buzz-1.50 | Décor-3.50 | Nightout for 2-₹4000

Open through the day (till 10pm), it's an ideal place for a relaxed, casual drink. A tastefully done wicker lounge complete with paintings of Mumbai is a cheery extension of the high-ceilinged lobby. Mojitos, caipiroskas, cocktails, and more... a library of Single Malts too for the discerning at Frederick's Lounge. A perfect place to conduct business discussions through the day over a glass of wine (hard drinks served after 11am) or a delicately brewed Darjeeling Summer Tips. They also have a tea rituals (4pm to 7pm) where they serve herbal teas, green teas and regular as well as high-tea snacks and savouries. They have cold sandwiches (which are popular here), grilled sandwiches, starters and dessert (Chocolate Walnut Brownie, Tiramisu and Baked Fruit Cheesecake). This open-through-the-day lounge at ITC Grand Central is dedicated to Frederick William Stevens who designed the Victoria Terminus Station.

HAPPY HOURS: 6pm to 8pm

■ **ITC Grand Central, Dr Babasaheb Ambedkar Road, Parel, Mumbai, Ph: 24101010, 40175117/5093**

Fuel – The Lounge

LOUNGE BAR — 6pm to 1.30am

Buzz-3.00 | Décor-3.00 | Nightout for 2-₹2000

It is bang opposite the the Powai Lake and it is one of few stand-alone bars in the area. Mood lighting and comfy leather seating and interesting starters make this joint popular amongst the Powaiites. They have quite a few cocktails, both exotic and the regular ones (Sex on the Beach, Tequila Surprise, etc). The range in mocktails is not bad either with Fruit Punch, Virgin Pina Colada, Virgin Mojito, Red Kiss, Tallish Man, Gigis and others. Cocktails are served along with complementary Cheeselings. A comprehensive menu consisting of Spanish Chicken Satay, Tex-Mex Sausages and Italian Pasta Alla Boscaiala. Fiery steaks, Chicken Pesto, Honey-glazed Ham and Hot 'n' Peppery Fish are new snacky additions to the menu. Pizzas (Hawaiian Chicken, Chicken Hot Pepper) too. Veggie food lovers need not worry for there's Flaky Chilli Paneer, Spicy Cheese Balls, Bruschetta, Spicy Mexi Veg Pizza, Exotic Veg Paprika for them. No DJ here.

HAPPY HOURS: 5.55pm to 8.55pm

■ **Jheel Darshan, Powai, Mumbai, Ph: 25705222/5333**

Fusion

RESTO-BAR — 7am to 11pm

Buzz-2.00 | Décor-3.00 | Nightout for 2-₹2000

Though Powai's resto-bar is mainly focussed on food, a few do drop by for pre- and post-dinner drinks. Try Fusion's specialities... Kiwi Margarita and Sweet Lime Caipiroska! Powai has a few places to boast about and one of them happens to be Residence Hotel's Fusion. The ambience is the greatest draw here with soft piped music, low lighting, Italian marble floors and fusion décor. A well-pruned garden gives a much-needed break from the hustle and bustle of the city. Classic cocktails like Side Car, Mint Julip, Manhattan, Margarita, Purple Cream, Coral Reef, Acapulco, Bloody Mary, Gimlet, Flying Grasshoper and Screwdriver are all on the menu. Mocktails such as Virgin Pina Colada, Fruit Punch and Donald Duck too. The food menu here offers Italian, European/Global, Chinese, Indian and Thai. All drinks come with complementary peanuts.

■ **The Residence Hotel, Saki Vihar Road, Powai, Mumbai, Ph: 28575000, 28578686-93**

Gadda Da Vida

LOUNGE BAR — 2pm to 1.30am

Buzz-3.00 | Décor-3.50 | Nightout for 2-₹4000

This Juhu Novotel's casual and comfortable (well-stocked) bar is ideal for an after-dinner drink, light snack or even a business meeting (good variety of coffee and tea too).... Ocean view (magnifique!), lighting that adjusts and changes, an alfresco area, an indoor area and a VIP seating for 12–15 people on a reservation basis. On Wednesday, Friday and Saturday evenings (10pm to 1.30am), this 60's style bar morphs into a hip and cool lounge. Come here to groove and rock as the DJ plays progressive house rock. The song is considered significant in rock history because, together with music by Blue Cheer, Jimi Hendrix and Steppenwolf, it marks the point when psychedelic music produced heavy metal. Insistently driving rhythms that typify music of the heavy metal style mark this music. On Friday, Saturday and Sundays there is a minimum bill of ₹1,000 per person.

HAPPY HOURS: 4pm to 8pm (Monday to Sunday)

■ Novotel Hotel, Balraj Sahani Marg, Juhu Beach Mumbai, Ph: 66934444, 66934343, M3 11

Gallops

RESTO-BAR — Noon to Midnight

Buzz-2.50 | Décor-3.50 | Nightout for 2-₹4000

South Mumbaikars meet here during the day or pop in from nearby offices for tea and even a drink after work. Old-world charm (complete with Western instrumental music lilting in the background) surrounded by the lush green of the Mahalaxmi Racecourse. Unwind in the English tavern-style atmosphere of this large, high-ceilinged restaurant done up in teakwood. Imported liquor, wine, spirits of all kinds and even a few cool cocktails (daiquiri and Blue Lagoon) and mocktails (Virgin Colada and Spice Girl) are on offer. Members of Royal Western Indian Trust Club (RWITC) can enjoy a 20 per cent discount on food and 15 per cent on liquor. For more details on food please see The Restaurant Guide.

■ Mahalaxmi Racecourse, Mahalaxmi, Mumbai, Ph: 23071448/1453/1258

Garden Bar

RESTO-BAR — 8am to 7.30pm

Buzz-2.00 | Décor-3.00 | Nightout for 2-₹4000

If at in the vicinity of the Sahar airport and looking for a calm and secluded bar, head to the Hilton. Choose to unwind here after a busy day at work and take a dip in the pool, sip your drinks and soak in the serene atmosphere with lush gardens surrounding the pool. The drinks and food can be ordered from the restaurants inside — right from starters to main course to desserts. Martinis, Pina Colada are some of the cocktails on offer. For mocktail lovers there's Virgin Pina Colada, Green Velvet and others.

■ Hilton, Opp. Escort Centre, Sahar Airport Road, Andheri (E), Mumbai, Ph: 28380000

Garden Court

RESTO-BAR — Noon to 3.15pm, 7pm to Midnight

Buzz-2.50 | Décor-3.00 | Nightout for 2-₹3000

Shimmering mirrors, reflecting surfaces, wooden ceilings will grab your attention immediately at this place. This family restaurant-cum-bar's Vashi branch at the Inorbit Mall doesn't fail to dazzle its patrons. Go for the milder mocktails like Litchi Punch, Fruit Punch, Virgin Pina Colada or Virgin Caipiroska (a popular here) or pick up your cocktails from Martini, Cosmopolitan, Mojito, Long Island Ice Tea, Screwdriver, Planters Punch, etc. Sip on some interesting cocktails mixed by the bartender. Munch on some stick salad and cheeselings (served complementary with your drinks) while you order drinks from their well-stocked bar menu. Whisky, beer and wine are served both by glass and bottle. Try their Veg Kurkure Kebabs, Veg Manchala Kebab, Chicken Tangdi Kebab, Chicken Sunhere Kebab for starters.

HAPPY HOURS: 11.30am to 3 pm, 7pm to 11.30pm (Only in the Ghatkopar Branch; on domestic liquor)

■ **Orlem 167, Marve Road, Malad (W), Mumbai, Ph: 28072973/8342**

■ **JP Road, Near Sports Complex, Andheri (W), Mumbai, Ph: 26770318/0253**

■ **Inorbit Mall, Vashi, Mumbai, Ph: 27810290/91**

■ **Neelyog Square Mall, Ghatkopar (E), Ph: 25010379-52**

Gaylord

RESTO-BAR 12.30pm to 3.30pm, 7.30pm to 11.30pm

Buzz-3.00 | Décor-3.50 | Nightout for 2-₹3000

Centrally located Gaylord has a mezzanine bar area and a few do drop in for a quiet drink here. In fact, Gaylord is an ideal place if you want to avoid smoky, crowded bars. Walk up to the mezzanine floor, which has a few bar stools and regular seating as well. Brandy, vodka, rum, tequila, gin, scotch, champagne, aperitifs, and liqueurs are all available in aplenty, besides kebabs. If you'd prefer a cocktail, you can take your pick from Margarita, Blue Hawaiian and Mojito. Minty Melon, Strawberry Frappe and Caribbean Medley are a few of the refreshing mocktails here. Nibble on the complementary peanuts. Popular starters include Murgh Pahadi Tikka and Tandoori Prawn. Non-Veg Tandoori Platter (₹710 onwards) and Veg Platter (₹300 onwards) too.

■ **20, Mayfair, Veer Nariman Road, Churchgate, Mumbai, Ph: 22821259, 22044693**

Geoffrey's

BAR 11.30am to 1.30am

Buzz-2.50 | Décor-3.00 | Nightout for 2-₹4000

Pip, pip, old chap! This "days-of-the-Raj" bar may not be as buzzing as it used to, but it still continues to be as popular as ever with the after-office crowd. Ole Geoffrey (whoever he is) must be thrilled with the very picture-book British look.... Warm, oakwood tones, gleaming brass, comfortable leather sofas, a sprinkling of colonial touches, sporty knick-knacks and a well-designed bar, all combine to create a mood that is informal enough for a pub and elegant enough for a gentleman's club. This ground-floored bar in Hotel Marine Plaza is great for business entertaining with its quiet alcoves. The afternoons are quiet and relaxed here. DJ Theron plays 7pm onwards. Go for the usual vodka, rum, tequila, Single Malts, cognacs, cocktails, mocktails, and more! Peanuts, salsa, nachos, wafers make up complementary snacks with your drinks (expect slightly higher prices at your next visit). A multi-cuisine menu of snacks and starters like Murgh Malai Kebab, Chicken Banno Kebab are recommended.

■ **Hotel Marine Plaza, 29, Marine Drive, Mumbai, Ph: 22851212**

The Ghetto

Pub — 7pm to 1.30am

Buzz-3.50 | Décor-3.50 | Nightout for 2-₹3000

Please note, ghetto means ghetto — the décor and even its entrance are very ghetto-like. Kick back, relax and do your thing in the Ghetto. This informal place is very ghetto with its graffiti walls, *et al*. Informal dress code (go as you are... in your flip-flops and shorts), reasonably priced drinks, no cover charges, a well-stocked bar makes this place as popular as ever. A varied range of cocktails (B52 shots, Blue Lagoon) and mocktails (Cool Rider, Fruit Punch). VFM, safe for women and sensitive to its clients' likes and dislikes. This seems to be the reason why this place still rocks even after so many years. Smoky, loud, chilled and neon-lit best describes this place. What can one do here? There's plenty... drink, dance to the rock music, play pool, chit-chat or just scribble on the walls here. Try their yummy starters which has the likes of Tangy Sausages, Stuffed Mushrooms, Chicken Fried Strip, Skinned Potatoes, and regular Indian starters too. Even the Hunters Chicken, Horn 'n' Blow, Casabia and Shephard's Pie are good too. They also have a separate room meant for smoking.

■ **30-B, Bhulabhai Desai Road, Near Mahalaxmi Temple, Breach Candy, Mumbai, Ph: 23538418, M2** 6

Ghost

Swish Privé shut down which was followed by the opening of Ghost. We now hear that it has shut down too... what else would you expect from a ghost?

■ **41/44, Ground Floor, Mon Repos, Minoo Desai Road, Colaba, Mumbai**

Goa Portuguesa

Resto-Bar — Noon to 3.30pm, 7pm to 12.30am

Buzz-3.00 | Décor-3.50 | Nightout for 2-₹3000

Get into the Goa spirit with a glass of feni in mini Goa! Walk into Goa Portuguesa with its old Goa-style façade, paintings of sunny Goa, blue pillars, picture windows and waiters in floral shirts. Don't miss the table mats featuring Mario's sketches of Goa. Get serenaded as you dig into delicious Gaon fare (a separate kitchen for veggie food). Do meet the flamboyant owner and his lovely wife, Dr Suhas and Deepa Awchat, before leaving. Try their new wines Nature's Bounty, French Root (French) & Soledoro (Italian), Filanda Vodka or Caribbean Ginestra. You can even bring your own imported booze here without paying for corkage! Sportsmen, doctors, journalists, senior citizens and physically-challenged are entitled to a 10 per cent discount.

SPECIAL NIGHTS: Guitarist (Wednesday & Friday-Sunday)

■ **Near Hinduja Hospital, TH Kataria Road, Mahim, Mumbai, Ph: 24440202/0707**

Gokul Rest & Bar

RESTO-BAR 11am to 1am

Buzz-3.50 | Décor-2.50 | Nightout for 2-₹1500

Go to Gokul for a taste of Mumbai's no-frills nightlife at its throbbing best. Check out their claim of serving the cheapest drinks and cold drinks. Rub shoulders with more than 500 people in this functional and bustling, twin-levelled restaurant, which sells alcohol by the "quarter". I find their air-conditioned section too cramped (drinks here are served by the "peg system" and include brandy, vodka, rum, tequila, gin, scotch and champagne). I enjoy the hum of humanity and watching them walloping down Fish Curry and Chicken Tikkas with gusto and can understand why this family-owned place has been popular for the past 35 years.

■ **Nawaz Bldg., 10, Tulloch Road, Behind Taj Mahal Palace & Towers, Colaba, Mumbai, Ph: 22848248**

Golden Chariot

RESTO-BAR 11.30am to 1am

Buzz-2.50 | Décor-3.50 | Nightout for 2-₹3000

Thane's Golden Chariot's *mehfils* (*ghazals* everyday, except Monday) are what keeps regulars coming back for more. DJ Mukesh also pumps up the tempo here. A well-stocked bar and a selection of cocktails (Strawberry Daiquiri, Lynch Burg Lemonade, Bikini Martini, Under Pressure, Kiss me Quick and Birthday Bash too). Mocktails (Virgin Navel, Cinderella, Thief) are recomended. Complementary snacks with selected items on different days like Chana Chaat, Aloo Chaat, cheeselings and potato chips. Popular food items include Subzi Uttranchali, Chicken Pahadi Kebab, Achaari Murgh Tikka, Veg Crispy, and assorted platters. They have mini-mall branches at Kalyan Metro, Kandivali Grover Mall, Metro Mall in Kalyan and Thakur Mall in Dahisar.

HAPPY HOURS: 6pm to 8pm

SPECIAL NIGHTS: Ghazals (8pm to Midnight) except Mondays

■ **The Hub Mall, 2nd Floor, Western Express Highway, Goregaon (E), Mumbai, Ph: 26866867/69, 67988777, 67988790**

■ **V Mall, 4th Floor, Thakur Complex, Western Express Highway, Kandivali, Mumbai, Ph: 28547258-59**

■ **Girnar Tower, Sai Baba Nagar, Mira Bhayandar Road and Off MTNL Road, Mira Road (E), Thane, Ph: 28124546, 9323338234**

Golden Wok

RESTO-BAR Noon to 3.30pm, 7pm to 11.30pm

Buzz-3.00 | Décor-2.00 | Nightout for 2-₹2000

Chembur's Golden Wok's make-shift interiors (wooden chairs and tables) has a no-frills bar too. Alcohol here is well-priced for guzzlers looking to tank up. Whisky,

Absolut Vodka and rum-based cocktails all for under ₹300. Sip on Bloody Mary, Screwdriver, Tom Collins, Pina Colada, Planter's Punch or Blue Lagoon. Mocktails available too... choose from Virgin Pina Colada, Green Chamber, Mickey Mouse or Virgin Margaritas. Head upstairs for a quiet and cozy meal with Kung Pao Chicken, Gullyan Chicken or the Crispy Spinach, which make for great appetizers.

■ **Sai Krupa Compound, Near Dukes Co., WT Patil Marg, Opp. Shatabdi Hospital, Chembur, Mumbai, Ph: 67974266, 67974267**

Grand Centre

RESTO-BAR 11am to 3.30pm, 6.30pm to 12.30am

Buzz-3.00 | Décor-1.50 | Nightout for 2-₹1500

Nightbirds looking for a non-smoky and noise-free bar, head this way please. Grand Centre is a hard-core drinker's paradise with decent selection of drinks to choose from. The orders are brought to your table by the waiters from the pantry as there's no bar counter. Litchi Punch is the winner here while other mocktails like Fruit Punch, Green Iceland, Pineapple Punch or Thumbs Up Float are refreshing options too. Popular cocktails include Grand Centre Kick, Blue Lagoon, Planter's Punch, Pink Panther and Chapman served along with complementary snacks like *chana, papad*, peanuts and salad. Try their Veg Platter (₹250), Non-veg Platter (₹375), Murgh Masala, Reshmi Kebab Masala, Veg Chop Masala, Assorted Vegetable, etc. to accompany your drinks.

■ **Kalakdina Terrace, August Kranti Marg, Gowalia Tank, Mumbai, Ph: 23805775/4787**

Green Jade Oriental Lounge & Bar

LOUNGE BAR Noon to 1am

Buzz-2.50 | Décor-3.00 | Nightout for 2-₹3000

Go to this cool, compact lounge bar in Andheri with low seating (uncomfy for a meal but comfy to lounge) and knockback the oversweet cocktails. The music is pretty good and the real fun starts at around 9pm when the house DJ belts out his favourites. There is no dance floor, but nobody minds if you are in a mood to jive a bit. Jager Bombs, Bull Frogs and Shangri La cocktails here are good to get your party started! Regular cocktails (Tequila Sun Rise, Mojito, Pina Colada, Black Russian, Old Fashion) and mocktails (Mango Bloom, Hawaiian Punch, Mickey toffee and White Cloud) available here along with complementary peanuts. Wok-smoked Lamb, dim sums, Mixed Fried Noodles and chicken dishes to choose from their okayish fine-tuned to the Indian palate. The Chinese menu is a bit over priced though. Service is pretty quick and the crowd is not bad either.

HAPPY HOURS: 6pm to Midnight

■ **34, Saffron House, Central Road, MIDC, Andheri (E), Mumbai, Ph: 65173131, 66880909**

H2O – The Liquid Lounge

DISCOTHEQUE/NIGHTCLUB 5.30pm to 1.30am

Buzz-3.50 | Décor-4.00 | Night out for 2-₹3000

Tucked into Bandra's Hotel Royal Inn, H2O offers a choice... it has two sections... a dance floor where the crowd is as loud as the music and a staircase leading to the the quiet lounge and the Standing Bar. As the name suggests, you stand in the Standing Bar. Water bounces off the walls and as you look down through the glass floor, you will notice the dance floor beneath. Try the cocktails mixed by the talented bartenders here (Tennesy Brunette, Salty Lips, H20 Martini, Wild On) or mocktails (Red Dream, Meri's Mellow, etc). Try the Bacardi Blaze, Goa Margarita, Rude Cosmopolitan, Joe Downer, Caribbean Rock, Linking Breeze, 3-in-1, BMW, TGV, Irish Fucker and KBV. Sony Sachdev's "Sheetal Bukhara" touch is evident in the succulent kebabs available from the extensive snack menu. Take your pick from Chicken Achaari Kebab, Chicken Shole Kebab, Mutton Kakori Kebab, Prawns in Hot Black Garlic, Fish Blackbean Dry, Fish Chilli Wine and Paneer Bukhara. They have projectors, big screens and Plasma TV that shows live matches.

■ **Hotel Royal Inn, Off Linking Road, Khar (W), Mumbai, Ph: 26495151, 9833625700, M3** 12

Hakkasan

RESTO-BAR Fri–Sun: Noon to 4.30pm, 7pm to 1am, Mon–Thur: 7pm to 1am

Buzz-3.00 | Décor-4.00 | Nightout for 2-₹7000

London's *Michelin*-starred Hakkasan, in the middle of 2011 made huge waves when it set up on the second floor in Bandra. However, it has not been rocking as it was when it first set up. Like the other Hakkasans, this one also has an uber-cool crowd in a sultry Oriental space, manned by stylish waitresses. And within the restaurant is Ling Ling... the Lounge which reflects the old-school decadence of Chinoiserie. Here, the 16-metre bar, a mystical melange of blue glass and stainless steel, is the centre of attention. An extraordinary wall of sawn slate provides a dramatic backdrop to the nocturnal bar activity. Ling Ling is punctuated with signature traditionally drawn panels. Profusion of intricately carved wooden screens, dim mood lighting, rich wood-panelled furniture and rippling light on the walls complete the décor. Over 900 bottles of wine and a selection of 125 labels especially chosen to complement Hakkasan's menu and the sommelier ably assists in doing so. Check out the elegant mirror-panelled whiskey cabinet with its exquisite selection of over a dozen rare old and exclusive Single Malts. Plenty of munchies with the drinks, from crispy rock shrimp and hand-pounded Rock Corn Cakes to Chilli Tamarind with (oven-roasted) Baby Aubergine. Salad Samplers and more. Do ask for over 35 varieties of cocktails prepared with seasonal fresh fruits exotic ingredients. Bartender will shake or stir your martini on your table too (the Litchi and Lemongrass Martini is recommended).

■ **Krystal Bldg., Above ICICI Bank, Water field Road, Bandra (W), Mumbai, Ph: 26444444, M3** 13

Harbour Bar

BAR

Buzz-3.00 | Décor-3.50 | Nightout for 2-₹7000

[Y] [card] [AC]
11am to 1.30am

Welcome to the city's oldest bar (bar license #1, 1933) and also the most relaxed bar! It's a great choice for pre- and post-dinner drinks with warm interiors, intimate seating, luxurious appointments and mood lighting comfort. Well-know for its collection of fine malts, international wines and global tapas, it continues to make James Bond proud (in fact, Pierce Brosnan has actually had his martini here). Soft jazz music playing in the background, elegant menu of starters, English-pub food and a view of the Gateway of India makes it the most relaxed bar in the city. Go for their "Martini Service" where the bartender creates classic, trendy and dessert martinis at individual tables. In true Bond-style, all martinis are shaken and not stirred! They are famous for their signature cocktails, champagne lounge, Single Malts and Cigars. Many a corporate deal have been struck here over a leisurely drink and dinner. Ask for 'From the Harbour since 1933', the signature cocktail, Asian Spice cocktails like the Paan Flip and with them the ever-popular, Golden-fried Prawns, Chicken Tikka, Minted Aioli Wraps, Satay Chicken Dry Red Chilli while Louisana-spiced Prawns, Sichuan Chilli Baby Corn are the latest additions. They have also introduced champagnes by glass (₹1,050–4,000) now.

■ **The Taj Mahal Palace, Apollo Bunder, Mumbai, Ph: 66653366**

Hard Rock Café

RESTO-BAR WITH LIVE MUSIC

Buzz-4.00 | Décor-4.00 | Nightout for 2-₹4000

[Y] [card] [AC]
Noon to 1.30am

I'm impressed. Hard Rock Café rocks. I pop in on a Thursday night and whoa! What energy. Friendly staff, lots of action, live band (not the greatest), Ladies Nite coupons being dished out for Wednesdays and much, much more. "It's fun to stay at the Y-M-C-A" belts out the enthusiastic staff of Hard Rock Café who pause on the hour to climb up and dance on the wooden panelling that segregates the bar floor from the rest of the restaurant to stir up the crowd, inviting patrons to sing and gesture along with them. Loud rock music and a bustling bar. A throbbing, noisy, boozy night *avatar* for you? Or a more sedate, quiet one through the day? Choose your time to match the schizophrenic personality of this centrally located café. Dramatically lit split levels characterize the warehouse-like look of this café that displays on its deep velvet walls memorabilia that most of the young rockers would appreciate — Eric Clapton's Versace suit, one of Tom Petty's guitars, Prince's Purple Rain military-style coat, and even one of David Bowie's signed suits! While these priceless pieces of Rock 'n' Roll history aren't for sale, the Rock Shop at the entrance offers pins, collectibles, those popular Hard Rock logo T-shirts, glasses, caps and other accessories for fans. Food isn't the focus here, the over-sized portions (with prices to match). Dry and stale Nachos with Sour Cream Jalapeños Cheese Sauce and Potato Skins stuffed with Dry Bacon Bits. Even the *aamchi mumbai*...

Paneer Kathi Roll Roomali with undercooked *kutcha masala*. It's the legendary 6-ounce Beef Burger in a warm bun that delights. Stody Apple Cobbler and okayish cheesecake.

Note: Shell out ₹65 for parking.

■ **Bombay Dyeing Mills Compound, Pandurang Budhkar Marg, Worli, Mumbai, Ph: 24382888, 66511209,** www.hardrock.com, **M2** 7

Harry's

PUB
Just Opened

Noon to Midnight

Powai is where Singapore-based pub chain, Harry's, has opened. As the book goes to press, Harry's is all set to offer international beers, interesting cocktails, wines and mocktails. Of course, the famous Dirty Harry and Caramel Popcorn Martini along with the Jazz Burger, Chicken Lollypops and Wasabi Paneer will be served too.

■ **IT Bldg., 1st Floor, 103, Ventura Park, Hiranandani Gardens, Opp. D Mart, Powai, Mumbai, M6** 2

Hawaiian Shack

RESTO-BAR
Buzz-3.50 | Décor-3.00 | Nightout for 2-₹3000

6.30pm to 1am

Get transported to the palm-fringed beaches at the Hawaiian Shack. This rocking bar in Bandra and now in Juhu also, with its wooden-floors, thatched-ceilings, loud music is a place to totally chill out. Summer Cooler (popular mocktail), Long Island Iced Tea or Sex Special (crowd-pleasing cocktails), inexpensive booze and bar snacks too (Spring Rolls, Crispy Chicken, Chicken Salt 'n' Pepper, Chicken Shashlik). Complimetary snacks can be anything from the menu of their choice.

P.S. I must admit, I enjoyed the cosy atmosphere and most of all, I lost my heart to the waiters in their colourful Hawaiian shirts and straw hats.

HAPPY HOURS: 6.30pm to 7pm (Bandra) , 6pm to 8pm (Juhu)

COVER: ₹500 (weekdays) & ₹1,000 (weekends) for Bandra ; Wed-Thurs ₹400, Friday & Saturday ₹1,000 for Juhu, Ladies free

SPECIAL NIGHTS: Ladies Night (Tuesdays), Messy Night (monkey nuts; Thursdays), Regular hip-hop & Commercial (Fri&Sat) on the 1st floor and Retro for ground floor for Bandra

■ **16th Road, Opp. Mini Punjab, Bandra (W), Mumbai, Ph: 26058753, 9967211694, M3** 15

■ **48, Gulmohar Road, 3rd Floor, Next to Costa Coffee, JVPD Scheme, Juhu, Mumbai, Ph: 33784444-47, 9619463371, 9967211694, 9619463413, M3** 14

The High Stake

BAR
Buzz-2.50 | Décor-3.00 | Nightout for 2-₹3000

11am to 1am

Soothing brown ambience with aromatic candles is what you will find in this open-through-the-day bar tucked away inside Hotel Bawa International. This place has a nice range of cocktails and drinks and it is also known for its intersting starters and kebabs. Match their popular Flamingo Cocktail, Blue Martini, Hight Stick Classic and Macko Martini with starters like Chicken Tikka, Chicken Chilli, Fish Tikka, Fish Chilli, Paneer Tikka or pakoras. A well-stocked bar (imported and domestic) and plenty of cocktails (Margaritas, Screwdriver, Bloody Mary, etc). Munch on the basic complementary snacks like salad and Hippo chips, or even more starters like Tandoori Pomphret, Hara Bhara Kebab, Paneer Tikka, Masala Papad and Veg Seekh Kebab. How about a Fruit Punch, fragrant Mango Gloom, Blue Dream, Millionaire or Tarzan for teetotalers. Peach Collins, Vodka Collins, Gin Collins, Strawberry Collins, Scotch Collins, ABC, Real Fighters are some more cocktails, and KBC, B52 and Day and Night Shooters — the barman also makes special requests for drinks. They have happy hours now where they offer 20 per cent discount.

HAPPY HOURS: 11am to 9 pm

■ **Hotel Bawa International, Nehru Road Extension, Vile Parle, Mumbai, Ph: 26113636/3856**

HQ's – City's 1st All Day Pub

Pub

Noon to Midnight

Buzz-3.50 | **Décor-3.50** | **Nightout for 2-₹3000**

Walk up the stairs into this British-style pub look alike. A well-lit space with wooden floors, green-and-oakwood, retro music and large TV screens flashing away welcomes you here. Large, glass ventilators look into Café Royal below. This old-fashioned, comfy and affordable pub happens to be the only place in the city where beer (Kingfisher, Stella and Hoegaarden) are available on tap! Even though the ceiling is a bit low and the air-conditioning a bit strained, there is something very comforting about this place. Grab a drink from any of the four sides of the island bar that sits in the heart of the pub. They also have absinthe and unique shots like Celtic 6. A Wi-fi enabled place, enjoy the sizzlers which are popular here along with sandwiches, burgers, pizzas and pastas.

HAPPY HOURS: Noon to Midnight (Monday to Thursday); Noon to 10pm (Friday to Sunday)

SPECIAL NIGHTS: Ladies' Night (Wednesdays)

■ **166, Indian Mercantile Mansion, Opp. Regal Cinema Colaba, Mumbai, Ph: 22883985, 65140197**

The Hub

Resto-Bar

11am to Midnight

Buzz-2.50 | **Décor-3.50** | **Nightout for 2-₹3500**

Check out their BOGO promotions (buy one get one), Special IPL promotions and even "classics in colour" (old Hindi songs live performances). Not a buzzing nightspot but more of an all-day resto-bar. Close to the airport and on the Western Express Highway, Ibis Hotel's Hub hums quietly. Double-height ceilings and a 16-ft wall of windows, low seating and an open layout bathed in natural light makes it a pleasant destination. It's ideal for a quick snack or even a healthy one. Open through the day, they offer their take on "happy hours"... complementary evening get togethers, food and beverage pairings topped off by their signature evening smoothie. Ask for the unusual Date and Olive stuffed Khajurbhari Aloo ki tikki and the Crispy Corn Kurkure Chaat. The non-veg dishes are not as good! Be it Batter-fried Prawns or Spicy Chicken Meatballs.

■ **IBIS Hotel Mumbai, Plot No. F-77, Junction of Nehru Road, Western Express Highway, Vile Parle (E), Mumbai, Ph: 67087777**

Hype

As the book goes to press, we are informed that Hype has shut down and is given out for private parties.

■ **Atria The Millennium Mall, R1, 4th Floor, Dr Annie Besant Road, Worli, Mumbai, Ph: 24813799, 67363799,** www.hypetheclub.com, **M2** 8

I-Bar

BAR Mon–Sat: 4.30pm to 1am; Sun: 12.30pm to 1am

Buzz-3.00 | Décor-3.00 | Nightout for-₹3000

As the book goes to press, I-Bar reopens after being closed for two months. And it gets even more high-tech and expands its space. I pop in for a quick *dekho*. The entire bar area is 3-D whirr of psychedelic images. This 3-D projection-mapped bar has been visually mapped by complete scenography by doing projection mapping and using infinite mirrors. The interactive table is fascinating and images dance and swirl and twirl as you move your fingers over the table top. You can also watch the table light up as your drink slides across the interactive "I-Bar Table", which, owners claim, is the first of its kind in India. Tucked away in a quiet and leafy lane of Bandra Reclamation, it is also known for its bartending workshops for women, Open Mic nights for poets, magicians, comedians and rappers alike. Keeping up-to-date with technology trends as well, they have an operational i-Pad ordering system where all your menu options are given, with perfect descriptions and pictures of dishes as well as drinks that will go well with them (ordering has also now become interesting!). Also a live juke box application that is installed for you to pick music! Molecular Mixology offers us Kamakaze Shots with beer and Lime Foam, Strawberry Margarita with Strawberry Foam and Berry Pearls, Pina Colada Shots with Coconut Foam, Vanilla Vodka with Kahlua Foam and more. Beyond the weekly featured foams (sometimes mint, sometimes others), they'll customize everything from strawberry and peach to apricot for froth fanatics. They also have fresh fruit special drinks that include Bailey's Banana Colada, Blackgrape Mojitos, Mandarin Caipiroska and Kiwi Margarita. It's definitely a place that brings an eclectic mix of people together. It remains an Interactive Bar with I-pad menus and the best part is that its rates make it nearly one of the most pocket friendly, yet futuristic bars!

■ **7-8, Gleki, ONGC Colony, Bldg. No. 2, Bandra Reclamation, Bandra (W), Mumbai, Ph: 9930588479**

Image

RESTO-BAR — 11.30am to 3.30pm, 6pm to 12.30am

Buzz-2.00 | Décor-3.00 | Nightout for 2-₹2000

Enjoy a candle-lit dinner every Tuesday in Image at Goregaon. Some cocktails to try are Goa Juice, Alwa Punch and Pink Lady. The bar menu includes mocktails like Bar Special, Strawberry Delight, Mango Delight and Sons of Wales. Nibble on Aloo Chaat, Roasted Papad, Chana, Bhujia, pakodas, cheeselings and Chana Chaat as you knock back Sea Breeze, Black Russian and Between the Sheets from their list of cocktails.

HAPPY HOURS: 6.30pm to 8.30pm

■ **Hotel Laxmi International, SV Road, Goregaon (W), Mumbai, Ph: 28741251, 28767225/7869**

Indigo

RESTO-BAR — Noon to 4pm, 7pm to 1am

Buzz-3.00 | Décor-3.50 | Nightout for 2-₹5000

I pop in to Indigo on a Saturday night, as the book goes to press. Zarir Warden's live band is pumping the energy and rocking the night. A much-older SOBO crowd is propping up the bar... ace-lensmen Atul Kasbekar and friends here too. Weekends find the bar empty. Stark walls, sandstone flooring, polished teak furniture, offset by brightly coloured surfaces and house music make up the ambience here. A wooden staircase against a blood-red wall leads you from the bar to the open-air terrace and into the cosy wooden-roofed lounge. However, the Burgundy Lounge on the terrace is desolate. It is now used for hosting wine dinners and has wine and Single Malts. Relax and nurse your Single Malt and order the finest wines as you munch on the antipasti menu of Poached Prawns Cocktail, Leek 'n' Gorgonzola Gnocchi, Roast Mushrooms 'n' Gruyère Crostini, Mushroom Almond Pâté, Grilled Artichoke, Yellow Fin Tuna Sashimi and more. It has bagged "Wine Spectator" awards and has blazed many a trail in the cocktail world. Step into Indigo to unwind with their Fresh Fruit Margaritas (they were introduced in Mumbai right here), grappas, cognacs and rare whiskies. The Sour Apple Martini tops the list here. Mojitos, Kiwi Margarita, Gooseberry Margarita and the magnificent list of wines are the stars here.

Note: They do provide a chauffeur if you can't drive back after all partying here, and also have small banquets on request and as per requirement.

■ **4, Mandlik Road, Off Colaba Causeway, Colaba, Mumbai, Ph: 66368999, 9820968555, 9702378664**

Indus – Cocktail Bar & Tandoor

RESTO-BAR — Noon to 3pm, 6pm to 1am

Buzz-3.00 | Décor-3.50 | Nightout for 2-₹2500

Shades of blue, a back-lit bar, a cramped dining area, mirrored wall and an impressively well-stacked bar is what you'll find if you do drop in at Hotel Diplomat's contemporary resto-bar Indus. Enjoy the numerous cocktails (Purple Rain, Black Magic, Island Affair, Fruit Martini) and refreshing mocktails (Virgin Mary, Spice girls, beachy Sunrise). Evenings are a bit more buzzy hence, reservations are advised. A pre-plated Indian fare too.

HAPPY HOURS: Noon to 3pm, 6pm to 8pm

■ **Hotel Diplomat, 24-26, BK Marg, Apollo Bunder, Behind Old Taj, Mumbai, Ph: 22021661**

Irish House

LOUNGE BAR — Noon to Midnight

Buzz-4.00 | Décor-3.50 | Nightout for 2-₹3000

Head to the packed Irish House for a cheery, beery VFM meal or snack. This pub has been modelled after traditional public houses of old Ireland and keeping with that spirit, it has a wooden décor sprawling under a green ceiling, brick walls and wooden floors. Along with your drinks and pub grub, you can enjoy favourite games on the giant screen in this rather boisterous club. From local favourites to Hoegaarden and Stella, you will find beers from all over the workd including Mexico, Japan and of course Ireland. Plenty of cocktails, international wines, Single Malts on the bar's extensive drinks menu... but it's the beer which is the main draw... Kingfisher, Stella and Hoegaarden are on tap and the international beers include Tsingtao, BiRra Moretti and Amstel Light. There's no Guinness, only Murphy's Irish Stout and the Irish Jameson whiskey and Bailey's. "Irish today, hungover tomorrow" and many such signs dot the space. Even the waiters wear funky T-shirts with taglines like "Free beer tomorrow". The pub grub includes Irish Sergeant Potato Skins (tasty coin-sized appetizers stuffed with corn and cheese) as well as nachos. Large platters of generous helpings of food with above-average, but well-priced fare. Not gourmet fare, some of it is patchy but pairs well with the alcohol here, be it the Crispy Duck Spring Rolls that come with two spicy dips; the large plate of Batter-fried Fish 'n' Chips; soggy fries, even the Grilled Chicken Spaghetti is worth trying. If you feel like testing your vocal chords at the start of the week, head here for Karaoke Nights on Mondays. They have happy hours from 5pm to 8 pm every night.

■ **Phoenix Mills, Senapati Bapat Marg, Lower Parel, Mumbai, Ph: 43471111**

HAPPY HOURS: 5pm to 8.30pm

Irish Pub

PUB — Noon to 1am

Buzz-2.50 | Décor-3.50 | Nightout for 2-₹2500

Wooden interiors, framed pictures and staple diet of Irish jokes, besides of course good old Irish drinks and pub grub is what you get in this pub at Ramee Guestline at Khar. With special offerings like Murphy Irish Stout Beer and Glenfiddich this place is bound to impressive with their collection. Good news for Foster's beer lovers... enjoy buy-two-get-one-free offer all through the day. Munch on complementary snacks like green salad and peanuts. Jamaican Coffee, Irish Kiss, Texan Coffee, Leprechauns Dance, Irish Sun Rise and Banana Nut Blast are some of the choices from their well-stocked bar. Take your pick from their Non-veg (₹650 onwards) or Veg (₹450 onwards) platters or Pepper Chicken and Pesto Chicken.

SPECIAL NIGHTS: Romantic Nights (Tuesdays; with candle light dinner, et al), Karaoke Nights (Thursdays), Princess Nights (Wednesday; two free drinks for ladies), Irish Nights (Fridays; rock music), House Party (Saturdays), Commercial Nights (Sundays)

HAPPY HOURS: Noon to 9pm; buy one get one free on Indian liquor

■ **Hotel Ramee Guestline, 757, SV Road, Khar (W), Mumbai, Ph: 61506688/66**

Ivy Bar & Bistro

Y ▭ AC

BAR, WINE BAR — 10am to 1am

Buzz-3.00 | Décor-2.50 | Nightout for 2-₹2500

A glass of wine and a happy bite in a casual atmosphere? You can enjoy a glass of domestic Indage wine (the cheapest priced at ₹120) and check out many more domestic wines by the glass too. Vickrant (Chateau Indage) Chougule's brainchild has maps of the wine regions sketched on the ceiling, wine shelves lining the walls, wine books to browse through and wine accessories to buy. There are 130 selections (their own and imports). Take your pick from White, Red, and Rose Wines like Tiger Hill Brutrose, Marquise de Pompadour, Indage Platinum series Sauvignon Blanc, Indage Vineyards Gold Series Chardonnay Semillion, Indage Platinum Series, Merlot Syrah, Indage Vineyards Gold series, Shiraz, Cabernet, Tiger Hill Vineyards, Merlot Shiraz. Chantilly, Chardonnay and Chantilly Cheninblanc, Chantilly Merlot, Chantilly Shiraz, Chantilly White Zinfandel, Ivy wine Zinfandel, and Tiger Hill Zinfandel. Pair your drink with Potato Wedges, Fish 'n' Chips, Cajun Chicken and Crispy Jalapeño Poppers. Do check out their ATMs (All Time Meals), which features dishes like Hyderabadi Keema Pao, Shephard's Pie, Bangers 'n' Mash with Onion Gravy, Seared Chicken with Mashed Potatoes and Veggies, and Chicken and Mushroom Pie. The service is pretty good and if you want assistance for pairing your wines and knowing the finer points of wine drinking, staff here is very warm and helpful.

PS: Check out the neighbouring "In Wine & Beer Shop", open from 10am to 11pm, which sells domestic wines and many international ones as well (from Barolo to Mateus Rose and Rioca). They do home delivery too.

■ **Indage House, 82, Dr Annie Besant Road, Opp. RBI, Worli, Mumbai, Ph: 66547939, M2** 9

■ **Seven Bungalows, Picnic Cottage, Aram Nagar, 1, JP Road, Andheri (W), Mumbai, Ph: 26395995, M5** 6

■ **Shop No. 6, Mangal Bhavana, Corner of Khar Pali Road, 14th Road, Khar (W), Mumbai, Ph: 65347788, M3** 16

Jalsa

Y ▭ AC

RESTO BAR — 5pm to 1.30am

Buzz-2.50 | Décor-3.00 | Nightout for 2-₹2500

From rustic benches to the typical cushions that are found in rural areas of India and other such things, it's a typical *dhaba* setting, but very sophisticated. This 60-seater resto-bar is cool and sophisticated with slow music playing in the background. Gulp down your favourite domestic liquor from the well-stocked bar. Pair them up with Indian snacks. A wide assortment of kebabs and platters available too. Their cocktails include Long Island Ice Tea, Margarita or Martini all of which go well with the complementary snacks (peanuts, cheeselings, papad).

HAPPY HOURS: 5pm to 8pm

■ **VITS Business Hotel, Andheri-Kurla Road, Andheri (E), Mumbai, Ph: 28270707, 61517555**

Jam Jar Diner

RESTO-BAR 9am to 1am

Buzz-3.50 | Décor-3.50 | Nightout for 2-₹2000

Looking for a relaxed drink in Versova? Enter the fairly new, small, blue bungalow with juke box (it works), the mixed print crockery and the crooked shelves grab attention. Climb the stairs to a mosaic-tiled, alfresco terrace. Sit on the charming alfresco terrace or while away the hours listening to golden oldies on the juke box. It's like coming to granma's cottage, a comforting feeling for some moderately priced, standard, comfort food. Open all day and serving American diner-style fare, Jam Jar also doubles as a nightspot with plenty of cocktails with a twist to them. The bar makes a small selection of the usual cocktails but with a "twist". American diner-style comfort food (burgers, hot dogs, pancakes, waffles, eggs) is far better than the Tex-Mex fare here. See the restaurant guide for more details.

■ **7-A&B, Aram Nagar 2, JP Road, Versova, Mumbai, Ph: 26358880, 26368880, M5 7**

Janata Lunch Home Restaurant & Bar

RESTO-BAR 11.30am to 1.30am

Buzz-3.50 | Décor-3.50 | Nightout for 2-₹800

Bandra's Janata Lunch Home is an appropriately named resto-bar. Here you will find men gulping down their chilled beer and popping pakodas till the wee hours of the night. Cheap booze is the main attraction here. Order anything from whisky, rum, beer or vodka. Well-worn formica adorned table tops, a blaring TV and an air-conditioned section to be found here. Order up a Butter Chicken or a biryani, both of which are popular here. A range of starters to fill your tummy like Chicken Tikka, Chicken Chilli, Chicken Manchurian, Chicken Crispy, Fish Tikka and Fish Chilli and in Vegetarian Paneer Chilli, Paneer Tikka, Paneer Manchurian, Veg Manchurian and Veg Crispy to name a few!

■ **Pali Naka, Bandra (W), Mumbai, Ph: 26004049/5180**

Jewel of India

RESTO-BAR 12.30pm to 3.30pm, 7.30pm to Midnight

Buzz-3.50 | Décor-3.50 | Nightout for 2-₹3000

Brilliantly located in Worli and with plenty of parking space! This handsome, tucked-away bar has many regulars. Breezy, plush interiors and very well stocked too.

It offers champagne, brandy, vodka, rum, gin, scotch, tequila, liqueurs and much more. Checkout their popular cocktails which include Tequila Sunrise, Sex on the Beach and Long Island Iced Tea. Or go for a glass of wine from their wide range of Sula wines available here (Ivy, Monkrock, Chantilly, Talasca and Belvedere). Chicken Tikka Kummel, Lobster Neerulli and Chicken Curry Melgu happen to be amongst their popular dishes. On many nights, this popular resto-bar remains packed.

HAPPY HOURS: 6.30pm to 8pm

■ **Nehru Centre, Dr Annie Besant Road, Worli, Mumbai, Ph: 24949217/9214/9435/9204/9219**

Karma

RESTO-BAR — Tue–Sun: Noon to 1am, Mondays Closed

Buzz-2.50 | Décor-3.50 | Nightout for 2-₹2500

Bean bags, sofas, dim lights, red candles on all tables and low-gadda seats with cushions in hues of purple greet you at Karma. They offer Horny Mary, B52, Kamasutra, Sex on the Beach, Abracadabra, Splendido, Nice 'n' Naughty, Virgin Margarita along with Caipiroska, Cosmopolitan and Long Island Iced Tea. Live DJ music from (7.30pm onwards). Their spciality is a 14-inch Milano Paper Pizza (₹469 inclusive of taxes). Select Indian snacks here but it's their Karma Diet Pizza, a 12-inch healthy pizza with soya-flour base which is the star here. They also have Veg and Non-veg Platters.

HAPPY HOURS: 6pm to 8.30pm

■ **534, SVP Road, Hughes Road, Opera House, Mumbai, Ph: 40287119, 40287116**

Kino 108

DISCOTHEQUE/NIGHTCLUB — 7pm to 3am

Buzz-3.50 | Décor-3.50 | Nightout for 2-₹3000

Andheri's rockin' zip code is worth checking out! Plenty of young crowd props up along the long, at Kino 108, knocking back many a Kino special (Banana Slide, Smoked Orange, Pomegranate Cooler, ₹250–500). Sip on the Apple or Hazelnut Martini (a bit too sweet, but refreshing) while the Espresso Martini has wonderful depth. Plenty of action here... huge game rooms, theme nights (Beer Bomb Night!) and special musicians to perform on weekends. A well-carved sculpture of Jim Morrison and a vintage-inspired Royal Enfield dominate the space which is alive with plasma screens and a rocking, young crowd. You may opt to sit on the booth by the cascading waterwall of the floor-to-ceiling glass windows overlooking the main road. There are two glass-walled private rooms (billing ₹20,000, seats 12) too. A large menu here, from succulent 108 Galouti to Moroccan-spiced Rawas. Pure-veg mock meats too... try the Zen Nizami Chicken, al dente Ravioli or Caribbean Chicken. Plenty of choice here and an excellent selection of food and flavour (many dishes priced between ₹200 and ₹500) not typically found at resto-bars or lounges that invites you to go from cocktails and conversations to dinner in the same space. No cover charges before 10.30pm, but on Fridays and Saturdays, the cover charges are after 10.30pm at ₹1,500 a couple and ₹1,000 for stag. Also, Mondays to Thursdays, couples are free. However, stags have to pay a cover of ₹500 after 10.30pm.

Note: No cover charges before 10.30pm, but on Fridays and Saturdays, the cover charges are after 10.30pm at ₹1,500 a couple and ₹1,000 for stag. Also, Mondays to Thursdays, couples are free. However, stags have to pay a cover of ₹500 after 10.30pm.

HAPPY HOURS: 7.30pm to 10.30pm (Sun-Thurs)

SPECIAL NIGHTS: Ladies Night (Wednesdays; 8pm to11pm)

■ **JP Road, Opp. Apna Bazaar, Versova, Andheri, Mumbai, Ph: 61620126, M5** 8

Koh

LOUNGE BAR 12.30pm to 3pm, 7.30pm to 11.45pm

Buzz-2.50 | Décor-4.00 | Nightout for 2-₹6000

Walk into the swanky lounge of New York's high-octane Ian Kittichai's (of Big Apple and Barcelona fame) restaurant. The small bar, at the entrance of the restaurant serves up many a classy cocktail, like Cosmopolitans and Scirotos. DJ Sumit comes in everyday except Monday (another DJ on Monday), plays house music which is lil' loud in the lounge but subtle in the dining area). Double Black Mojito Signature cocktails and sophisticated starters are served with elegance here. Gojiberry Bellini merges fruit from Tibet as well as Peach Schnapps and is topped off with champagne; Jasmine 'n' Honey Martini combines Jasmine-infused vodka, honey and kaffir lime leaves. Dragon Fly is a delicious blend of watermelon, Thai sweet basil and vodka while the Koh Bloody Mary kicks up the classic with Sriracha (an imported chilli sauce from Thailand) that re-invents the flavour and texture of the drink. Soothing music pipes in the background of this cosy lounge that also serves Glenfiddich (40 years), Glenfarclas (42 years), Girvan (1964), and Ladyburn (1973) as part of an exquisite Single Malt collection. Kauffman Vintage, Roberto Cavalli, Jean Marc XO, Martell XO, and Hennessey XO showcase a few of their premium labels. Koh has changed its iKoh digital menu to include Crispy Tiger Shrimps, Soup-spiced Tiger Prawn Soup and Wok-fried Asian Pomfret in burnt lemon in the main course options.

■ **InterContinental Marine Drive, 135 Marine Drive, Mumbai, Ph: 39879999, M1** 9

Kolonials

RESTO-BAR 11am to 1.30am

Buzz-3.00 | Décor-3.00 | Nightout for 2-₹2000

As the book goes to press, the former Cool Chef Café, known for its music nights, is now specializing in local cuisine with a well-stocked bar for those who need their daily quart. Drawing corporate diners and after office tipplers this recently christened haunt amazes you both with its prices and tasty cuisine. They serve fresh catch of seafood daily along with their own special sauces.

■ **Thadani House, 329/A Gulphadevi Mandir Road, Worli Village, Mumbai, Ph: 32231199**

The Lazy Dog (TLD)

Bar — 6pm to 12.30am

Buzz-3.50 | Décor-3.50 | Nightout for 2-₹2400

Every dog has his day. But this Lazy Dog has a night also. And what a pleasant surprise it is too. Many a reason: the clever dual system of booze-pricing, which makes it affordable coupled with a glassed-in handsome and comfy ambience in its first bar at Fort. We are charmed by the spartan cream-and-wood-décor. Walk past the glass exterior into the ground-floor's long bar, the mezzanine lounge bar is replete with art déco-themed rose and teak tall tables, sofas, armchairs and benches. You can get drinks at approximately half price by becoming a member and paying a one-time patron card fee of ₹500 topped up by ₹2,500 (minimum amount) which is redeemable. For instance, Smirnoff is priced at ₹115 (otherwise ₹250), Red Label ₹165 (₹350), Ciroc for just ₹275 (₹500)... all inclusive. Okayish cocktails, be it a Mojito or Cosmo. It's the signature *chatpata* ones like the Kala Khatta Chuski, Peru Martini (rimmed with *hing* and *amchur* powder) that are worth trying. As is the mocktail, Cranberry Breezer. The chalked in menu on the blackboard has just a few snacks and though we had heard mixed reviews, we are delighted with their robust spicing, be it the Mutton Boti or the Tandoori Aloo. The other finger-foods include Dahi Kebab, Chicken Seekh, Omelette Pao Kebabs and Rolls. Just like Tsar, the dog (in whose memory the bar is dedicated), liked to do nothing but just laze around, people do the same here. The most recent TLDs to open are at One India Bulls and at India Bulls Finance Centre, Lower Parel... smaller but equally pleasant Dogs.

■ **24-A, Rajabahadur Mansion, Bombay Samachar Marg, Horniman Circle, Fort, Mumbai, Ph: 9167949940, M1** 18

■ **Lobby Level, Tower Two, One India Bulls Centre and India Bulls Finance Centre, Elphinstone Road, Lower Parel, Mumbai, Ph: 9167942041**

■ **9th Floor, Tower 2, Indiabulls Finance Centre, Senapati Bapat Marg, Parel, Mumbai, Ph: 9167942947**

Leopold Café

Resto-Bar — 7.30am to 12.30am

Buzz-3.50 | Décor-2.00 | Nightout for 2-₹1500

This cherished Colaba café (144 years and counting) is a beloved Mumbai landmark and historical icon both rolled into one. Cheap and cheerful, buzzing and bustling, this high-ceilinged café serves beer towers (two pitchers), glasses of draught beer and, of course, complementary peanuts to go with it all. Cocktails include Hakoona Matata (yes, Lion King-inspired), Between the Sheets, Dart in the Dark and Cupid's Arrow. Mocktails like Fruit Punch and Tropicana and more. A DJ rocks the house from 7pm onwards; the first floor pub is where all action takes place - they stay open from 1pm and keep going past midnight. Nibble on reasonably priced and generous portions of sandwiches, Chicken Tikka Masala and Beef Chilli Fry and a new Chinese menu too. Dishes are varied and range from Toast Butter and Akuri to noodles, pastas and even

Chicken Biryani. Tourist guides and history books have this place down thanks to the terror attack which began here and also the noteable mention in *Shantaram*.

■ **Colaba Causeway, Next to Regal Cinema, Colaba, Mumbai, Ph: 22020131, 22828185, M1** 10

Levo Restaurant & Lounge

[Y] [card] [AC]

RESTO-BAR 11am to 3pm, 7pm to Midnight

Buzz-3.00 | Décor-3.50 | Nightout for 2-₹3000

Walk into the sprawling 20,000sq ft restaurant and the sheer scale (indoors and alfresco) and the sophistication of décor sets the tone for the food. The high-ceilinged restaurant is done to international standards by the Japanese architect who has also done Hyatt's China House and is clad in wood and style. A wood-fired oven takes pride of place and DJ music fills the air. Yet to take off, the Levo bar, has a huge collection of liquor ranging from international brands (Dom Perignon, Castello Banfi Brunello di Montalcino, whiskey, scotch, beer and liqueurs, *et al.*). Suffice it to say that the most important element here is the brilliant chef's ability and determination to amplify the charms of whatever lies at the center of a dish and masterfully balancing its flavours and textures. Award-winning Canadian masterchef, Rajeev Arora, pays more heed to emphasizing two or three flavours than to inventing oddball pairings or imagining eureka flourishes. It's too early to tell how the bar will take off.

■ **Mukti Business Park, Model Town, 4 Bungalows, Behind Kokilaben Dhirubhai Ambani Hospital, Andheri (W), Mumbai, Ph: 65571234, M5** 9

Li Bai

[Y] [card] [AC]

BAR, LOUNGE 11.30am to 1am

Buzz-3.00 | Décor-4.00 | Nightout for 2-₹6000

This new swish bar raises the bar (literally) as it opens on the 37th floor of the Palladium Hotel (erstwhile Shangri La). It is aptly named after the exalted booze-loving eighth-century Chinese poet Li Bai. As the book goes to press I pop in here, to find it buzzing (though not packed). Take the direct elevator up (the wrong one will take you to the ninth floor and you'll have to change elevators there). The dimly lit sprawling space throbs to loud DJ music. Feast on the stunning and magnificent view of the Mahalaxmi Racecourse on one side and the Arabian Sea on the other. A wire mesh sculpture of Li Bai lords over the bar, which has a dedicated cigar and cognac section and two (minimum-spend-requiring) semi-private seating areas. Molecular mixes, foams, smoking guns are all used to create cocktails here. Fog, Asian-inspired cocktails such as the Du Fu (sake, orange liqueur, fresh lime and sugar); Smoking China (gin, green tea, apple juice and lime juice with apple smoke); Li Bai (served in a mojito jar, Kaffir lime pomegranate juice), Lonely Bird (with jalapeño infusion), Spring Wind (vodka, jasmine tea, cinnamon syrup and lime juice) do the rounds as do Chinese, Thai and Vietnamese starters. Kung Pao Potatoes, Sesame

Chicken and Sizzling Prawns are must tries. DJ Anurag Chadha spins house music and mixes it with hip hop. The bar lounge rocks with a few youngsters and some families who've stopped by after dinner at the neighbouring Mekong restaurant. The swanky new bar lounge has yet to pick up steam.

■ **Level 37, Palladium Hotel, Mumbai, Ph: 61628000**

Lido Bar

Resto-Bar
Under Renovation

Currently closed for renovation, this used to be a cosy, quiet place in the Ritz Hotel.

■ **Ritz Hotel, 5, Jamshedji Tata Road, Churchgate, Mumbai, Ph: 22820141, 22850500**

Liquid Lounge – The Bar

Bar — Noon to 1.30am
Buzz-3.00 | Décor-3.50 | Nightout for 2-₹3000

A casual lounge bar at the Grand Sarovar Premiere, it is considered an ideal place for guests and visitors alike in this business hotel. This place looks chic with brilliant and creative use of wood, marble and glass in its interiors. Besides an elaborate liquor menu and interesting snacks, it is also known for its private area where you can smoke cigars from around the world. Three different types of cuisines, cocktails, mocktails and more can be had here. Sip on their house speciality '180' while you munch on complementary *masala* nuts and cheeselings or B52 or other cocktails (Caipiroska, Mojito, Manhattan) and mocktails (Spring Blossom, Coco Colada, Blue Lagoon). Snacks menu (Nachos with cheesy Garlic Dip, Chilli Cheese Toast and Chilli Chicken), and piped music. The attractions here are the reasonably priced European/Global, Oriental (Thai and Chinese) and Indian fare from their extensive menu and a VFM buffet through the day in which they have Indian, European and Chinese fare.

HAPPY HOURS: Noon to 9pm

■ **Grand Sarovar Premiere, AK Plaza, SV Road, Goregaon (W), Mumbai, Ph: 28718000, 42158000**

LIV

Pub — Wed–Sat: 9.30pm to 1am
Buzz-4.50 | Décor-4.00 | Nightout for 2-₹6000

South Mumbai's comatose nightlife injected with life is now rocking away. As the book goes to press, on a Saturday night, I pop into this signature statement nightclub for 25 and above. Lines outside Kala Ghoda's first-floored nightclub keep growing. Inside, it's one amazing sight: the LED lights on the glamourous ceiling dance in synchronization with the hip-hop and electronic music as the sea of crammed and jammed youngsters bob and sway in a happy, heady haze. The dramatic black metalla marble walls, and the custom-made floating chandelier criss-crosses the entire ceiling. There are mirrors on both sides of the club and the VIP room with its reflective walls and fibre optics recreates a starry night. VIP tables (ranging from ₹50,000 for the Royal Room to ₹35,000 for the Crystal tables) are squeezed in too. It takes four young and innovative owners to breathe this energy into LIV. Red Light's décor, menu, and target demographics have been revamped with the setting up of this boutique nightclub. In addition to the premium alcohol and usual concoctions, there are also unique signature drinks named after the owners (Aneeni, Crackling Shash, Sunny All Night Long and Jageritz.) A global food menu of small plates here. LIV is open from Wednesday to Saturday and can be reserved for private parties from Sunday till Tuesday. Entry ₹1,000 per head.

■ Next to Khyber Restaurant, Mahatma Gandhi Road, Fort, Mumbai, Ph: 66346248, 66346247

The Lobby Lounge

BAR — 7am to 11pm

Buzz-2.50 | Décor-3.50 | Nightout for 2-₹5000

Whether it is for a business meeting or an informal drink or for a relaxed evening, head to Lobby Lounge in one of the best business hotels in the city. Brocade tapestries and ethnic bronze statues add an Indian touch and the view of the lush outdoors and picturesque setting of the azure poolside, cascading fountain, floating lotus plants, and verdant gardens adds to the charm. It has an eclectic mix of drinks and food. On its beverage menu is premium selection of Eau de Vie and the Indian single estate teas. Tea or coffee is served with cookies on the house. Single Origin Coffee and International Teas include Jamaican Blue Mountain, Monkey Pick Tea, and White Ambrosia. They have cocktails like Blue Lagoon, Flavour of Scotland, LIT, Black Russian and Talk of the Town. Try their Platter, wraps and classic bagels, toasties and BLT to go with your drink. Perfect accompaniments with your tea are samosas, Chicken 65, crêpes and pancakes. They also serve whisky, gin, vodka with complementary Pringles and peanuts and wines with complementary canapés. High Tea can be enjoyed from 3pm to 5pm where you can add a tea trolley which comes with tarts, macaroons, scones, quiches, veg and non veg sandwiches and tea forte — the works. Enjoy Live Piano Music play from 7pm to 10pm by Mr William McRae.

■ The Leela Mumbai, Andheri-Kurla Road, Sahar, Andheri (E), Mumbai, Ph: 66911355-56,
www.theleelamumbai.com, **M4** 6

Loca Loca

BAR — 7pm to 1.30am

Buzz-4.00 | Décor-4.00 | Nightout for 2-₹3000

Crazy crazy (read loca loca) the Cuban-themed colourful bar slam dunks my adrenalin with its infectious energy and affordable prices. It sprawls under a banyan tree and colourful drums, broken door frames, suspended Cuban movie posters seem to be rocking to the new-age disco. Vibrant, blue, green and yellow painted walls, murals plastered all over. Prop up the bar in the verandah, push open double doors to the air-conditioned section bar or sink into soft sofas in the seated section... all thoughtful options. The brainchild of Kishore DF (WTF, which Loca Loca replaces and The Big Nasty), this place has all the right notes to make it rock. From their cocktails in a jar Fresh Strawberry Cubanito (₹385 for a glass and ₹1,000 for a jar) also available in pineapple and watermelon flavours. Ditto for Mojitos and Daiquiris. The good Lord be praised, they don't take the Cuban theme seriously. *Kya* snacks! Spicy and tasty. Andhra vegetables, *chatpata*, filling and totally non-Cuban. Paneer Wrap, Mushroom Baby Salt 'n' Pepper, Chilli Cauliflower, Spicy Mayo, Fried Calamari Pot Roast Beef and many more. Must ask for the Loca Cuscurro (crouton in Spanish) with *kairi* which is their version of a Mexican *chaat*, with broken tortilla pieces and salad but is basically bhelpuri with a fancier name. Popular, packed, colourful and tasty, well-priced booze and snacks.

■ 8, Vora House, 3rd Road, Off Station Road, Khar (W), Opp. Mumbadevi School, Mumbai, Ph: 26486233, 9833243071, M3 17

The Local

RESTO-BAR 6pm to 1.30am, Sunday Jam Session: Noon to 4pm

Buzz-4.00 | Décor-3.50 | Nightout for-₹2000

You gotta go! Brand new The Local at Fort is already packed. Ooof! ho! but you can't get in without a password. So is it snooty? No way! It's a relaxed, very casual hangout and if you love music, VFM booze, and spicy, robust food then this is your *adda*. What is truly "local" about the bar is the famous Mumbai quarter system. Kachchi Kairi, Imli ka Nasha and such like cocktails and most of all, competitively priced booze here. DJ Marciano plays retro and on Sunday, the lively Flypside Band is a must to dance to. Deliberately grungy look in the small, dimly lit, split-level room, industrial unfinished wood, exposed water pipes and Banksy's street art splattered all over. Clement D'Silva and Sabina Singh add on a barber's chair and a tap with running water in a basin and nudge in even more funky features. Ignore cranky cribbers ("The Local tries too hard to be cool") and locate the nondescript door behind the bus-stop opposite the University. Having logged on to their FB, key in the password onto a computer at the entrance. On offer are high-end booze by the bottle for the party goers, but it's the Great Indian Cocktails (served in two measures 'cutting' and 'full') that have caught everyone's fancy. The food menu is bar food that varies from snacks to light meals. The Local favourites are Butter Popcorn, Chorizo Pao, Sri Lankan Beef Chilli with Neer Dosa, Lamb Chops, Nachos, and the recently introduced Fun Fries and crusty Crostini on weekends. The Local plays mostly retro music with a mix of latin and spanish. Wednesdays it's Over the Hump with DJ Sandy (of Olive fame) playing his signature tunes, Thursdays are Jukebox Nights where guests bring their own music and play their favourite tunes. Fridays and Saturdays are retro nights and Sunday afternoons have the 60's live jam session with a lunch menu featuring

Soul Fry's favourites. The *chatpata* food is not gourmet (Sri Lankan Beef Curry and Railway Mutton kind of fare... for more details check out the restaurant guide), but it's tasty. The all-day Sunday jam session, the casual, affordable hang-loose vibe make The Local a much needed, refreshing new arrival. Whoopeee!

■ 111 -A, Currimjee Bldg, MG Road, Opp. Mumbai, University, Fort, Mumbai, Ph: 22671421, M1 19

Long & Short – The Gastro Bar

Y ▭ AC

RESTO-BAR 7am to 1.30am

About to Open | Nightout for 2-₹2500

As the book goes to press, Marine Drive's first-floored restaurant, Long & Short – The Gastro Bar, is all set to open. The evenings promise to buzz with an interactive stage where there will be live music (four times a week), stand-ups and anyone and everyone can go up and take part in the fun. It's all ready to serve up Global street food, comfort food (Asian, flat breads, burgers, pizzas) through the day but also huge dollops of fun.

■ InterContinental Marine Drive, 135, Marine Drive, Mumbai, Ph: 39879999

Lounge Bar

Y ▭ AC

BAR 11am to 8pm

Buzz-3.00 | Décor-3.50 | Nightout for 2-₹4000

A rare collection of Single Malts at 'The Bar' like Glen Fiddich, 50 years old and Lady Purn. Very contemporary and chic. Not for you if you are looking for a quiet hideaway! Set in the midst of the gleaming lobby of the Grand Hyatt, this sexily dim-lit bar is an ideal place for pre- and post-dinner drinks. It has impeccable attention to detail — temperature-controlled, bookshelf-style glass cabinets with separate sections for whisky, Red and White wines; cigar and cigarette Ritznhorf ashtrays and even a special ice-cube machine. An impressive drinks menu with 40 martinis, popular cocktails (Cosmopolitan, Journalist, Hot 'n' Dirty), Single Malts (hot sellers) and exquisite wine (Bentley Australian Shiraz, Oxford Landing Shiraz and Santa). The usual quick bites on the menu (bruschetta, nachos, samosas, chicken wings, calamari), but the service is fantastic.

HAPPY HOURS: 6pm to 8pm

■ Hilton, Sahar Airport Road, Andheri (E), Mumbai, Ph: 28380000

Madness

Y ▭ AC

DISCOTHEQUE/NIGHTCLUB

Mon–Wed: 3.30pm to 11pm, Thu–Sun: 3.30pm to 1.30am

Buzz-3.00 | Décor-3.00 | Nightout for 2-₹3000

Curacao Punch, Four Score, Piscola are some of the popular cocktails in this dimly lit bar in Hotel Ramee Guestline. A VIP lounge, separate bar area and special smoking zone keep the enthusiastic crowd happy. The bar

Smoke House Deli

[Y] [card] [AC]

EUROPEAN, FAST FOOD 9am to Midnight

Buzz-3.00 | Décor-3.50 | Nightout for 2-₹3000

Open through the day, it's a packed, popular and well-priced place where you can stroll in anytime for a drink. Not a frenetic night out place at all, but people do drop by for a pre-dinner drink. It's their unusual Cucumber, Basil, Lavender + Vodka, the refreshing Kiwi, Melon, Jasmine + Vodka; and the Californian Plum, Star Anise, Lily + Vodka that are recommended. The mocktails of choice are the Apple Soaked Mojito, Two Tango and More Melon. It's not so much of a deli as a café. Crammed into the cacophonic Phoenix High Street mall, this all-white, whimsically done up restaurant soothes. As the book goes to press, we pop in here and loved the whimsical black-and-white doodles that cover every inch. Papier-mâché telephones and gramophones too. Within Riyaz Amlani and Kiran Salasker's easy going café, you'll find plenty to eat, whether you're hungry for something delicate or blunt. True to it's name smoky flavours infuse many a dish. Please see the restaurant guide for more details.

HAPPY HOURS: 4.30pm to 6.30pm and 10.30pm to 12.20 pm; Unlimited cocktails and sangrias for ₹950++ everyday.

■ **Unit No. 9G, Block No. 3, High Street Phoenix, Lower Parel, Mumbai, Ph: 24933222, 9320098621**

Smooth

[Y] [card] [AC]

BAR 11.30am to 3pm, 6pm to 1am

Buzz-3.00 | Décor-3.00 | Nightout for 2-₹2500

Tucked away into Kemps Corner's Shalimar hotel, this lounge bar promises the best spirits, exciting pours, inventive mixes and chart-busting music. And not to forget some good food. Try their Long Island Iced Tea, Classic Daiquiri, Caipiroskas, Irish Whisky, Blue Lagoon, Bloody Mary or mojitos. Thursdays have a 20 per cent discount for doctors on food and beverages. Nibble on some Indian food... kebabs, platters and more. They have a multi-cuisine menu that features European/Global and Chinese but are well known for their Indian fare. They also bring in a DJ on weekends who spins house mixes. Chicken Makhanwala, Mutton Seekh Kebab, Tandoori Veg Platter and Paneer Chilli are of the dishes that you could enjoy with your drinks. Ladies can buy a drink and get one free on Wednesdays.

HAPPY HOURS: Tuesdays and Fridays 7pm to 1am (Buy 2, get 1 free)

■ **Hotel Shalimar, August Kranti Marg, Mumbai, Ph: 66641000**

Soul Fry

[Y] [card] [AC]

RESTO-BAR 12.30pm to 3pm, 7.30pm to 12.30am

Buzz-2.50 | Décor-3.00 | Nightout for 2-₹2500

Although Soul Fry has lost its initial sparkle, it still succeeds in attracting people mainly for its cheerful and happy ambience, delicious coastal fare, margaritas and flavoured iced teas. We miss the live music they once played here. An adequately stocked brick-and-wood bar is chock-a-block with glasses and racks (a practical approach indeed). Try their popular starters: Bombil Fry, Squid Green Chilli Garlic, Prawn Loncha and the Konkan speciality, Sol Kadi.

SPECIAL NIGHTS: Karaoke Nights (Mondays)

■ 1/2, Silver Craft, Pali Mala Road, Opp. Pali Market, Bandra (W), Mumbai, Ph: 26046892

The Spare Kitchen

Resto-Bar Noon to Midnight
Just Opened

As the book goes to press, The Spare Kitchen opens in Juhu and replaces Don Giovanni. It sprawls into an alfresco section and has a bar area too. The brick-walled and dark-wood tables inner section lends it a young look with white faux leather seating and flat-screen TV sets. A fully stocked bar and cocktails will be on offer along with the multi-cuisine snacks.

■ 5, King's International Hotel Compound, Ground Floor, Opp. Juhu Church, Juhu Tara Road, Mumbai, Ph: 65893333, M3 33

Splash

AC

Poolside Bar 9am to 9pm
Buzz-2.00 | Décor-3.00 | Nightout for 2-₹4000

Located beside the pool in a manicured garden at The Westin, Splash has the atmosphere that of a resort more than anything else... all in the middle of one of the busiest places in the city. With a well-stocked bar, Splash serves popular cocktails like Mimosas, Bellini, Sangria, Martinis (Lemon, Dirty Martini, Smirnofftini), Hurricane (a concoction of White Rum, Dark Rum and Passion Fruit Juice), Mojitos, Long Island Iced Tea, flavoured diaquiris and margaritas. Health buffs can try their popular Heavenly Spa Breakfast smoothie from their Smoothie selection. Open through the day, they serve salads, burgers, wraps, tea and coffee. Buffalo Wings, Potato Wedges, sandwiches, burgers, Chicken Caesar Salad, tomato and cheese salad are some of the delectables that you can enjoy here. They even have a kiddy zone (a foosball table, play stations, games and even a television tuned to Cartoon Network and more) to keep your children occupied. You can enjoy yourselves in this informal setting.

■ The Westin Mumbai Garden City, International Business Park, Oberoi Garden City, Goregaon (E), Mumbai, Ph: 61470000

Sports Bar Express

As the book goes to press, we hear that Colaba's once popular Sports Bar Experss has downed its shutters.

■ Regal Cinema Bldg., Shaheed Bhagat Singh Road, Colaba, Mumbai, Ph: 66396682-84

Starboard

Bar with Live Music Sun-Thurs: 5pm to 12.15am, Fri-Sat: 5pm to 1.30am

Buzz-3.00 | Décor-3.00 | Nightout for 2-₹6000

Shake a leg (7.30pm to 10.30pm; Tuesday through Friday) to the live band. Different genres of music on each day of the week. This stylish, off the lobby bar of the Taj offers exclusive Mexican cuisine, DJs and live bands too. Popular with more of an older crowd, Starboard is well known for its expensively priced range of Single Malts, vodkas and liqueurs. During the day, a feeling of calm pervades the carpeted bar as its large glass windows let in daylight. A well-stocked "Mexican Bar" too. Mojitos include unique flavours (Betel Leaf, Green Tea) as do the margaritas (try the almond one). Kamakaze, Lemon Grass Martini, Litchi and Ginger Litchi Martini, Tequila Sunrise and Executive Martini are all on offer. Discover 101 Margaritas... one for every season, mood, and occasion... and pair it perfectly with Mexican Quesadillas, Burritos or Enchiladas. The all-time favourites are the Jalisco Fruit Cocktail, Don Julio Tequila, Guacamole, Tortilla Chips, Taco Tica Gambas and Ranchero Quesadilla.

HAPPY HOURS: 5pm to 8pm; 50% discount on alcohol

SPECIAL NIGHTS: Rewind Nights on Fridays; RSVP Saturdays where you can choose your preferred music.

■ **The Taj Mahal Palace, Apollo Bunder, Colaba, Mumbai, Ph: 66653366 (Extn. 3391), M1** 15

Stax

Bar 5pm to 1.30am

Buzz-3.50 | Décor-4.00 | Nightout for 2-₹5000

If you want to relax and enjoy a drink and you happen to be near the Sahar Airport, then come to this first-floored bar. Stax now also gives us Red Corvet, Spiced Caipiroskas, Mind Space, Greenday and Grappa Frappe. Walk through the dramatic walkway leading you to this warm, inviting ambience with slow lounge music, and glamorously lit up with "stacks" of glass, stones, *et al*. There's a stand-alone island bar and lounge seating too. Explore the extensive beverage list which includes champagnes, imported beers and wines of the world (more than 90 labels, plenty of them Italian) and premium Single Malts as slow lounge music lilts in the background. All drinks are served with complementary snacks (fried cashew nuts, almonds). With these, enjoy Chicken skewers, Lamb Kebabs, Panko Crumbed Fried Prawns, Parmesan Crusted Chicken and Soy Polenta to balance out the alcohol! My only problem is its location (near the international airport) and the fact that it is open only for dinner!

HAPPY HOURS: 5pm to 7pm (Single Malts, wine and cognac not included)

■ **Hyatt Regency Mumbai, Sahar Airport Road, Andheri (E), Mumbai, Ph: 66961631, M4** 11

Stella

As the book goes to press, we are informed that Stella has closed to give way to Le Cirque Singature.

■ **The Leela Mumbai, Sahar, Andheri (E), Mumbai, Ph: 66911344-45, M4** 12

Step Iin Bar & Kitchen

RESTO-BAR Noon to Midnight

Buzz-3.00 | Décor-3.00 | Nightout for 2-₹3000

This new, small, boxed-in, Mahim eatery with a bar has yet to hit its stride. It offers standard Mughlai fare (at ₹1,000 meal for two) and slow service. It's wedged into a *galli* opposite Paradise cinema in Mahim and is a functional, grey-and-white eatery (fish tank, *et al.*). Waistcoated waiters with ties scurry around and serving food in steel platters. "Buffalo soldier" and such like songs play in the background. On the weekend, Nalli Nihari and Laal Maas are on the menu. A well-stocked, well-priced bar with *chatpata* snacks. As the book goes to press, we are informed that they will be introducing Chinese food soon.

■ 1-3, Green Lawn CHS, Kapad Bazaar Lane, Opp. Paradise Cinema, LJ Road, Mahim (W), Mumbai, Ph: 24452516, M3 34

Sutra – The Night Lounge

DISCOTHEQUE/NIGHTCLUB Fri & Sun: 10pm to 1.30am, Sat: 10pm to 2am

Buzz-3.00 | Décor-3.50 | Nightout for 2-₹5000

Walk in to The Lalit's nightclub on a Friday and you'll think it's a sedate lounge bar, but on Saturday and Sunday, get your groove on at this discotheque (Bollywood fans, this way please!). Spread over 2,450sq ft, Sutra's dance floor with glass flooring, laser lights, a projector screen, mirror balls and thumping, pumped-up music are bound to get you up and dancing the night away. To add to the party mood or to help you relax after a hard day's work, Sutra offers a diverse mix of cocktails, an extensive wine list and premium spirits. Try the margaritas, daiquiris, Sutra Special, and Chicken Tikka and Veg Spring Rolls. Apart from celebrity DJ Akhtar and DJ Suketu (once a month on Saturdays) there are special performances by other known DJs and guest DJs. The in-house DJ Wiliam, rocks the house on all other days. Both lounge and private seating areas are available.

Note: Cover charge ₹1,000 for a couple.

■ The Lalit, Sahar Airport Road, Andheri (E), Mumbai, Ph: 66992222

Suyog Rest. & Bar

RESTO-BAR 11am to 3pm, 6pm to 12.30am

Buzz-2.00 | Décor-2.50 | Nightout for 2-₹2000

They call it a family restaurant, sure it is, but it's a tippler's paradise too for the residents of Wadala... both the sections are well separated. And hence, not a problem at all. It has a well-stocked bar offering a varied range of drinks. Whisky, rum, Blenders's Punch, Gimlet, Tom Collins as well as the Roadmaster, Rainkiller and Roadkiller do the rounds here. Enjoy complementary snacks like Chaklis, Schezwan Sauce and Green Chutney along with the drinks. Others can try mocktails like Virgin Pina Colada and Fruit Punch along with the (popular) Tandoori Platter, Chicken Tikka, Paneer Tikka, Veg Shashlik and Veg Platter.

■ Near Wadala Market, Katrak Road, Wadala, Mumbai, Ph: 24131879, 24189221

The Table

Resto-Bar Noon to 3.30pm, 7pm to 11.30pm

Buzz-3.00 | Décor-3.50 | Nightout for 2-₹4000

Curacao Punch, Four Score, Piscola are some of the cocktails you can enjoy at this three-year-old, simply and yet unpretentiously named resto-bar. Though it has a well-stocked bar, it still remains a place for a serious meal. Go for a quick tipple, sit at the community table, enjoy the buzz and the chic décor... from the black-and-white-striped floor to the comfy mezzanine level. A global wine list, even wines by "half glass" (a welcome addition) here. They have recently started stocking up on spirits of premium brands like Blue Label, Glenfiddich, Johnny Walker series, Jack Daniel's, Grey Goose, Belvedere and more. Some of their mocktails include Mojitos, Shirley Temple and Lime Cola. Must nibble on perfectly made, crisp, fluffy Cheese Goujères. Superb Chicken Liver Pâté and plenty of small plates tango beautifully with a drink. The Californian chef, Alex Sanchez, serves food in "small plates" and "large plates" and focuses not on fanciful adornment but simple sophisticated flavours.

■ **Ground Floor, Kalapesi Trust Bldg., Apollo Bunder Marg, Behind Regal Cinema, Colaba, Mumbai, Ph: 22825000, M1** 16

Tamarind

Resto-Bar 7am to 11pm

Buzz-2.00 | Décor-2.00 | Nightout for 2-₹3000

In spite of its all-jazzed-up décor, Tamarind is primarily a dinner restaurant. A quiet and stylish place, it has a live band performing all days except Tuesdays. A well-stocked bar with vodka, rum, whisky, cocktails and mocktails like Capriccio, Kiwi Delight, Virgin Pina Colada, Summer Show, Caipiroska, Mojito, Cinderella Shoe, Virgin Caipiroska, Fruit Punch and Planter's Punch. The usual Indian and European dishes are on offer and there are VFM buffets as well.

HAPPY HOURS: 2pm to 8pm

SPECIAL NIGHTS: Live band on all nights (except Tuesdays) from 7.30pm to 11pm

■ **The Fariyas Hotel, 25, Off Arthur Bunder Road, Colaba, Mumbai, Ph: 22042911**

Tamnak Thai

Resto-Bar Noon to 3.30pm, 7pm to 12.30am

Buzz-1.50 | Décor-3.00 | Nightout for 2-₹3000

Tamnak Thai at Shivaji Park, Dadar does hold a few surprises with its huge, well-stocked bar of wines, cocktails (Strawberry Punch, Thai Champagne, The Man About Town, Mojito, Green Cooler, Sweet Sixteen, Chocolate Martini), mocktails (Pink Lady, Green Cooler, Virgin Mary) and martinis. Try their signature drink, the Tamnak Mojito as you relax and enjoy Thai instrumental music and mouth-watering Thai food. Sample their Chicken Black Pepper Sauce with Lemon Grass Sweet 'n' Sour Veg Crispy, Fish Cakes, Stir-fried Prawns and Crispy Lamb. Try their collection of vodkas: chocolate-flavoured vodka and Ed Hardy, wines from France, Italy, South

Africa, Chile and Single Malt whiskies (Glennfiddich, Glenmorangie) too! No Happy hours here.

■ **274, VS Marg, Shivaji Park, Dadar (W), Mumbai, Ph: 24474949/4646**

The Tavern

BAR — 1pm to 1am

Buzz-3.00 | Décor-3.00 | Nightout for 2-₹3000

Colaba's Tavern retains its cool, relaxing, pleasant décor along with well-priced, imported liquor. Find yourself at the Tavern enjoying their Rock music till midnight on Fridays and Saturdays and their House music after midnight. On other days, their in-house DJ spins mostly rock music and other songs on request. They also have Draught Beer towers here. Gulp down Sex on the Beach, Grand Cosmopolitan or Sea Breeze at good prices. Teatotallers can opt for the Belly Button, Kahlua Cow or Peach Sunrise, Summer Snow or Land of Paradise, accompanied by their tasty Kebab Platter. Cocktails like Incredible Hulk, Piscola and Savoy Affair enjoy repeat orders from patrons. Their mocktails such as Tornado Twist and Cherry Fizz are not bad either.

HAPPY HOURS: 8pm to 10pm

SPECIAL NIGHTS: Retro Nights (Mondays & Tuesdays), Rock (Wednesdays), Hip-hop (Thursdays), Commercial (Fridays & Saturdays), House (Sundays)

■ **The Fariyas Hotel, 25, Off Arthur Bunder Road, Colaba, Mumbai, Ph: 22042911**

Temptation

BAR — Noon to 1.30am

Buzz-3.00 | Décor-2.50 | Nightout for 2-₹3000

Bandra's Hotel Metro Palace's well-stocked bar lures the crowd with its karaoke nights, happy hours and cocktails and mocktails. It's dimly lit and with comfortable seating and a jukebox. It's a good way to spend an evening here. Enjoy the multi-cuisine dishes (Indian, Chinese and European) along with cocktails and mocktails like their popular Brain Freezer, AK47, Blue Frog, Long Beach Iced Tea, margaritas, martinis, Blush on Ice (smoothie strawberry muddled with lime and fresh mint topped with Sprite Cooler). The Chicken Kali Miri Kebab, Mutton Kakori Seekh, and Tandoori Platter (both veg and non-veg) are quite popular.

HAPPY HOURS: Mon-Tue: 8.30pm to 9.30pm, Wednesday: 9.30pm to 10.30pm, Thursday: 10.30pm to 11.30pm

SPECIAL NIGHTS: Karaoke Nights (Fridays, 9pm onwards)

■ **Hotel Metro Palace, 355, Ramdas Nayak Road, Opposite Globus Shopping Mall, Off Hill Road, Bandra (W), Mumbai, Ph: 67744555, 9930972112**

TGI Fridays

RESTO-BAR — Noon to Midnight

Buzz-3.50 | Décor-3.00 | Nightout for 2-₹3000

With their wide screen TVs, sports paraphernalia all over the walls TGI fridays continue to be testosterone-fueled drinking places! Vodka (flavoured Absolut, Grey Goose, Belvedere) and whisky (Jack Daniel and Chivas) are popular besides, of course, the beer that flows through out the evening. Share the fun of Fridays every day at Andheri's Infiniti Mall and Lower Parel's High Street Phoenix. The happy crowd here grabs Long Island Iced Teas, margaritas and classic cocktails such as Pisco Sour and Zombie. Not much by way of wine or champagne (only three domestic varieties and one from which to choose, respectively), but plenty of mocktails, cocktails, liquors and beer to keep the spirit of the weekend alive. Munch on nachos, Onion Rings, Chilli Cheese Toast, Chicken Bites with Blue Cheese while you kick back with "Fridays' Classics" (cocktails). From south-west and sizzling to seafood, they serve it all in a kick-back, casual "weekend's-almost-here" kind of relaxed and lively ambience.

■ **F-11/12/13, 1st Floor, Palladium Mall, Phoenix Mills Compound, 462, Senapati Bapat Marg, Lower Parel, Mumbai, Ph: 66155687,** www.tgifindia.com

■ **2nd Floor, Infiniti Mall, Oshiwara, New Linking Road, Andheri (W), Mumbai, Ph: 26367047, 67032063/65**

■ **R City Mall, Ghatgopar (W), Mumbai, Ph: 65612659**

Three Wise Men

RESTO-BAR — 7pm to 1am

Buzz-3.50 | Décor-3.00 | Nightout for 2-₹2500

It has hit the sweet spot! Santacruz's Three Wise Men has been packed from the day it opened. So what if it's all part to the formula... an all-black décor, a few booths and bar stools littered about, the mandatory big screen TV, retro playlist and the usual multi-cuisine snacks. Retro pop (ABBA), retro rock (Guns N' Roses), retro hip hop (Salt N' Peppa) here. Framed paintings on the ceiling (you read that right) Big Ben and Trafalgar Square and the Union Jack posters dot the bar. And here's the best part... the moderately priced booze... Kingfisher pints for ₹165, cocktails at ₹395 onwards and imported beers ₹350 each. Check out the standard cocktails... TWM Sangria okayish, Rusty Nail better... but it's more the regular booze that one goes here for. Okayish Chicken Wings, Burritos, Batter-fried Prawn Tempura, golden and crisp Fish 'n' Chips, Chicken Satay to Veg Tempura and mini Falafel Rolls. To sum it up, it is relaxed and casual with slow service. But no one seems to mind.

Note: Three Wise Men is named after the whisky shot featuring Jim (Beam), Jack (Daniels) and Johnnie (Walker).

SPECIAL NIGHTS: Mondays: Karaoke Nights; Wednesdays: Ladies Nights; Thursdays: Comedy Nights

■ **Sujata Rajpipla, Opp. Santacruz Police Station, Santacruz (W), Mumbai, Ph: 26614792, M3** 36

Tippler's Lounge

LOUNGE BAR — 3pm to 11.30pm

Buzz-3.00 | Décor-3.00 | Nightout for 2-₹2000

Rather aptly named. If in Vashi and looking for creative bartenders whipping up an array of tasty cocktails and shooters as well as fun bar games, head here. This dignified-and-elegant-by-the-day and gorgeous-and-glamorous-by-night bar offers both bar and lounge seating with comfy sofas.You can enjoy a wide range of beers and international wines here. Some of Tippler's Lounge's signature cocktails include Moonwalk, Americano, Negroni, Burbondaisi and Cosmopolitans. A well-stocked bar with Indian (Vinsura and Riveillo) and international wines (Jacob's Creek, Georges Duboeuf Marlot, Broken Wood and Oxford Landing). Beers like Kingfisher, Budweiser, London Pride and Murphy's English Trout too! Enjoy your drink with Achari Jhinga, Mediterranean Chicken, Barmushai Tangdi, Mexican Bruschetta Veg Julians with Cheesy Dip and Golden-fried Cauliflower. The booze comes with complementary peanuts, chips and dried green peas. Classic cocktails to choose from: daiquiris, mojitos, etc. and teetotallers can order their signature Four Point Special. They have signature coffees too with alcohol like Irish, Jamaican and Mexican, to name a few.

HAPPY HOURS: 4pm to 6pm

■ **Four Points by Sheraton, Plot 39/1, 6 to 15, Sector-30A, Vashi, Navi Mumbai, Ph: 27817777, M6** 8

Tote Bar

BAR

Buzz-3.00 | Décor-4.50 | Nightout for 2-₹5000

8pm to 1.30am

Everything about it is text-book perfect... location... Turf Club, looks... brilliant design, a dramatically lit, high-ceilinged, wooden field of energy. Add to this all triangular and trapezoid panels of polished teak wood which form jagged planes and embrace a 40ft vaulted interior, designed to mirror the trees outside and the high-profile owner, Rahul Akerkar. Set amidst a lush canopy of 101-year-old rain trees, with a stunning backdrop of historic buildings and the green of the Mahalaxmi Racecourse, it is a beauty. As the book goes to press, I pop in here to find it desolate. With concoctions of champagne cocktails, Cosmopolitans and Jager Bombs, among others, you can also order from their menu at the bar which is only that from their companion restaurant Neel on the Turf. Mumbai street *tawa* food like Baida Roti, Kathi Roll and Butter Bheja to Jaituni Khumb Tikka, Murgh Karachi Kebab and Ajwaini Rawas Tikka. A great wine list and bar menu here.

Note: It usually picks up late at night and mainly on weekends. Call and check for themed nights.

■ **Mahalaxmi Racecourse, Opp. Gate Nos. 5&6, Keshva Rao Khadye Marg, Mahalaxmi, Mumbai, Ph: 61577777, M2** 19

Toto's Garage

BAR

Buzz-3.50 | Décor-3.50 | Nightout for 2-₹2500

6pm to 1am

Bandra's cosy themed bar continues to be popular. A Beetle car still looms over this bar (for more than 20 years now!). And nothing much has changed here, and the people here like it that way it seems. DJ Colin occupies the seat in the Maruti van hanging near the ceiling and plays rock with no space for Hindi tracks. Bandra-ites mingle to gulp down Brandy Sour, Jack Rose, Bloody Mary, Kamakaze and B52 shots amidst the dangling tyres and the number plates stuck on the walls. In mocktails, you can try their speciality, Toto's Special (orange, pineapple, mango, and fresh cream blended together). Greasy Chinese fare is on offer here. No dress code for entering... wear whatever you want as nobody would notice in this small and smoky bar.

■ **30, Lourdes Heaven, Pali Junction, Bandra (W), Mumbai, Ph: 26005494/6429**

Town House Café

RESTO-BAR — Noon to Midnight

Buzz-3.00 | Décor-3.00 | Nightout for 2-₹2500

As the book goes to press, Town House Café opens in the heart of town. It replaces Crepe Station, and Malt & Pepper. A perfect location for office goers, this open-through-the-day café has wooden-beamed high ceilings, and is dotted by ornate frames of vintage advertisements. Leather-clad seating adds a cosy charm, while DJ music fills the air. Ask for the favourites... Guava Mary, Orange 'n' Basil Martini, Red Wine Sangria and Tropical Mojito. Plenty of well-priced fare for vegetarians is offered by the Spanish, French and Italian inspired menu. Try the range of handmade pastas (Pappardelle, Maccheroni and Linguine, in a choice of Pesto, Alfredo, Arrabbiata, Carbonara and Primavera)... all of which are somewhat oversauced. Be it the Crusted Mushroom with Romesco Dip or the Pan-seared Basa with Beans Ragout and Chilli Mango Reduction all are on the menu. We just hope it has a longer life than its predecessors.

■ **16, Murzban Road, Near Sterling Cinema, Fort, Mumbai, Ph: 22037356-57, M1** 20

Trader Vic's Mai Tai

RESTO-BAR — Noon to 1am

Buzz-3.00 | Décor-3.50 | Nightout for 2-₹4000

Stroll in here for a drink, should you be in the Phoenix Mill mall, or before or after going for a movie. Bang opposite the PVR Phoenix, the international chain of Trader Vic's Mai Tai Lounge sets up. It is part of the 75-year-old American chain of Trader Vic's (which invented the original Mai Tai cocktail in 1944). The unique Tiki-culture inspired lounge with its tropical décor serves up refreshing delights. Sit amid the plant-filled Caribbean-themed space, ask for the tangy Spicy Lemongrass Potatoes and Tofu, even the Kona Vegetable Skewers & Bloody Mary Prawns are worth trying. Vegetarians are well taken care of here. Ask for the Caribbean Cottage Cheese Steak, Harrisa Mushroom Skewers and non-veggies can go for Kahuna Grilled Basa, and Chargrilled Harissa and Lime Chicken to name a few. With decent food and an array of drink choices, this open-through-the-day lounge can get crowded as it is plonked on the main thoroughfare. Also warm as half the lounge is not airconditioned.

■ **Opp. PVR Phoenix, Phoenix High Street Mall, Lower Parel, Mumbai, Ph: 67734949, M2** 20

■ **F-81, 81A, 82, Phoenix Market City Mall, Bandra Kurla Complex, Mumbai, Ph: 61801615**

Trilogy

NIGHTCLUB — 9pm to 3am

Buzz-4.50 | Décor-4.50 | Nightout for 2-₹6000

Whoa! It's now officially open till 3am. Trilogy reopens after 18 months. As the book goes to press, I pop in unannounced for a quick check out on a Friday night. Its psychedelic wave of sugar-cube like ceiling lights and plush elevator that leads up to 4,000sq ft of split-level space (great sea view) are as spiffy as ever. The first-floored wooden bar and lounge area are uninspired. Walk up the flight of shimmering ruby red stairs (heaven help you if you are high or wearing high heels) scattered with mini VIP lounges and onto the large dance floor, vibrant bar and smoking room with ocean view. Their Mojitos and Martinis reign supreme. As does sushi, Salt 'n' Pepper Prawns and Mongolian Chicken from the menu. It's ₹2,000 entry (not cover) charge per couple on Fridays and Saturdays.

■ **Hotel Sea Princess, Juhu Tara Road, Santracruz (W), 26469500**

Tryst

NIGHTCLUB — Wed-Thur: 10.20pm to 1.30am, Fri-Sat: 10.30pm to 2.30am

Buzz-4.50 | Décor-3.50 | Nightout for 2-₹5000

High-energy, throbbing and packed with young 20-something year olds! High-ceilinged, futuristic interiors, dark and bathed in hi-tech spinning, dancing (synchronized to the music) 16-million coloured lights... Tryst swings as I pop in here at 1am on a Saturday night. The DJ console is perched at a commanding height and I teeter and totter my way to the most expensive table (where Tusshar Kapoor, Urmila Matondkar, Manish Malhotra are having a good time). It's difficult to find my way amidst swaying youngsters (the whole nightclub is a dance floor). From Ra to Play to Ra again and now Tryst... this space has seen many a shift in concept and change in *avatar*. Exclusivity at every turn... from the guest list-only entry to the eight VIP tables stacked across three levels (minimum billing ₹30,000). Their USP is their private tables that sell from ₹35,000 going up to ₹75,000 with a minimum of 12 to 15 people on each table (personal bartender, bouncer, *et al.*). The DJs spin popular dance anthems and international club music like Hip-Hop, RnB, and varied genres of house music. A 27-foot long, creatively constructed bar, besides a smaller bar is accessible to guests serving signature Tryst cocktails. The young brigade go there to be seen; food and drinks are secondary to that experience. Trio Cheese Fried Ravioli Corn & Caper Bruschetta, Tryst Chicken, Oriental Chicken and Wasabi Prawns are the hotsellers. Shots are the popular drink of choice in this rocking Rishi Acharya's nightclub. Go for the fast-moving cocktails, Long Island

Iced Tea and Flavoured Caipiroska. An exclusive list of Single Malts, cognacs, beer, wine and, of course, champagne.

Note: Entry is just as exclusive as everything else. Please call in advance; ₹2,000/couple (entry through guest list only). No stags allowed.

■ **Phoenix Mill Compound, High Street Phoenix, Senapati Bapat Marg, Lower Parel, Mumbai, Ph: 66614366, 66614365**

Two One Two Bar & Grill

RESTO-BAR 12.30pm to 2.30pm, 7.30pm to 11.30pm

Buzz-2.50 | Décor-3.50 | Nightout for 2-₹4000

There's "Sex on the Beach" and there's also "Safe Sex on the Beach" here. Ever since this Worli bar and grill opened a few years back, it has been making waves because of its food. However, the buzz in the bar seems to have slowed down somewhat in this smart, sassy and handsome space offset by unfinished black marble tables. It's a three-levelled restaurant serving Italian-European fare with a global sensibility. The glassed-in show kitchen stands prominently at the entrance and overlooks the alfresco terrace with its white umbrellas (a boon in the cool winter months). Well known for its martinis especially the Watermelon, Basil, Ginger and Pomegranate Sour Apple, Cucumber, Choco Vanilla and Thyme, it has a well-stocked wine bar too. Enjoy cocktails such as Black Velvet or Flirtini while the DJ plays retro numbers.

■ **12-A, Hornby Vellard Estate, Near Nehru Planetarium, Worli, Mumbai, Ph: 24901994, M2** 21

Unplugg Wine & Dine

RESTO-BAR 1pm to 1.30am

Buzz-3.00 | Décor-3.00 | Nightout for 2-₹2000

As you enter Malad's red-hued, deep wooden-toned lively joint, you will be greeted by life-size posters of Michael Jackson and Elvis Presley, and realize that at this joint, rock 'n' roll and retro rule supreme. Try the Liquid Marijuana, made of Blue Curacao, Malibu, Bacardi and Pineapple Juice combined together in a potent fashion, which you can enjoy during their happy hours which are from Monday through Thursday. A large plasma screen to keep you entertained with classic rock to heavy metal and everything in-between. Purple Rain, Frozen Peach Tree and mojitos like Apple Manhattan (Scotch and Apple Liqueur) popularly make the rounds. Margarita fans can try the Absinthe Margaritas (Absinthe and Triple Sec), while hard-core heavy metal fans could order Bloodbath (Raspberry Liqueur, Red Wine, Cranberry Juice) at the well-stocked bar where a brightly lit guitar hangs that reads "Jim Beam". Cajun Chicken Drumsticks to Buffalo Strips and Quesadillas, you have some interesting dishes to go with the drinks here.

HAPPY HOURS: 4pm to 6pm (Monday through Thursday)

■ **Uncle's Kitchen Junction, Mitch Chowki, New Link Marve Road Malad (W), Mumbai, Ph: 28443686, 9821516388**

Upper Deck

BAR Noon to 3pm, 5pm to 11.30pm

Buzz-1.50 | Décor-3.00 | Nightout for 2-₹3000

A long drive away from the city, this seaside hotel's bar overlooks the swimming pool and the sea. You can spend the weekend here and chill in its rustic interiors to Western pop, country, Western classical and regular bar music. It's a long drive away from the city, but a visit to this seaside hotel is worth the effort. Their unique cocktails (Blue Neon, On Aksa Beach, Sinking Sand, Beach Cooler, Hawaiian Punch) or some interesting mocktails (Shirley Temple, Golden Beach, Senorita, Sun Bathing). Complementary snacks like peanuts and wafers are served with the drinks. DJ Clyde spins here from 8pm to 11.30pm. Try Mozzarella Cheese Sticks, Cajun-spiced Potatoes, Nachos with Salsa and Pepper Blasted Chicken as all these starters enjoy repeat orders by patrons.

HAPPY HOURS: 5pm to 8pm

■ **The Resort Hotel, Aksa Beach, 11, Madh-Marve Road, Malad (W), Mumbai, Ph: 28808888, 28447777**

Veda

BAR Mon–Fri: Noon to 3.30pm, 6.30pm to Midnight, Sat-Sun: Noon to Midnight

Buzz-2.50 | Décor-4.00 | Nightout for 2-₹4000

More of a dining destination than a drinking one, nonetheless, Rohit Bal, hailed as "master of fabric and fantasy" by TIME has created a dramatic bar and the interiors here. These bear his flamboyant signature: long bar, draped in gold leaves, dark, black tones of magenta and dramatic gold flourishes everywhere. Pink and black chandeliers gleam. There's a mirror-walled private dining room too. Get into the spirit(ual) with "Veda"? How about some Indian-inspired flavours under "Vedanta"? Chatka Mary (liquid vodka and spiced guava with chilli) or Mumbai Lassie with a scotch and cumin twist? Munch on Veda Curry Leaf and Lotus Steam Chips. Check out the mocktails under "Unzipped" and classic cocktails under "Pure Culture". "Significance of Vedas" lists on refreshing combinations of tropical passion and other fruit with rum and vodka. Martinis in various fruity flavours... Appletini, Melontini, Italian Peachitini and even Espressotini comprise the "Essences of Vedas". Veda offers premium liqour, Ed Hardy Vodka and Dom Perignon as well as fine wines and Single Malts. Kick back with Blues Brothers (peachy blue rum chased by iced orange juice). Flavoured vodka shots, Red Devil, spiced and iced vodka with a bite and many more. "Sutras" like Rita in Paradise (tequila, litchi and strawberry), Dead Woman Walking (a very blue Rita) and Acapulco Gold (tequila, peach, apricot and mint) aim to seduce. The very Indian Mughlai menu serves up Crispy Spinach Chaat and the famous Veda Rahra (Lamb special) and more.

■ **2nd Floor, Palladium Mall, Senapati Bapat Marg, High Street Phoenix, Lower Parel, Mumbai, Ph: 24900055, 9873655216,** www.vedarestaurants.com**, M2** 22

Velvet Lounge

NIGHTCLUB
Under Renovation

As the book goes to press, Powai's Renaissance Hotel's Velvet Lounge is under renovation. .

▪ **Renaissance Hotel & Convention Centre, 2&3-B, Near Chinmayanand Ashram, Powai, Mumbai, Ph: 66927576**

Vicinia Café & Bar

BAR
8am to 1am
Buzz-3.00 | Décor-3.50 | Nightout for 2-₹3000

Open through the day, this new café and bar (only beer, wine and wine cocktails) is cosy and cute. Wedged between Warden Road's shoe shops, this small, twin-levelled, 40-seater café (replaces Subway) is cosy with its exposed brick walls, photos of Bombay and white wooden tables and chairs. The bar promises to pick up as the owner, Gaurish Rangnekar, has done his masters in mixology from the New York bartending school and along with his wife, Akanksha, runs the interesting "bar mobile". The boozy Pina Colada and mojito-soaked cupcakes make for an interesting finale. It fumbles on some of its dishes and most desserts. A sure hit with canoodling couples, or those looking for a bite in a restaurant in the vicinity (that's where the Latin word "vicinia" derives from).

▪ **Ground Floor, Chinoy Mansion, Near Gangar Opticians, Kemps Corner, Mumbai, Ph: 23681010, 9167194784**

Vie Lounge & Deck

As the book goes to press, we are informed that Vie Lounge has shut down and is open only for private parties.

▪ **Roop Leela Bungalow, Juhu Tara Road, Opp. Little Italy Restaurant, Mumbai, Ph: 26603003/4884**

Vinoteca by Sula

RESTO-BAR
Noon to 4.30pm, 6pm to 12.30am
Buzz-3.00 | Décor-3.50 | Nightout for 2-₹4000

This tiny tapas and wine bar is all about low-impact pleasure rather than high-wattage excitement or gourmet fare. Rajiv Sula Samant's Spanish tapas bar's casual, relaxed ambience, VFM lunch, moderate pricing, wines by the glass, grazing menu, lift what might otherwise be just another neighbourhood charmer into a loftier league. It's tiny, has an alfresco wrap around bar and the centerpiece is made of 300 Sula Riesling wine bottles that light up the bar. Ritu Nanda and Elsie Nanji have even managed to nudge in a sofa seating in to the burgundy-walled and wood-floored tapas and wine bar. A must try is the Sangria made with Silvia's

Sparkling Wine, equally popular is the Cointreau Side Car, whiskies and Single Malts. The food is enlivened with flavours of Spain, garlic and olive oil and the deft use of pine nuts and figs. With your drinks, ask for the Tabla (platter with salami and serrano ham and chorizo with dill hummus), moist meaty Albondigas and the robust Chicken Chillindron. Ask for the new menu's Tuna Tartare with Guacamole and refreshing watermelon. Go for the Quinoa Salad with Walnuts, while the Lamb Burger is moist and succulent, it's the aubergine bristling with the vigorous flavours of the Mediteranean that delights. The fitting finale in a wine bar? A selection of wine-infused sorbets and gelatos... gelato with wine (Blush, Cab Shiraz), wine-flavoured Chenin Blanc Choc Mousse. Outstanding, bespoke Chocolate Truffles from Zeba Kohli's Fantasie Fine concludes the meal on a high note.

■ Ground Floor, Sunville Bldg., 9, Dr Annie Besant Road, Worli, Mumbai, Ph: 40046234

Waves

LOUNGE BAR

Buzz-3.00 | Décor-3.00 | Nightout for 2-₹2500

11am to Midnight

This open-through-the-day lounge bar has a relaxed and pleasant vibe, dotted with TVs and filled with piped music. Located in Thane's four-start hotel, United 21, this green-hued, 42-seater's popular cocktails are Cosmopolitan and Long Island Iced Tea. In the mocktail range, ask for the Blue Lady or the Cranberry Cooler. Pair these with Hakka Cottage Cheese (veg) or Hazari Murgh Kebab (non-veg). All this in a very cosy, warm atmosphere. All IMFL and varieties of international liquor brands available. Prices... Indian beer ₹225 (pint), IMFL ₹175 (30ml), Imported ₹450 (30ml).

HAPPY HOURS: Buy 2, get 1 free

■ 29, LBS Marg, Gokul Nagar, Near Castle Mill Circle, Thane (W), Mumbai, Ph: 41579999. 61165999

The White Owl

RESTO-BAR

Buzz-3.00 | Décor-3.50 | Nightout for 2-₹3500

Noon to 1.30am

Walk through the gleaming lobby of One India Bulls into the new White Owl. Here, in this warehouse-like brewery bistro, garage-meets-living room, factory-meets-kitchen, grunge-meets-shabby-chic. Antique smoked-mirror tabletops and metal chairs with patent leather upholstery complete the ambience. An innovative menu and food that has many peaks and valleys. Even the humble Potato Gratin is given a gourmet twist with blue cheese, caramelized onions and chives. Pesto Chicken Skewers are spiked with chilli. While the Devilled Eggs are lacklustre the Jalapeño Cheese Dumplings are overdone. Mains, like the Pepper-crusted Rawas are small portioned and just about okayish. But more than the food, The Owl is about popping in for an "Owltail" or more. These are poured on the double, each Owltail uses a double shot of the liquor. Check out the Biddy (whisky;

triple sec; fresh orange chunks; egg white), the Tanner (tequila; freshly-cut pineapple wedges; mixed bell peppers) or the Socialista (vodka; fresh pomegranate & mint juice). The music is modern and lively. The Owl is awaiting it's microbrewery, and is in the process of handcrafting the finest brews. Best for an easy going and chilled out afternoon or late evening. This open-through-the-day owl is a boon for the office-goers in the vicinity. It has yet to hit its stride.

■ **One Indiabulls Center, Lobby Level, Tower 2-B, Senapati Bapat Marg, Lower Parel (W), Mumbai, Ph: 24210231, M2** 18

Wink

BAR — 6pm to 1am, Mondays: 6pm to Midnight

Buzz-4.00 | Décor-4.00 | Nightout for 2-₹6000

Wink makes it to our must-visit list for several reasons! Plenty of action here... and sophistication... for a price, of course. Monthly events, Molecular Mixology, aged barrel cocktails (first bar to do so in Mumbai) and infusion cocktails too. Here, vibe is still chilled out, there are no hassles getting in and the music is pumped-up as the night wears on. Distinctive elixirs, the latest music and mouth-watering eats in a vibrant setting come together to provide a spirited experience. Flirtatious black *jalis* create private spaces between the high-octane bar area and the more sedate comfy seating one. Wink provides a smooth transition of two interconnected spaces, allowing guests to shift from the high-energy bar area with its glass bar, stone flooring and brick walls to the more intimate, carpeted lounge area in an instant. With no doors or separate entrances to each area, guests can move from one to the other in the 'wink' of an eye. Therein lies its magic. Winkitinies, Vivanta private reserve aberlour 17 years, Wink infusions, sushis are the old favourites here. What's new? You name it, they got it, including Remy Martin Louis XIII Cognac and fancy cigars. The bar opens in the evening and it's the older crowd nursing their Single Malts till 9.30pm post which the younger lot floats in to party.

■ **Vivanta by Taj – President, 90, Cuffe Parade, Colaba, Mumbai, Ph: 66650808, M1** 22

Woodside Inn

RESTO-BAR — 10am to 1am

Buzz-3.50 | Décor-3.50 | Nightout for 2-₹2500

This tiny little place, opposite Regal, is the spot for "pregaming". "This is where we pop in for many a well-priced drink before going nightclubbing", explain my young buddies. And sure enough it is packed with energetic, enthusiastic crowds swaying and singing to the retro music near the bar downstairs. Woodside Inn exudes a happy, warm, pubbish kind of enthusiastic vibe. In the afternoons, the wooden tables and leafy peepul trees provide a quiet retreat from the bustle of the city during the day. And it comes alive at night with plenty of fairy lights twinkling on the trees outside the South

Mumbai location. The booze is inexpensive (vodka: ₹100; glass of wine ₹225), Goat Cheese Bruschetta, Grilled Harissa Chicken are as popular as ever.

■ Indian Mercantile Mansion, Wodehouse Road, Opp. Regal, Colaba, Mumbai, Ph: 22875752

Woodside – All Day Bar & Eatery

RESTO-BAR 10am to 1am

Buzz-3.50 | Décor-3.50 | Nightout for 2-₹2500

It's the relaxed vibe and comfy space which makes Andheris Woodside bar a popular watering hole. Its fans swear by Spicy Rum Mojito and you should try it too when you are here! Woodside has a separate section in the menu (Woodside Concoction) dedicated to their exclusive/signature drinks like Bloody Maria, Espresso Martini, La Boheme, Absent Tango, Tanqueray Melon Fizz, Tennessee Hot Toddy, Green Apple Martini (cocktails) and Muskmelon 'n' Mint Lassi; Banana 'n' Almond Granola Shake; Papaya, Coconut 'n' Soy Smoothie; Fresh Watermelon 'n' Cucumber Juice; and Pineapple 'n' Ginger Fizz (mocktails). Keep a tab on their events like Beer Event, Beer 'n' Burger Event and Cycling Tour Event too. You could try their Napolitano Parmesan Chicken Burger served in Ciabatta Bread with fries and coleslaw or Chicken Pesto Pizza.

■ New Link Plaza, Oshiwara Link Road, Next to Oshiwara Police Station, Andheri (W), Mumbai, Ph: 26328963, 26336549

WTF!

BAR 7pm to 1.30am

Buzz-3.50 | Décor-3.50 | Nightout for 2-₹3000

Exuberant, grungy, relaxed and affordably priced... are a few words which describe Versova's WTF. Take your pick... relax on the charpoys and cushions in the outdoor section with relaxing soft music playing in the background. Interesting art walls and a bar placed on a handcart make this a fun place to hangout. Or choose to go into the air-conditioned section and chill on the grungy, old-coloured wooden furniture, the red couch pop-culture area and a Rajanikanth image with a guitar in the DJ console. Textured walls and unconventional bar stools greet you inside, and to the extreme right, a loud red seating area canvassed with witticisms, designs, pop culture and blaring music playing retro, hip-hop and popular hits. *Chatpata*, robustly spiced starters and well-made cocktails here. Only starters served here from the Mean Ass Chicken Chilli to Vada Pao (yes, seriously... and ₹75 only), Aloo Chaat and Quesadillas (all under ₹200) along with VFM drinks like mojitos, Long Island Iced Teas, Caiprioska, shots, and shooters (around ₹200)... they have them all! Wine by glass and bottle too. A packed, casual hangout.

■ 12, Mahal Shopping Center, Seven Bungalows, Near Seven Bungalow Garden & Bus Stop, Versova, Andheri (W), Mumbai, Ph: 9967893416, M5 18

Yauatcha

RESTO-BAR

11am to Midnight

Buzz-3.00 | Décor-3.00 | Nightout for 2-₹6000

The bar rocks mainly on the weekends... all other days, it is mainly for the outstanding dim sum and Chinese fare that it draws packed houses. Yau-wow-atcha is how I'd like to rename this London's Michelin-starred restaurant of the Hakkasan-fame maestro Alan Yau. Walk into one of those gleaming Bandra-Kurla buildings, go past the white-marble counter patisserie and tea counter and up the stairs into a large, urban canteen-like space with a slim aquarium, back lighting, communal bar table and uncomfy seating too. Don't let that put you off in this fabulous, modern, two-storey tea house (24 varieties of tea) and twice as many dim sum (steamed, baked and fried) are served. The well-stocked bar offers many a choice but it's the Lalu (vodka-based cocktail enlivened with litchi lemon grass oolong tea) which is the hotseller and definitely worth trying.

■ **Raheja Towers, Right from ILFS Bldg., Bandra Kurla Complex, Mumbai, Ph: 26448888**

Zenith Party Suite

WINE BAR

About to Open

As the book goes to press, we are informed that the Palladium Hotel is all set to open Zentih Party Suite with 360 glass views and a glass box at the top of it all.

■ **Palladium Hotel, 462, Senapati Bapat Marg, Lower Parel, Mumbai, Ph: 61628000, M2** 23

What are you looking for today? Golas? Mulberry Ice Cream? Falooda? Malai Rabadi? Green Chilli Ice Cream? Jackfruit Ice Cream or a glass of hygienic Sugarcane Juice? Or maybe it's the American-style stone creamery? Italian gelato? Or the latest craze for frozen yoghurt? You'll find all the answers here.

While the old-fashioned, typically mumbaiya *juice and icecream shops continue to throb with life on the streets and serve up comfort on the car bonnets, the glitzy new international brands muscle their way. Behind the fruits (which are strung on the forehead of these shops) lurk many a surprise. Ginger Lemon, Herbal Juice and Dry Fruit Ice Cream. What names — Munna Munni and Maara Maari! Ginger Ice Cream, hand-churned fresh fruit flavour, too! Tried Malai Golas? Must not miss Mumbai's faludas (including Gadbad Faluda). Did I forget to tell you about Chinese Grilled Sandwiches and idlis? I am sure you knew that Haji Ali Juice Centre accepts credit cards too (but other than this exception, most of them are cash only). Open late into the night, these are Mumbai institutions...*

P.S. Did we call this chapter "Ice Cream & Juice Parlours"? As you can see, it's all that and much more. Much much more.

Achija Juice Centre

10.30am to 1am

You can walk in to Achija at the middle of the night and still find something worth munching. Their dry fruit creamy shakes (₹165), cold coffee with ice cream (₹75), jelly with fruit custard, ice-cream combinations (Watermelon Blossom, Bunty aur Bubbly Blossom, Rim Zim Blossom), *chatpata chaats* and the ever-famous *masaledaar* Pao Bhaji are all worth a try. Since 1986, this Ghatkopar institution is serving freshly squeezed juice cocktail combinations. Also a hit with the regulars are idlis, dosas, pizzas and the Chin-dian fare. But it's for their Pao Bhaji and juice combos that you would want to "come again" (literal meaning of Achija). Not surprisingly, their catering is in demand too (100+). They are planning another branch very soon in Vikrant Circle.

■ 13, Vasant Nivas, Tilak Road Naka, Ghatkopar (E), Mumbai, Ph: 21024909, 21027359, 21025982, 9892515373

Amar Fast Food & Restaurant

10am to 12.45am

Vashi's Amar Juice Centre's juices and creamy milkshakes are not to be missed. Try their Pao Bhaji, Butter Idlis, sandwiches, pizzas and more.

■ Satra Plaza, Sector 19, Palm Beach Road, Vashi, Navi Mumbai

vehicle. The staff also likes it that way. Amar's thick and creamy milkshakes (Chocolate, Chikoo, Pista, Kesar, Pineapple, Sitaphal, Strawberry, Mango) and refreshing juices (Munna Munni, Maara Maari, Grape and more) are a hit at this landmark. Bite in the Grilled Sandwiches, Pizza (including Special Amar Pizzza), Pao Bhaji (₹85; the star here), dosas, or idlis. Order for bonnet service or just enjoy slurping the shakes and juices on the footpath. Catering too for over 100 people.

■ **Shop No. 3, RN Cooper Hospital Compound, Gulmohar Road, Vile Parle (W), Mumbai, Ph: 26247917, 26243863**

Amore

10am to 6pm

More happiness in every scoop! Flavour of the Month at ₹30, fruit sorbets (try refreshing pineapple and strawberry) at ₹50, special flavours at ₹50 and premium at ₹70. Cakes (₹460/half kg) for celebrations, gelato on a stick (₹59) and new flavours (banana, toffee) have been added to the menu. Try the luscious Belgian Chocolate, sinful Bombay Double Fudge, heavenly Ferrero Rocher or the award-winning Masala Latte and Passagio to Indian flavours (18 available including yoghurt-based and sugar-free flavours) at these tiny, cosy outlets and kiosks. Vegetarian, natural, organic, always fresh, award-winning gelato from a socially engaged company that donates a part of its profits to orphanages and NGO's... that's Amore for you! No seating area, but they offer home delivery (carefully packed in dry ice) to make up for that.

■ **Vivivana Mall, Eastern Express Highway, Thane (W), Thane,** www.amoregelato.com

■ **R Mall, Near Food Court, Mulund Check-Naka, Mulund (W), Mumbai, Ph: 9167394314**

■ **Haiko Mall, Ground Floor, Opp. Rodas Ecotel, Hiranandani, Powai, Mumbai, Ph: 9167394316**

■ **Kiosk No. 229, 2nd Floor, Infiniti, Link Road Oshiwara, Andheri (W), Mumbai, Ph: 9167394320**

■ **Shop No. 4, Gokul Park Co-operative Housing Society, Ambadi Road, Near Manav Mandir, Vasai (W), Mumbai**

■ **Kakson Holdings, Ground Floor, Plot No. 80, Sion-Trombay Road, Opp. RK Studio, Chembur, Mumbai, Ph: 64577272**

■ **Growel's, 101, Mall Kandivali (E), Mumbai**

■ **Big Cinema, R City Centre, Ghatkopar (W), Mumbai, Ph: 9167394319**

■ **Sangam BIG Cinemas, 127, Opp. ACME Plaza, Chakala, Andheri Kurla Road, Andheri (E), Mumbai**

■ **Equinox, Food Court, Indulge, Unit No. 09, Ground Floor, East Wing (P3), Tower-3, Peninusula Techno Park Complex, AH Wadia Marg, Kurla, Mumbai, Ph: 9167394312**

■ **2nd Floor, Fame Multiplex, In-Orbit Mall, Malad (W), Mumbai, Ph: 9167394323**

■ **Unit No. 338, 3rd Floor, Infiniti Mall, Malad (W), Mumbai, Ph: 9167740056**

■ **BIG Cinemas, 1st Floor, I- Max Adlabs, Wadala, Mumbai, Ph: 9167394311**

■ **R City Center, LBS Marg, Ghatkopar (W), Mumbai, Ph: 9167394318**

■ **BIG Cinemas, 1st Floor, Metro Adlabs, Dhobi Talao, Marine Lines (E), Mumbai, Ph: 9167394310**

Anando

10am to 12.30am

With a specialization in flavoured milk products, within a price range of ₹51–63, Anando is a fifty-two-year-old all-sides-open, L-shaped parlour at Chowpatty Seaface! No sitting and no home delivery either, but people come by dozens for the tempting thandais (₹51), ice creams (Kwality Walls), milkshakes (Sitaphal, Mango or Choco Almond) and flavoured milk (Choco-Almond/Special Masala or the new Sugar-free Masala). Enjoyed by corporates and chauffeurs alike, Anando is open late into the night. Grilled Veg Sandwich (₹25) too, 100 per cent Jain like everything else available here. They have opened quite a few new outlets in several places in Mumbai.

■ **Near Purandare Hospital, Chowpatty Seaface, Girgaon, Mumbai, Ph: 23690221, 9819992201**
www.anando.in

Apsara Ice Creams

9am to 11pm

Hugely (and justifiably) popular hand-churned ice creams here. Also, a paradise for Jains! Jayanti Bhai and his family have been churning all-natural Jain seasonal fresh fruit ice-creams (Paan Masala and Red Peru, ₹40/scoop) and seasonal milkshakes for over forty years now. Other flavours are Cinnamon Walnut Crunch, Orange Apricot, Orange with Chocolate Chips, Thandai and Veriali Pista. Of the 25-30 flavours available, Ferrero Rocher, Sitaphal and Roasted Almond are my favourites. The regulars enjoy South Indian snacks, *chatpata chaats*, Pao Bhaji at this delightful Jain ice-cream parlour.

■ **74/76, Walkeshwar Road, Near Birla Public School, Mumbai, Ph: 23680294, 23617410**

■ **Vasani Cottage, Opp. McDonald's, Vile Parle (W), Mumbai, Ph: 26188253, 26144990**

■ **Kakad Estate, RG Thadani Marg, Opp. Poddar Hospital, Worli, Mumbai, Ph: 24968386, 9892077330**

Baba Faluda

2pm to 1am

Masha Allah! Their tall glass of Special Baba Faluda (₹80) and Double Special Baba Faluda (₹110), (named after Baba Maqdom Shah Dargah at the end of the lane) pulls in people late into the night. Loaded with ice-cream, faluda (Royal Double, Black Currant, Chocolate; or any of the 15 flavours available), Takhmariya and (home-made) syrups of your choice, ice cream (₹25-30 and there are 30 seasonal flavours too), kulfi, cassata, fresh Pineapple Roll, all ₹35 onwards. Lucky Mahim residents get home delivery too.

■ **52, Bell View Bldg., Shop No. 2, LJ 2nd Cross Road, Mahim, Mumbai, Ph: 24473813**

Bachelorr's Juice House

11pm to 1am

This city institution on a pavement has been a fixture since 1940 and remains as popular as ever and it's not Bachelor but Bachelorr. Amidst the hustle and bustle of Chowpatty, hit Bachelorr's for the frothy milkshakes (₹126 Choco Chip, ₹150 for Sitaphal and Mango), cream-based desserts (Fresh Strawberries and Cream), ice creams and fresh fruit juices. Bachelorr's Rocher (₹45, chocolate infused with hazelnut), Mango (₹41), Dry Fruits (₹35), Fresh Fruits (₹30), Green Chilli and Ginger (₹30), along with other seasonal flavours are all worth a try. Regulars dive into sandwiches, Pao Bhaji, thin-crust pizzas and more late into the night. Do say hello to the cheerful AA Agarwal, who joyfully narrates the tale of his father's late marriage, which gave the place its name.

■ **45, Sattar Sea View, Opp. Birla Krida Kendra, Chowpatty, Mumbai, Ph: 23682211, 23681408**

Badshah

7am to 12.30am

Nobody here seems to mind sharing a table with strangers for their fix of the sugary-sweet Faluda (try SP Irani's Royal Faluda, ₹51), laced with in-house ingredients. You'll have to wade your way through the crowds at Crawford Market and wait in queue to get a seat at this cramped and crowded eatery. Snacks offered include pizzas, sandwiches, dosas, Pao Bhaji and *chaats*. Milkshakes are popular too — the famed Chocolate Milkshake (₹85), ever-popular Masala, or a host of fruit-based flavours. I recommend home delivery.

■ **152/156, LT Marg, Opp. Crawford Market, Mumbai, Ph: 23425950, 23449316**

Baskin Robbins

11am to Midnight

Critics may complain about the synthetic taste or the imported tag, but there is no denying the popularity of this mega chain. It makes its presence felt throughout the city with more than 75 parlours and menu appearances at many five-star hotels and high-end restaurants. The iconic pink spoon and thirty-one pure vegetarian flavours (made with cows' milk) are here to stay. Mississippi Mud and Fig 'n' Honey are new flavours while the Cotton Candy and Pink Bubblegum evoke childhood memories. Bavarian Chocolate and Chocolate Chip Mousse are the most popular by far. They even have high-end favourites like Gold Medal Ribbon and Alphonso. Ice-cream Sundaes begin at ₹120 (Thanda Hot Fudge with Vanilla) and go up to ₹213 (Build Your Own

Sundae). To keep footfall high, Baskin Robbins has a flavour of the month. Pop into a parlour and give them your mobile number to get on the list of their ice-cream lover's club and get exclusive offers daily!

■ **Ph: 42313131, 42315008,** www.baskinrobbins.com

Bharat Dairy and Juice Centre 10am to 1.30am

The Gupta brothers' four decade strong thriving Chowpatty-based snack centre is characterized by long lines of cars snaking around the lanes of the Bharatiya Vidya Bhavan. *Fatafat* service and *chatpata* snacks. Pao Bhaji (₹80); Idli (₹35); Dosa (₹60); Grilled Toast (₹115), pizza (₹110), Paneer Roll (₹55) and more. Milkshakes (₹110), freshly squeezed juices (even Anjeer and Grape), Kesar Lassi (₹45), seasonal fruits with cream and lassis are all served in largish beer mugs and more than sufficient for one.

■ **Opp. Bharatiya Vidya Bhavan, Chowpatty, Mumbai, Ph: 23689072, 65720413**

Broadway Juice Centre 7am to 10pm

For more than 30 years, Broadway has been serving sandwiches, milkshakes and juices to the locals of Dadar TT. Relax on chairs placed on the footpath and gaze at the star-studded sky as you enjoy their famous Cheese Toasted Sandwich, Milkshakes (Seasonal and Dry Fruit) and seasonal fresh fruit juices (in cocktail combinations).

■ **Dr Ambedkar Road, Next to Babubhai Jagjivandas, Dadar TT, Mumbai, Ph: 9619132427**

Café Chokolade (Formerly Cad-B) 11am to Midnight

On offer here are Chocolate Sandwiches (₹50 and satisfyingly consistent), brownies (₹80–160) and Chocolate Shots (₹40–60) and much more. It's all about chocolate at Café Chokolade. But what exactly is their signature Chokolade? Served as a shake, it is so thick that you would need a spoon. It's frozen but it definitely doesn't have the consistency of an ice cream — a brilliant-sounding concept. Try their Cad-B (more chocolate, less cream) or Cad-M (less chocolate more cream) as you like. There are times when the chocolate tastes watered-down because of the ice. They are in more than 15 locations across Mumbai now.

■ **Gagangiri Society, Shop No. 4A, Next to Open Affair, Union Park, Carter Road, Khar (W), Mumbai, Ph: 9167384868,** www.cafechockolade.com

■ **Shop No. 10, Next to VIP, Nebula Cooperative Housing Society, Crossroad No. 4, Lokhandwala Complex, Andheri (W), Mumbai, Ph: 9167384868**

■ **4, Ashok Enclave, Chincholi Bandar Signal, Near Evershine Mall, Next to Javed Habib Saloon, Malad (W), Mumbai, Ph: 9920478307, 9322992427**

■ **Shop No. 4, Block No. 1, Hiranandani Meadows, Off Pokhran Road No. 2, Thane (W), Ph: 9322335881, 9920478307**

■ **6, Parmar CHS Limited, Paranjpe B-Scheme Road 1, Vile Parle (E), Mumbai, Ph: 9821999981**

■ **11, Golden Willows, Vasant Garden, Off LBS Road, Mulund (W), Mumbai, Ph: 21641265**

■ **5, Bethlem Premises, Ground Floor, Next to Domino's Pizza, Borivali (W), Mumbai, Ph: 28930892**

■ **77, Bldg. 42, Phase 5, Insat CHS, Thakur Village, Kandivali (E), Mumbai, Ph: 65044444**

■ **6, Happy Homes, Tilak Road, Ghatkopar (E), Mumbai, Ph: 9892724045**

■ **9, Neelkanth Darshan, Old Mumbai Pune Highway, Panvel, Navi Mumbai, Ph: 27483233**

■ **CB-7, Thadani Apts., Gol Maidan, Ulhasnagar, Kalyan, Mumbai**

■ **7, Sorti Somnath CHS, Link Road, Kanderpada, Dahisar, Mumbai, Ph: 65615701**

■ **3, Darya Darshan CHS, JP Road, 7 Bungalows, Mumbai**

■ **Food Court, Growels, 101 Mall, Akurli Road, Kandivali (E), Mumbai, Ph: 65044444**

■ **6, Vani Apts., Near Basant Cinema, CG Gidwani Road, Chembur, Mumbai, Ph: 9833777224**

■ **6&7, Asmita Orient Bldg., Next to Café Coffee Day, Mira Road (E), Mumbai, Ph: 65090001, 9869669869**

■ **53, Shreeji Heights, Opp. Mumbai High Restaurant, Sector 46-A, Seawoods, Navi Mumbai, Ph: 9594202628**

Cocoberry

10am to 1am

New flavours to try at Cocoberry include Peach, Chocolate and Mango! They make all the health claims yoghurt would — good for digestion and your skin with substantial calcium content. For a guilt-free cool dessert, head to Cocoberry and try their 98 per cent, low-fat with a strong and very familiar aftertaste of unsweetened dahi in every flavour. Sip a splash (₹99; for all flavours, their recommendation is Blueberry and Berry Blast) or dive into a scrumptious Parfait which is a layer of muesli, yoghurt, topping (of your choice), yoghurt and again muesli served in large and tall glasses. Choose from 24 available toppings. Exotic toppings are premium fruits like strawberries and chocolates. Ranbir Kapoor, Karan Johar, John Abraham have all sampled the healthy goodness on offer.

■ **Shop No. A4, Gagangiri Premises Cooperative Society, Carter Road, Khar (W), Mumbai, Ph: 26058611 ,**
www.cocoberry.co.in

■ **Shop No. 2, Juhu Princess, Next to Bru World Café, Juhu, Mumbai, Ph: 26123099**

■ **Shop No. TF309, Infinity 2, New Link Road, Malad (W), Mumbai, Ph: 28894974, 9819683819**

■ **Shop No. 7, Dream Ville, Swami Samarth Nagar, Lokhandwala, Andheri (W), Mumbai, 26323031, 8879449496**

■ **41/C, Shop No. 3, Opp. SoBo Centre, Tardeo, Mumbai, Ph: 23531905**

■ Level 9, Platina Bldg., Block G, Plot C 59, Bandra Kurla Complex, Bandra (E), Mumbai

Das Fast Food and Juice Centre 11.30am to 11.15pm

It's the Malai Kulfi Mixed Ice Cream Faluda (₹50) that's the star here. Mosambi Juice available here only from June– September (₹30/glass) and two seasonal add-ons at other times of the year. Unlike most juice centers, they serve non-veg snacks too. You'll see patrons slurping on *golas* ₹25 for plain and ₹50 for milk-based flavours. Take your pick from Grilled Cheese Sandwiches (₹45), dosa, *chaats*, Pao Bhaji (₹50) or even Chinese (veg and chicken). They also have Das Special Jain Pav Bhaji (₹70). Thin-crust pizzas come in both chicken and veg variants in small and large sizes.

■ Shop No. 11, Unity Apts., B-39, Vaishali Nagar, Jogeshwari (W), Mumbai, Ph: 26779588, 26769853

Dinshaw's Xpress 11.30am to Midnight

Well-priced desserts and ice creams here. Chocolate fondues to sundaes topped with Oreo cookies, Ferrero Rochers, fruits and marshmallows and many a ice cream flavour choices... Melba, Figs 'n' Almond, Pistachio and Chocolate Brownie too. Smoothies fans must try their Black Currant Ice Cream and Cranberry Juice Blend. The rest of the menu offers the usual pastas and burgers too.

■ Shop No. 3, Canvera, JP Road, Versova, Andheri (W), Mumbai, Ph: 9323737337, 9820636865

FroYo Mon–Thurs: 11am to 12.30am, Fri–Sun: 11am to 1.30am

A smiling watermelon, an enthusiastic strawberry, a banana playing tug-o-war... colourful posters like these adorn the brightly lit (flagship) Andheri and Bandra outlets. Check out the Kibanana flavour, a combination of kiwi and banana. Triple Treat begins at ₹100 (with two regular and one premium topping), while Jus for You (includes three regular and one premium topping) costs ₹100 onwards. The taste of yoghurt is very apparent but it's not as sweet as most ice creams would be. It's pure veg, low-fat and made with all-natural ingredients. Frojitos, smoothies, juices and soda-based refreshers too! Try their waffles such as Chocolate Waffles and Choco O Banana starting at ₹40 onwards.

■ Shop No. 4, Silver Pearl, Opp. Harley Davidson, Waterfield Road, Bandra (W), Mumbai, Ph: 26443020, 9820889960, www.letsgofroyo.com

■ Shop No. 4, MHADA Complex, Link Road, Oshiwara, Andheri (W), Mumbai, Ph: 9920885559

■ Shop No. 9, Gagangiri Bldg., Off Carter Road, Near CCD, Bandra (W), Mumbai, Ph: 8879363088

■ Shop No. 48, G Wing, Raj Arcade, Mahavir Nagar, Opp. D'Mart, Kandivali (W), Mumbai, Ph: 9920885559, 977349729

Froot Café

10am to 10pm, Mondays Closed

Juices, froothies, milkshakes and frootzz — it's all about fruits at Borivali East's Froot Café where they have 60 varieties of them. They have a limited snack menu (all vegetarian) offering Aloo Tikki (₹35), Nuggets Surprise (₹35), sandwiches (₹40), burgers (₹40) and pizzas and pastas. Seasonal fruits make their way to customers freshly squeezed (₹50). Froothies (fruit smoothies) are all for ₹65 of which Red Gold, Apple Berry and Berry Banana are popular. Frootzz, soda-based mocktails, are available too in flavours like Strawberry Cockail, Deep Purple and Ocean's Legend and their best seller Mango Berry Blast.

■ **Shop No. 18, Koyna CHS, Near Borivali National Park, Shantivan, Borivali (E), Mumbai, Ph: 9833039639, 9833441156**

Gelato Italiano

Noon to Midnight

There are more than 30 locations across Mumbai of this brand that offers pure vegetarian and 97 per cent fat-free gelato! But the bigger news is that you get a gelato for as low as ₹9 on the 1st of every month! Every month beginning, Gelato Italiano launches a brand new flavour and you can find long lines outside the brilliantly designed, hi-tech and contemporary ice cream parlour's outlets. It's only on the first day that these flavours are sold at ₹9, which on other days cost you ₹40. Over two dozen flavours, shake-a-lattos (gelatos blended with milk/sorbet blended with ice; available at select outlets only) and special waffle cones ensure that there is something tantalizing for every tastebud. Diet Lite flavours are made with fructose and has flavours like Limoncello, Chocolate, Coffee and others made with seasonal fruits. Bulk ordering available for restaurants and occasional promotional discounts for those signed up on their facebook page.

■ **Ph: 8080888441, 8080788441**

Gogola

11am to Midnight

Mineral water, attendants with gloves, natural-flavoured syrups made from pure sugar... all this and more offered at Gogola, the logo of which reminds you of the google homepage. Their range includes twenty exciting flavours like Litchi, Blue Lagoon, Fruit Twist, Anar and even Anarapple. Milkmaid Golas too! All reasonably priced at ₹80, served in a specially designed glass with a plate embedded on it so that children don't spill on their clothes and their hands don't get dirty. Ask them for a portable ice-crushing machines and throw a gola party at home. They have a presence in Bengaluru, Pune, Essleworld and Water Kingdom.

■ **Hanuman Road, Opp. Bal Vidhya Mandir, Vile Parle (E), Mumbai, Ph: 9930810915, 9820729994**

Gokul Ice Cream

Noon to 11.30pm

Seasonal fresh fruit flavours like Mulberry, Jackfruit, Kala Jamun and Litchi lead the list amongst others. The late Gundraya Kamath perfected the art of rich Shrikhand (₹120/500gm for kesar) and hand-churned ice creams back in 1970. Today, his legacy continues at four retail outlets that serve an array of indulgent flavours (18 choices; ₹45/scoop or ₹200/500gm). Chocobite and Butterscotch are very popular. Other combinations offered are Orange Pineapple, Kesar Pista, Kesar Badam Pista and the innovative Kesar Thandai. Thick ice cream shakes too!

■ **71-C, Ajay Apts., Saraswati Road, Santacruz (W), Mumbai, Ph: 26497755, 26052128, 26487755,** www.gokulicecreams.in

■ **Gokul Foods & Dairymade Products, New Sonal Link Indl. Estate, Bldg. No. 1, Gala No. 39, Kachapada, Link Road, Malad (W), Mumbai, Ph: 28826857**

■ **Warm Treat, C/5, Bhakti Palace Society Ltd., Bhakti Nagar, Kandar Pada, Dahisar (W), Mumbai, Ph: 28959333, 28959335**

■ **Shop No. 83, Marwadi Chawl, Near Empire Chemist, Opp. Petrol Pump, Irla, S V Road, Vile Parle (W), Mumbai, Ph: 26711022, 26714443**

Gupta Sugarcane

10am to Midnight

Head to Gupta, near the Gateway of India, for the most hygienic glass of sugarcane juice in town! Special discounts for students and Defense personnel too. Topped with refreshing ginger and lemon and cooled down with filter-cube ice, it's incredibly rejuvenating. At ₹20 for a small, ₹25 for medium and ₹37 for a large, it's well priced too. They adhere to high hygienic standards here. After thoroughly cleaning and washing the sugarcane, they crush it once (for 35 seconds) with stainless steel equipment, so the juice is untouched by hand. Within 15 minutes they can get 100 glasses ready for pickup! No delivery though.

■ **Ground Floor, Dhanraj Mahal, Chhatrapati Shivaji Road, Gateway of India, Mumbai, Ph: 22023124**

Häagen-Dazs

10am to 11.30pm

I dip fruits, cookies, sponge cake and mini ice-cream scoops into the pot of hot chocolate in the (more than enough for four) Häagen-Dazs Fondue (₹1,395). A palette of flavours... Dulce de Leche and Strawberry Cheesecake, but the must try is the innovative Häagen-Dazs Dolce, a multi-layered flavour sensation inspired by desserts of the world. Some of the flavours require fine tuning and some are over-the-top exotic. I love their meticulous attention to the source of ingredients: be it the six years taken to find strawberries sweet enough to carry the Häagen-Dazs name or the fresh-from-the-dairy cream of the highest quality, vanilla from Madagascar and chocolate from Belgium. It's the slow magic of the gentle blending of these fine ingredients that results in the minimizing of air. The result? Each scoop is dense and creamy. It melts slowly, lasts longer and redefines super-premium. Sure, all this comes with a big price tag and the ice creams are expensive. Häagen-Dazs comes in with its supreme combination of substance with style, tradition with modernity and service with a smile.

■ **G-36, Oberoi Mall, Oberoi Garden City, Off Western Express Highway, Goregaon (E), Mumbai, Ph: 40233700**

■ **High Street Phoenix, Opp. Croma, Senapati Bapat Marg, Lower Parel, Mumbai, Ph: 43474449, 43474445**

■ **Ground Floor, City Park, Hiranandani Gardens, Powai, Mumbai, Ph: 40222096**

Haji Ali Juice Centre

5am to 1am

Celebs like Farooq Abdullah and even Amitabh Bachchan have stopped by Fareed Noorani's humble tea stall that has blossomed into a city landmark and an institution that was established way back in 1937. Cherries 'n' Cream and Kesar Royal Faluda are the favourites here. Veg Pizza remains the most ordered snack. The brightly lit shop at the main Haji Ali junction is the only juice centre to accept credit cards. Ask for the bespectacled Aslam, waiter no. 1 (first to join in 1969) who will not only serve efficiently, but also regale you with colourful anecdotes.

■ **Lala Lajpat Rai Road, Haji Ali Circle, Haji Ali, Mumbai, Ph: 23510957, 23517632**

Hokey Pokey

11am to 10.30pm

America's cold stone creamery has come to India in a Hokey Pokey *avatar*. And they are in 11 locations in Mumbai now. A daily bonanza from 2pm to 5pm — 25 per cent discount on all cool creations! Also have everything from Tangy Lemon to Chocolate with Chikoo being the latest addition to the menu. Select your ice cream, add mix-ins and watch as the friendly folks behind the counter deftly and delicately swirl them all together. Wonderland Magic, Brownie Break, Black Forest Blend and Choco Coffee Crazy are all served in both cones and cups. Sip on their blended shakes priced at ₹80 and ₹240.

■ **Shop No. 3, Shroff Tower, Sodawala Lane, Near Prabodhan Thakray Hall, Borivali (W), Mumbai, Ph: 8879465027**

■ **Shop No. 4, Ground Floor, Lourds Heritage Bldg., Marve Road, Opp. Orlem Church, Malad (W), Mumbai, Ph: 9619484816**

■ **Korum Mall, 3rd Floor, Food Court, Unit No. K3, Cadbury Compound, Mangal Pandey Road, Off Eastern Express Highway, Thane, Ph: 25450880, 9619484818**

■ **Phoenix Market City, Level 2, Atrium 2, LBS Marg, Kurla (W), Mumbai, Ph: 9619484814**

■ **Shop No. 35, Bldg. No. 38, Evershine Milennium Paradise, Thakur Village, Kandivali (E), Mumbai, Ph: 28463696, 9619484817**

■ **Shop No. 2, Ground Floor, Kalpitan CHS, 16th Road, Bandra (W), Ph: 9619484811**

■ **17th,Marzaban Road, Opp. Pizza Hut, Next to Sterling Cinema, Chatrapati Shivaji Terminus, Mumbai, Ph: 7506065959**

■ **1, Garden Apts., Diamond Garden, Sion Trombay Road, Chembur, Mumbai, Ph: 25201198**

■ **Shop No. 4, Sainath Apts., Ground Floor, Near Turning Point, Chopra Court Road, Ulhas Nagar Station Road, Ph: 8554054054**

■ **1st Floor, Haiko Mall, Hiranandini Business Park, Powai, Mumbai, Ph: 7506045959**

■ **Inox, Raghuleela Mega Mall, Off Swami Vivekananda Road, Behind Poisar Depot, Kandivali (W), Mumbai**

Ice Cream Works

Noon to 1am

Creative and dedicated to the pleasure, romance and ceremony of eating ice creams, yoghurts and more. There's a sleek and elegant, yet warm and cheerful energy in these parlours. They have been steadily spanning the city. Enlivened with 150 inch screens and 60 inch plasmas, wi-fi and lively music, the stage is set for a "cool" experience. ICW offers adventure for those who want it and comfort for those who don't. The exquisite and unusual Calcutta Meetha Paan is a must try. Chocolate to Die For, Madagascar Choco-Nut, Sicilian Pistachio, Double Strawberry Chocolate Chip, Mint Brownie Fudge are popular too. Do lookout for the sundae menu here; especially the kiddy special. Elaborate, creative and innovative sums up this place. The sundaes not to be missed are Before I Die (eight scoops of chocolate sundae); Ice Cream Fondue (16 mini scoops of ice cream, fresh fruit, cookies etc); Nuts About Kulfi (crispy sevia in a rich rabdi sauce, milk burfi and hot mini gulab jamuns). Yoghurt fans this way please... Yogorto Humble Fruit Bowl or Healthy Habit Yogorto are worth trying. Most ingredients are imported from Italy, France, Belgium and Spain and the difference shows.

■ **Shop No. 1, Shiv Kutir, Near Natural Ice Cream, 278, Veer Savarkar Marg, Shivaji Park, Mumbai, Ph: 24462626,** www.icecreamworks.com

■ **Glamour Ice Cream, Near Café Coffee Day, Chowpatty, Mumbai, Ph: 23620104, 23690104**

■ **Unit 2, 1st Floor, Opp. PVR Multiplex, The Phoenix Mills, Senapati Bapat Marg, Lower Parel, Mumbai**

K Rustom Ice Cream Parlour

9.30am to 11pm

I have many fond memories of biting into an Ice Cream Sandwich and, more recently, enjoying some sweet set *dahi*, served in a tall glass, at this nearly 60-year-old city landmark. It's one of those VFM places that also proves that old-fashioned hospitality and good quality never go out of style. With more than a dozen flavours you're sure to find your favourite. Kiwi, Chocolate Walnut, Chocolate Nuts, Kesar Pista, Bitter Chocolate and Black Currant are some of them. The attractive array continues with Green Mango, Coconut Pista, Toffee, Coffee, Litchi, Peach, Rum 'n' Raisin, Anjeer, Nutty Bake, Mint Crunch, Pineapple,

Raspberry, Vanilla, Peppermint, Lime 'n' Lemon and Badam. I scream, you scream, we all scream for ice cream!

■ **87, Stadium House, Veer Nariman Road, Opp. Lladro Showroom, Churchgate, Mumbai, Ph: 22821768**

Kalpana's Tastee

10am to 11.30pm

This five-decade-old Worli wonder offers favourites like idlis, dosas, pizzas and chaats. While here, try their sizzling and tastee Pao Bhaji (₹65). Wash it all down with freshly squeezed seasonal fruit juices (₹55–105) or milkshakes (₹55–145). Top it off with ice cream (Kwality Walls) to beat that Mumbai heat!

■ **Nadava Bhavan, Dr Annie Besant Road, Opp. City Bakery, Worli Naka, Mumbai, Ph: 24920118**

Kulfi Centre

10am to 1.30am

Since 1960, they've come a long way and have even catered for the Raj Bhavan! Attack their Matka Kulfis or relish the seasonal fruit flavours, ever-popular Special Malai, Royal Banana, Zaffrani Rogan, Badam Pista Kesar, Sugar free and Badam Pista Elaichi. They have also introduced Sugar-free Kulfis priced reasonably.

■ **SVP Road, 556, Marina Mansion, Girgaon Chowpatty, Mumbai, Ph: 23684291, 23689059**

Mango Forest

11am to 11.45pm

Hygienic and freshly squeezed juices are the USP of this Andheri juice bar. Not as much variety here though. Try their Apple, Orange, Sweet Lime, Watermelon and Kiwi juices. Cocktail Juice and a Mango Milkshake too. Mix Fruit Chaat and Veg Cheese Grilled Sandwich are also available.

■ **Windermere, 1-A, Shop No. 4, Off New Link Road, Oshiwara, Andheri (W), Mumbai, Ph: 7208409015**

Melting Munch

11am to Midnight

Of the 25 perennial flavours and 10 seasonal favourites, Green Chilli, Ferrero Rocher and Orange Chocolate are crowd favourites. It serves (all-natural and eggless) flavours of Aspara ice creams. Order ice cream cakes for those special occasions or ask about those specialized photo cakes (1kg min; 6 days' notice) and personalized photo chocolates (with nuts ₹100/150gm). Many creamy mikshakes too! Get your birth date or anniversary day printed on a special ten rupee note (check their website under "birth note" for details).

■ **Shop No. 6, Meher Premises, Ranade Road, Shivaji Park, Dadar (W), Mumbai, Ph: 22920628, 24382268, 9821154430,** www.meltingmunch.com

Microwave Snacks & Juice Centre

9am to 9pm

When they began more than thirty years ago, it wasn't as common as it is today to have a microwave handy to heat snacks on the spot and that's how it got its name.

Amazing rock-bottom prices at this best value-for-money place in the city! Captain Godbole's silver goody, a modest Worli joint, serves up amazing value and flavours in milkshakes (₹30 and under), freshly squeezed juices (₹20 and under), lassi (₹15), Energy Drinks (₹19), Masala Milk (₹20) and snacks (samosas, vadas and mutton patties). No ice creams here! It closes earlier than most juice centers (at 9pm), but it's worth heading there for good juice and good eats at those awesome prices.

Opp. Satyam Cinema, Worli, Mumbai, Ph: 24983685

Natural Ice Cream

10.30am to 12.30am

We all know that Natural's is everywhere, but with nearly 60 outlets(!) everywhere isn't and apt enough word! Handmade ice creams that convert fruits into light, fluffy and dreamy ice cream flavours through traditional methods and modern technology with Indian-sourced vegetarian ingredients. Outstanding flavours that have Sanjeev Kapoor, Shilpa Shetty and more digging into fruity (Sitaphal and Chikoo are my picks) and chocolate-y goodness (Choco-everything is popular here). Eye-catching, mouthwatering posters in these elegant, clean parlours (visit their "web parlour" online for locations) will tempt you to walk out with a tub for family, or an indulgent rich ice cream shake (₹125) for yourself.

13th North South Road, Juhu Scheme, Mumbai, Ph: 26206053, 26707558, 32977272, 28696851-53,
www.naturalicecreams.in

Noorani Milk Centre

5.30pm to 1.30am

Open 24/7 during Ramzan, try the Malpuas (₹80 for single and ₹100 double) at this tiny little place in Minara Masjid neighbourhood. The very popular Fruitella is not a candy, but their very own creation which is a Rabadi-like custard made of milk and fruits. Masala Milk and the Special Milkshake (hot: ₹26, cold: ₹22) are served in glasses by the dozens throughout the day. More milk-based goodness: Dry Fruit Halwa (₹400/kg), Mango Malai Halwa (₹340/kg), Butterscotch Halwa (₹340/kg), and Phirni (₹25 onwards) are all worth savouring. Dudhi Halwa (₹220/kg) too.

157, Ebrahim Road, Minara Masjid, Mumbai, Ph: 23464361, 23443751

Pankaj Juice Centre

8am to 2am

When in Matunga, pile on at Pankaj's! Lap off their newly introduced Chocolate Fudge Sundae, soothing and smooth. Juice cocktails, milkshakes, handmade ice creams and kulfis (try mango and strawberry) keep this place packed. They've got a host of interesting juices and fruit punches — Bhoom, Cinderella, Karishma and Sunshine (very popular orange-based drink). Late-night snackers feast on everything from Pao Bhaji to Veg Grilled Sandwich and pizzas and footlongs.

Bhaudaji Road, King's Circle, Matunga, Mumbai, Ph: 24016654, 24013685, 24142009, 24161010

Park Malai Gola

6pm to 11.15pm

Go for the *golas*. Manish Thakur's Park Malai Gola (evenings only) is just as famous as the neighbouring Shivaji Park. Order a good ol' plain Thand Gola (multiple flavours), a yummy *malai*-based (various flavours) or a Dry Fruits one . Watch them grate the ice, shape it efficiently into balls and lace it all with syrup and malai goodness. Royal Cashew and Kala Khatta (thand) are the most popular flavours, with English Strawberry and Faluda close behind. Only natural ingredients and fresh fruits here. The crowning glory is the American Gola and it also happens to be Manohar Joshi's personal favourite.

■ **Near Patkar Nursing Home, Shivaji Park, Dadar (W), Mumbai, Ph: 9869186711**

Pinkberry

Noon to Midnight

Dhokla Yoghurt anyone? And that too from the US-based, internationally famous yoghurt Pinkberry. They have specially introduced *desi* yoghurts like Khatta Meetha and Dhokla. If you are feeling adventurous, you could go for the Dhokla Yoghurt with its green chutney, masala, farsan mix and yellow dhokla cubes. Ask for the savoury and unusual Tomato 'n' Basil Yoghurt (regular yoghurt; topped with coriander, basil and cherry tomatoes with mildly herbed dressing). The hot-selling Salted Caramel Yoghurt is a must try. Drinks like Pineapple Coconut Lassi and Pomegranate Shake too. Many more regular froyo flavours with a wide range of toppings and their internationally popular milkshakes.

■ **Dheeraj Swapna, Near Costa Coffee, Pali Naka, Bandra (W), Mumbai**

Rasana Juice Centre

11.30am to 12.30am

No powder-based Rasana here (thank goodness!) — just nutritious and refreshing seasonal juices. Go for plain or cocktail mixes. Peach and Plum being the new flavours. My fave? Litchi! Sitaphal Supreme too is worth a try. Fabulous range of munchies... French, Masala or Veg Rolls; sipping and munching continues late into the night.

■ **Shop No. 2, MG Road, Parvati Nivas, 5 Rasta, Mulund (W), Mumbai, Ph: 25643394**

Right Place

9am to Midnight

Long lines, but *fatafat* service! Here you can munch on veg pizzas, rolls and burgers or a Chicken Mayonnaise Roll (all for just ₹60). *Chaats* too! Paani Puri, Bhelpuri and Sevpuri are all available at ₹60 each. Your search for a perfectly grilled Veg Cheese Sandwich ends here, at Right Place. The Double Decker Sandwich (₹100) with Green Chutney, your choice of veggies and a generous helping of their renowned Sandwich Masala makes it a mini meal in itself. Wash it all down with slushes (Orange and Kala Khatta) or cool it off with jumbo ice cream scoops (₹40) or softies available in Vanilla, Chocolate, Strawberry,

Butterscotch, Custard Apple or twin flavours (₹50 each). Ice Cream Sundaes, Black Magic or the Chic Choc (₹100) is enough for 2-3 people to share.

■ **Opp. Breach Candy Hospital, Warden Road, Kemps Corner, Breach Candy, Cumballa Hill, Mumbai, Ph: 23670885, 23683374**

Sancha Ice Creams
11am to Midnight

It has developed a legion of fans and one can see people lining up for Ganesh Kamat's hand-churned ice creams. My picks are Roasted Almond and Choco Chip, but many regulars love the seasonal favourites. Milkshakes in many fruity flavours and other unique ones like Badam Dry Fruit and Kesar Pista.

■ **Shop No. 5, Fantasy Bldg., Picnic Cottage, Seven Bungalows, Versova, Andheri (W), Mumbai, Ph: 26314500, 26344500**

Sanjay Ice Cream
11am to 12.30am

They started with Kandivali and Malad, but they have now expanded into many more outlets. Walk in at any time and enjoy the Rose Faluda, Malai Rabadi (₹90 and ₹95 respectively), Black Grape (in season), Kesar Rabadi (₹85), Kesar Faluda (₹85), Choco Almond (₹155/half kg) or Roasted Almond (₹33 on stick; ₹40 in cup) that are doled out by the dozens. Home delivery for orders above ₹150 too!

■ **7, Shreeji Sagar, Junction of SV Road & Sainath Road, Near Nataraj Market, Malad (W), Mumbai, Ph: 28886190**

■ **SV Road, Next to Season's Hotel, Across from Bata Showroom, Kandivali (W), Mumbai, Ph: 28073947, 28074141**

Snow Bite Natural Ice-cream
11am to Midnight

This very utilitarian ice-cream parlour now has one more outlet in Jogeshwari besides the Bandra one. Snow Bite offers you carefully hand-churned ice creams, whipped up creamy for the Indian palate, with less sugar than their competitors. Walk in and try the Watermelon, Chikoo, Mango Pulp or any of the popular chocolatey favourites. Milkshakes are an excellent value for money. Faluda too! Rose, Kesar and Special Snowbite with dry fruit toppings.

■ **241, 7 Hill View, Opp. Mehboob Studio, Bandra (W), Hill Road, Mumbai, Ph: 66764556, 26510031, 26416010**

■ **1/A, Devraj RamrajCompound, Opp BMC bank, SV Road, Next to Pakezah Restaurant, Jogeshwari (W), Mumbai, Ph: 26785229/3373**

Sukh Sagar Juice Centre
9.30am to 1.30am

Pop into the popular Chowpatty landmark for its variety of juices (Watermelon, Apple, Mosambi). When Sukh Sagar first set up shop years ago, former Union Defence Minister

George Fernandes used to enjoy their Lime Juice priced at ₹1! It's just as refreshing today and at ₹55. Their milkshakes (Mango, Strawberry, Sitaphal, Anjeer, Kesar, Badam, and Pista), fresh and creamy, served in large beer tankards and tall glasses are VFM to the max! Fruits topped with fresh fruit cream and faludas here are fabulous too. They can seat up to sixty, but their popularity exceeds far beyond that and runs late into the night!

■ **SVP Road, Girgaon, Chowpatty, Mumbai, Ph: 23640088**

Tastings

9am to 12.30am

Feast on Chembur's Tastings' Sizzling Brownie with Ice Cream (₹125). Premium London Dairy ice creams as well as handmade ice cream in 26 flavours, such as Blueberry Yoghurt, Tiramisu, Biscotti, Banana Strawberry and Tender Coconut are popular. Delicious cakes and pastries in flavours like Fruit Cake with Caramel, Dutch Truffle and Chocolate Mousse are all popular. However, the chart toppers are the Blueberry Cheesecake and Apple Pie. Frothy milkshakes, pizza, Grilled Sandwiches (Mushroom Cheese, Veg and Chilli Cheese Garlic) and Chinese too.

■ **Opp. Diamond Garden, Sion-Trombay Road, Chembur, Mumbai, Ph: 25288978, 25290404**

Temptation

11am to Midnight

As the book goes to press I pop in to the Andheri Temptations to find it packed with long queues outside it. First set up in Hyderabad, this award-winning ice-cream parlour now has three branches in Mumbai. IHow about some Yours Butterly, Chocolate Vampire or Blue Berry Venom for you? None of these? Then try some Double Trouble or Nutty Gritty, both of which are hot favourites here. ts original menu of sundaes like Fruit of Fun, Hot Choco Fudge, Made for Each Other, Awesome Twosome, Bluffmaster, Death by Chocolate, Dark Devil and Titanic shot to immediate popularity. The choice is enormous... pastries, brownies, chocolate cakes, milkshakes and soda pops to name a few. Trip out on a wide variety of ice creams, from the regular flavours of vanilla, strawberry, chocolate, fresh mango to many a delight on a stick... Crunchy Bar, Mango Bar, Orange Bar, Kulfi Stick, King Cone and much more. The latest is the cold stone... a teppanyaki version of ice cream, which is mashed and combined with a variety of fruits, nuts, chocolate and various goodies which result in a lip-smacking dessert. The cold stone chocolate creations include Oreo 'n' Cookies, Black Forest Passion, Melting Brownie, Ferrero Rochers, Chocolate Fifa, Kiddy Candy Land, Fresh Fruit Exotica, Pink Panther, Belgium Hot Waffles and much more.

■ **Shop No. 5, Below Irla Nurshing Home, SV Road, Vile Parle (W), Mumbai, Ph: 9324772857**

■ **Shop No. 8, Shroff Arcade, Sodawala Road, Borivali (W), Mumbai, Ph: 9323908007**

■ **Near Shoppers Stop, Andheri, Mumbai, Ph: 9322479773**

Temptation Ice Cream Parlour 10am to 11.15pm

Thane's Temptations take the form of Gulkand, Jamun, Ginger and Chilli ice creams. Grab a scoop, pair it with (eggless) cake and create what they call a Cake Sundae or top off your ice cream with a few toppings. Sugar-free Anjeer, Mastani Milkshake with Ice Cream and Swingers too!

■ **Shop No. 3, Nav Madhuban Apts., Ram Maruti Road, Opp. New English School, Naupada, Thane (W), Ph: 65159997**

Top 'n' Town

From its humble beginnings in Bhopal under the guidance of late Balchand Kukreja (first opened in 1970), this chain has grown to 7,500 outlets all over the country with a production of 1lakh litres a day! More than 10 in Mumbai alone. Order their Ice-cream Cakes (Black Forest and Gold Moment for ₹300 each) for those special occasions. Flavours for scoops are may but the famous ones include Belgian Chocolate and unique ones like Date With You, Mello Jello, Kaju Draksh, Raj Bhog and Rajwadi Kulfi. Kiwi, Litchi, Mango and Strawberry are popular in Ice-cream Shakes while Waffle-O-Choc, Blind Love, Dream Boat and Temptation are the stars in Sundaes.

■ **Shop No. 11, Mira Tower, Off New Link Road, Oshiwara, Andheri (W), Mumbai, Ph: 26332298,** www.topntown.com

■ **Shop No. 9&10, Off SV Road, Mangal Arambh Bldg., Near Kora Kendra, Borivali (W), Mumbai, Ph: 28997690**

Yogurtbay 11am to Midnight

When the two young friends, Robin Chatterjee and Viral Jhaveri, set up Yogurtbay Off Carter Road, I was immediately informed by my young Foodie reader Shilpa Chawla. "It's healthy yet fabulously tasty" she gushed. The crowds never stopped packing in. And just when I was planning to go to Bandra, Yogurtbay opened in Breach Candy. I popped in there and what do I find? Offputting catchwords like "skimmed milk", "low in sodium and cholesterol" and "virtually fat free". But one scoop of the swirl of frozen yoghurt and I got addicted to the stuff. Not only is it the closest you can get to ice-cream, but also has a texture and a after finish which is restrainedly sweet and not cloying. Go for the Mango Froyo and their signature topping of Fruit Poppers, translucent pearls which explode with juicy flavour in the mouth (Litchi, Passion Fruit and Strawberry) and are made of tapioca (but don't let that put you off, try them). Strawberry or Blueberry Cheesecake Yoghurt (add cheese crust and jam). Chocoholics go for the Chunky Monkey. Plenty of flavours. The regulars include Plain, Mango, Strawberry and Chocolate variants. Check out the huge choice of toppings. Downsides? The unusual Acai Berry, Green Tea, Mojito Mint and Apple Pie were not our favourites. Frozen yoghurt can't be stored for long. The stamp-sized Breach Candy store should be enlarged. And they have another outlet in Versova now.

■ **11, Gagangiri, Off Carter Road, Bandra (W), Mumbai, Ph: 30629191, 9833360235,** www.yogurtbay.com

■ **Shop No. 1A, Sagar Vilas CHS, Opp. Navroze Apts., Near Mahalaxmi Temple, Warden Road, Breach Candy, Mumbai, Ph: 9833360235**

■ **JP Road, Versova, Andheri (W), Mumbai, Ph: 9833360235**

Yogos Ice Cream

Andheri's Lokhandwala market gets its own frozen yoghurt place. Its colourful interiors dotted with the Panda mascot instantly set the tone. Choose from four basic flavours... Original, Strawberry, Chocolate, and the Flavour of the Day. Load it with a choice of toppings like almonds, hazelnut fudge, nutella, granola, brownie muffin, etc. Skip the disappointing Blueberry Yoghurt and go for the preset menu recommendations, Hazelnut Nutella Mix and Strawberry Delight (a blend of Strawberry Yoghurt topped with fresh fruits and candy floss on a vanilla muffin base) recommended.

■ **Unit 7, Greenfields Society, Lokhandwala Market, Andheri (W), Mumbai**

Zelos and Zest

11am to Midnight

It is toppings galore at Zelos and Zest. Begin with the 18 flavours available (of the 180 on the list) with the obvious seasonal sorbets like Plum 'n' Peach, and novelty gelato like Paan, Cookies 'n' Cream, Hazelnut, Whisky on the Rocks, Italian Cassata and even Targola! Zelos and Zest is made for the Indian palate, a bit thicker (creamier) than the gelatos normally available. Fun creations like Devil's Own (most popular), Brownie Drownie, Nut Job, Fairytale (kids' special), Gelato Indulgence, Dark Knight (with Oreo), or create your own. Gelato shakes and smoothies for ₹120 each. You can make your favourite gelato into a thick shake or order your own customized Cold Stone. They now have another outlet at Ghatkopar.

■ **Shop No. 65, Harmony, Ranade Road, Next to SBI, Near Shushrusha Hospital, Shivaji Park, Dadar (W), Mumbai, Ph: 64274075, 9833064174**

■ **Phase 2, R City Mall, LBS Marg, Ghatkopar (W), Mumbai, Ph: 9869120212, 9869397890**

PARTY MAKERS

Here it is... the ultimate party kit.... and it's all sorted under useful and usable categories for you. We show you how to be a guest at your own party. You may want to do things your way and just look for that added frill or thrill. Invites to return gifts... it's all here. Lady magicians to mehndiwalis too. Need live musicians, ventriloquists, jugglers, magicians? Customized return gifts and invites, balloons, fireworks, neon fireworks, corporate logos in fireworks, ice? Or is it fancy food for you? From Arabian to French, chaats to Kashmiri (look under the Caterers section)? Bar managers, event managers and more to take charge of it all? All you need to do is just turn the pages and enjoy your own party!

- Planners (party, event management, wedding);
- Party Supply Stores;
- Decorations, Invitations and Fireworks;
- Music; Entertainment Acts, Mehendi Art & Calligraphy;
- Food; Gifts; Bartending Services, Wine Tasting and Wine Tours, Party Safe

Here's how you use all three volumes of The Times guides for all of your planning.... this section for decorators, music and entertainment; dessert section for cakes; caterers for food; party halls for venues and for return gifts etc. please see White Book Food Shops Gift section.

PARTY PLANNERS

Fun 4 U

CORPORATES/CHILDREN/ANNIVERSARIES — Notice: 2 Days–1 Week

Fun 4 U has now exclusively come up with XD Motion! They also have exciting new concepts for décor. If you want to pop that question to your beloved at a romantic yet secluded place, Fun 4 U is the place to contact! Swapnil manages operations at Fun 4 U and has even organized a boat party for two to create the perfect, most romantic wedding proposal. Themed parties, unique entertainment acts and lavish decorations all come with a personal touch. They also hold an impressive clientele list and have arranged birthday parties for the children of Jackie Shroff, Shaan, Roshan Abaas, Roopali Piramal, Gayatri Ruia and Sharda Agarwal, just to name a few.

■ **Swapnil Shah, 87-89, Sitaram Poddar Road, Pramod Nivas, Ground Floor, Mumbai, Ph: 9820078188, 9223371050,** partyups@gmail.com, partyups2@gmail.com

Karishma Party Organiser

Min: 10 people

CHILDREN/CORPORATE GIFTS — Notice: 7–10 Days

Appropriate catering, party shows, return gifts, décor, ventriloquist shows, contacting artists for tattooing, braiding and balloon crafting for theme parties? Popcorn for toddlers and tattoos for teens? Want a birthday bash that can appeal to one and all? Well, then, call Karishma Party Organiser where she will happily arrange all solutions for your child's party! She also organizes fabulous corporate events with the same flair, corporate gifts, handmade chocolates, *et al*.

■ **Dhamini Shah, 14/15, Rekha No. 2, 46, Ridge Road, Mumbai, Ph: 23620320, 9870429202,** dhaminimshah@gmail.com

Party Planet

CORPORATES/CHILDREN — Notice: 1 Day-2 Months

New themes for children parties like inflatable cakes, tiger, rainbow, fairy themes and football games at Party Planet! They also have mermaid themes as well as inflated black tunnel for a Halloween theme for children. Corporate theme parties and children's birthday party is what Meghna has a knack for. Ask about Halloween, Jungle, Mermaid, Barbie and Hawaiin themes with live toons. From invitation cards and décor to audio-visuals and sets with lights or sound effects for weddings, pre-wedding functions, casino parties, corporate events, and birthdays — you name it and she will manage it all for you!

■ **Meghna Chitalia, 6, Precious House, Near Khanna House, MIDC, Andheri (E), Mumbai, Ph: 28263658, 9820059512,** www.partyplanetindia.com, partyplanet@gmail.com

Radhika Events Service

CORPORATES/CHILDREN/WEDDINGS — Min: 10 people — Notice: 1 Day

Birthday parties, corporate events, wedding planning, theme parties, product launches, exhibitions — they do it all! A walking-talking cartoon character for your kid's birthday party? Call up Radhika Events Service for they have imported toon mascots which can get that expression of exciting disbelief on your child's face! Radhika plans everything... from invitations to gifts, including catering for corporate events or children's parties (popcorn and candy floss too!). Cartoonists, imported toon mascots, caricature/tattoo artists and balloon sculptors, along with electronic rides on toy elephants, horses and engines (₹4,000 for 3) keep children squealing for more.

■ **Radhika, 57, Dadiseth Agyari lane, Vyas Bldg., 2nd Floor, Kalbadevi, Mumbai, Ph: 22033353, 65042881, 9820139949, 9320139949,** radhikadisneyplay@yahoo.com

Wanna Party

WEDDINGS/THEME PARTIES — Min: 20 people — Notice: 1-4 Weeks

Wanna party? You can get anything and everything to organize your dream party, all under one roof! They have it all covered, from selection of venue to catering, entertainment or décor. It is definitely a one stop shop here! More than 70 themes to choose from... you can create the charm of early 90s, retro night or a crazy casino themed night. Dial Vishal and Sushma of Wanna

Party and your party wishes will be answered. From children's parties, to baby showers, sweet sixteen and the big 50! Wanna Party, apart from organizing events, also has retail stores both in Delhi and Mumbai. They supply and offer more than 3,000 products for parties to other vendors as well as to their clients. To organize your party you have the choice to go in for their package system which starts from min ₹50,000 or decide and select each item as per your choice. They also have an online portal for your convenience. Now your event or party is just a click away.

Vishal Lakhwani, Shop No. 28, Bldg. No.9, Lakshami Plaza, New Link Road, Andheri (W), Mumbai, www.i-wannaparty.com, www.wannaparty.in

Bungalow No. 3, A1 Piaza, Thakur Complex, Kandivali (E), Mumbai, Ph: 9004646700, 9415223287, www.i-wannaparty.com, vishal@i-wannaparty.com

EVENT MANAGEMENT

3 Charlie

THEME PARTIES/CORPORATES/WEDDINGS

Min: 25 people

Notice: 2 Days

New decoration themes and ideas for children parties! Your friend's getting married and you want to have a crazy night? Organizing bachelor parties is the new thing here. It's not too often to find that right blend of class and excitement when you are planning for your next bash. But with 3 Charlie you are assured of all this and much more! With their pulse on new and upcoming trends, they will offer you everything — from corporate meetings to destination weddings to college prom nights all with an interesting twist. They have even created the illusion of multiple images of a single celebrity simultaneously performing on stage! So look no further and get in action!

Varun and Tejashree V. Gaikwad Inamdar, C/002, Baba Sadan, Ratan Nagar, Four Bungalows, Andheri (W), Mumbai, Ph: 9619256293, 9619256293 www.3charlie.co.in, varun.pgi@gmail.com

Apex Entertainment

LAUNCHES/PROMOTIONS/MARKETING/FASHION SHOWS/PARTIES

Min: 25 people

Do you want your fashion show to be devoid of any faux pas? Or a brand launch without a glitch? For big ticket events like fashion shows, brand launches, promotions, road shows and the like, Apex Entertainment is your best bet. To their credit are some high-profile events. They have seen an upswing in their operations over the past four years. Especially skilled at handling corporate luxury events, this team will make sure that your event is a raging success! They also have new year's bash for 7,000 odd fine-wine diners at Indigo and Blue Frog to their credit!

Nidhi Shetty, Bina Apts., Level 2, Room No. 6, 6th Road, Khar (W), Mumbai, Ph: 9820025414, 9820055414, www.apexent.in

Catalyst – Event & Design Solutions

Min: 50 people

CORPORATES/BIRTHDAYS/WEDDINGS/PRODUCT LAUNCHES

Notice: 2–20 Days

Running out on days and still haven't finalized your bookings? Worry not for Catalyst Event & Design Solutions is there for your rescue! They shall take care of your conferences, product launches, brand marketing, corporate annual days, fashion shows, or exhibitions. All these are taken care with insightful and simple solutions. They also do thematic set designing, entertainment, sound, permissions/licenses, décor and customized giveaways too. You want an example? They've taken care of it all for the Aditya Birla Privilege Club product launch. In just six days they planned and executed a launch that spanned five cities. Others to their credit are Firestone Diamonds launch for Nirav Modi's collection via a fashion show with Marc Robinson choreographing and Gavin Miguel styling the gowns for the international models and the 40th birthday celebration of an industrialist.

■ **Jaya B. Kewalramani, 3003, Phoenix Towers, B Wing, SB Marg, Lower Parel, Mumbai, Ph: 24954601, 9821456909,** www.catalysteds.com, jaya@catalysteds.com

Cupid

Min: 10 people

EXHIBITIONS/DISPLAYS/LAUNCHES

Notice: 1 Week–3 Months

Anything that defines event, Cupid aims its arrow at! They handle corporate events, weddings, theme parties, product launches, birthdays, anniversaries, children parties! Of course, you have heard about Coca Cola, Cadbury India, Frito Lays, Tata AIG, ITC, HDFC etc. But now you know who handles their macro-level events too. Clyde Dias' 22-year-old advertising and event management company, Cupid, has many corporate bigwigs to its kitty. They do exhibitions, displays, glow signs, product launches, conferences, road shows and set designs to promote their products and services, nationwide. Cupid also caters to birthdays and wedding parties as well providing suggestions on catering as deciding the venue for the event.

■ **Clyde Dias, 27-B, Allwyn Villa Terrace, New Kant Wadi, Perry Cross Road, Bandra (W), Mumbai, Ph: 26424293, 26454667, 9820022636 (Clyde),** clydedias@gmail.com

Fun Time

CORPORATES/ENTERTAINMENT ACTS/LAUNCHES

Entertainment equals Fun Time! They are also into decorations. Be it the celebrity bling or stiff ironed tucked corporate shirts — Deepak Raj's Fun Time has handled them all! Adding feathers to his cap are events for the top corporate honchos of financial firms like Deutsche Bank and UTI Securities to the complete opposite clients like Rakshanda Khan and Javed Jaffery. Fun Time covers parties, picnics, seminars and brand promotion events, as well as birthday parties. As per the requirement of the event, they handle décor, shows, rides and can make DJ arrangements with flair.

■ **Deepak Raj, B- Sankalp, Flat No. 001, Pratiksha Nagar, Sion East, Mumbai, Mumbai, Ph: 9820080860, 9833647263,** funtimeindia@gmail.com

Klass Entertainment

Min: 20 people

LAUNCHES/SHOWS/WEDDINGS/CORPORATES

Notice:3-4 Weeks

Entertainment, entertainment, and entertainment! With the music scene in India growing by leaps and bounds and international acts flying from abroad, do you want someone who can handle each facet of such events? Klass Entertainment has a knack for arranging events like album launches, *ghazal* nights, fusion bands, and they also take care of licensing requirements, professional sound, theme décor, stage and kiosk set-ups. Apart from this, they are also in to product launches, movie promotions, brand positioning, baby shower, fashion shows, teenage socials, weddings, movie launches, road shows, workshops, stage shows, corporate magic shows or themed entertainment evenings, conferences, team-building activities, celebrity management, celebrity singers and stand-up comedians.

■ **Mrs. Sanah Mansukhani, 244, Shantivan Bldg., New Link Road Extension, Oshiwara, Andheri (W), Mumbai, Ph: 9820105393, 9820055393**

Leolans International

Min: 10 people

CORPORATES/WEDDINGS/LAUNCHES

Notice: 1 Day–1 Week

With 18 albums to his credit, Rodrigues, previously a singer, has now taken up full time event management which comes with a difference. Want someone who is backed with an experience of performing onstage and thus knows the nitty-gritties all the more in detail? Birthday parties, weddings, picnics, and product launches for the likes of UB Group, Alkem Laboratories, The Resort and even Pepsi, have been arranged by them. Big events require a week's notice but smaller ones like birthday parties can be arranged in a day, subject to schedule availability.

■ **Leo Rodrigues, Flat No. 2, Rose Land Apts., Lourdes Colony, Orlem, Malad (W), Mumbai, Ph: 9821982055, 9960483397,** leolansintl@gmail.com

National Institute of Event

Min: 10 people

MANAGEMENT/CORPORATES/HIGH-PROFILE PARTIES

Notice: 3 Days

Help comes from the experts themselves! Head towards the National Institute of Event Management where diplomas in event management are available on a full-time and part time basis. As part of their education, students complete on-the-job training module wherein they receive hands-on experience by managing large-scale events. Their clientele includes The Times of India, CineYug and Zee Telefilms.

■ **Ground Floor, Nandanvan Bldg., Vile Parle (W), Mumbai, Ph: 26282928, 26716676,** www.niemindia.com, support@niemindia.com, niem.events@gmail.com

Omega Event Management

WEDDINGS/FAMILY PARTIES

Notice: 5 Days

Omega now also does Corporate events like corporate holistic development, corporate rejuvenation camp and other programmes, in order for one to increase their efficiency 10 times more! Omega provides it all — from celebrity duplicates to hair-braiding artistes. They can even plan picnics, theme parties, spiritual outings and honeymoons for you! Urmila, head of a catering college in Thane that is affiliated with Mumbai University and the woman behind this firm, comes with a mission. She aims to educate and empower men and women through the catering field. Those who have their secondary education can contact her and she will give them the means to earn an independent living through this profession. Flaunt a chocolate fountain with a whopping variety of twenty flavours!

■ **Urmila, B5/301, Vijay Park, Kasarwadavli, Thane, Ph: 65998280, 9820389125, 9819743601,** omegaeventmgt@yahoo.com

Party Cruisers Pvt. Ltd.

Min: 5 people

DESTINATION WEDDINGS/LAUNCHES/CORPORATES — Notice: 1 Week–6 Months

From designer weddings at the Taj to product launches, celebrity performances, road shows, theme parties, corporate picnics and more, the charming duo have been successfully planning parties for years, with an impeccable attention to detail. This one comes with a personal experience! When I called Rachna and Juzer Lucknowala of Party Cruisers Pvt. Ltd. for a photo shoot at my house, they obliged at short notice. They did an outstanding job of turning my home into a café — with Kashmiri, Thai, European and Marwari sections of the table with the right drapes, artefacts, cutlery, *et al*. Their wedding division, Vivah, specializes in destination weddings. Call them when you want the best for your engagement, *sangeet*, wedding reception, *mehendi* ceremony, cocktail party, bachelor party and more.

■ **Rachna and Juzer Lucknowala 203, Dhiraj Arcade, 2nd Floor, Pali Naka, Bandra (W), Mumbai, Ph: 9821124040, 9820402897,** www.partycruisersindia.com, vivah@partycruisersindia.com, eventfactory@partycruisersindia.com

Party Hites

Min: 10 people

LAUNCHES/CORPORATES/WEDDINGS/PRIVATE PARTIES — Notice: 3 Days-1 Month

For a dazzled night full of fireworks call Party Hites. Alwyn and Ziren Coelho can plan all types of parties and have a zing for arranging large scale fireworks on request! They will take care of all details — from designing and printing invitation cards, getting live bands that play your favourite music, planning the perfect menu and setting the mood with fabulous décor. Whether it's a private or corporate party, sales or product launch, wedding or a promotional event, they can carry them all with élan.

■ **Alwyn & Ziren Coelho, 33-A, Kalpana, 2nd Pasta Lane, Colaba, Mumbai, Ph: 22845159, 9821224698, 9867052007,** www.partyhites.com, coelhoalwyn@hotmail.com

Red Om Entertainment (ROE)

Min: 20 people

CORPORATES/PREMIERS/LAUNCHES/ WEDDINGS — Notice: 1 Week–3 Months

They do high-profile club parties, social events and specialize in organizing Christmas and New Year parties. Attention, all nocturnal creatures who love their night lives, look no further! Red Om Entertainment specializes in turning your nights even wilder. This company has organized some of the best dance parties in Mumbai and New Year's bash at Taj Lands End. Nightclub gigs, theme parties, weddings, fashion shows, concerts, grand openings, corporate symposiums, product launches, exhibitions, movie premiers, artist/celebrity management... they will organize, arrange and decorate for it all with one week's notice. They have two sections, one for nightclubs and the other for wedding events.

Vikram Mehta & Sapna Lulla, 201, Meena Mahal, Pali Road, Near Almeida Park, Bandra (W), Mumbai, Ph: 9820091731, 9820394716, www.redomentertainment.com, vikram@redomentertainment.com, redomentertainment@gmail.com

Showtime Events India Pvt. Ltd.

Min: 20 people

SPORTS/TELEVISION/LAUNCHES/EXHIBITIONS — Notice: 1 Week–2 Months

Showtime has now started organizing wedding events as well, and many will be glad after they made us proud with the astounding laser show at the Commonwealth Games. Showtime Events India Pvt. Ltd. has a penchant for high profile events that want their audiences to have a memory of the event for years to come! One peek at their impressive website and you'll know why they were hired for the laser shows at the Commonwealth Games. They've got the world's largest xenon projector and work with two of the best laser systems in the world. For a prior event with the Taj, they brought in water screens and fountains from France. It's the world-class facilities and that attention to detail which makes each of their high-profile events (Jaguar and Land Rover launches, new identity of ICC Cricket World Cup, 2011) unique and absolutely unforgettable. Mobile stages, display and backdrop systems, state-of-the-art video screens, masking systems and mobile, soundless generating sets — name it and they have it!

Deryl Rodrigues, 801, Leo Bldg., Kohinoor CHS, 24th Road, TPS 3 Road, Khar (W), Mumbai, Ph: 26008393, www.showtimegroup.in, derylrodrigues@showtimegroup.in, showtimeevents@showtimegroup.in

Wizcraft International Entertainment

MUSIC CONCERTS/BOLLYWOOD EVENTS/LASER SHOWS — Notice: 1 Day–6 Months

Who, in India, can forget the breath-taking Mumbai concert of none other than the King of Pop, Michael Jackson? Events from A to Z, with different teams and staff for each event, all spectacular in scale and impeccable in detail. Large-scale concerts, film awards, Bollywood star nights, international events, and television parties — they've done it all. They specialize in doing things creatively and spectacularly be it sound, lights, lasers, video, décor or webcasting. With a presence in every metropolitan in India and global associates in the UK, UAE; Sabbas Joseph and company cater to many blue-chip clients with almost two events daily!

Sabbas Joseph, 5th Floor, Satyadev Plaza, Behind Bhagwati House, Off New Link Road, Fun Republic Lane, Andheri (W), Mumbai, Ph: 42001400, 66915072-81, 9820042872, www.wizcraftworld.com, wizcraft@wizcraftworld.com

Zara Hatke – The Party Managers

Min: 5 people

CORPORATES/LAUNCHES

Notice: 1 Day–3 Months

Specializing in creating themes for boat parties, children's parties and live shows, Zara Hatke! Now there's no need to get bogged up with statutory permits and licences Zara Hatke – The Party Managers handle it all for you! From set designs to theme setups, taking care of all the statutory licenses and permits, arranging entertainment acts, catering and bar services. The expert planners of Zara Hatke have done it all for Bank of America, Godrej, Mahindra, Metlife, Ernst and Young, Citigroup and more. Creative head Dipanker Nag, ex-banquet manager of Sea Rock Sheraton, offers a million ideas a minute.

■ **Dipankar Nag, A-71, Highland Glory, Charkop Village, Kandivali (W), Mumbai, Ph: 9819176998, 9820865568,** www.zarahatke.net, zara.hatke@gmail.com , dipankardnag@gmail.com, dipankar@zarahatke.com, www.zarahatke.net

WEDDING PLANNERS

Gurleen Manchanda & Geeta Samuel

WEDDINGS/PARTY PLANNERS

Notice: 1 Week–6 Months

Gurleen and Geeta, wedding planners known for their eye for detail and a flair for panache, create magic with their well-executed classic designs and innovative themes for events and parties. The oohs and aahs are obvious when someone comes across the signature style of Gurleen and Geeta! Godrejs trusted her with one of their wedding celebrations. Even the launches of CNBC and NBC... all by the wonderful duo! The brilliant signature touch shines through at yacht parties, conferences and especially the big, flamboyant weddings that they organize.

■ **Gurleen Manchada & Geeta Samuel, 204, Shalaka, Near Santacruz Police Station, Santacruz (W), Mumbai, Ph: 26053139, 9820189494,** www.gurleenmpuri.com, gurleenmpuri@gmail.com

PARTY SUPPLY STORES

Party Hunterz

PARTY SUPPLIES

Notice: 1–3 Days

Finding that perfect Halloween hat and outfit for your themed night out was never so easy! Look no further because Party Hunterz has it all for you! Costumes for Halloween and creative elements that add personal touches to any celebration big or small, accessories for golden and silver jubilees, baby showers and more! They also have Mardi Gras beads, return gifts galore and everything else you need from cups to plates and spoons. Order online for accessible value and do ask about their annual 50 per cent off sale.

■ **Shop Nos.1, 2&2A, Shabistan CHSL 312-A, Dr Ambedkar Road, Opp. Brownie Point, Bandra (W), Mumbai, Ph: 65250747**

■ **20, Shreeji Heights, Sector 46-A Seawoods, Nerul, Navi Mumbai, Ph: 9819083622, 9819831406, 9819220040,** www.partyhunterz.com, sales@partyhunterz.com

SG Imani & Sons

DECORATIONS/DISPOSABLE PLATES & GLASSES — **Notice: 1 Hour**

Agreed! Washing utensils after the party is a nightmare for the hosts! But with disposable plates and glasses you can enjoy a no-mess, no-fuss affair even after the party! SG Imani provides paper/plastic plates, glasses and other disposable crockery, all at wholesale prices! Thermocol products don't flip or cave in and are quite convenient. Plates are ₹150 onward for a pack of hundred (depending on size) and thermocol glasses are ₹50 for a pack of hundred. You can also pick up decoration items for birthdays, parties, Diwali, Christmas and New Year.

■ **18, Sutar Chawl, Near Crawford Market, Mumbai, Ground floor, Ph: 23445010, 23427293**

Shraddha Charitable Trust

LEAF PLATES, GIFT ARTICLES, CASH ENVELOPES, ETC. — **Notice: 1 Week**

Go on, do your bit! Part of all purchases made at the Shradha Charitable Trust support autistic children and mentally-challenged adults. Go green is the latest fad plus a lifestyle that everyone needs to take up before it's too late. Shradha Charitable Trust has on offer a variety of rangoli designs, incense stands, leaf plates and envelopes, bowls, table mats, cash envelopes, gift articles, gift boxes, paper bags, floating lotuses, patravali plates (microwavable and recyclable), garlands, canvas bags, jute bags, jute bottle bags, gajra bags, bangle bags, mobile bags, paper bags and much more! Most of these are eco-friendly products.

■ **14-19, Mahalaxmi Municipal School Bldg., 3rd Floor, Bhulabhai Desai Road, Next to Mahalaxmi Temple, Mumbai, Ph: 23513735, 23524463, 9820904079,** www.shraddhamumbai.org

Sona Stores

PARTY SUPPLIES/ENTERTAINMENT — **Notice: 2 Days**

The fun people at Sona Stores can suggest and arrange entertainment acts to match your theme and preferences. Charlie Chaplin shows, clowns, jugglers, or anything else on your wish list! They also arrange for games, decorations, gifts, and more, at wholesale prices for birthdays, theme parties and all other special celebrations.

■ **Jayanti Shah, 76-A, Hill Road, Bandra (W), Mumbai, Ph: 26402493, 26420356/3407, 9820249253**

SPK Engineering

FLAVOURED TOOTHPICKS, COFFEE STIRRERS, ICE-CREAM SPOONS — **Notice: 15 Days**

A strawberry toothpick anyone? Personalized/flavoured toothpicks, or personalized nitty-gritties for your party,

Prakash shall provide it all! He supplies to the Taj, McDonald's, Baskin Robbins, Häagen-Dazs and Barista. Enjoy a dessert even without biting into one! That's the fun of flavoured toothpicks from Prakash's SPK Engineering. Ask him about coffee stirrers, ice-cream spoons and plastic straws too.

■ **Haroon Bldg., Ground Floor, 190, Princess Street, Mumbai-2, Ph: 22085293, 22004913, 9820146918** spkeng@mtnl.net.in

INVITATIONS, DECORATIONS AND FIREWORKS

2DAY-IS-4EVER

BALLOON BOUQUETS & DÉCOR — Notice: 1 Week

2DAY-IS-4EVER can print names, logos and messages on balloons! So, if you fancy a balloon, up in the sky, that will declare your love for your girlfriend, you know who to call. That is not all — your special day will be even more special with their exclusive balloon décor ideas for theme, birthday, corporate, Christmas and New Year parties. Balloon bouquets for celebrations, balloon decorations in malls and Dahi Handi designs are their speciality. No party-planning services, however, if you have a specific entertainment request, they can help you with those arrangements.

■ **Rajiv Ahuja, 401, Jaymala Apts., Evershine Nagar, Marve Road, Malad (W), Mumbai, Ph: 9820198082, 9819121182,** todayis_forever@rediffmail.com

Classic Concepts

PARTY DÉCOR & ENTERTAINMENT — Notice: 3 Days

For now over 50 years, Classic Concepts has been offering innovative displays and themes best-suited for each client's event. Party décor based on the theme of your choice (for weddings and parties) with innovative and creative touches. Since the age of nine, Nazneen has cultivated her aesthetic sense from her mother, Perine Irani, the pioneer of show-window design in Mumbai. Customized invitation cards and return gifts as well as entertainment acts (magician, DJ, party host and/or games) can be arranged on request.

■ **Flat No. 4, 1st Floor, Sonawalla Bldg., 67, Marine Drive, Mumbai, Ph: 22816069/4861, 9820045100, 9867299454 (Nazneen),** www.classicconcepts.co.in

■ **4/65, AH Wadia Bldg., Parel Tank Road, Mumbai, Ph: 24714287, 9820026385,** gamadia@gmail.com

Entertainment Design Co.

INVITATIONS/STATIONERY

If you got an invitation for Bachchan Junior's wedding, you ought to know that it was Reita Singh's Entertainment Design Co. who created and delivered that invitation in style! Even Manish Arora has commissioned her to design many a party invite. Also, personalized stationery on request.

■ **Reita Singh, Dheeraj Arcade, Opp. Tava Restaurant, Turner Road, Bandra (W), Mumbai, Ph: 9833003999,** www.edc.co.in, reita@edc.co.in

Inflates

BALLOON SCULPTING & DÉCOR **Notice: 1 Week**

Balloon art at its sculpted best! Trees, animals, letters, toon characters and real products — they twist and turn balloons into everything imaginable. Almost forty years and going strong. Inflates proudly caters to prestigious clients like Sony, McDonald, Pizza Hut, 360 Degrees, Pantaloons, Standard Chartered, HSBC and HDFC. Kuleen, who now runs the business set up by her dad, offers screen-printed and PVC balloons for personal and commercial use.

■ **Kuleen, 2, Ram Nivas, Hanuman Road, Opp. Loop Gallery, Vile Parle, Mumbai, Ph: 9820805800,** ballonmail@gmail.com

Morani Fireworks

FIREWORK DISPLAYS **Notice: 1 Day–3 Weeks**

The 2010 Commonwealth Games in Delhi, as well as many beauty pageants, award ceremonies, weddings, products and movie launches feature their creative displays. Call India's premier pyrotechnicians for a spectacular aerial fireworks show. They've organized, designed and executed major displays for Air India's golden jubilee celebration, major airlines, hotels, corporates, TV channels, clubs, gymkhanas, amusement parks and shopping malls. The Moranis are known for delivering the best. Company logos, luminescent slogans (environment-friendly) and corporate mottos glowing in neon fireworks are all here, for every budget too!

■ **Amir Morani, 709, B-3, B-Wing, Ankur, Gokuldham Kanya Pada, Goregaon (E), Mumbai, Ph: 28493187, 9821032029,** www.moranifireworks.com, amirmorani@moranifireworks.com

Party Warty

INVITATIONS & RETURN GIFTS **Notice: 1 Week**

Party Warty can take care of the start and the end of your party! They arrange designer personalized invitation cards for your birthdays, weddings, baby showers, engagements, sangeets, anniversaries, theme parties, or any other such ceremonies.

■ **Neetu Gogoi, 204, Garden View, Shastri Nagar, Lokhandwala, Andheri (W), Mumbai, Ph: 26366877, 9920723755, 9323055992,** info.partywary@gmail.com

Satwant Singh Bhatti

LIGHTS & SOUND **Notice: 1 Day**

Satwant Singh Bhatti has top-of-the-line audio and visual equipments with clarity in audio-visual effects and awesome pulsating lights and sounds. Sound systems and lighting available for all occasions from all kinds of events - conferences to product launches and college festivals. Basic services begin at ₹1,500 and go up to ₹30,000 including stage lights, effect lights, dance floor lighting. Translation sets also available for conferences.

■ **Satwant Singh Bhatti, 5/I, Veena Beena Apts., Acharya Dhonde Marg, Mumbai, Ph: 24131341, 24153767, 9892201341**

South Indian Flower Shop

FLOWER DÉCOR — Notice: 3 Days

For your wife, sister, girlfriend or mother — all women love flowers! Are Amaryllis and orchids their favourite flowers? Exotic is what they swear by? Allow the experienced Devika to guide you through to ensure the best selections from their collection for car décor, garlands, wedding décor, and Indian classical dance performance décor. Special customized bouquets too!A parade of designs and themes to choose from at this 46-year-old store.

■ **Bhandarkar Road, Near Post Office, Matunga, Mumbai, Ph: 24021074, 8080737510**

MUSIC

A to Z Entertainment

LIVE MUSIC, DANCE, DJ — Notice: 1 Day

Giving your event a professional touch with choreographed dancers and even *kavi sammelans, ghazals, antaksharis,* or *qawwalis*, this outfit is determined to make your party a memorable one. Do you want to give your event a professional touch by choreographed dances and all? As the name says it all — A to Z Entertainment shall arrange anything and everything for you. They are a company that will arrange for a DJ, live bands or solo/group performances and also organize dandiya nights for your special occasions!

■ **Girish Thapar, 902, Tejas Bldg., Plot No. 245, Sion (E), Mumbai, Ph: 24012921, 9820166162,**
showmangirish@gmail.com

Ernie

MUSICIAN — Notice: 1-2 Days

Ernie, the creative genius, has had a career that spans 160 poems, 90 songs and two albums: "Sweet Sweet Goa" in 1997 and "Tell Me Lord" in 2000. It is hardly possible that you've been party hopping all these years and do not know about Ernie! May be you do, but you don't know he is the one yet! Ernie plays the bass/acoustic guitar or the keyboards as he belts out over 2,000 tunes at the Indigo Sunday Brunch or at friend's homes. He has been following his heart's passion since 1976, with bands all over India and abroad (London, New York, Chicago, Dubai, Muscat, Abu Dhabi and Hong Kong). Every weekday evening, he plays the grand piano at the Il & FS building atrium (Bandra-Kurla complex).

■ **Ernie, 1804, Rushabh Tower, Jakaria Bunder, Cross Road, Sewri (W), Mumbai, Ph: 65253630, 9820304040,** www.erniethesongster.com, ernie_songster@hotmail.com

G Stringz (Groove)

LIVE BAND

Notice: 5-6 weeks

A versatile six-member Western Band — Rahul Cardoza and company play retro, jazz, funk, pop and even Indipop. They'll have you grooving to the beat at your next Christmas, New Year, or corporate bash. They play at the Indigo Sunday Brunch and perform nationwide.No one can deny that the most impromptu salsa performances end up happening where live music makes its presence felt!

■ **Wilburn D'Costa & Rahul Cardoza, 2, Convent View Society, NB Patil Marg, Ghatla Road, Chembur, Mumbai, Ph: 9820044326,** www.wilburn.co.in, wilburndecosta@yahoo.co.in, wilburn.decosta@ymail.com

Novalis Rodricks

DJ

Notice: 15 Days

DJ Noel has an impressive resume gathered over 17 years, having worked with many high profile DJs and independently in many nightclubs. His journey spans different genres like retro, hip-hop, commercial dance, house, Bollywood and lounge (hip-hop and R'n'B are his personal favourites). He has been the in-house DJ for Escobar, Zenzi Mills, Hawaiian Shack, Hype and High Spirit. He has been at New Year's eve bashes at China House and Hyatt Regency; and performed at theme nights at Enigma, Velvet Lounge (Mumbai), Athena (Leela, Bangalore), Butter (Goa), Tantra (Hyderabad), High Spirit (Pune). Corporate clients like Fountain Head Entertainment and Wizcraft Entertainment.

■ **Novalis Rodricks, 310, Gautam Kripa Dheeraj Grand, 3rd Floor, Corner Of 16th/33rd Road, Bandra (W), Mumbai, Ph: 9820852959,** djknite@yahoo.com, novalis.rodricks@gmail.comnot

Percussionist & Djembe Drum Player

Min: 100 people

PERCUSSIONIST

Notice: 2 Weeks

Jonqui Dutta has performed at Blue Frog, Tote and Wink on the djembe, darbuka, bongu, conga, timbale, *tabla*, *nagada*, *bhur taal* and more. He has delighted his audiences nationwide and all over the world. Book him for your next event or party and let the vibrations flow. Percussion fans, kindly pay attention! Because this is the man that is never far away from an event that hosts the best percussionists from all over the country!

■ **Jonqui Dutta, Manasmoti CHS, Flat No. A-202, Behind Dindoshi Bus Depot, General AK Vaidhya Marg, Goregaon (E), Mumbai, Ph: 9821196905,** jonqui_xmuz@rediffmail.com

Shylite Creations Inc.

Min: 10 people

Singer/Band

Notice: 3 Days

A lively Shiamak Davar trained compere, Sharmilla, following her ten-year career at the Apollo Bar of the Taj Mahal Hotel has her own band that performs in India and abroad. Sharmilla's fabulous retro, contemporary pop and rock shows at weddings, product launches, corporate celebrations and theme parties aim to "redefine the art of the moment".

■ **Sharmilla Dias, 702, Wavelash Perry Crossroad, Bandra (W), Mumbai, Ph: 9821085040,** www.sharmilladias.com, shydiaz@hotmail.com

ENTERTAINMENT ACTS (MAGIC, JUGGLING, CLOWNS, RIDES), MEHENDI ART AND CALLIGRAPHY

Akshmey Universal Magical Entertainer

Magician/Illusionist

Notice: 1 Week

Magic's a way of life in this family that consists of four magicians and counting! With many national awards under his belt and exotic performance venues to his credit worldwide, Vinay Kumar is always in huge demand. For jaw-dropping entertainment acts call this third generation magician. Sleight-of-hand, hypnotism, ventriloquism and illusion acts are his speciality and he can perform anywhere in the world. Cutting a lady in half, haunted houses, X-Ray Eyes and more! Complexity of the program and venue determine cost.

■ **Vinay Kumar, 1401/A, Kingston High Street, Hiranandani Garden, Powai, Mumbai, Ph: 25704007, 9819599389, 9869064761,** www.akshmey.com vinaykumarsarang@yahoo.co.in

Candy Floss

Min: 10 people

Buffet Counters, Moonwalkers, Toys

Notice: 2 Days

Moonwalkers, the big air-filled balloons, are huge hits with children at parties, as are the electronic toys that Tarla Ben provides. For weddings and other events involving catering, she works on the set-up of the buffet counters in various designs. Rates vary according to the location and nature of the service. Here, they have plenty of them — not versions of Michael Jackson but giant air-filled balloons whom they call Moonwalkers!

■ **Tarla Ben, B/3, Mangalam Apts., Irla Lane, Vile Parle (W), Mumbai, Ph: 26710092, 9819242891, 9930539809**

Charlie Entertainment

Min: ₹1,000

Magicians, Jugglers, Puppets, Toons, Rides

Notice: 1 Week

They have every kind of entertainment act possible. With over two dozen people dedicated to providing the best entertainment with state-of-the-art equipments, all you can expect is a flawless fun-filled event! From moonwalkers and magicians to mimicry acts and jugglers. Disney cartoon characters to please the children, mini-trains and live toons to thrill their friends... this is indeed a one-stop shop for your child's birthday bash, variety shows, corporate events, get-togethers, birthday parties, anniversaries and engagements, weddings and corporate parties.

■ **Ganesh Kumar, 353, D-44, Nanda Deep Cooperative Housing Society, Sector-3, Charkon, Kandivali (W), Mumbai, Ph: 28694035, 9820283064, 9220585460,** ganeshcharlieg9@rediffmail.com

Fun Magic Show

Min: 5 People

MOONWALKERS, JUGGLERS, TATTOO ARTISTS, MAGICIANS, DJ, CIRCUS & CARNIVAL ACTS

Notice: 3 Days

From mimicry artists and moonwalkers to mascots? With over a thousand magic tricks, Chandresh is a show-stopper on his own. Add to that moonwalkers, popcorn and candy machines, jugglers, tattoo artists, balloon décor, DJs, hair-braiding, nail art, bangle stalls, rope and stilt walkers, giant wheels, golas, puppet shows, firework shows or game stalls and you'll have one amazing party. Chandresh trains aspiring magicians and sells/exports educational magic toys too!

■ **Chandresh, 311, MS Ali Road, Mumbai, Ph: 23851686, 23877827, 22075456, 9820026949,** funtimeindia@gmail.com

Joyride

Minimum: ₹2,000

GIANT WHEEL, ELECTRONIC TRAINS & ENTERTAINMENT ACTS

Notice: 1 Week

At Joyrides there is something for everyone! Azim lets adults have their share of fun too! Get on to the Giant Wheel and for children (or the child in you), he's got merry-go-rounds, mini trains, swings, moonwalkers and electronic trains (featured in movies like Sagar and Mela). Pair them up with entertainment acts like magicians, tattoo artists and *mehendi* artists for an incredibly memorable party.

■ **Azim Bhai, 53, Kapad Bazaar, Opp. Royal Guest House, Mahim, Mumbai, Ph: 24441107, 9821341346**

Just Smile

ENTERTAINMENT, DECORATION

Notice: 2 Weeks

Just Smile, known for its exquisite backdrops, cutouts and balloons, is on the panel of many clubs, restaurants and banquet halls. As their name suggests, they do just that... makes everyone smile! DJ, games, compare, magic shows, puppet shows, jugglers, outdoor play equipment and carnival-like activity stalls keep children enraptured for hours. They've also organized events conducted in malls and events organized by companies for children (Diwali parties, Birthday parties, Christmas parties).

■ **Shraddha Dhoot, Khar, Mumbai, Ph: 40101437, 9820252556,** dhoot.shradha@gmail.com, shradha_dhoot@yahoo.co.in

Marigold & Jaygold

MAGICIANS Notice: 3 Weeks

Siblings Marigold (India's first female magician) and Jaygold have performed all over the world for over 50 years! They even offer lessons to those who wish to learn. Lady-cutting, Zigzag Lady, driving blindfold and other illusions will keep the audience gasping, guessing and asking for more.

■ **Marigold & Jaygold, 2nd Floor, The Cliff, 8, Raghavji Road, Gowalia Tank, Cumballa Hill, Mumbai, Ph: 9869505700, 9510166947,** marigoldjaygold@indiatimes.com

Mehendi Art

MEHENDI ART Notice: 1 Month

The Discovery Channel has crowned Usha Shah as the world's best *mehendi* artist. Even if you live in the USA, you can call them to get your *mehendi* makeover! Designs, in all their gorgeous glory, are on the website. Kajol, Hrithik Roshan, Jackie Shroff and Demi Moore — Usha Shah and (more recently) daughter Ekta have a number of celebrity clients to their credit.

■ **Usha & Ekta Shah, Ground Floor, Pattharwala Bldg. No. 2, Loyalka Compound, Dadiseth Lane, Chowpatty, Mumbai, Ph: 23692976, 23680619, 9821121221,** www.mehendiart.com, usha@mehendiart.com

Party Time

DECORATION, ENTERTAINMENT ACTS Notice: 1 Week

One phone call and you shall get it all! Call Party Time for theme decorations and entertainment acts to match. Magicians, tattoo artists, balloon sculptists, jugglers and more for corporate parties, annual functions, product launches and more.

■ **Sandeep Kumar, 404, Saikrupa Bldg. No. 1, Off Veera Desai Road, Andheri (W), Mumbai, Ph: 26773333/3535, 9820133999,** partytime.sandeep@gmail.com

Payal Bhattacharya

CALLIGRAPHY & PAINTING Notice: 2-3 Days

Multi-talented Payal Bhattacharya now also paints! From murals, to installations (3D art) and paintings. You can see her painting hung up at Hotel Sea Princess too. With regards to her calligraphy, she makes the art of handwritten expression come alive as her audience watches with utter fascination. She can write the invitations for your next party or write your guests names in the colour, font and style of their choice at your party. Wedding invitations, or those for social, academic and business functions, invitation envelopes, table cards, short letters for birthdays or anniversaries, name cards for hotels, thank you cards, lunch/dinner menus, family tree, CD or book covers and degree/diploma certificates all look brighter with her personal touch and calligraphic art. Ever thought that words could be written in such a way that they seem alive and dancing? At 24, she watched an artist in Dubai work on Arabic calligraphy and she was mesmerized beyond belief and captivated beyond words. That was the moment Payal Bhattacharya decided to pursue her career as a calligraphist. She teaches her art and takes classes for the same (Basic: ₹3,500, and Advance: ₹5,000).

■ **Payal Bhattacharya, Madh Island, Mumbai, Ph: 9930144828,** www.calligraphersink.com, info@calligraphersink.com

Pleasure Group

ENTERTAINMENT ACTS, LIVE BAND

Min: 20 people

Notice: 1 Day–1 Week

Did you just see a skeleton dancing somewhere in the background? No, you're not drunk! It is Pleasure Group that organises ghazals to dancing skeletons and talking puppets. Ask about magician Charlie's (53 years of experience) customized magic show, party games, jugglers, tattoo and caricature artists. Décor, invitation cards and all party details taken care of on request. Kohinoor, the in-house band, is available for shows, or if you prefer, they can arrange artists to sing regional music programmes in Punjabi and Gujarati too. They also do birthday parties and have an orchestra.

■ **208, United Tennence, Parsiwada, Sahar Road, Andheri (E), Mumbai9, Ph: 28386166, 9892255512, 9892531393**

Ramesh Magician

MAGICIAN

Notice: 1 Week

Ramesh is the magician to hire when you want a performer to wave his wand and keep people guessing. Thirty-nine years of experience and counting... both in India and abroad. He is fluent in three languages and practices mimicry and ventriloquism. Charges depend on location and the type of party, but generally vary from ₹1,500 to ₹10,000.

■ **104, Sahi Shradha Society Opp. Gagan Giri Park Society Sumita Nagar, Thane (W), Mumbai, Ph: 9322401558,** www.tradelinkin.com/magicianramesh

Sunil, the Magician

MAGICIAN

Min: ₹1500

Notice: 1 Week

Magic that comes in three languages! Ventriloquist shows, illusions and a magician who teaches his audience the tricks of the trade! He can perform in three languages — English, Hindi and Marathi. His tricks always put the audiences on a perpetual "wonderment" mode!

■ **Sunil Kamath 231, Narayan Nivas, LJ Road, Shivaji Park, Mumbai, Ph: 24305852, 9869009313,** kamathsunil@rediffmail.com

FOOD

(For detailed information on cakes and caterers, please refer to the White Guide)

Bhagwati Fruit Juice

PARTY SNACKS, REFRESHMENT — Notice: 2-4 Weeks

Their homemade kulfis can give Baskin' Robbins a run for their money! Sachin delivers happiness in every flavourful glass, with a lemon and ginger twist. And nostalgia served in every earthen pot... choose your favourite flavour! Nothing can beat a glass full of ganne ka juice! Strict hygiene followed.

▪ **Sachin Bhagwati, Nana Chowk, Jyoti Studio Compound, Behind Lal Bungalow, Grant Road, Mumbai, Ph: 23881981, 9821050009**

Maido Enterprises Pvt. Ltd.

Min: 5 people

SUSHI — Notice: 1-2 Weeks

Maido brings Japan closer to India through food, art, culture and more. They organize events connected to any Japanese theme (food festivals, exhibitions, fashion shows and more). For private parties, Harry Chang will send a Japanese chef to your home with authentic ingredients to prepare sushi on the spot and can even temporarily install a moving sushi conveyor belt. Call for a party with a difference!

▪ **Harry Chang, 133, Hyatt Regency Hotel, Andheri (E), Mumbai, Ph: 66961585, 9870003267,** www.maidoindia.com, aj@maidoindia.com

Party Time Ice Pvt. Ltd.

Min: 1 kg

ICE — Notice: 2-3 Hours

Ice, ice baby! Making life convenient for you, grab it by the kilo with doorstep delivery for 20kg and above. Enjoy many rounds of drinks "on the rocks". A simple, inexpensive and "cool" solution from Party Time Ice Pvt. Ltd.

▪ **D-29/12, TTC MIDC Industrial Area, Turbhe, Near Allana Cold Storage, Navi Mumbai, Ph: 27614801, 65131986, 9821123341**

GIFTS

(For detailed information, please refer to the White Guide, "Food Shops", subsection Gifts for more suggestions)

Creative Awards & Rewards

GIFTS, CORPORATE EMPLOYEE RECOGNITION — Notice: 10 Days

Now with another branch in Pune, Creative Awards and Rewards are such a perfect token for appreciation!

Corporates looking for employee recognition plaques, trophies and more... this is the place you had been looking for! Unique personalized gifts for children's birthdays, festivals and other occasions too, are available. Silver coins, Feng Shui pieces, candlesticks, wrought-iron artefacts, handicrafts, medals, badges, cups and corporate gifts in metal, marble, granite, fibre glass, wood, acrylic and resin. They also offer laser engraving. Give them at least ten days' notice for personalization and delivery.

■ **Prashant More, 124, Andheri Industrial Estate, Off Veera Desai Road, Andheri (W), Mumbai, Ph: 26730193, 9821110207**

Creative Chase

CUSTOMIZED GIFTS, INVITATION CARDS

Dhwani Doshi, creative head, certainly thinks ahead about everything you'd need at your next party. From invitation cards, thank you tags, gift cards and envelopes, menu tags, name tags, gift tags, posters to pop corn tubs, mats and coasters, paper bags, wrist bands, sippy cups and bottles to customized puzzles — she plans it all even before you will ask for it!

■ **Dhwani Doshi, 5/B, 31, Mittal Industrial Estate, Saki Naka, Andheri (E), Mumbai, Ph: 9820515351,**
www.creativechase.in, info@creativechase.in, dhwanid_2000@rediffmail.com

Digital Fantasty Birthday World

Min: 100 people

CORPORATE GIFTS, RETURN GIFTS, BIRTHDAY GIFTS

Notice: 4-5 Days

Personalized photo souvenirs is what they specialize in. What's more? Gift your guests photos clicked and framed instantly in the party itself. With over 1,400 backdrops (exotic locations, wanted posters, movie posters and more), the selection is infinite! Get yourself printed on the magazine cover while shaking hands with a celebrity or get your kid's picture while posing with their favourite comic book hero. They also have on offer customized books, photo albums, family albums (with your story) and customized cartoon movies which can feature your children! Send in a photograph of your child, select a story and you will have a DVD delivered, with your child's picture on the cover. Your loved one's name on sand, personalized Monopoly board with photos, cushions, T-shirts and more. They also organize parties from invitations to return gifts.

■ **Viral Shah, Shubangini, Ground Floor, Santacruz (W), Milan Subway, Mumbai, Ph: 9820088566,**
www.digitalfantasyin.com, www.mycartoonmovies.com, digitalfantasyin@gmail.com

Learning Ladder Comet Media Foundation

EDUCATIONAL TOYS, HANDMADE CRAFTS

Learning Ladder Comet Media foundation stocks handmade crafts, toys and books sourced from NGO's who work with traditional craftspeople. Heart-warming gifts including educational toys do double up the blessings! Orders of ₹1,500 and above come with doorstep delivery. The store disseminates ideas, information and alternative viewpoints on education and technology. Health, environment and gender issues are all discussed.

■ **Sangeetha, Topiwala Lane, Municipal School, Lamington Road, Mumbai, Ph: 23869052, 23826674, 9860509129**

Witty Gift

GIFTS — Notice: 1–10 Days

Something for everyone! For the people in your life who have been blessed with everything, gift them an experience. For best quality of experiences, the best value and the best brands in elegantly packaged boxes, Witty Gift to provide a well rounded solution for every gifting need. For adventurists, there is parasailing, skydiving, white-water rafting. For those who love the spa, there are massages and other customizable packages. Culinary lovers can choose from tossing a pizza with a chef to cooking in a famous kitchen. Partners Samuel Ziza and Manvinder Kohli put together the best brands in elegantly packaged boxes. Witty Gift puts together forty unique experiences in broad categories - culinary, leisure, wellbeing, cultural, sports and adventure, and offers a choice of unforgettable experiences in each one.

■ **Samuel Ziza and Manvinder Kohli, 3rd Floor, Kohli Villa, 130, SV Road, Andheri (W), Mumbai, Ph: 67109423/29,** www.wittygift.com, info@wittygift.com

BARTENDING SERVICES/WORKSHOPS, WINE TASTING/TOURS

All Things Nice

SOMMELIER – WINE APPRECIATION & CONSULTANCY SERVICES — Notice: 1 Week

Not sure which wine goes with the dinner you're preparing? With eleven years of experience with industry giants, Nikhil Agarwal, trained sommelier from the Wine and Spirits Education Trust, is your best bet for everything related to wine. All Things Nice, his personal venture, was started to promote wine culture in India. A platform to fine-tune your taste for the finer things in life such as wines, whiskies, single malts and gourmet experiences. Wine tasting events, introduction of quality international wine labels into the market and consultancy services for importers, hoteliers and restaurateurs are a few of the many services they offer. Recent events have been held at Pali Village Café, Tote, Intercontinental (Marine Drive), Chez Vous and Sahara Star. Shine Nights are designed to be a celebration of food and drink experiences. Consultancy Services include training programs and menu engineering for hotels, restaurants, modern retail chains and airlines.

■ **Nikhil Agarwal, Near Shiv Sagar, Bandra (W), Mumbai, Ph: 9820704500,** www.allthingsnice.in, info@allthingsnice.in

Art Loft

Bartending

A unique space that allows you to explore your artistic side in everyday life, through various workshops and cultural and wellness programs. Their mission is to cultivate creativity through art. One of their creative pursuits is their cocktail making class. A signature cocktail of your own for your next party! Now that's called partying in style! Learn to make cool and great impromptu cocktails. They teach you how to pick cocktails by the occasion, design a menu and even how to pair cocktails with food. And at the end of the workshop, create your own signature cocktail! Wine appreciation workshops slated on occasion too. Creative mavens at Bandra's Art Loft organize and conduct workshops, exhibitions, featured events and conferences that create a common platform for professionals and amateurs belonging to diverse backgrounds who share common love of art and creativity to get together. Course duration 2-4 hours and fees ₹1,200–3,000 per workshop.

■ **37, Waroda Road, Off Hill Road, Behind Stanislaus School, Bandra (W), Mumbai, Ph: 69996663, 9819132958,** www.theartloft.co.in, contact@theartloft.co.in

Barwings Hospitality

Bartending Services, Training Academy

Notice: 2 Days

Planning a rocking party at home? Barwings will handle any kind of professional bar set up. Your drinks will be devoid of any synthetic ingredients and made fresh and live. Ever heard of White Tea Parties? Well, Barwings Hospitality comes with that unique streak! A fresh twist to all of the classic cocktails with many innovative firsts like "ice bars" with superior quality and excellent value as well as service, a Barwings promise. Heading operations is Ankit Negandhi who has won numerous national and international mixology awards after acquiring a dozen years of experience with Marriott. In addition to a training academy which runs a three-month course to elevate the industry in India, his team staffs for major corporate heads and hotels including Marriott Courtyard, Holiday Inn and more.

■ **Ankit Negandhi Shop No. 1, Radhika Niwas, Opp. Vishal Hall, AK Road, Andheri (E), Mumbai, Ph: 26845416,** www.barwingasia.com, barwings@asia.com

Flaming Trio

Bartending Services, Training Academy

Min: 5 people

Notice: 1-3 Months

Faming Trio's flaming shots will most certainly rock any party. Binny and Mehdi have been in demand for flavoured and flaming shots, called hot shots, and have taken their expertise as far as Colombo, Malaysia, Bali,

Indonesia, and Spain for the Diwans, Ambanis and Vardhans. Their bartending schools and offices are all over the country – Mumbai, Pune, Kolkatta, New Mumbai and even Dubai. They also provide skillful bartenders for weddings, corporate events, promotions and even consultancy.

■ **Shop No 11 Below Solitare Hotel Sahar Road Andheri (E), Mumbai, Ph: 9820613404 (Binny), 9820429908 (Mehdi),** www.flamingtrio.com

Fratelli Wines

WINE TOURS — Notice: 1 Week–1 Month

Long strolls through the vineyards, starlit dinners, wine-tasting with an expert and watching the sunset over a glass of wine... sounds dreamy! Doesn't it? But that's what Fratelli (Indo-Italian wine) promises to give you! They have day packages, rejuvenation packages, couple and family getaways. All these range from ₹2,000–50,000 with personal chefs and neighbourhood tours included, depending on the package selected. Visitors are invited to get involved in the full experience of wine-making, as part of Fratelli's efforts to promote wine tourism in the rural heartland of Maharashtra.

■ **512, Janki Centre, 29, Shah Industrial Estate, Off Veera Desai Road, Andheri (W), Mumbai, Ph: 9833368727, 9821289846,** www.fratelliwines.in, info@fratelliwines.in

STIR Academy of Bartending

BARTENDING SERVICES, TRAINING

Their "minimal wastage and zero pilferage" policy keeps the young bartenders from STIR Academy in demand for many high-profile events. Show-stopping performances, flamboyant cocktails and mocktails, interactive bars with innovative themes, fantastic shows and bar performances. Those who wish to learn the tricks of the trade can sign up for a six-month course in bar designing for parties and party beverages.

■ **7-8, Joel Apts., 3rd Floor, St Michael School Marg, Mahim (W), Mumbai, Ph: 24452750/1033,** www.shatbhibasu.com, www.shatbhitalkies.wordpress.com

Wasted Fish

BAR ACCESSORIES, GIFTS, MUSIC, PARTY PLANNER — Notice: 3-4 Weeks

A High-heeled Wine Stopper? Wasted Fish, started by Chandni Shahani & Imran Rizvi, offers unique ideas to make your drinking experience a little more enjoyable! It seemed criminal to them to pour alcohol out of impeccably designed bottles into the same banal barware. They got their artist friends together to help design unique, quirky, peculiar shot glasses, and kept going with everything from upscale wine glasses, stoppers, racks and decanters or beer mugs and whisky glasses to ashtrays and even matchboxes. It's a range that's individualistic, can be customized and definitely unlike anything seen in your uncle's stuffy bar. Bulk orders, customized party orders and drinking games too.

■ **Varsha Kalani, 36-A, Luisa Apts., Ground Floor, St. John Baptist Road, Bandra (W), Mumbai, Ph: 9820592199,** www.wastedfish.com, varsha.wastedfish@gmail.com

Wine Warehouse

WINE TASTING

India's first temperature-controlled wine warehouse (walk-in; 1,000sq ft) located in a bustling Andheri neighbourhood offers information via leaflets, pamphlets and books and a trained sommelier to help guide you through your selection. They import wines directly from many countries like France, Italy, South Africa, Argentina, Chile and California. The warehouse is packed to the rafters with many private labels. To help make wine a part of everyday life, they offer wine recommendations (₹1,400 and up) and fortnightly wine tastings (see website for details; entry fee redeemable against purchase of three bottles).

■ **23, Keytuo Estate, Kondovita Village Road, Andheri (E), Mumbai, Ph: 42639200,** www.thewinesocietyofindia.com

PARTY SAFE

Party Hard Drivers

CHAUFFEUR SERVICES

Min: 1 person

Notice: 1 Hour

Need to go out? Get a PHD! Not what you're thinking — Get your license to party with Party Hard Drivers! Call Party Hard Drivers, a service that rents out chauffeurs to drive your car. They charge just ₹500 and work for the night in five-hour shifts (7pm to Midnight, 8pm to 1am, 9pm to 2am and 10pm to 3am). Powai, Wadala, Kandivali, Borivali, Dahisar, Navi Mumbai and Thane residents will have to pay ₹650 for the privilege. Party Hard Drivers has an elaborate screening process. They take drivers with reliable references only and after checking their police and driving records. So, worry not and party all night long...!

■ **207, Perin Nariman Street, Near Apna Bazaar, Fort, Mumbai, Ph: 65256522-21, 43331333**
www.partyharddrivers.com

Safe T drive

CHAUFFEUR SERVICES

Notice: 2 Hours

Don't want to get into trouble? Safe T sees to your safety, literally! Temporary and permanent drivers on call... at your doorstep, 24X7. If required, they can provide cars with the drivers for airport transfers, outstation trips and even for daily use. Pay ₹500 for 8 hours for a day service. Night rates vary by distance as they want as many people as possible to avail of this service.

■ **102, Sadhbhavna Apts., Kajuwadi, Near Maharaja Restaurant, Chakkala, Andheri (E), Mumbai, Ph: 65222257/58, 65274374, 9821604411, 9920804411, 9594244411,** safetdrive@gmail.com

24-HOUR CAB SERVICES

■ **Meru Cabs: 44224422,** www.merucabs.com

■ **Cool Cabs: 22164466,** www.citycoolcab.in

■ **VIIRA Cabs: 61206120,** www.viiracabs.com **(female drivers)**

■ **Priyadarshani Cabs: 9320845064 (female drivers)**

You're looking for a venue. Where do you begin? Anniversaries, birthdays, weddings, cocktails, corporate bashes, celebrations, or just mood hai yaar! *Need a grand one? Inexpensive one? For 10 people or for thousands? We have combed the city and come up with some options for you. Of course, we haven't (and cannot possibly) include them all. From garden-fringed bungalows in Malad, to terraces in Bandra and catamarans in Apollo Bunder... they're all here! Many a new venue too...*

Abott Hotel

MULTI-CUISINE (NORTH INDIAN, MUGHLAI, SOUTH INDIAN, THAI, CHINESE, EUROPEAN)

Capacity: **Chanakya:** 150–175 people; **Chandragupta** (AC): 80 people; **Shweta** (AC): 350 people (floating) or 250 people (sitting); and **Rooftop:** 30–40 people.

■ **Plot No. 25, Sector-2, Vashi, Navi Mumbai, Ph: 27826677**

Ajanta Restaurant

MULTI-CUISINE (NORTH INDIAN, CHINESE, GUJARATI, MARWARI, SOUTH INDIAN)

Capacity: **Hall 1:** 40 people; and **Hall 2:** 150 people.

■ **Sumer Nagar, Adjacent to Flyover, SV Road, Borivali (W), Mumbai, Ph: 28064449, 28629979**

The Ambassador

MULTI-CUISINE (INDIAN, EUROPEAN, ITALIAN)

Capacity: **Panorama:** 30–100 people; and **Shiva:** 30–150 people. They book the hall for minimum 30 people.

■ **VN Road, Churchgate, Mumbai, Ph: 22041131, 61416141**

Astoria Hotel Banquet Hall

MULTI-CUISINE (INDIAN, CHINESE)

Capacity: **Hall—Theatre:** 60–70 **Floating:** 100. For business purpose only.

■ **Astoria Hotel, J Tata Road, Churchgate, Mumbai, Ph: 66541234, 66541212, 9223308888, 9892024444**
www.astoriamumbai.com

Bageecha

MULTI-CUISINE (NORTH INDIAN, MUGHLAI, RAJASTHANI, GUJARATI, CHINESE)

Capacity: **Hall** (AC): 50–250 people; and **2 lawns:** 300–800 people.

■ **Bageecha Complex, Madh-Marve Road, Malad (W), Mumbai, Ph: 28832671, 28832672**

Bawa International

FUSION (INDIAN, CHINESE, EUROPEAN, CONTINENTAL, ITALIAN)

Capacity: **Senate** Hall: 80–100 people; **White House:** 50 people.

■ **Nehru Road Extn., Near Domestic Airport, Vile Parle (E), Mumbai, Ph: 26113636, 9820641676, 9324953222 (Girish Solanki)**

Bhasin Resort

MULTI-CUISINE (INDIAN, SOUTH INDIAN, CHINESE)

Lawns 1–5 (tennis court and swimming pool): 500 people per lawn; 2,500 people total.

■ **Malti Cottage Bus Stop, Madh-Marve Road, Madh Island, Mumbai, Ph: 9820069252**

Blue Grotto

MULTI-CUISINE (INDIAN, SOUTH INDIAN, CHINESE, ITALIAN), JAIN

Capacity: **Banquet Hall:** 100 people.

■ **3rd Floor, Above Goa Portuguesa Restaurant, Near Versova Tele Exchange, Mumbai, Ph: 26313222/777, 9167096460, 9619961818,** info@culturecurry.com

Blue Sea Banquet

MULTI-CUISINE (ORIENTAL, MEXICAN, LEBANESE, ITALIAN, THAI, SOUTH INDIAN, NORTH INDIAN, MAHARASHTRIAN, GUJARATI)

Rocking with many a happening party, Blue Sea Banquet has three indoor rooms — **The Glass**, **The Silk** and **The Mezzanine**, and two outdoor spaces, **The Waterfront** designed to accommodate 25–600 people. The main banquet hall can accommodate 300–350 people. **Patio** (open lawn): 150–200 people.

■ **11, Khan Abdul Gaffar Khan Road, Worli Seaface, Mumbai, Ph: 24902222, 24903333**

The Club

AS PER THE CLIENT'S REQUIREMENT

Capacity: **COLONIAL HALL — U-shaped:** 60 people; **Theatre:** 200–250 people; **Classroom:** 90 people; **Informal:** 275 people.

HARMONY — Boardroom: 16 people; **U-shaped:** 14 people; **Theatre:** 20 people; **Classroom:** 15 people; **Informal:** 20 people

MAHOGANY — Boardroom: 40 people; **U-shaped:** 30 people; **Theatre:** 80 people; **Classroom style:** 60 people; **Informal:** 100 people.

SYMPHONY — Boardroom: 30 people; **U-shaped:** 32 people; **Theatre:** 50 people; **Classroom:** 24 people; **Informal:** 60 people.

SENATE WITH TERRACE — Boardroom: 20 people; **U-shaped:** 20 people; **Theatre:** 25 people; **Classroom style:** 20 people; **Informal:** 35–45 people.

MAHOGANY TERRACE — Theatre: 80 people; **Informal:** 100 people; **Boardroom:** 40 people; **U-shaped:** 30 people.

Garden View: 175 people with Garden Grill; 75 people garden only (not a part of banquet).

Bowl O' Drome: 150 people, **Courtyard 1&2:** 2,000 people (all in informal style).

■ **197, DN Nagar, Andheri (W), Mumbai, Ph: 66939999 (Extn. 115)**

Courtyard By Marriott

MULTI-CUISINE (INDIAN, CHINESE, THAI, CONTINENTAL)

Capacity: **AMBER 1 — Theater:** 70 people; **Classroom:** 24 people; **Roundtable:** 30 people; **U-shaped:** 20 people; **Boardroom:** 26 people; **Cluster:** 24 people.

AMBER 2 — Theater: 70 people; **Classroom:** 24 people; **Roundtable:** 30 people; **U-shaped:** 20 people; **Boardroom:** 26 people; **Cluster:** 24 people.

AMBER 3 — Theater: 150 people; **Classroom:** 52 people; **Roundtable:** 80 people; **U-shaped:** 40 people; **Boardroom:** 52 people; **Cluster:** 64 people.

AMBER (1–3 COMBINED) — Theater: 300 people; **Classroom:** 100 people; **Roundtable:** 160 people; **U-shaped:** 80 people; **Boardroom:** 110 people; **Cluster:** 128 people.

JADE — Theater: 70; **Classroom:** 36 people; **Roundtable:** 40 people; **U-shaped:** 21 people; **Boardroom:** 21 people; **Cluster:** 32 people.

PEARL 1 — Theater: 80 people; **Classroom:** 51 people; **Roundtable:** 60 people; **U-shaped:** 32 people; **Boardroom:** 27 people; **Cluster:** 56 people.

PEARL 2 — Theater: 70 people; **Classroom:** 38 people; **Roundtable:** 40 people; **U-shaped:** 21 people; **Boardroom:** 21 people; **Cluster:** 32 people.

PEARL 3 — Theater: 30 people; **Classroom:** 24 people; **Roundtable:** 20 people; **U-shaped:** 15 people; **Boardroom:** 15 people; **Cluster:** 16 people.

SAPPHIRE — Boardroom: 12 people.

TOPAZ — Theater: 24 people; **Classroom:** 12 people; **Roundtable:** 10 people; **U-shaped:** 15 people; **Boardroom:** 15 people; **Cluster:** 8 people.

POOL LAWNS — Roundtable: 100 people; **Cluster:** 80 people.

COURTYARD MARRIOTT LAWNS — Roundtable: 80 people; **Cluster:** 64 people.

■ **Courtyard Mumbai International Airport, Andheri Kurla Road, Andheri (E), Mumbai, Ph: 61369999, 61366990,** www.courtyardmarriottmumbai.com

CT Chatwani Hall

MULTI-CUISINE (INDIAN, CHINESE, ITALIAN), MUGHLAI, SNACKS, CHAATS

Capacity: **Sitting:** 500–600 people; **Floating:** 1,000–1,200 people.

■ **Chatwani Hall, Telli Gali, Andheri (E), Mumbai, 26843051, 9819511286**

Dios

MULTI-CUISINE (INDIAN, CHINESE, THAI, CONTINENTAL)

Capacity: **Sitting:** 60 people; **Floating:** 200 people.

MOROCCAN TERRACE — South Terrace: 150–175 people; **Greek Terrace:** 40–50; **Dance Floor:** 60–70 people.

Total venue capacity is 400 people and food is put out on the terrace areas.

■ **Konarkshram, 5th Floor, Behind Everest Bldg., Tardeo Road, Tardeo, Mumbai, Ph: 67446969, 9820721555, 9930330053**

Diplomat

INDIAN (NORTH INDIAN, CHINESE)

Capacity: **Noble Room:** 80–100 people; **Fiesta (Terrace):** 200–300 people.

■ **24-26, BK Boman Behram Marg, Apollo Bunder, Mumbai, Ph: 22021661**

Dragon Fly

MULTI-CUISINE (THAI, INDIAN, CHINESE)

Capacity: **Hall 1:** 350 people (can be divided in to three separate sections). Sophisticated bar-like ambience with separate bar area.

■ **Express Tower, 1st Floor, Nariman Point, Mumbai, Ph: 2287 5633-35, 9321369773**

Executive Enclave

MULTI-CUISINE (INDIAN, CONTINENTAL, CHINESE)

Capacity: **MEMORY 1 — U-shaped:** 50-60 people; **Cocktail Dinner:** 150–180 people; **Conference:** 25–80 people.

MEMORY 2 — U-shaped: 50–60 people; **Cocktail Dinner:** 150–180 people; **Conference:** 25–80 people.

■ **The Elegant Corporate Hotel, 331, Dr Ambedkar Road, Pali Hill, Bandra (W), Mumbai, Ph: 66969000, 26490227,** enclave@vsnl.com

Fortune Select Exotica

MULTI-CUISINE (INDIAN, CONTINENTAL, ITALIAN, CHINESE)

Capacity: **HELIOS — U-shaped:** 55–60 people; **Theatre:** 200–220 people; **Classroom:** 55–60 people.

ZEUS — U-shaped: 40-45 people; **Theatre:** 180–200 people;

Classroom: 45–50 people.

VENUS — U-shaped: 40–45 people; **Theatre:** 160-180 people; **Classroom:** 40–45 people.

APOLLO — U-shaped: 40–45 people; **Theatre:** 160–180 people; **Classroom:** 40–45 people.

PRE-FUNCTION: 200 people.

■ **Plot No. 16, Sector 19-D, Vashi, Navi Mumbai, Ph: 39884444,** www.fortunehotels.in, exotica@fortunehotels.in

Four Points by Sheraton

MULTI-CUISINE (INDIAN, CHINESE, THAI, ITALIAN)

Capacity: **UNISON (1,2&3-each) — Freeflow:** 150 people; **Theatre:** 130 people; **Sit-down:** 75 people; **Classroom:** 75 people; **U-shaped:** 75 people.

UNISON (1&2 combined) — Freeflow: 300 people; **Theatre:** 275 people; **Sit-down:** 155 people; **Classroom:** 160 people; **U-shaped:** 115 people.

UNISON (1,2&3 combined) — Freeflow: 500 people; **Theatre:** 450 people; **Sit-down:** 230 people; **Classroom:** 250 people; **U-shaped:** 175 people.

Boardroom 1: 10 people; **Boardroom 2:** 12 people; **Boardroom 3:** 10 people; **Boardroom 4:** 8 people.

■ **Plot 39/1, 6-15, Sector 30-A, Vashi, Navi Mumbai, Mumbai, Ph: 27817777**

Four Seasons Hotel

MULTI-CUISINE (INDIAN, ASIAN, EUROPEAN)

Capacity: **LOBBY LEVEL — PAVILLION — Classroom:** 120 people; **Hollow Square:** 60 people; **U-shaped:** 60 people; **Theatre:** 250 people; **Reception style:** 300 people; Banquet **Rounds:** 150 people; **Boardroom:** 60 people.

Level II :

HEMANT — Classroom: 30 people; **U-shaped:** 26 people; **Theatre:** 70 people; **Reception style:** 50 people; **Banquet Rounds:** 40 people; **Boardroom style:** 30 people

BASANT — Classroom: 26 people; **U-shaped:** 24 people; **Theatre:** 60 people; **Reception style:** 40 people; **Banquet Rounds:** 30 people; **Boardroom:** 25 people.

TAPAN — Classroom: 16 people; **U-shaped:** 14 people; **Theatre:** 30 people; **Reception style:** 25 people; **Banquet Rounds:** 20 people; **Boardroom:** 12 people.

Level VI :

SHARAD — Classroom: 24 people; **U-shaped:** 20 people; **Theatre:** 40 people; **Reception style:** 35 people; **Banquet Rounds:** 30 people; **Boardroom:** 18 people.

SHISHIR — Classroom: 20 people; **U-shaped:** 16 people; **Theatre:** 35 people; **Reception style:** 30 people; **Banquet Rounds:** 20 people; **Boardroom:** 15 people.

GRISHM — Boardroom: 10 people.

■ **114, Dr E Moses Road, Worli, Mumbai, Ph: 24818000, 24818058,** www.fourseasons.com/mumbai

Gateway Rooms

MULTI-CUISINE (INDIAN, CHINESE, CONTINENTAL)

Capacity: **Buffet:** 130 people (seating); **Theatre:** 150 people; **Classroom:** 130 people.

Hall 1 — Buffet: 60 people (seating); **Theatre:** 60 people; **Classroom:** 48 people; **U-shaped:** 35 people.

Hall 2 — Buffet: 48 people (seating); **Theatre:** 48 people; **Classroom:** 28 people; **U-shaped:** 19 people.

Hall 3 — Buffet: 36 people (seating); **Theatre:** 40 people; **Classroom:** 24 people; **U-shaped:** 16 people.

■ **1st Floor, Narang House, Chatrapati Shivaji Maharaj Marg, Colaba, Mumbai, Ph: 22852582, 22829934-35, 9867505999,** www.mars-world.com

Golden Orchid

CUISINE (CHINESE, INDIAN)

Capacity: **Hall:** 50–75 people (Theater-style); 100 people (Standing & Floating).

■ **155, Waterfield Road, Bandra (W), Mumbai, Ph: 26402256-57**

The Gordon House Hotel

ORIENTAL (CHINESE, THAI)

Capacity: **Discotheque:** 700–800 people.

■ **5, Battery Street, Apollo Bunder, Colaba, Mumbai, Ph: 22894400, 22871122**

Grand Central

MULTI-CUISINE (INDIAN, CHINESE, THAI)

Capacity: **Banquet Hall:** 60–80 people; **Rooftop:** 150–160 people.

■ **Central Avenue Road, Chembur, Mumbai, Ph: 25283911, 67611999**

Grand Hyatt Mumbai

MULTI-CUISINE (INDIAN, EUROPEAN)

Capacity: **Boardroom** 1&2: 30 people each; **Drawing Room:** 70 people; **Grand Ballroom:** 1,000–1,200 people; **Mahogany:** 80 people; **Grand Salon:** 150 people; and **Courtyard:** 300–400 people.

■ **Off Western Express Highway, Santacruz (E), Mumbai, Ph: 66761234**

Grand Sarovar Premiere

MULTI-CUISINE (INDIAN, CHINESE, CONTINENTAL)

Capacity: **SENATE 1 — U-shaped:** 48 people; **Boardroom:** 48 people; **Theatre:** 120 people; **Reception style:** 250 people.

SENATE 2 — U-shaped: 18 people; **Boardroom:** 18 people; **Theatre:** 60 people; **Reception style:** 100 people.

Banquet Hall: 250 people.

■ **AK Plaza, Junction of SV Road & Veer Savarkar Road Flyover, Goregaon (W), Mumbai, Ph: 28718000**

Green House

Multi-Cuisine (Indian, Chinese, Seafood, Continental)

Capacity: **Hall:** 70–80 people. Garden has been converted into a restaurant.

■ **Rao Apts., Nehru Road, Vile Parle (E), Mumbai, Ph: 26102593, 26151104, 26179712**

Hilton Mumbai International Airport Hotel

Multi-Cuisine (Indian, Global)

Capacity: **CHANCELLOR 1 — Classroom:** 35 people; **Theater:** 65 people; **Banquet Rounds:** 30 people; **Reception style:** 60 people; **Conference:** 22 people; **U-shaped:** 28 people.

CHANCELLOR 2 — Classroom: 48 people; **Theater:** 100 people; **Banquet Rounds:** 48 people; **Reception style:** 100 people; **Conference:** 28 people; **U-shaped:** 34 people.

CHANCELLOR SUITE — Classroom style: 35 people; **Theater:** 65 people; **Banquet Rounds:** 30 people; **Reception style:** 60 people; **Conference:** 22 people; **U-shaped:** 28 people.

COUNTESS — Classroom: 35 people; **Theater:** 65 people; **Banquet Rounds:** 30 people; **Reception style:** 60 people; **Conference:** 22 people; **U-shaped:** 28 people.

VICTORIA (Marquee) — Classroom: 35 people; **Theater:** 65 people; **Banquet Rounds:** 30 people; **Reception style:** 60 people; **Conference:** 22 people; **U-shaped:** 28 people.

VISCOUNT — Classroom: 35 people; **Theater:** 65 people; **Banquet Rounds:** 30 people; **Reception style:** 60 people; **Conference:** 22 people; **U-shaped:** 28 people.

■ **Sahar Airport Road, Andheri (E), Mumbai, Ph: 28380000**

Holiday Inn

Multi-Cuisine (Indian, European)

Capacity: **Meeting Rooms** (1-4): 20–50 people (each X 4); **Ballroom:** 500 people; **Ballroom Terrace:** 140 people; Sky **Terrace:** 150–200 people. Business Centre facilities for in-house guests.

■ **Holiday Inn, Mumbai International Airport, Saki Naka Junction, Andheri (E), Mumbai, Ph: 40851800, 61161800**

Hotel Bawa International Private Limited

Multi-Cuisine (Indian, Chinese, Continental)

Capacity: **Ballroom:** 200 (sitting) and 260 (floating), **Boardroom:** 150 (sitting), 200 (floating); **Discovery:** 100

(sitting), 140 (floating); **Mehfil:** 80 (sitting), 110 (floating).

■ **256-E, Bellasis Road, Near Best Bus Depot, Mumbai Central, Mumbai, Ph: 23081481**

Hotel Marine Plaza

MULTI-CUISINE (INDIAN, EUROPEAN)

Capacity: **Bayview Section 1:** 30–35 people; **Allamanda Terrace:** 250–300 people (evenings only); **Plaza Room:** 300 people.

■ **29, Marine Drive, Mumbai, Ph: 22851212,** hotelmarineplaza@vsnl.com, fb@hotelmarineplaza.com

Hotel Royal Gardens

MULTI-CUISINE (INDIAN, CHINESE)

Capacity: **Banquet Hall:** 200–300 people; **Small Hall:** 20–55 people.

■ **Juhu Tara Road, Juhu, Mumbai, Ph: 26602954-55, 26603516**

Hotel Sea Princess

MULTI-CUISINE (INDIAN, CONTINENTAL, ASIAN)

Capacity: **Sea Facing Lawn:** 500–800 people; **Crystal Banquet Room:** 250–400 people.

CHANCELLOR 1 — U-shaped: 36 people; **Classroom:** 30 people; **Theatre:** 55 people.

CHANCELLOR 2 — U-shaped: 42 people; **Classroom:** 30 people; **Theatre:** 65 people.

REGAL I&II: U-shaped: 73 people; **Classroom:** 60 people; **Theatre:** 116 people.

BUSINESSCENTRE — Interview Room: 6 people; **Meeting Room:** 15 people.

■ **Juhu Tara Road, Juhu Beach, Mumbai, Ph: 26611111, 66924455,** www.seaprincess.com, banquets@seaprincess.com

Hyatt Regency Mumbai

WORLD CUISINE

Capacity: **Regency Ballroom 1,2&3:** 75 people each-classroom seating; **Emerald:** 44 people; **Sapphire:** 30 people; **Topaz:** 16 people; **Jade:** 12 people; **Opel:** 24 people; and **Pearl:** 16 people.

■ **Sahar Airport Road, Andheri (E), Mumbai, Ph: 66961234, 66961411**

Ikxia

MULTI-CUISINE (INDIAN, CHINESE)

Capacity: **LEVEL 1 — Classroom:** 34 people; **Boardroom:** 30 people; **Theatre:** 100 people; **Cluster:** 35 people.

LEVEL 2 — Classroom: 24 people; **Boardroom:** 15 people; **Theatre:** 50 people; **Cluster:** 28 people.

■ **Barot Hotels Pvt. Ltd., Chowpatty Seaface, Mumbai, Ph: 23696991,** www.ikxia.com

Image

MULTI-CUISINE (INDIAN, CHINESE)

Capacity: **Hall:** 40 people; **Lobby Area:** 100 people.

■ **Hotel Laxmi International, SV Road, Goregaon (W), Mumbai, Ph: 28741251, 28767225, 28767869**

Imperial Banquets

AS PER CLIENT'S REQUIREMENT

This banquet has two halls by the name of **Grand I, II.** The total capacity of both halls combined is 100–800 people. Separate Capacities are as follows: **Grand I:** 300 people (floating); **Grand II:** 500 people

■ **Opp. Raghuleela Mall, S Pranavanandji Marg, Vashi, Navi Mumbai, Ph: 66908900**

InterContinental Marine Drive

MULTI-CUISINE (INDIAN, EUROPEAN)

Capacity: **Onyx:** 70–80 people. **Dome:** 150–175 (rooftop).

■ **135, Marine Drive, Mumbai, Ph: 39879999**

InterContinental The Lalit

MULTI-CUISINE (INDIAN, EUROPEAN, CHINESE, PAN ASIAN)

Capacity: **MAJESTIC — Theatre:** 800 people; **Reception-style:** 1,500 people; **Classroom:** 300 people.

ROYAL — Theatre 35 people; **Reception-style:** 15 people; **Classroom:** 15 people.

REGAL — Theatre: 45 people; **Reception-style:** 40 people; **Classroom:** 21 people.

Quorum 1, 2 & 3: 10–12 people each.

Quorum Skydo: 18-27 people.

Garden: 1,000–2,000 people.

■ **Sahar Airport Road, Mumbai, Ph: 66992222**

ITC Grand Central

AS PER CLIENT'S REQUIREMENT

Capacity: **TERRACE GARDEN — Theatre:** 400 people; **Round table:** 150 people; **Floating:** 500 people.

MAIN BALLROOM — Theatre: 400 people; **Round table:** 150 people; **Floating:** 500 people.

CJ's — Theatre & Round table: 50–60 people each.

■ **Dr Ambedkar Road, Parel, Mumbai, Ph: 24101010**

ITC Maratha

MULTI-CUISINE (INDIAN, EUROPEAN)

Capacity: **BALLROOMS 1,2&3 — Theatre:** 650 people; **Royal Garden**: 1,500–1,700 people.

■ **Sahar, Andheri (E), Mumbai, Ph: 28303030**

Juhu Hotel Pvt. Ltd.

MULTI-CUISINE (NORTH INDIAN, CHINESE)

Capacity: **Banquet Hall:** 80 people; **Lawn** (evenings only): 450–500 people.

■ **Juhu Tara Road, Juhu, Mumbai, Ph: 26184014**

JW Marriott Hotel

MULTI-CUISINE (INDIAN, EUROPEAN, JAPANESE, ITALIAN)

Capacity: **Sangam Ballroom:** 500 people (sitting); 1000 people (floating); **Kaveri:** 125 people; **Terrace:** 180 people (cluster) and 250 people (floating); and **Salt Water Pool:** 65–70 people (sitting) and 150 people (floating).

■ **Juhu Tara Road, Juhu, Mumbai, Ph: 66933000**

Kohinoor Hall & Banquet

MULTI-CUISINE (INDIAN, CHINESE)

Capacity: **Kohinoor Hall:** 250 people; **Kohinoor Banquet:** 80 people; **Terrace area:** 250 people.

■ **Kohinoor Corner, Veer Savarkar Marg, Prabhadevi, Mumbai, Ph: 24226743, 24372441**

Krishna Palace Residency

MULTI-CUISINE (INDIAN, CHINESE, ITALIAN, MEXICAN, SOUTH-INDIAN, COTINENTAL)

Capacity: **RAAS 1 — Theater:** 125 people; **Reception style:** 200 people; **Classroom:** 80 people; **U-shaped:** 70 people.

RAAS 2 — Theater: 80 people; **Reception style:** 100 people; **Classroom:** 60 people; **U-shaped:** 40 people.

RAAS (full) — Theater: 200 people; **Reception style:** 400 people; **Classroom:** 150 people; **U-shaped:** 100 people.

RAAGA — Theater: 200 people; **Reception style:** 250 people; **Classroom:** 100 people; **U-shaped:** 85 people.

HAVELI 1 — Theater: 50 people; **Reception style:** 50 people; **Classroom:** 40 people; **U-shaped:** 35 people.

HAVELI 2 — Theater: 35 people; **Reception style:** 35 people; **Classroom:** 30 people; **U-shaped:** 30 people.

Raas 1 Terrace: 50 people; **Raas 2 Terrace:** 150 people.

n Hotel Krishna Palace Residency Pvt. Ltd.,

■ **Nana Chowk, Mumbai, Ph: 66293333,**
www.krishnapalaceresidency.com,
info@krishnapalaceresidency.com

The Leela Mumbai

MULTI-CUISINE (INDIAN, EUAROPEAN/GLOBAL, CHINESE, ITALIAN, INDONESIAN, THAI)

Capacity: **Grand Ballroom:** 1000–1,200 people. The Grand Ballroom can be divided into five sections.

MEETING ROOMS — Kamal: 16 people; **Nidhi:** 12 people; **Nithya:** 16 people; **Diya:** 12 people; and **Maya:** 12 people.

■ **Sahar Airport Road, Andheri (E), Mumbai, Ph: 66911234**

The Liquid Lounge

MULTI-CUISINE (INDIAN, ITALIAN, LEBANESE)

Capacity: **Liquid Lounge:** 150 people; **Bellessima:** 100 people.

■ **534, SVP Road, Near Sukh Sagar, Opera House, Mumbai, Ph: 40287171, 40287106 (Padmini)**

Mayfair Rooms

MULTI-CUISINE (INDIAN, EUROPEAN, CHINESE, ITALIAN, MEXICAN)

Capacity: **Mayfair South:** 300 people; **Mayfair North:** 125 people; **The Lounge:** 90 people; **Odyssey:** 125 people.

■ **Ground Floor, Indian Oil Bldg., 254-C, Dr Annie Besant Road, Worli, Mumbai, Ph: 40501111**

Mirador

MULTI-CUISINE (INDIAN, CHINESE, CONTINENTAL)

CRIMSON (1,2,3&4 each) — Theatre: 60 people; **Classroom style:** 25 people; **U-shaped:** 30 people; **Cocktail:** 50 people; **Boardroom:** 30 people.

CRIMSON (1,2,3&4 combined as ballroom) — Theatre: 275 people; **Classroom style:** 130 people; **Cocktail:** 350 people.

MEDLER — Theatre: 40 people; **Classroom style:** 25 people; **U-shaped:** 22 people; **Cocktail:** 30 people; **Boardroom:** 20 people.

PRUNELLA — Theatre: 30 people; **Classroom:** 15 people; **U-shaped:** 15 people; **Cocktail:** 15 people; **Boardroom:** 15 people.

BIANCA — Boardroom: 10 people.

■ **131/B, New Link Road, Chakala, Andheri (E), Mumbai, Ph: 42485000,** www.themirador.com, themirador@themirador.com, banquets@themirador.com

Natraj Lawns

MULTI-CUISINE (INDIAN, CHINESE, MONGOLIAN, MEXICAN, THAI, ITALIAN, BURMESE)

Capacity: **AC Hall 1:** 200 people; **Open Ground:** 600 people; **Hall 2:** 200 people; total capacity for venue: 1,000–1,200.

■ **B-165, Chembur Colony, Opp Basant Cinema, Dr CG Road, Chembur, Mumbai, Ph: 25204762, 65816536, 9820282583**

Novotel

MULTI-CUISINE (INDIAN, CHINESE, MEDITERRANEAN, ITALIAN)

Capacity: **CHAMPAGNE I — Reception style:** 150 people; **Theater:** 100 people; **U-shaped:** 32 people; **Boardroom:** 40 people; **Classroom:** 60 people; **Cluster:** 60 people; **Roundtable:** 60 people.

CHAMPAGNE II — Reception style: 250 people; **Theater:** 200 people; **U-shaped:** 40 people; **Boardroom:** 60 people; **Classroom:** 100 people; **Cluster:** 60 people; **Roundtable:** 60 people.

CHAMPAGNE (I&II combined) — Reception style: 600 people; **Theater:** 350 people; **Classroom:** 200 people; **Cluster:** 180 people; **Roundtable:** 200 people.

BURGUNDY — Reception style: 100 people; **Theater:** 80 people; **U-shaped:** 30 people; **Boardroom:** 33 people; **Classroom:** 32 people; **Cluster:** 30 people; **Roundtable:** 50 people.

BORDEAUX — Reception style: 60 people; **Theater:** 50 people; **U-shaped:** 25 people; **Boardroom:** 28 people; **Classroom:** 30 people; **Cluster:** 30 people; **Roundtable:** 40 people.

Sea-facing Rerrace (I&II): 50 people.

■ **Balraj Sahani Marg, Juhu Beach, Mumbai, Ph: 66934444,** h6926-re@accor.com

The Orchid

AS PER CLIENT'S REQUIREMENT

Capacity: **Chambers 1,2&3:** 150 people (floating), 100 people (sitting); can be further divided into three of 60 people each; **Senate 1,2&3:** 15 people each; **Cascade** (rooftop; evenings only): 250–300 people.

■ **70-C, Nehru Road, Vile Parle (E), Mumbai, Ph: 26164040**

Pali Presidency

MULTI-CUISINE (INDIAN, CHINESE)

Capacity: **Hall:** 100 people (lunch); 40 people (dinner).

■ **Bandra Parimal Tank, Pali Naka, Pali Road, Bandra (W), Mumbai, Ph: 26439726, 26413446**

Pan Street

MULTI-CUISINE (INDIAN, CHINESE, EUROPEAN)

Capacity: **Concord:** 350 people; **Garnet:** 70 people. They serve two rounds of tea and coffee with buffet lunch packages for conferences.

■ **Peninsula Grand Hotel, Saki Naka Junction, Andheri (E), Mumbai, Ph: 28519191**

The Park

As Per Client's Requirement

Capacity: **MEETING ROOM — Theatre:** 30 people; **U-shaped:** 15 people; **Box:** 15 people.

MEETINGROOM 2 — Theatre: 30 people; **U-shaped:** 15 people; **Box:** 15 people

ROSEWOOD — Theatre: 250 people; **Classroom style:** 135 people; **U-shaped (single):** 75 people; **U-shaped (double):** 125 people; **Casual:** 350 people; **Sit-down:** 136 people; **Cluster:** 102 people.

BANYAN (I&II each) — Theatre: 50 people; **Classroom style:** 25 people; **U-shaped:** 15 people; **Casual:** 40 people.

BANYAN (I&II combined) — Theatre: 75 people; **Classroom style:** 50 people; **U-shaped:** 25 people; **Casual:** 60 people.

BANYAN III — Theatre: 50 people; **Classroom style:** 25 people; **U-shaped:** 15 people.

BANYAN (I,II&III combined) — Theatre: 150 people; **Classroom:** 75 people; **U-shaped:** 60 people; **Casual:** 250 people; **Sit-down:** 56 people; **Cluster:** 50 people.

Garden: 175 people; Terrace: 500 people.

■ **No. 1, Sector 10, CBD Belapur, Navi Mumbai, Ph: 67589000, 27589000, 67589032,** www.theparkhotels.com

Peninsula Next

Multi-Cuisine (Chinese, North Indian)

Capacity: **Peninsula Gold:** 100 people; **Peninsula Platinum:** 150 people.

■ **118, Thomas Villa, Opp. Cine Planet, Sion, Mumbai, Ph: 24078200, 24070150**

Pritam da Dhaba

Indian (North Indian)

Capacity: **Hall 1:** 70 people; **Hall 2:** 70 people; and **Full Hall** (without divider): 140 people.

■ **32, Dharamputra, Pritam Estates, Dadar, Mumbai, Ph: 24143311, 24145555, 24143817**

Puranmal

Multi-Cuisine (Chinese, Indian, South Indian), Fast Food

Capacity: **Rasraj:** 100–150 people.

■ **V Mehta Road, Vile Parle (W), Mumbai, Ph: 26716939**

Quality Inn Parle International

Multi-Cuisine (Indian, Chinese, European)

Capacity: **CRYSTAL HALL** — 40–400 people **(Reception style:** 300 people; **Boardroom:** 80 people; **Summit:** 40–70 people); **NEW HALL:** 400 people.

■ **BN Agarwal Commercial Complex, Vile Parle, Mumbai, Ph: 26102122**

Rajhans Hotel

MULTI-CUISINE (INDIAN, ORIENTAL, MUGHLAI, THAI)

Capacity: **Top Terrace:** 250 people; **Mini Terrace:** 60–80 people; **Banquet Hall:** 50–60 people; **Long Garden:** 50–60 people.

■ **15/16, NG Acharya Marg, Opp. Railway Station, Chembur, Mumbai, Ph: 67856600**

Ramada Plaza Palm Grove

MULTI-CUISINE (INDIAN, CHINESE, ITALIAN, THAI, CONTINENTAL)

Capacity: **CONCORD I — U-shaped:** 25–30 people; **Boardroom:** 25–30 people; **Cluster:** 25–42 people; **Classroom style:** 25–42 people; **Theater:** 25–65 people.

CONCORD II — U-shaped: 35–40 people; **Boardroom:** 35–40 people; **Cluster:** 35–56 people; **Classroom style:** 35–60 people; **Theater:** 35–100 people.

CONCORD (Full) — U-shaped: 75 people; **Boardroom:** 75 people; **Cluster:** 75–85 people; **Classroom style:** 75–90 people; **Theater:** 75–250 people.

ORIENTAL BOWL — U-shaped: 15–20 people; **Boardroom:** 15–20 people; **Cluster:** 15–25 people; **Classroom style:** 15–27 people; **Theater:** 15–35 people.

CHANCERY — U-shaped: 12-15 people; **Boardroom:** 12-15 people; **Cluster:** 12-15 people; **Classroom style:** 12-15 people; **Theater:** 12-20 people.

■ **Ramada Plaza, Palm Grove, Juhu Beach, Mumbai, Ph: 26112323**

Ramada Powai Hotel & Convention Centre

MULTI-CUISINE (INDIAN, CHINESE, THAI, MEXICAN, ITALIAN, CONTINENTAL), **JAIN**

Capacity: **CRYSTAL —** (can be divided into three separate halls) Theater: 500 people; **Reception style:** 700 people; **Garden, pool and waterfall area:** 2,000 people.

EMERALD — (can be divided into three separate halls) **Theater:** 500 people; **Reception style:** 700 people.

SAPPHIRE — Theater: 100 people; **Classroom style:** 45 people.

EMBASSY — Boardroom: 15 people.

Poolside lawn and garden: 2,000 people; **Poolside Garden:** 100 people.

■ **Near The Residence Hotel & Convention Centre, Before Vihar Lake, Powai, Saki Vihar Road, Mumbai, Ph: 67776000,** info@ramadapowai.com, reservation@ramadapowai.com

Ramee Guestline

MULTI-CUISINE (INDIAN, CHINESE, EUROPEAN)

Capacity: **Regal Room:** 40–50 people; **Rooftop:** 80–90 people.

■ **Plot No. 3, Kohinoor Road, Opp. Swami Narayan Temple, Dadar (E), Mumbai, Ph: 24115657, 24177900**

Ramee Guestline

As Per Client's Requirement

Capacity: **REGENT — Theatre:** 300 people; **Floating:** 400 people; **Madness A:** 150 people; **Madness B:** 100 people.

■ **757, SV Road, Khar (W), Mumbai, Ph: 26485421**

Rangsharda

Multi-Cuisine (Indian, European, Chinese, Mexican)

Capacity: **Embassy 1:** 50 people; **Westerlies (Terrace):** 1,000 people; **Rangsharda Auditorium:** 800 people.

■ **Near Lilavati Hospital, Bandra Reclamation, Bandra (W), Mumbai, Ph: 26401919, 26438120-27**

Renaissance

As Per Client's Requirement

Capacity: **GRAND BALLROOM — Theatre:** 1-1,200 people; **Classroom style:** 350 people; **Banquet:** 350 people; **Boardroom:** 225 people; **U-shaped:** 225 people; **Reception style:** 2,000 people.

POWAI BALLROOM — Theatre: 200 people; **Classroom style:** 80 people; **Banquet:** 80 people; **Boardroom:** 65 people; **U-shaped:** 65 people; **Reception style** (can be booked separately also): 250 people.

LOTUS & JASMINE — Theatre: 40 people; **Classroom style:** 20 people; **Banquet style:** 25 people; **Boardroom:** 20 people; **U-shaped:** 20 people; **Reception style:** 40 people.

RENAISSANCE GARDEN: 5,000 people (both in Reception style).

TERRACE — Banquet: 400 people; **Reception style:** 1,200 people.

ASHRAM LAND — Also known as Gauri Point, takes around 150 floating crowd.

Meeting Room 1: 15 people, **Meeting Room 2:** 12 people, **Meeting Room 3, 4, 5**: 8 people.

Terrace Garden: 500 people (floating).

■ **Renaissance Hotel & Convention Centre, 2&3 B, Near Chinmayanand Ashram, Powai, Mumbai, Ph: 66928888, 66927777, 66927060**

The Residence Hotel

Multi-Cuisine (Indian, European, Chinese)

Capacity: **Jasmine 1&2:** 25 people each; **Poolside Lawn:** 1,000 people; **Poolside Garden:** 150–175 people; **Garden:** 50–100 people; **Crystal Ballroom:** 450 people; **Sapphire Ballroom:** 45 people; **Emerald Ballroom:** 450 people.

■ **Saki Vihar Road, Powai, Mumbai, Ph: 28578686**

The Resort

MULTI-CUISINE (INDIAN, EUROPEAN, CHINESE)

Capacity: **CONFERENCE HALLS — Ripples:** 25 people; **Coral:** 100 people; **Anchor:** 75 people; **Harbour:** 90 people; **Waves:** 20 people; **Pebbles:** 50 people; **Oyster:** 20–25 people; **Pearl:** 25 people.

PARTY VENUES — RBC Lawn: 300 people; **Queen's Lawn:** 150 people; **Waterworld:** 75 people; **Resort Garden:** 1,000 people.

■ **Aksa Beach, Madh-Marve Road, Malad (W), Mumbai, Ph: 28823331, 28808888**

Retreat

MULTI-CUISINE (NORTH INDIAN, MUGHLAI, CHINESE, EUROPEAN)

Capacity: **CONFERENCE HALL — Assembly:** 150 people; **Wharf Site:** 150–180 people; **Summit:** 80–100 people; **Fraternity:** 15–20 people; **Tete 1&2:** 15 people each.

OUTDOOR PARTIES — Ocean Terrace: 80–200 people; **Pool Garden:** 700 people; **Water Edge:** 50–150 people; **Volley Ball:** 700 people.

■ **Erangle Beach, Madh-Marve Road, Malad (W), Mumbai, Ph: 28813500**

Ritz Hotel

MULTI-CUISINE (INDIAN, EUROPEAN, CHINESE, ITALIAN)

Capacity: **Lotus Room:** 40–50 people; **Lounge:** 20 people; **Aaina Khana:** 60–80 people.

■ **5, Jamshedji Tata Road, Churchgate, Mumbai, Ph: 22820141, 22850500, 22837623**

Rodas Ecotel Hotel

MULTI-CUISINE (INDIAN, EUROPEAN)

Capacity: **PAVILION — U-shaped:** 78 people; **Theatre:** 289 people; **Classroom style:** 108 people; **Round table:** 176 people. The Pavilion can be divided into four parts.

PAVILION 1 — U-shaped: 35 people; **Theatre:** 90 people; **Classroom style:** 30 people; **Round table:** 76 people.

PAVILION 2 — U-shaped: 20 people; **Theatre:** 50 people; **Classroom style:** 24 people.

PAVILION 3 — U-shaped: 30 people; **Theatre:** 70 people; Classroom style: 30 people.

■ **Central Avenue, Hiranandani Gardens, Powai, Mumbai, Ph: 66936969, 40075555**

Sahara Star

MULTI-CUISINE (INDIAN, GLOBAL)

Capacity: **Aces (Presidential Boardroom):** 77 people

PEARL — Theatre: 30 people; **Classroom style:** 30 people; **U-shaped:** 25 people; **Boardroom:** 25 people; **Cluster:** 25 people; **Banquet:** 30 people.

OYSTER — Theatre: 100 people; **Classroom style:** 50 people; **U-shaped:** 30 people; **Boardroom:** 30 people; **Cluster:** 70 people; **Banquet:** 120 people.

BUSINESSCENTRE — Clubs: 7 people; **Spades:** 7 people; **Hearts:** 14 people; **Diamonds:** 14 people; **Kings:** 16 people.

Banquet Hall: 300 people; **Terrace Banquet:** 200 people.

■ **Opp. Domestic Airport, Ph: 39895000, 1800226645,** www.saharastar.com, reservations@saharastar.com

Samrat

INDIAN (GUJARATI THALI, NORTH INDIAN)

Capacity: **Umang:** 25–35 people; **Utsav:** 60–80 people.

■ **Prem Court, Jamshedji Tata Road, Churchgate, Mumbai, Ph: 42135401**

Sannidhi

MULTI-CUISINE (NORTH INDIAN, SOUTH INDIAN, CHINESE)

Capacity: **Celebrity:** 250 people; **Samarambha** (non-AC): 300 people.

■ **Payyade International, VL Road, Kandivali (W), Mumbai, Ph: 28010732, 28012876, 28011468**

Shabri

MULTI-CUISINE (NORTH INDIAN, CHINESE)

Capacity: **Panchavati:** 50–90 people.

■ **148, Nehru Road, Vile Parle (E), Mumbai, Ph: 26177777, 26178888**

Shagun

MULTI-CUISINE (GUJARATI, NORTH INDIAN, SOUTH INDIAN, CHINESE)

Capacity: **Hall:** 60–70 people.

■ **M-61, Shivlal Motilal Mansion, DB Road, Central Junction, Mumbai, Ph: 23084444, 23091515**

Shatranj Napoli

MULTI-CUISINE (INDIAN, ITALAIAN)

Capacity: **Ground Floor** — restaurant Shatranj; **First Floor** (AC): 70–90 people banquet hall. As the book goes to press, this place is under renovation.

■ **Hotel Oscar, 12, Union Park, Carter Road, Khar (W), Mumbai, Ph: 26498458, 26499844, 26499865**

Shiv Krishna

MULTI-CUISINE (INDIAN, CHINESE)

Capacity: **Shiva:** 50 people; **Krishna:** 40 people.

■ **55, Ranchhod Bhawan, JSS Road, Opera House, Mumbai, Ph: 23823966, 23813882, 23813884**

Siddhartha

MULTI-CUISINE (GUJARATI, NORTH INDIAN, SOUTH INDIAN), **SNACKS**

Capacity: **Hall:** 700–800 people, depending on the size of the gathering.

■ **368, SV Road, Near Bandra Lake, Bandra (W), Mumbai, Ph: 26428718, 26554013**

Silk Route

CHINESE, THAI

Capacity: **Julianas:** 20–25 people.

■ **38, K Dubash Marg, Kala Ghoda, Fort, Mumbai, Ph: 22844324, 22818572**

Silver Coin

MULTI-CUISINE (NORTH INDIAN, CHINESE), **SIZZLERS**

Capacity: **Hall** (afternoons only): 40 people; **Garden:** 75–100 people.

■ **RSK Apts., IC Colony, Borivali (W), Mumbai, Ph: 28939763, 28951410, 28933413, 65280028**

Sitara

MULTI-CUISINE (NORTH INDIAN, CHINESE)

Capacity: **Hall:** 50 people.

■ **Dhiraj Annexe, Sarojini Naidu Road, Mulund (W), Mumbai, Ph: 25618758, 25641242**

Sun-n-Sand

MULTI-CUISINE (INDIAN, EUROPEAN, CHINESE)

Capacity: **JUBILEE — Reception style:** 130–150 people; **Open Lawn:** 800 people.

ANCHOR — Room A: 45 people; **Room B (Conference style):** 20 people.

■ **39, Juhu Beach, Mumbai, Ph: 66938888, 26201811**

Sunville

MULTI-CUISINE (INDIAN, MEXICAN, EUROPEAN, CHINESE)

Capacity: **Orchid:** 125–150 people; **Royal — Annexe & Terrace:** 300 people; **Imperial:** 150 people; **Executive Room:** 40–50 people.

■ **9, Dr Annie Besant Road, Worli, Mumbai, Ph: 24978082, 24935546, 24934637**

Svenska Design Hotel

MULTI-CUISINE (INDIAN, CHINESE, ITALIAN, SPANISH, MEDITERRANEAN, CONTINENTAL)

Capacity: **BANQUET HALL — Theatre:** 120 people; **Floating:** 150 people.

■ **F 73/74, Oberoi Complex, Off Link Road, Andheri (W), Mumbai, Ph: 44310000, 9167707013, 9820711110**

Symphony

MULTI-CUISINE (INDIAN, CHINESE, EUROPEAN)

Capacity: **Hall:** 35 people.

■ **72, Sheredon House, August Kranti Marg, Mumbai, Ph: 23862231, 23876238**

Taj Lands End

MULTI-CUISINE (INDIAN, EUROPEAN, CHINESE)

Capacity: **Ballroom 1&2:** 1,000 people; **Salcette I,II&III:** 50–60 people each; **Malabar & Konkan:** 70 people each; **Sea Side Lounge & Poolside Lounge:** 3,000 people each; **Garden View:** 250 people.

■ **Band Stand, Bandra (W), Mumbai, Ph: 66681234**

Taj Mahal Palace

AS PER CLIENT'S REQUIREMENTS

Capacity: **BALLROOM — Classroom style:** 200 people; **U-shaped:** 75 people; **Theatre:** 450 people; **Round table:** 300 people; **Floating:** 650 people.

CRYSTAL CENTRAL — Classroom style: 120 people; **U-shaped:** 75 people; **Theatre:** 400 people; **Round table:** 220 people; **Floating:** 450 people.

CRYSTAL NORTH & SOUTH — Classroom style: 45 people; **U-shaped:** 35 people; **Theatre:** 60 people; **Round table:** 80 people; **Floating:** 80 people.

EMERALD & JADE — Classroom style: 20 people; **U-shaped:** 16 people; **Theatre:** 30 people; **Round table:** 40 people; **Floating:** 40 people.

GATEWAY ROOM — Classroom style: 35 people; **U-shaped:** 35 people; **Theatre:** 70 people; **Round table:** 80 people; **Floating:** 100 people.

GOLDEN ROOM — Classroom style: 15 people; **U-shaped:** 17 people; **Theatre:** 30 people; **Round table:** 30 people; **Floating:** 40 people.

PRINCES ROOM — Classroom style: 15 people, **U-shaped:** 18 people; **Theatre:** 30 people; **Round table:** 30 people; **Floating:** 60 people.

RUBY ROOM — U-shaped: 7 people.

SAPPHIRE ROOM — Classroom style: 18 people; **U-shaped:** 14 people; **Theatre;** 24 people; **Round table:** 16 people.

■ **Apollo Bunder, Opp. Gateway of India, Colaba, Mumbai, Ph: 66653366**

Tamarind

AS PER CLIENT'S REQUIREMENTS

Capacity: **Poolside area:** 50 people.

■ **Fariyas Hotel 25, Off Arthur Bunder Road, Colaba, Mumbai, Ph: 61416141**

Time and Again

MULTI-CUISINE (INDIAN, CHINESE, CONTINENTAL)

Capacity: **Hall:** 400 people.

■ **9, Raheja Classique, Opp. Cinemax Adlabs, Oshiwara Link Road, Lokhandwala, Andheri (W), Mumbai, Ph: 26339997**

Tote on the Turf

WORLD CUISINE

With 8,000sq ft of dedicated banqueting space... Tote on the Turf impresses one and all. The entire events venue can be used in as one large space, or sub-divided into several smaller spaces, with or without attached open-air garden areas to spill over in to. On offer is: World-class cuisine from the deGustibus Hospitality catering arm, Moveable Feast, which customizes multi-cuisine menus with a variety of artful serving options, from banquet buffet-style formats to intimate, sit-down dinners.

■ **Mahalaxmi Racecourse, Opp. Gate Nos. 5-6, Keshav Rao Khadye Marg, Mahalaxmi, Mumbai, Ph: 61577777**

Trident Hotel

MULTI-CUISINE (INDIAN, EUROPEAN)

Capacity: **REGAL ROOM — Theatre:** 550 people; **Classroom style:** 250 people; **Reception style:** 1,000 people (informal); **Banquet:** 250 people.

ROOFTOP — Theatre: 200 people; **Classroom style:** 110 people; **Reception style:** 225 people; **Banquet:** 120 people.

GULMOHAR — Theatre: 80 people, **Classroom style:** 50 people, **Reception style:** 125 people, **Banquet:** 80 people.

JACARANDA — Theatre: 45 people; **Classroom style:** 25 people; **Reception style:** 50 people; **Banquet:** 40 people.

MALABAR ROOM — Classroom style: 35 people; **Reception style:** 50 people; **Banquet:** 40 people.

LOTUS ROOM — Theatre: 100 people; **Classroom style:** 60 people; **Reception style:** 120 people.

SUNSET LOUNGE — Theatre: 85 people; **Classroom style:** 50 people; **Reception style:** 120 people.

Sunset Boardroom: 14 people.

■ **Nariman Point, Mumbai, Ph: 66326585, 66325757**

Trident Hotel (Bandra-Kurla)

MULTI-CUISINE (INDIAN, EUROPEAN)

Capacity: **4 Boardrooms:** 8-12 people each; **6 meeting rooms:** 6-14 people each.

ORLOFF — Theatre: 100 people; **Classroom style:** 45 people; **U-shaped:** 32 people; **Sit-down:** 48 people; **Cocktail dinner:** 120 people.

CULLIAN — Theatre: 100 people; **Classroom style:** 45 people; **U-shaped:** 32 people; **Sit-down:** 48 people; **Cocktail dinner:** 120 people.

ORLOFF& CIULLIAN (combined) — Theatre: 280 people; **Classroom style:** 105 people; **U-shaped:** 62 people; **Sit-down:** 96 people; **Cocktail dinner:** 300 people.

GOLCONDA BALLROOM (I-III) — Theatre: 120 people; **Classroom style:** 45 people; **U-shaped:** 30 people; **Sit-down:** 48 people; **Cocktail dinner:** 150 people (each X 3).

GOLCONDA BALLROOM (I&II combined) — Theatre: 300 people; **Classroom style:** 105 people; **U-shaped:** 60 people; **Sit-down:** 96 people; **Cocktail dinner:** 350 people.

FULLGOLCONDA BALLROOM — Theatre: 450 people; **Classroom style:** 180 people; **U-shaped:** 90 people; **Sit-down:** 168 people; **Cocktail dinner:** 550 people.

■ **C-56, G Block, Bandra Kurla Complex, Mumbai, Ph: 66727777**

Tunga International

MULTI-CUISINE (INDIAN, CHINESE, EUROPEAN), COASTAL

Capacity: **Tribune 1:** 150–200 people; **Tribune 2:** 30–35 people; **Terrace — Blossom:** 150–200 people.

■ **B-11, MIDC Central Road, Andheri (E), Mumbai, Ph: 66921212**

Turf Club

AS PER CLIENT'S REQUIREMENTS

Capacity: **LAWNS — Members' Enclosure:** 2,000–2,500 people; **Enclosure 1:** 1,500 people; **Enclosure 2:** 1,500 people.

P.S. Do remember that they don't look after catering requirements.

■ **Royal Western India Turf Club, Mahalakshmi Racecourse, Mumbai, Ph: 23071407, 23071401**

United-21

MULTI-CUISINE (NORTH INDIAN, MUGHLAI, SOUTH INDIAN, THAI, CHINESE, EUROPEAN)

Be it any occasion to celebrate, banquets @ United-21 is the ideal place for you. This place can accommodate a guest list of around 1,000 pax. On offer is are a variety of cuisines, conference facility, theme décor, games and DJ.

■ **29, LBS Marg, Gokul Nagar, Near Castle Mill Circle, Thane, Ph: 41579999,** banquets@united21.in

VITS Business Hotels

MULTI-CUISINE (SOUTH INDIAN, NORTH INDIAN, EUROPEAN, CHINESE)

Capacity: **Topaz:** 15 people; **Coral:** 25 people; **Ruby:** 25 people **Emerald:** 50 people; **Sapphire:** 140 people; **Crystal:** 200 people, **Roof top:** 300 people, **QDR:** 25 people,

Onyx 1: 25, **Onyx 2:** 25, **Onyx 3:** 30, **Big Onyx:** 70 (all in Theatre style).

■ **Andheri-Kurla Road, International Airport Zone, Andheri (E), Mumbai, Ph: 28270707, 61517555, 60017555**

Vivanta by Taj – President

MULTI-CUISINE (INDIAN, EUROPEAN, CHINESE)

Capacity: **PRESIDENTIAL BALLROOM — Theatre:** 425 people; **Classroom style:** 180 people; **U-shaped:** 75 people; **Boardroom:** 165 people; **Floating:** 475 people; **Round table:** 225 people.

CAPITAL & FORUM — Theatre: 80 people; **Classroom style:** 30 people; **U-shaped:** 30 people; **Boardroom:** 30 people; **Floating:** 70 people; **Round table:** 40 people.

ASSEMBLY — Theatre: 60 people; **Classroom style:** 25 people; **U-shaped:** 30 people; **Boardroom:** 30 people; **Floating:** 30 people; **Round table:** 80 people.

SENATE — Theatre: 40 people; **Classroom style:** 20 people; **U-shaped:** 22 people; **Boardroom:** 22 people; **Floating:** 50 people; **Round Table:** 35 people; **Poolside:** 150 people.

Terrace: 100–125 people.

■ **90, Cuffe Parade, Mumbai, Ph: 66650808**

Westin

MULTI-CUISINE (INDIAN, ASIAN, EUROPEAN)

Capacity: **Ground Level:** WESTIN GRAND BALLROOM — **Classroom style:** 216 people; **U-shaped:** 60 people; **Theatre:** 400 people; **Reception style:** 450 people; **Banquet Rounds:** 300 people; **Dinner Dance style:** 350 people.

WESTIN I&II — Classroom style: 105 people; **U-shaped:** 30 people; **Theatre:** 200 people; **Reception style:** 220 people; **Banquet Rounds:** 150 people; **Dinner Dance style:** 150 people.

PRE-FUNCTION AREA — Reception style: 180 people

WESTINGARDENS — **Reception style:** 350 people

CHAFA — Classroom style: 24 people; **U-shaped:** 20 people; **Theatre:** 60 people; **Reception style:** 60 people; **Banquet Rounds:** 40 people.

CHAFA I — Classroom style: 12 people; **Hollow Square:** 12 people; **U-shaped:** 16 people; **Theatre:** 20 people; **Reception style:** 36 people; **Banquet Rounds:** 20 people; **Boardroom style:** 12 people.

CHAFA II — Hollow Square: 8 people; **U-shaped:** 8 people; **Theatre:** 20 people; **Reception style:** 20 people; **Banquet Rounds:** 10 people.

MOGRA — Classroom style: 24 people; **Hollow Square:** 20 people; **U-shaped:** 20 people; **Theatre style:** 60 people;

Reception style: 60 people; **Banquet Rounds:** 40 people; **Boardroom style:** 18 people.

MOGRA I — Classroom style: 12 people; **U-shaped:** 12 people; **Theatre:** 20 people; **Reception style:** 36 people; **Banquet Rounds:** 20 people.

MOGRA II — Classroom style: 8 people; **Hollow Square:** 8 people; **U-shaped:** 8 people; **Theatre:** 20 people; **Reception style:** 20 people; **Banquet Rounds:** 10 people.

TAMAN — Classroom style: 24 people; **Hollow Square:** 20 people; **U-shaped:** 20 people; **Theatre:** 60 people; **Reception style:** 60 people; **Banquet Rounds:** 40 people; **Boardroom style:** 18 people.

TAMAN I — **Classroom style:** 12 people; **Hollow Square:** 12 people; **U-shaped:** 12 people; **Theatre:** 20 people; **Reception style:** 36 people; **Banquet Rounds:** 20 people.

TAMAN II — **Hollow Square:** 8 people; **U-shaped:** 8 people; **Theatre:** 20 people; **Reception style:** 20 people; **Banquet Rounds:** 10 people.

BOARDROOM — U-shaped: 14 people.

EXECUTIVE 1-4 — U-shaped: 8 people.

■ **International Business Park, Oberoi Garden City, Goregaon (E), Mumbai, Ph: 61470000, 67361101-04, 67361122,** www.starwoodhotels.com/westin

Woodland Retreat

MULTI-CUISINE (INDIAN, CHINESE)

Capacity: **Hall:** 250 people (sitting); 450–500 people (floating).

■ **Near Mulund Check Naka, LBS Marg, Thane (W), Mumbai, Ph: 25800088-89**

Zodiac

MULTI-CUISINE (INDIAN, CHINESE)

Capacity: **Hall:** 300 people.

■ **15, Brindaban, Poonam Nagar, Off Mahakali Caves Road, Andheri (E), Mumbai, Ph: 28346143, 28341708**

THE GREAT BAR GUIDE

- A Beginner's Guide to Champagne
- Wine? Cheers! My Introduction to Wine
- A Beginner's Guide to Beer
- A Beginner's Guide to Single Malts
- A Beginner's Guide to Cognac
- A Beginner's Guide to Sake
- A to Z of Wine Terms
- Setting up a Bar at Home
- Cocktail Recipes, Tips and Guidelines
- Eric Lobo's Cocktail Recipes
- Shatbhi Basu's Cocktail Recipes
- Mix of Recipes from Mumbai's Bars
- Wine-based Cocktails
- Shooters
- Pairing Indian Food with Wine
- Fine Wines for Profit and Pleasure — Wine as an Investment
- Music

A BEGINNER'S GUIDE TO CHAMPAGNE

I raise a toast (with sensuous bubbles, of course!) and present to you "A Beginner's Guide to Champagne". I get cheeky and ask the most obvious questions... only to get you the answers from the most knowledgeable, respected and charming sources of all. From the direct descendant of the Moët & Chandon family, Jean Berchon, Brand Ambassador, Moët & Chandon, the world's leading Champagne house, synonymous with fine Champagne since 1743 and with its own vineyards in the Champagne district of France.

The charming Frenchman's passion for Champagne bubbles as he along with the knowledgeable and dapper Gaurav Bhatia, Director, Marketing, Moët Hennessy India take me lyrically through the art and science of Champagne drinking — starting with the popping of the Champagne.

HOW TO SERVE?

"The ideal way to chill your champagne is to put it in a ice bucket. The trick is to do 50% water and 50% ice up to its neck. 30 minutes should do it. For an extra kick of chill, you can add some salt in the ice water and you will see your bottle chill down even faster!" say the gentlemen. But if that's not practical, place the bottle in the refrigerator 24 hours prior to serving.

Here is the best way to open a bottle of Champagne: remove the foil and wire, keeping your thumb firmly in place on the cork in case the bottle has been shaken and is itching to explode (Berchon's tip: Don't shake or move the bottle too much to prevent the Champagne from spraying all over). Now, cover the cork with a towel or cloth, grip this with one hand and with the other, turn the bottle, not the cork! Celebrate!

Serve in a flute-shaped glass to concentrate the flavour of the wine. Do not fill it to the top — pour only two-thirds of the glass. The drinking temperature should be 8-10 degrees.

HOW TO STORE?

Lay the bottles flat in a dark and cool place. If you have opened a bottle but are unable to finish it, you can put a resealer and store it in the fridge for two or three days. It's a good idea to refrain from keeping it in a fridge for more than six months to prevent it from getting too dry.

HOW TO TASTE?

"First... you must look at the glass and enjoy the ballet of bubbles, three hundred years of history bubbling in it," advises Jean Berchon. Then "nose" or smell it and take small sips. The most noteworthy quality of a good

Champagne is that it should be "crisp". "It should also be a mouthful, talk to your full palate," explains Berchon.

HOW TO PAIR CHAMPAGNE AND FOOD?

Champagne is easily drunk with a wide variety of cuisines including the spicy ones as it is well balanced, light, and elegant. It goes well with fish, poultry, and desserts too so long as they aren't too sweet (avoidable with ice cream, chocolate; light, fruity desserts work best).

WHY CHAMPAGNE?

Made with the cool climate-grown Chardonnay, Pinot Noir and Pinot Meunier grapes, the history of Champagne is as romantic as the drink itself but since we are short on space, I will be happy to share that with anyone who is really interested. Please send an e-mail to me.

TYPES OF CHAMPAGNE

- Brut Impérial implies a dry Champagne with a sugar content of 11-13gm/l;
- Rosé Impérial is a unique blend of Red Wines & White Wines that give it its unique, radiant & sensual colour.
- Nectar Impérial is the sweeter (40-45gm of sugar per litre) and more popular Champagne; the name of the category is Demi Sec
- Vintage is blended from grapes harvested in the same year.

DO'S AND DON'TS

- Don't call any beverage with bubbles Champagne. Champagne is a sparkling wine produced from grapes grown only in the Champagne region of France following rules that demand secondary fermentation of the wine in the bottle to create carbonation. Some use the term Champagne as a generic term for sparkling wine.
- Don't add anything to Champagne (ice, fruit, etc);
- Do hold the stem of the glass while drinking;
- Do not chill the glasses in the fridge as it kills the bubbles;
- Do rinse the Champagne glass well and ensure no washing liquid is left in it;
- Do remember that smaller bubbles in the Champagne indicate it's of a finer quality. This often implies longer ageing.
- Do remember Champagne is the perfect aperitif to begin your evening or a brunch with and that it is a wonderful wine that can be paired with meals.
- Do remember you don't always need a special occasion to open a bottle — the 'pop' of Champagne turns the ordinary to the celebratory in a flash!

As the book goes to press, Veuve Clicquot champagne honored Shobhaa De with a special Tribute by for her remarkable accomplishments in the field of writing and her contributions to the cultural landscape of India.

Speaking on the occasion, Gaurav Bhatia — Marketing Director for Veuve Clicquot in India said, "The perfect combination of boldness and elegance, Veuve Clicquot has been synonymous around the world with outstanding luxury and only one quality, the finest since 1772.
With this special recognition, Mrs. De remarked, "I believe there is a little bit of Madame Clicquot in every woman. It is her unique spirit of audacity and gutsiness that defines this prestigious, international Award. I feel deeply honoured by the Tribute. To me, quite simply: an empowered woman equals an empowered world. By honouring me, Veuve Clicquot has honoured the half- a - billion women of India. Here's to the spirit of female entrepreneurship and success. "

WINE? CHEERS!
MY INTRODUCTION TO WINE

Your attention, please! What follows is the single-most, enjoyable introduction to wine that you are ever going to read. It's honest, to the point and (here's the best part) it has been shared by an internationally well-known twosome. Ch'ng Poh Tiong is the publisher of South-East Asia's oldest wine magazine, The Wine Review, the regional Chairman of the UK Decanter's magazine World Wine Awards, a judge of wine around the world and an international speaker on the subject.

So you can imagine my delight when I attend a French wine and food pairing session conducted by him. It is witty and down-to-earth, takes the mystery and intimidation out of wine-drinking and quite clearly points out that wine-drinking is all about "yum and yuck". If you like it , it is "yummy" and if you don't, it is "yucky".
Over to Ch'ng Poh Tiong...

UNRAVELLING THE MYSTIQUE AND MYSTERY OF WINE

I have never come across something as a snobbish bottle of wine. Only wine snobs who masquerade as wine lovers! It's a con job because these people do not take wine seriously. On the contrary, it's only themselves that they take seriously. Sure, wine is special and interesting but it is never excluding. Wine has always been made for family and friends to gather around to have a good time.

WHY WINE?

In the very first place, don't drink wine unless you enjoy it! Don't drink it if you don't like the taste but because it's the "in" thing to do. Unless, of course, you are a masochist. If, on the other hand, you enjoy wine and want to learn more, there's no substitute to investing in a good, reliable book (Hugh Johnson, Jancis Robinson and Steven Spurrier) or subscribing to a magazine (it's too presumptuous to suggest my own The Wine Review, but the Decanter from the UK is great).

HOW TO PAIR WINE WITH FOOD?

If you are thirsty, and I were to offer you mango or lime juice, which one would you choose? Lime Juice will be the drink of choice because it is refreshing, dry, and acidic. Mango Juice, on the other hand, is sweet, flabby, rich, and thick. My analogy here is to suggest to you that a dry, acidic, crisp white wine is more refreshing than a full-bodied, overly-oaked white Chardonnay. And that refreshing White Wine will pair better with deep-fried foods like pakodas and dim sums. The okay white Chardonnay pairs well with Salmon and Japanese food.

HOW TO STORE?

Storing wine is a big problem in hot climate. If you cannot re-create a special cellar or get a customized wine fridge, store all your wines in the domestic fridge. Enjoy them straight out of the fridge. Warm up only the Red Wine to room temperature.

DOS AND DON'TS

- Don't tell a guest how much the bottle of wine costs you (unless you want to show off how crass you are.)
- Don't "Bottoms Up" with wine.
- Do not add ice or water to any wine.

A BEGINNER'S GUIDE TO BEER

"Beer is living proof that God wants us to be happy," said Benjamin Franklin. There are plenty of people who echo his sentiment. It may have started as "beer and barbecue" but we've happily adapted it and altered it to "beer and biryani" and "beer and bhelpuri". I attended the Oktoberfest in Munich and revelled in the wealth of beer in its homeland. The House of Budweiser shares with us some interesting notes on how to sniff, sip, swallow, and taste beer...

HOW TO POUR?

Pouring beer properly allows the carbon trapped in the bottle after fermentation to escape, carrying the beer's aroma up to your nose. It produces a tight and proper head of foam and enhances the beer's flavour. Here's how:

- Start with a beer-ready glass. Clean the glass with mild soap and rinse well with warm water. Dry the glass with a clean, lint-free towel. Pouring beer into an improperly cleaned glass can create flat beer or a false head that dissipates rapidly and can cause bubbles to stick to the side of the glass or an off taste.
- Remove the cap from the bottle.
- Place the glass on a flat surface. Begin pouring the beer by placing either the neck of the bottle or the lip of the can over the edge of the clean glass.
- Quickly raise the bottom of the bottle or can to high angle, causing the beer to agitate into the glass.
- Lower the bottom of the bottle or can to reduce the flow until the head rises to the rim of the glass.
- Wipe away any of the head that might run over the rim of the glass with a cotton towel.

HOW TO TASTE?

Tasting beer isn't fussy or formal. It's just a matter of paying attention to three basic components: The beer's scent, or "nose", its taste, and its body or weight. Start with perfectly clean glasses, matched to the type of beer and begin sniffing and sipping.

SNIFF!

The first step in tasting is to use your nose. The scent of beer has two components, aroma and bouquet. Aroma is derived from the toastiness of malt, while bouquet describes scents caused by fermentation, such as the banana-like scent of some wheat beers.

Floral: Floral aromas are frequently derived from hops, which impart a complex range of scents, and are especially common in pilsners.

Fruity: Fruity aromas, as in citrusy pale ales, are derived from hops. Fruity bouquets stem from esters created in fermentation and are common in ales, stouts, and doppelbock.

Grassy: As well as contributing fruity and floral notes, hops contribute grassy aromas to beer, characterized by a fresh, "green" scent or a herbal quality.

Toasty: Malt, especially if darkly roasted, contributes this rounded, rich aroma, found most prominently in brown ales, stouts and dark lagers.

Yeasty: It is a complex, sometimes bready aroma that may accompany hints of fruitiness; yeastiness is more predominant in ales than in most lagers.

SIP!

The next step is to take a sip. Roll the beer in your mouth, so that it hits all your taste buds, and consider what sensations you perceive.

Fruity: Fruit flavours in beer convey a light tartness; examples include the lemony, citrusy taste of wheat beers and the cidery notes of lambics.

Roasted/malty: These flavours come from beer's main ingredient, malted barley, and may range from bready to deeply chocolaty. They leave a sweet impression.

Spicy/hoppy: The characteristic note contributed by hops is a spicy edge, found particularly in heavily hopped beers, such as pale ales, bitters and porters.

Sweet: Although most beers are fermented until dry, some, like barley wine, have residual sugars. In other beers, such as cream stouts, sugar may be added.

SWALLOW!

As you swallow beer, assess its body or weight, textural qualities linked to its alcohol level, carbonation, and density. Is the beer rich and mouth-filling, clean, and refreshing, or is it somewhere in-between?

Light bodied: Light-bodied beers like German pilsners, some wheat beers, many Americans lagers and ordinary bitter, leave a clean finish after swallowing.

Medium bodied: Weightier on the palate, medium-bodied beers include pale and brown ales, porters, American premium lagers and amber lagers.

Full bodied: Rounded, mouth-filling, and sometimes creamy-textured, full-bodied beers may be higher in alcohol. Examples include stouts, extra-special bitter, dark lagers and some bocks.

HOW TO PAIR BEER AND FOOD?

Whether you are grilling in the backyard or dining with guests, beers seem to fit in with the way Americans cook and entertain today. It partners naturally with food and its varied flavours can be matched to any menu, as long as you keep the principle of balance in mind.

To understand why a particular beer pairs well with an arrangement of food flavours, take time to taste the beer carefully and appreciate its nuances. A process for savouring beer flavours described above will give you a deeper understanding of the beer and enable you to seek the right balance with the food.

Anheuser-Busch's brew masters and chefs find balance by looking for either contrasting or complementing flavours in the food.

TYPES OF BEER

What's the difference between an ale and a lager? Why was beer served at Oktoberfest traditionally made in March? Upgrade your knowledge on beers by reading the glossary entries listed below.

Ale: Beer produced using warm (65°F) top fermentation, in which the yeast rises to the surface. Many ales use roasted malts, lending them a dark colour and full flavour, as well as plenty of hops. Types include malty British ale and English brown ale, hoppy American ale, pale ale and Belgian ales such as Trappist and abbey ales.

Amber: Describes a copper-brown or reddish tone found in certain lagers and ales. Amber beers are typically in aroma and may have a hint of sweetness.

American ale: Ales made in America come in a range of styles, including American brown ale, which is generally hoppier than its English counterpart; pale ale, which is quite hoppy and may have a fruity aroma; and amber ales.

American lager: Clean, crisp, and more carbonated than European lagers, American lagers and premium lagers are mild, with low hopping, and are known for smooth drinkability. Premium lagers are distinguished by their more flavourful, full-bodied character and often have a deeper colour than other American lagers. Still deeper in colour are American amber lagers, which also have a slightly maltier aroma and dark lagers. American lagers may use adjunct grains, such as corn or rice, in addition to barley.

Barley: The basic grain used in brewing, barley is malted before use. Brewers use two types, defined by the number of kernels on the stalk: Two-row barley, which results in a smooth, sweet brew; and six-row barley, which contributes crispness.

Barley wine: A sweet, high-alcohol speciality beer that uses wine or Champagne yeast and offers a fruity and malty flavour profile. Barley wines may range in colour from copper to dark brown.

Beer: The first-known alcoholic beverage, beer is brewed from malted barley (and sometimes other grains), fermented with yeast and flavoured with hops. Beer may be categorized into two lagers and ales.

Bitter: Traditionally English ale made with low carbonation. It is typically highly hopped. Usually served at room temperature, bitter comes in three styles: hoppier special, full-bodied and malty, extra-special bitter.

Bock: A sweet, often dark lager that originated in Germany as a seasonal beer served in spring. Types include malty traditional bock; pale, hoppier Helles bock; and sweet, strong, deeply-coloured doppelbock.

Golden ale: Also sometimes creamy ale, this crisp, floral, light-golden style of ale, which is commonly brewed in Canada, shares many floral characteristics with lagers.

Hops: The flowering hop vine produces cone-shaped

blossoms that add a unique aroma and spice to beer and have been used for centuries as a preservative and flavouring agent. Hops are grown in Germany and in North-west America and render the beer a "hoppy" characteristic. Brewers blend different varieties of hops to attain the desired flavour and aroma profile for their beers.

Ice beer: Crisp, clean-tasting ice beers are made using a distinctive process in which ice crystals are formed in the beer and then removed, resulting in a smoother taste.

India pale ale: Originally developed with a high alcohol content and heavy hopping to survive the sea voyage from Britain to colonial India, pale ale is now brewed the world over.

Lager: Beer produced using cold (45°F) bottom fermentation, in which the yeast settles at the bottom after fermentation. There are many styles of lager, but the best known are pale in colour and crisp in flavour, with mild hops character. Lager means "to store" in German, and lager beers are aged for a period of time in lager tanks at low temperatures. Many lagers are pale in colour and crisp in flavour, but their colour and flavour can range from the snappy, crisp qualities of American lagers to hoppy European pilsners and rounder, dark lagers and bocks.

Lambic: A Belgian-style of beer, often fermented with fruit, lambics are distinguished by using open-tank fermentation and wild yeasts, resulting in a sharp, tart, fruity-flavour profile. They use both malted barley and unmalted wheat in brewing; fruit lambics typically feature cherries or raspberries.

Light lager: An American style of low-calorie beer that is extremely pale, with light body, high carbonation and a mild and smooth flavour.

Maerzen/Oktoberfest: Before the advent of refrigeration, beers were necessarily made seasonally. Originally, lager served at Oktoberfest had been made in March (Maerzen is German for March) from new malt and aged until October, to be served at harvest festivals. Traditional Maerzen is golden brown in colour, with a balanced maltiness and hoppiness. Today, Oktoberfest lagers range from golden to red-brown.

Malt: Barley that has been soaked in water, germinated and then kiln-dried is known as malt. It contributes a characteristic sweet, "malty" flavour to beer. Malt may be roasted to varying degrees; the darker the malt, the darker the beer.

Pale ale: A light-coloured, hoppy ale with medium body and little maltiness. English pale ales are typically very hoppy and spicy, whereas the pale-to-light copper American pale ales feature American-style hopping and a fruity bouquet. Similar but slightly darker and maltier in character are American amber ales.

Pilsner: A classic European type of pale lager, German pilsners tends to be very pale lagers worldwide. Bohemian pilsners, which take their name from the town of Plzen, are slightly darker and balance the hoppy and malty characters.

Porter: An extremely dark ale made from heavily roasted

malt, porter may range from sweet to very hoppy. This style of beer originated in London and is medium bodied with a crisp finish.

Speciality beers: Also called flavoured beers, many brewers add fruit, vegetable or spice flavours, ranging from pumpkin to Chile peppers, to their brews. Some of these, such as fruits, may be added as an adjunct in fermentation; others may be added after brewing. A traditional German beer, Rauchbier, is smoke-flavoured by smoking some of the malt.

Steam beer: A style originating in 19th-century California. As ice was unavailable, lager yeasts were fermented at the warmer temperatures typically used for ales, resulting in a beer with both ale- and lager-like flavours.

Stout: Distinguished by the use of unmalted, darkly roasted barley among its grains, stout tends to be low in hops, with malty and caramel aromas. Styles include dry Irish stout, sweet or cream stout and oatmeal stout.

Strong beer: Beers with more than 6 per cent alcohol by volume are generally referred to as strong beers. Any type of ale or lager can be brewed to this higher strength; some of the most common types of strong beers include doppelbocks, pale ales, stouts and porters.

Wheat beer: Found under several names — Weizen, Weissbier, or the popular Hefeweizen — these beers are made using wheat as part of the grain profile. They tend to be refreshing, pale in colour, and highly carbonated, with fruity flavours and little hoppiness.

BEGINNER'S GUIDE TO SINGLE MALTS

I got my first formal introduction to this "water of life" in its birthplace. It was at the celebration of Chivas Regal's 200 years in Leith, Scotland, that I learnt all about single malts and blended Scotch whiskies. The dedication and devotion to whisky borders on religious fervour: it is not to be dismissed lightly. Especially for single malts. And so from Scotland's The House of Banffshire's The Glenlivet come tips and guidelines on ways to nose and taste whisky. Should you drink it neat or with water? Read on and find out more...

A single-malt Scotch whisky is the product of one specific distillery and has not been mixed with whisky from any other distillery. The greatest concentration of malt whisky distilleries can be found in the Speyside region of North-east Scotland, with Highland, Lowland, Campeltown and Islay being the other main malt whisky-producing zones. Each of these regions has its own particular distinctive style of malt whisky and although it is not possible for two malts to be identical — even if the distilleries that produce them happen to stand side by side — it is usually possible to distinguish in which region of Scotland a particular whisky was made. This is not such an accurate statement nowadays as styles are very diverse across the country but a good place to start for beginners.

BLENDED MALT SCOTCH WHISKY

A vatted malt will contain a number of malt whiskies that have been skilfully blended together or "married", to create a consistent whisky with its own distinct, identifiable character. Such a malt can also consist entirely of single malt whiskies of various ages from the same distillery. However, blended malts will never contain any grain whisky.

A single-grain whisky is the product of one-grain distillery and is usually made from wheat, corn or unmalted barley. There are about eight operating grain distilleries in Scotland, the majority being in Central Scotland with the exception of Invergordon in the northern highlands and Girvan in the far south. There are of course, more grain distilleries, which are now either closed or mothballed.

In the production of malt Scotch whisky the basic raw materials are limited and consist of barley, water, and yeast.

HOW IS IT PREPARED?

The entire process of preparation comprises five stages:

- Malting, which converts barley to malt
- Mashing, which produces wort (sugar solution) from ground or crushed malt
- Maturation, which transforms the new make spirit into whisky.

In two of the above stages, the malster is concerned with the behaviour of living organisms. In malting, these organisms control germination of the barley corn and in fermentation, yeast acts when placed in a solution rich in fermentable sugars and growth factors. All living organisms are susceptible to conditions of their environment and many of the distiller's problems arise from there.

Every single-malt distillery produces its own distinctly flavoured whisky depending upon its location, water source, type of barley, size, and shape of the stills and style of maturation. As a result, two distilleries 500 yards apart in the same region can produce entirely different malts. Single malts in Scotland vary according to the regions in which they are produced.

Lowland Malts are generally found in a line running from Greenock to Dundee, and include the major urban areas of Edinburgh, Glasgow, and the South. Overall, this style of whisky lacks a signature subtle delicate aroma. Their light, and sometimes sweet and more delicate character makes them popular for use in blending.

Island Malts can be recognized by their peaty smell. The taste is an acquired one and perhaps best exemplified by Laphroaig and Lagavulin. If they originate from Jura or Mull, there can be a hint of saltiness, even a kippery flavour in the after taste.

Highland Malts come from one of the most beautiful areas of Scotland, where a gentle blend of altitude and mountain water imparts a depth of flavour and quality.

Speyside Malts are acknowledged as perhaps the most outstanding of the single malts. Classic malts, such as Aberlour are the result of a combination of natural elements that have set the region apart from all others.

Each natural constituent along with every man-made vessel contributes to the final taste of Scotland's individual single malts. Some are more fortunate than others in their choice of water and location. When this is combined with the dedication of the distiller and careful and generous patience of the proprietor, the result will delight the most discerning palate. To find it and to taste it is to appreciate the art of single-malt whisky-making.

HOW TO TASTE?

It should be noted that there is no "right" or "wrong" way to drink Scotch whisky. It is very much down to a question of personal taste. However, let us offer a few basic suggestions especially for those interested in pursuing the pleasures of "nosing" and "tasting".

Many who drink Scotch whisky neat say they do not want to spoil the taste by adding water. However, an equal number will say that adding a touch of water, particularly if it is pure, soft spring water, (ideally the same spring water used in the making of the particular whisky!) serves to enhance the distinctive aroma and flavour of a whisky. Tap water may contain high amounts of chlorine and therefore would not complement any whisky. Your best bet is to opt for bottled Scottish mineral whisky!) serves to enhance the distinctive aroma and flavour of a whisky. Tap water may contain high amounts of chlorine and therefore would not complement any whisky. Your best bet is to opt for bottled Scottish mineral water!

Adding ice to a whisky can provide a refreshing drink but it should be noted that it will dull the fine taste and wonderful aromas and so should never be contemplated when conducting a "whisky nosing and tasting" session. Similarly, carbonated water is not an ideal accompaniment for whisky as it will also interfere with the aromas.

The addition of mixers such as ginger ale, soda, and even cola is a popular trend. (Disagree, long drinks are very effective and recommended way to drink scotch whisky.)

"NOSING" AND "TASTING"

The sense of smell is one of the most sophisticated of all the senses, and the pleasure that can be gained from "nosing and tasting" the many wonderful and varied Scotch whiskies available is an experience that should be treasured. This is particularly true if it is experienced in a convivial atmosphere with a group of friends — old or new.

A BEGINNER'S GUIDE TO COGNAC

Mention the word and cognac lovers will wax lyrical. They will say that cognac is at once a place, a drink, and a state of mind. However, the place is simply described: it's the region surrounding the town of the same name, the only region in France entitled to bestow the name "cognac" on the unique style of brandy it produces. The oldest of the great cognac houses (founded in 1715 in the Charente region by Jean Martell) shares its tips and information with us.

By 1721, Martell was already exporting more than 2,00,000lt of cognac to the United Kingdom. By 1868, Martell cognacs could be found as far afield as China, Japan, and Hong Kong. Then, in 1912, Edouard Martell kept the family tradition going by creating Cordon Bleu, which today has become a classic amongst the truly great cognacs. Martell is today a part of the Pernod Ricard Group.

HOW TO SERVE?

The best way to drink cognac is from a Brandy Balloon or from a Brandy Snifter, where the lip just curls inwards. This helps preserve the aroma and the initial bouquet. It is ideally drunk on its own or mixed with warm water in equal quantities.

HOW TO TASTE?

Hold the base of the glass and allow the palm of your hand to impart a little warmth to the spirit. Swirl for 30 seconds, sniff, inhale and just lace it around the top part of the tongue to get the slightly woody and crispy feel. You can feel the smoothness as it flows down.

HOW TO STORE?

Similar to whisky, cognac can be stored upright as it is a finished product inside the bottle. However, it needs to be stored in cool place away from sunlight. Cognac is served at room temperature and does not require refrigeration.

GOOD COGNAC VS BAD COGNAC

Initially, check for the Appellation d'Origine Contrôlée. This would mean that the cognac has been made as per standard norms, which have been set historically and have only improved over time.

APPELLATION D'ORIGINE CONTRÔLÉE

All cognacs must be produced in strict accordance with the conditions set out in the 1909 decree governing the Appellation d'Origine Contrôlée. Across centuries, Martell has developed and perpetuated its know-how and tradition at each stage of the cognac-making process. This gives it the unique Martell taste.

HOW IS IT PREPARED?

The Wine: The raw material for cognac is the grape. It is important to select the best wines for distillation. The quality of wines should be excellent because some of them will become 100-year-old eaux-de-vie (spirits).

Double Distillation: The wine is distilled using a technique dating back to the 5th century. It has to be distilled twice in Charentais alembics or pot stills to extract the eaux-de-vie or quintessence of the wine. After the distillation process, the so-called Heads and Tails are again distilled with the wine. This distillation process, a Martell specificity, gives a particularly delicate, smooth and lighter eaux-de-vie.

Ageing: Once distillation is over, the eaux-de-vie ages in oak barrels stored in chais or warehouses — for a minimum of two years. These barrels are handmade by coopers. Martell uses only fine-grained Tronçais-type oak, which gives a mellower, lighter and more fragrant eaux-de-vie. During the ageing process, the eaux-de-vie is enhanced by compounds from the wood; it becomes concentrated by the evaporation effect, and over time, acquires its amber colour and its aromas.

The Art of Blending: The next step is to combine the eaux-de-vie to create cognac. Each cognac is a specific blend of eaux-de-vie from different years and different crus or growth areas.

Only the best growth areas — Borderies, Grande Champagne, Petite Champagne, and Fins Bois — are used to make Martell cognacs. Martell has always favoured a predominance of eaux-de-vie from the Borderies area in its blends: they confer finesse, lightness, and a matchless floral character. The combination of these growth areas gives cognac a richness, complexity and balance.

The Cellar Master's Role: The cellar master is the person who judiciously selects and blends the various eaux-de-vie and ensures the unique quality and consistency.

Serving Suggestions: Purists will say either neat or with a splash of water and/or ice. But cognac styles such as VS or VSOP (eg, younger eaux-de-vie) blend beautifully with fruit juices to make mouth-watering cocktails; the Maison Martell is a new trend-setting favourite.

First club of its kind in the country. Join the club! It's absolutely free. The Japanese Consul-General Hagiuda inaugurated the Sake Club of India spearheaded by Harry Cheng. All sake buffs are rejoicing. And there are plenty in Mumbai and even as I write this, their tribe is increasing! More and more foodies are getting excited about Japanese food and sushi as they are about the Japanese wine.

WHAT IS THE TRADITION OF SAKE?

The world of sake combines an age-old tradition in Japan, bringing together the spiritual, the mysterious and the magical. The magic of Japanese food is exciting the palates of gourmet Indians, and as the boom of Japanese food is ignited, so is the keen interest in sake.

Japanese sake has played a long and distinguished role in the evolution of Japanese tradition and culture. Sake reflects the appreciation of the Japanese for the ebb and flow of the seasons and is enjoyed and shared among friends.

WHAT IS THE HISTORY OF SAKE?

Many ancient records mention sake. Sake production, using rice and koji, or malted rice, is considered to have begun between 300 and 200 BC. Given its long history, it is no surprise that sake-brewing evolved to take on local and regional variations. Different regions developed their own distinctive types of sake traditions that are faithfully carried on today.

WHY SAKE?

Japanese sake is perhaps unique in the world, in that it is delicious both when warmed and chilled. Sake can be enjoyed across a wide range of temperatures, anywhere between 5 degrees and 55 degrees Celsius. Moreover, Japanese law strictly defines the ingredients and production methods acceptable for making sake. Unlike wine, sake doesn't contain anti-oxidizing agents such as sulfites, or any other additive or preservative. Moreover, even in this modern age, much of the sake production process is done by hand. The type of rice used and the degree to which the rice grains are milled both affect the personality of the resulting sake, carefully nurtured in the hands-on production process.

HOW IS IT MADE?

Although sake is defined as a brewed alcoholic beverage, the brewing process is more complex than that employed for beer and wine. In the wine-production process, the crushed grapes ferment naturally after yeast is added. In the case of beer, similarly, fermentation takes place after yeast and hot water are added to crushed malt. But the rice used to make sake does not begin to ferment with the addition of yeast alone.

Sake brewing begins with the introduction of koji, which breaks down rice starch into glucose in a process known as saccharification. Next, sake yeast is added and fermentation begins. This process, in which saccharification and fermentation take place in the same vat at the same time, is called multiple parallel fermentation. This is a unique feature of sake brewing that distinguishes it from every other brewing process.

The longer fermentation process — which can be as much as three to four times that of wine — produces a wide variety of amino acids, giving sake a balanced, rounded taste and fresh flavour.

WHAT IS KOJI?

Koji are microbes that are good for the health, similar to those used in blue cheese production. Shouyu (soya sauce) and miso (soyabean paste) are also produced using similar beneficial microbes.

BREWING

Controlling the complex sake-brewing process requires intuition as well as knowledge of special techniques. For this reason, every sake maker has its own brewery master, known as toji. The toji manages not only the sake-brewing process but also the activities of his brewing team, including their work shifts and living arrangements. Maintaining a good team spirit is essential to sake brewing. The toji lives at the work site as long as he is in control of the brewing process. When he grows old, he appoints a hand-picked successor, to whom he has passed on his brewing know-how and techniques.

HOW TO SERVE WARM?

Enjoyable either warmed or chilled to complement the season, traditional Japanese sake can be savoured across a wide range of temperatures. The different temperatures provide a changing array of flavours for the palate to appreciate. Warmed sake is rather unusual in the world of alcoholic beverages, but it has a long history. Drinking warmed sake spread from the aristocracy to the common people during the middle of the Tokugawa period (1600-1867), when the drinking of sake itself became popular with the masses. The real pleasure of drinking warmed sake is in savouring the complexity of the rice-derived flavour brought out by the heating. Heating enhances the impact of naturally occurring glutamic and saccinic acids, imbuing the sake with a pleasant mellowness. Warmed sake aids in digestion and is mild on the body. It is a drink to warm the hearts of those who share a glass.

HOW TO SERVE COLD?

When chilled, sake is known as Reishu, and when drunk at room temperature, it is called Hiya. In general, sake types such as freshly pressed Namazake or the cloudy

Nigorizake, and highly fragrant premium sakes are best enjoyed as Hiya or Reishu. A temperature change of just a single degree can cause subtle changes in the flavour and aroma of a sake, demonstrating the depth and complexity of this ancient drink. Sampling sake at different temperatures to find a favourite flavour is yet another way to enjoy sake.

THE A TO Z OF WINE TERMS

In 30 years of journalism, Vinod Advani has written over 1,000 articles on travel, wine, music, and health. Vinod is also a radio jockey on Mumbai's popular FM Rainbow since 1993. For many years he worked in advertising and now, Vinod represents the State of South Australia in the capacity of Tourism Ambassador. Vinod travels the world and distils for us the A to Z of wine terms.

Romance. Magic. Poetry. These are the words that my mind associates with wine. To some, it may connote fermented grape juice. That much is true. To others, it may mean a healthy way of getting high. That is true too. But, pause for a moment and think. A grape on a vine. A single grape by weight, 75 per cent pulp, 20 per cent skin and 5 per cent seeds. The pulp is the soft thing that finally becomes wine. So simple and yet so very complex. How to get that perfect balance of alcohol, acid, tannins, fruitiness and sweetness or dryness!

Now think about this: Vit is the Latin root of the word viticulture. Vit is also the source of Vita, life itself. How fitting. And how amazing that there are certain places on our planet where grapes and earth are transformed into thrilling wine!

India too is experiencing the romance of wine; exploring the different oaked tastes of a Chardonnay from France, California or Australia; and sipping with delight the fleshy flavours of a Barossa valley Shiraz . For those adventurous ones, here is a brief guide to help you along. And to play wine connoisseur when the occasion demands. Santé.

GLOSSARY OF WINE TERMS:

Accessible: The wine is approachable. Its flavours and feel are balanced. Also when it is ready to drink.

Aftertaste: The lingering flavours and impressions of a wine.

Aroma: What your nose senses first. Smells in the bouquet, specially those associated with the grape.

Attack: First sensations on palate/nose — pungent, aggressive, quiet and so on.

Backbone: When the wine has taste and power and is neither flabby nor insipid.

Balance: A desirable attribute. When the wine's chief constituents — alcohol, acid, tannin and fruit — are in harmony.

Bead: The bubbles you see in sparkling wine or Champagne. Fine beads are formed.

Botrytis Cinerea: When fungus strips grapes of water, thus raising relative sugar content. Also known as Noble Rot. In this condition, wine-makers can produce stunning dessert wines.

Brut: Very dry Champagnes and sparkling wines.

Corked: When a wine's flavours have been tainted by the cork. Fungal and bacterial infections from the cork damage the wine. In a restaurant, a corked wine should be rejected and returned immediately.

Crisp: When the wine is refreshing and tarty.
Dessert Wine: General term for a wine that is sweet and, as such, could accompany, or be, a dessert. There are many ways of making dessert wines. Two of the world's most famous dessert wines, French Sauternes and German Trockenbeerenauslesen, came from grapes that are infected with the noble rot Botrytis Cinerea (described above).
Dry: Used to describe any wine that doesn't contain significant grape sugar, less than 0.2 per cent. A wine can be dry and taste fruity at the same time.
Earthy: Usually positive, wine showing its origins from soil, minerals, damp leaves, mushrooms and so on.
Esters: Scents and smells, usually generated by alcohols and acids in wine. A wine can be described as "estery" when these characteristics are prominent.
Fat: Big, full, ample in the mouth.
Fleshy: Very positive, meaning a wine is well-fleshed out with warm texture and grape flavours.
Gravelly: With suggestions of minerally, earthy quality; also firm texture.
Grip: Often almost literally, gripping, firm on palate. Acid, tannin, alcohol are contributors.
Hollow: Empty of substance, flavours on palate; dumb, retiring.
Hot: When the alcohol leaves a burning sensation in finish.
Intensity: Also concentration, no flab, plenty of driving flavour.
Isinglass: A gelatinous material, obtained from the air bladders of sturgeons and other fish, that is used in clarifying wine. It is not left in.
Leesy: Lees look like custard lying at the bottom of barrels, tanks. They are the taste-imparting dead yeast cells. The longer the wine is "on its lees", the more richness and flavour it should absorb.
Lively: Wine with bounce, the mix of fruit and other flavours refreshing on the palate.
Mousse: Froth or foam in sparkling wines. Usually refers also to quality, size and effervescence of the bubbles.
New World Wine Style: A loose term. Generally meant to include the accessible, bold and often uninhibitedly fruity wines of America, Australia, Chile, Argentina, India and so on.
Palate: What you feel on your tongue. The flavour, taste, texture.
Porty: Heavy, overdone — sometimes, over-ripe.
Rough: When a wine feels like your throat is being sand papered.
Structure: A vague wine-tasting word, usually referring to acid, tannin and alcohol make-up; as in "it has the structure to age" means that these principal preservatives are in place.
Supple: Very desirable friendly, refined texture, and flavours.
Tannin: A vital preservative in wine, which derives from grape skins, necessary for a wine's longevity. No Red Wine matures into a great one without some tannin.

Texture: The tactile "feel" in the mouth — hard, acidic, smooth, velvety and so on.

Toasty: Frequently used term for barrel-fermented and aged wines. After some years in bottle, a toasty aspect develops to enrich a quality wine.

Unfiltered: Used to describe a wine that has not been filtered to clarify it. Wine-makers who believe that filtering strips wine of some flavours and texture may leave their wines unfiltered and may even label them as such.

Vitis: The genus of the plant kingdom to which grape vines belong. Within the genus Vitis, there are some sixty separate species. The most famous species — and the only one to have originated in Europe — is Vitis Vinifera, which includes all of the well-known wine grapes: Chardonnay, Pinot Noir, Cabernet Sauvignon.

Vegetal: Grassy, leafy, herby flavours or aromas.

Wood Fermented: When wines are stored or aged in oak barrels to add cedar or vanilla flavours.

Xynomavro: A well-known Red Wine grape from Greece.

Yeasty: In still wines, yeasty describes an aroma suggestive of the yeasts used in fermentation.

Yield: The measure of how much a vineyard produces. In general, very high yields are associated with low-quality wine, and low yields are associated with high-quality wine.

Zinfandel: The second-most, widely planted red grape in California. It's a versatile grape, can be made into White Wine, sweet Port-style Wine, dry Red Wine and even light Pink Wines!

SETTING UP A BAR AT HOME FOR STARTERS...

Here's an open invitation! Come, create excitement at home, get bar savvy as I distil for you some tried, tested and tasted tips. Excuse me if I get a bit carried away, but I really do believe that a bar is the stage for many a performance and this is a guide for the "home stage" and the "home bartender".

Do you agree with me when I say that the bartender is a psychologist and psychiatrist, rolled into one? He or she has to keep a finger on your pulse and know exactly what you want and serve up the right dose. Whether that makes any sense or not, I am sure you agree that making cocktails and mocktails at home can add a real zing to your evening!

HOME BAR BASICS

Here are some very basics to begin with.

I requested bar consultant Eric Lobo, who has not only worked with Indigo and Chateau Indage but has also consulted with Olive, Absolut Vodka, Mainland China group, Brittos and Goa and is currently setting up a large nightclub and fine-dining space in New Mumbai.

Here is his suggestion for the glasses you need to keep in your bar. You do not need to get all and you can get them from anywhere, but I have added names and phone number of wholesalers at the end of this note.

- **GLASSWARE**
  Hi-ball (200ml glass whisky, water; ₹156/doz)
  Collins (300ml glass for tall drinks; ₹156/doz)
  Brandy Balloon (200ml; ₹156/doz)
  Zombie (300ml, slick and tall; ₹350/doz)
  All-purpose Wine Glass (180ml glass for Sangria, wines; ₹156/doz)
  Liqueur Glass (₹144/doz)
  Shot Glass (60ml glass for shooters and slammers; ₹132/doz)
  Cocktail Glass (like a martini stemmed glass, 200ml; ₹156/doz)
  Rock or Old-fashioned Glass (200ml whisky on the rocks, ₹240/doz)
  Champagne Tulip (150ml, ₹240/doz).

- **LIQUORS**
  Gin, rum, brandy, white rum, vodka, whisky, and wine liqueurs

- **MIXERS**
  Lime juice, lime cordial, sugar syrup, rose syrup, khus syrup, orange squash, grenadine syrup, and kokum syrup

- **JUICES**
  Mango, pineapple, orange, tomato, cranberry, grape, grapefruit, and coconut water

- **OTHERS**
  Soft drinks, vanilla ice cream, and fresh cream

- **EQUIPMENT**
  Salt/pepper shakers, wine opener/bottle opener, glass water jug, glass decanters, stir sticks, chopsticks, ice pail, small refrigerator, cocktail shaker, glass or stainless steel mixing jar, peg measure, plastic juice pourers, carving knife, chopping board, blender cups, and hand blender.
  For bar equipment, Eric suggests you go down to Badshah Kulfi House (near Crawford Market). "On the pavement there, you can pick up imported muddlers, carving knives and boards at really reasonable rates," he says.

- **FOR GLASSWARE, CALL**
  Sariya Stores: Mr Ali, Ph: 22082314, 22066311, 9820229850
  Taheri Saifee Palace: Mr Mohammedali, Ph: 23422713, 23433961
  Arif of Sparkle: 9833150307

COCKTAIL RECIPES, TIPS AND GUIDELINES

GET STARTED...

Making cocktails is an art; it's like theatre. Of course, a good cocktail should be pleasing to the nose, eye, and palate. It should be a crescendo of colour and flavour and that's why I have requested the great bartenders of the city to share their recipes with us.

Interestingly, the word "cocktail" has many different origins. Legend ascribes it to a Mexican princess Xocti, another to race-goers who likened the mixing spoon to the tails of the non-thoroughbred horses and etymologically, it derives from "coquete" — a French recipe which contained a concoction of wine. Many a legend ascribes the origin of the word to an actual cock's tail. Interestingly, the first cocktail book — The Bon Vivant's Guide or How to Mix Drinks — was published in the 1860s by legendary bartender "Professor" Jerry Thomas. Harry Johnson's Illustrated Bartender's Manual is another landmark. Prohibition in the US made cocktails popular and alluring, and many of the world's favourite cocktails were invented before the 20th century had begun — Mint Julep, Daiquiri, Gin Fizz, Corpse Reviver, and Martini. Most owed their origin to the roaring 1920s.

While "Professor" Jerry Thomas was the pioneer, there was also the charming Harry Craddock, bartender at London's Savoy. Victor Bergeron (also known as Trader Vic), Johnny Brooks, well known for his charm and great personality and Martini with a twist of lemon, Guiseppe Cipriani (creator of Bellini), and the creator of the Bloody Mary at Harry's Bar in Paris — Fernand Pete Petiot. Let"s toast them all!

Let's hope you get inspired and primed up to produce some great masterpieces of your own. Here's a little help...

TIPS AND TECHNIQUES...

...that I've imbibed along the way, from bartenders, enthusiasts and experts.

- Do chill the glass before serving a cocktail. Place it in the freezer half an hour before use or fill with crushed ice, just before use. Throw away the ice when you make the drink.
- To give the glass a sugar-frosted look, dampen the rim of the pre-chilled glass with a slice of lemon and lip the rim into a saucer of castor sugar.
  Handle the glass by its stem or its bottom.
- Do not shake a fizzy drink.
- Always squeeze fresh juice just prior to the occasion and keep in the fridge. The fresher the juice, the better the cocktail will be.

Some cocktail terms you might come across are as follows:

Build: To pour the ingredients directly into the glass.

Mix: To pour the ingredients into the cone of an electric drink mixer and mix. Then strain into appropriate glass.
Shake: To pour the ingredients into a cocktail shaker with ice.
Stir: Put ice into a mixing glass, add the ingredients, stir for about 10 seconds until chilled and then pour into the appropriate glass.
Straight up: A drink that is mixed and served without ice.

- Do serve a cocktail immediately. If left standing around, it will separate.

INFUSED VODKAS

Make your own flavoured vodkas...

- Pop 15 star anise and 1 tbsp of saunf into a bottle. Keep it for a couple of days. Watch it deepen in colour and get aromatic in flavour. Drink it on the rocks.
- Make a Jeera Vodka (pop in 1½ tbsp jeera into the bottle) for your Bloody Mary.
- The Sindhi Vodka with strands of saffron and elaichi (15 elaichi and a dash of saffron) is very delicious too.
- For a spicy peppery taste, make the Three Peppercorn Vodka with pink, green, and black peppercorns (six peppercorns each).
- Take two jalapeños and one fresh green chilli and pop into a bottle of vodka for a spicy Bloody Mary.

FROZEN DELIGHTS

FROZEN LEMON

Even housewives can make this. It can be used as a base for any spirit and is equally refreshing sipped as a mocktail," points out Eric.

Ingredients: 15 ice cubes, crushed; 15 seedless nimbu slices; 4 tbsp sugar.

Method:

- Put into the mixer and blend.
- Add a few mint leaves while blending.

FROZEN LITCHI

Ingredients: 15 ice cubes, crushed; 150ml litchi crush.
Method: Blend in the mixer till frozen. Scoop into glass and top with litchi juice. Add spirit of choice.

GARNISHING YOUR COCKTAIL GLASS

Keep it simple and use pineapple, sweet lime, sour lime, oranges, cherries, and olives. Eric advises being creative and carving a beach girl out of cucumber or even a seahorse. "Combining colours, like the brilliant red of a cherry with the yellow of the sweet lime is always a good idea," he says.

ERIC LOBO'S COCKTAIL RECIPES

ERIC LOBO PH: 9870260409, 9819862621

Eric Lobo, talented mixologist and bar consultant, runs his own beverage academy BACCHUS (bacchus.co.in) in the World Trade Centre. He takes time off from his busy schedule to share his creations with us.

All these unusual creations serve one person only.

CAIPIROSKA

Ingredients: Wedges of 6 lemons (seedless); 7 mint leaves; 3 tbsp sugar; 60ml vodka.

Method:

- Pour all in a mixing jar with 4-5 crushed ice cubes.
- Muddle with wooden muddler.
- Use an old-fashioned glass for the purpose.

CARIBBEAN DAWN

Ingredients: 60ml pineapple juice; 5ml lime juice; 10ml grenadine; Sprite and soda for topping; 10ml orange squash

Method:

- Top the Tom Collins glass with ice cubes.
- Pour grenadine first, then orange squash, then lime.
- Pour pineapple juice and top with Sprite and soda
- Suggestions for Serving: Sweet lime slice dropped in the glass with cherries.

FRUIT PUNCH

Ingredients: 60ml orange juice; 60ml mango juice; 60ml pineapple juice

Method: Pour all in a Tom Collins glass with 3 cubes of ice and stir till chilled.

Garnish: 2 cherries passed through a straw, straw passed through a sweet lime and pineapple slice which sit on the rim of the glass.

Suggestions for Serving: Drop 15ml grenadine; float 15ml of cream or ice cream; fizz with soda.

HAWAIIAN ICED TEA

Ingredients: 40ml peach and apricot crush; 45ml Bacardi rum/gin/vodka.

Method:

- To the peach and apricot crush, add Bacardi, or gin or vodka.
- Squeeze lime, top the glass with ice and pour room temperature Iced Tea.

KIWI MARGARITA

Ingredients: 20ml lime juice; 30ml tequila; 10ml sugar syrup; 60ml kiwi pulp; 30ml Kiwi liqueur.

Method: Blend with three crushed ice cubes.

Suggestions for Serving: Pour into a cocktail glass rimmed with salt.

MANGO SIN

Ingredients: 180ml mango juice; 10ml fresh cream; 10ml khus.

Method:

- Stir in a glass jar with 4 cubes of ice.
- Pour into a hi-ball glass.

Suggestions for serving: Garnish with 2 cherries passed through a straw, a mint leaf stuck on the cherries which sit on the rim of the glass.

MARGARITA

Ingredients: 30ml tequila; 30ml lime juice; cointreau; 20ml sugar syrup.

Method:

- Blend in the mixer with 3-4 cubes of ice.
- Pour in a salt-rimmed cocktail glass. "Cheers!"

PERU PYALA

"This recreates that guava (peru) we used to eat in school with lal mirchi," says an excited Eric. "It is refreshing and chatpata."

Ingredients: 150ml guava juice; 4-5 dashes of tabasco sauce; 45ml vodka; 4 cubes of ice.

Method: Mix and shake into a salt-rimmed glass.

PINA COLADA

Ingredients: 90ml coconut water; 60ml white rum; 90ml tinned apple juice; 15ml fresh cream; 30ml Malibu.

Method: Blend in a mixer with 4 cubes of ice.

Glass: Tom Collins.

Suggestions for serving: Garnish with cherries passed through a straw; straw passed through a pineapple slice which sits on the rim of the glass.

SANGRIA

Ingredients: 1 bottle red wine; 100ml tequila; 1lt red grape juice; ½ bottle vermouth; ½ bottle sweet port; 100ml cointreau.

Method:

- Mix all ingredients together in a glass jar.
- Chop fruits like apples, pears, grapes, and pomegranate.
- Soak in the jar overnight and serve the next day.

VIRGIN PINA COLADA

Same as Pina Colada, only without the alcohol.

SHATBHI BASU'S COCKTAIL RECIPES

Shatbhi Basu, Master Mixologist and savant on all things spirited, has spent three decades pursuing her passion. An alumnus of IHM Mumbai, class of 1980, she started her career as a chef with the Centaur Hotel. Along the way, she founded India's first and most respected institute of bartending — STIR in 1999. Shatbhi consults in setting up and designing bar work areas, menus, and training in all aspects of bar operations.

Shatbhi is a consultant to some of the top beverage brands of the world, innovating and educating trade and consumers alike, having worked with brands like House of Johnnie Walker, Ciroc, Vat 69, Smirnoff, Jose Cuervo, Skyy, Campari, Cutty Sark and others. She conducts workshops on de-mystifying wine, scotch and single malt, world whiskies and more — reaching out to a wide group of people in a completely unpretentious style. Her irreverent approach and wit always leaves her audience thirsting for more!

Shatbhi also writes extensively in trade and mainstream press and has just finished three seasons of one of NDTV Good Times' most appreciated shows — "In High Spirits". She is currently working on two more shows for television, food and drink, and hopes to continue doing what she does best for as long as possible!

Surprisingly, she grins, recognition of her contribution to education in beverages came, not from the hospitality industry as one would have thought but from media (woman achievers) and even better, from consumers — The Rotary Club of Bombay Airport — Vocational Excellence Award 2009-2010 for permanently raising the bar of a career in hospitality.

She shares with us the recipes of the Classical and Contemporary hits.

Shatbhi Basu
Ph: 9820220424; 022-24451033
stiracademy@gmail.com;
shatbhibasu@gmail.com
www.shatbhibasu.com

Here are some classical and contemporary recipes from Shatbhi Basu's; STIR, the Academy of Bartending…

APPLE PIE MOJITO

Ingredients: 45ml spiced rum; 6 lime wedges; 4/5 slice of apple;10ml Monin/Teisseire Cinnamon syrup; 10 mint leaves; Appy Fizz to top; 2 cinnamon sticks.

Method:

- Squeeze and drop lime wedges into glass.
- Tear mint leaves over the lime and cinnamon. Muddle.
- Fill the glass with crushed ice. Add spice rum, cinnamon syrup and stir.
- Top with more crushed ice and top with Appy Fizz.

Glass: Collins.

Garnish: Slice of apples.

BLONDE SANGRIA

Ingredients: Cut fruits (litchi, kiwi, pineapple, strawberries, green apple); 375ml chilled white wine; 75ml citrus vodka — to soak fruits; Sprite and Appy Fizz or apple juice.

Method:

- Soak all the fruits in citrus vodka overnight.
- Add the soaked fruits and ice in the pitcher.
- Fill with white wine and top it up with Sprite and Appy Fizz half-and-half.

Glass: Pitcher, AP wine5

BLUE COSMO ON THE ROCKS

Ingredients: 30ml Finlandia cranberry vodka; 30ml Smirnoff orange vodka; 10ml lime juice;10ml blue Curacao syrup

Method:

- Fill the shaker 3/4 with ice.
- Add all the ingredients, squeeze a wedge of lime and drop it in. Shake and pour into an old fashioned glass.
- Garnish.

Glass: Old fashioned

Garnish: Slice of orange

CHATKA MARY

Ingredients: 45ml regular vodka; 150ml guava juice; 15ml lime juice; a wedge of lime; 1/3tsp Worcestershire Sauce; 1tsp or more of Tabasco Sauce.

Method:

- Take a tall glass; rim the glass with salt and red chilli powder.
- Fill it with ice cubes, add all the ingredients except vodka, squeeze a wedge of lime and drop it in.
- And then gently slide in the vodka to form a clear layer. Place a green chilly in the glass instead of stirrer.

Glass: Tall/Collins glass.

Garnish: Green chilli, red chilli powder, and salt rim.

DRUNKEN ARCHER

Ingredients: 60ml vodka;10ml Monin/Teisseire Peach syrup/Archer's Peach Schnapps.

Method:

- Fill the shaker ¾ with ice.
- Add all the ingredients and shake.
- Strain it into a pre-chilled Martini glass.

Glass: Pre-chilled Martini glass.

Garnish: Two whole almonds.

ESPRESSO MARTINI

Wake up to some holiday cheer!

Ingredients: 45ml vanilla vodka; 30ml black coffee; 15ml Kahlua; 5ml Monin/Teisseire hazelnut syrup or Frangelico.

Method:
- Take mixing tin with ¾ ice and pour vanilla vodka, Kahlua, coffee and hazelnut syrup.
- Shake and strain into a pre-chilled Martini glass.
- Glass: Pre-chilled Martini glass.

Garnish: Polo and Coffee Bite.

LYNCHBURG LEMONADE

Ingredients: 60ml Jack Daniel's; 15ml triple sec; 10ml lime juice; lemonade to top.

Method:
- Fill the glass with ice.
- Pour JD, triple sec on ice.
- Squeeze a wedge of lime and drop it in.
- Top it up with lemonade.
- Glass: Footed Pilsner.

Garnish: Sprig of mint/slice of sweet lime or orange.

MANHATTAN

A very chewy kind of drink! There's lots of flavour and character. It was invented in the mid-19th century. Has always vied for top spot with the Martini.

Ingredients: 45ml Bourbon whisky; 2-3 drops Angostura bitters; 15ml sweet Vermouth (optional)

Method: This one can be made either like a Martini or served on the rocks.
- Chill Martini glass with ice. Fill shaker with ice, pour ingredients and stir with bar spoon. Strain into the pre-chilled glass.
- Fill whisky tumbler with ice cubes. Pour ingredients over ice and stir. Top with more ice if necessary.

Glass: Martini or old-fashioned whisky tumbler.

Garnish: Cherries and orange peel.

MARTINI

The Martini is regarded as the king of cocktails. It is to mixed drinks what Rolls Royce is to cars and Tiffany's is to diamonds! A classic — stirred with lots of iced gin and a hint of dry vermouth. James Bond was a big fan of the Martini. He, of course, preferred his with vodka, shaken not stirred. The question to consider is how dry you like your Martini — the drier it gets, the higher the amount of gin/vodka, the lesser the vermouth. Flavoured martinis are very "in" too.

Ingredients: 60-90ml gin/vodka; 10ml dry vermouth.

Method:
- Chill the glass by packing it with ice. Fill ¾ mixing glass or cocktail shaker with ice cubes.
- Pour the ingredients over ice.
- Stir with a long bar spoon or shut the shaker and shake.

Glass: Martini.

Garnish: Green stuffed olives, lime peel.

Suggestions for Serving: Strain without the ice into the pre-chilled glass. Stick the olives in.

ORANGE & CRANBERRY CAIPIROSKA

Ingredients: 45ml orange vodka; 4 lime wedges; 2 slices fresh orange; 30ml cranberry nectar; 10ml sugar syrup; 10 mint leaves; crushed ice.

Method:

- Squeeze and drop lime wedges into glass.
- Tear the mint leaves, add oranges and muddle.
- Fill glass with crushed ice. Add sugar syrup, vodka.
- Stir. Top with more crushed ice. Splash in the cranberry nectar.

Glass: Old-fashioned.

Garnish: Fresh orange/mint sprig.

PASSION & COCONUT CAIPIRINHA

Ingredients: 45ml Cachaca; 6 lime wedges; 30ml Monin Passion purée; 10ml Monin coconut; crushed ice.

Method:

- Squeeze and drop lime wedges into glass and muddle.
- Fill glass with crushed ice. Add Passion purée and Monin coconut syrup.
- Stir and taste to adjust. Top with more crushed ice.

Glass: Old-fashioned.

Garnish: Half-a-slice of coconut.

PINEAPPLE & BELL PEPPER MARGARITA

Ingredients: 45ml tequila; 20ml lime juice; 10ml sugar syrup; 30ml pineapple juice; 2 slices pineapple (cubed); 6 pieces of bell peppers (red, green, yellow).

Method:

- Rim a Margarita/Rocks glass with salt.
- Take a mixing can, add all the bell peppers, pineapple and muddle.
- Fill the can half with ice cube. Pour tequila, lime juice, pineapple juice, sugar syrup and shake.
- Adjust taste and double strain into salt-rimmed Margarita glass or on the rocks.

Glass: Margarita glass/Rocks glass

Garnish: Stripes of red, yellow and green bell peppers.

RUSTY NAIL

From the Scottish Highlands comes this phenomenal drink. Tastes best on the rocks and even better chased with a pint of beer!

Ingredients: 30ml Scotch whisky; 30ml Drambuie.

Method:

- Fill the glass with ice cubes.
- Pour in the ingredients and stir.

Glass: Old-fashioned/heavy bottom whisky tumbler.

Garnish: Cinnamon stick/orange peel.

Suggestions for Serving: Top with more ice if needed. Drop the garnish on top.

UTTERLY SIMPLE

Ingredients: 30ml dark rum; 150ml apple juice; cinnamon stick.

Method:

- Rim the glass with cinnamon and sugar.
- Steam the apple juice with the cinnamon sticks.
- Pour dark rum in the rimmed glass and pour the hot apple juice in the glass with a cinnamon stick.

Glass: Wine glass.

Garnish: Cinnamon stick and apple slice.

WHITE RUSSIAN/DIRTY BIRD

Known by either name, it is very popular in US bars.

Ingredients: 30ml vodka; 30ml Kahlua.

Method:

- Fill glass with ice. Pour in the vodka and Kahlua.
- Top with your favourite of the three!

Glass: Rocks.

Garnish: KitKat.

Suggestions for Serving: Dip in the KitKat. Top up with cream or half and half (half milk and half cream) or milk.

CONTEMPORARY CLASSICS

These are truly current across the world. Frozen and flavoured Margaritas and Daiquiris, Long Island Iced Tea, Caipirinha, Caipiroska, Mojito, and Cosmopolitan.

CAIPIRINHA

A Brazilian classic made with their local spirit "Cachaca" (ka-sha-sa).

Ingredients: 60ml Cachaca; 15ml sugar syrup or 4tsp brown/demerara sugar; 6 lime wedges.

Method:

- Put the lime and sugar in the glass and muddle them together to release the juice, and a little oil from the skin.
- Crush the sugar if using the brown one. This can be done with a muddler — a wooden pestle — or the back of a tablespoon.
- Fill the glass with crushed ice, top with Cachaca and stir.

Glass: Rocks/ Old-fashioned.

Garnish: Sprig of mint leaves/ slice of orange.

CAIPIROSKA

There are two versions — Mumbai and Delhi. The Delhi one is simply a Caipirinha made with vodka instead of Cachaca. We, in Mumbai, think differently!

Ingredients: 45ml vodka; 12-15 fresh mint leaves all torn up; 6 lime wedges; 15ml sugar syrup.

Method:

- Put the lime, mint, and sugar in the glass and muddle them together to release the juice, a little oil from the skin and the aromatics of the mint. This can be done with a muddler — a wooden pestle — or the back of a tablespoon.

- Fill the glass with crushed ice, top with Cachaca or vodka and stir.
- Add more ice if required.

Glass: Rocks/old-fashioned.
Garnish: Sprig of mint leaves/slice of orange.

COSMOPOLITAN

Very hot if made right. Is becoming increasingly popular. Has been on the top-five world favourites for a while.

Ingredients: 45ml citrus vodka; 15ml cointreau/triple sec syrup; 45ml Dabur Real cranberry nectar or better still 30ml Smirnoff citrus; 30ml Smirnoff orange; 15ml lime juice; 60ml Dabur Real cranberry nectar, splashes of lime juice and sugar.

Method:
- Fill ½ of the cocktail shaker with ice and pour all ingredients in.
- Shut the shaker well and shake vigorously for 20 seconds.
- Strain without the ice or pour with the ice into the glass.

Glass: Large — Martini/Margarita/Cocktail.
Garnish: ½ slice of orange.

FROZEN MARGARITA

Flavoured or uncluttered, do what you like with them. A few mistakes, a little adventure and experiment will get them perfect.

Ingredients: 45ml tequila; 20ml cointreau/triple sec; 2 tsp powdered sugar or 10ml sugar syrup (optional); 20ml lime juice; 2-3 glasses, crushed ice.

Method:
- Take a shaker can. Add crushed ice. Pour in all ingredients and blend with a hand blender, or in a mixer jar.
- Pour the slush into a salt-rimmed Margarita glass.

Glass: Margarita.
Garnish: Slice of orange/appropriate fruit.
Tip for Flavoured Margarita: Add fresh fruit — enough for a portion. Eg: Half a kiwi or 4-5 strawberries. Add more sugar and less lime as they are both tart.
Fruit Concentrate: Omit the sugar. All else constant.
A Daiquiri is made with white rum instead of tequila and cointreau. A Moskowski uses vodka.

LONG ISLAND ICED TEA

This is how we make it. Equal measures of 4 white spirits and a clear orange liqueur over ice in a tall glass topped with cola and a splash of lime juice.

Ingredients: 15/30ml gin; 15/30ml cointreau/triple sec; 15/30ml vodka; 15/30ml white rum; 15/30ml tequila; splash of lime juice; cola.
Method: Fill a very tall glass with ice. Pour everything in and top with cola. Use a really tall straw.
Garnish: Fresh mint leaves, slice of orange/sweet lime.

MOJITO

A Cuban favourite with all kinds of rum, though popular with the white!

Ingredients: 45ml white rum; 12-15 fresh mint leaves all torn up; 6 lime wedges; 20/30ml sugar syrup; top with soda.

Method:

- Put the lime, mint, and sugar in the glass and muddle them together to release the juice, a little oil from the skin and the aromatics of the mint.
- This can be done with a muddler — a wooden pestle — or the back of a tablespoon.
- Fill the glass with crushed ice, add rum, and stir.
- Top with soda.

Glass: Tall Chimney/Zombie/Collins.

Garnish: Sprig of mint leaves/slice of orange, 2 cherries.

A MIX OF RECIPES FROM MUMBAI'S BARS...

ALMOND JOY

Ingredients: 30ml malibu; 15ml crème de cacao; 15ml amaretto; a splash of cream.

Method: Shake with lots of ice.

Suggestions for Serving: Serve in a cocktail glass.

Bartender's Tip: Add choco rim in the glass from inside.

APPLE A DAY

Ingredients: 90ml apple juice; ½tsp egg white; 90ml cranberry juice; 30ml fresh lime juice; and 30ml sugar syrup.

Method: Blend.

Suggestions for Serving: Apple slice and cherry served in a tall glass with lots of ice.

BLUE LAGOON

Ingredients: 25ml vodka lemonade; 25ml Blue Curacao.

Method: Pour vodka and Curacao over ice in a tall glass. Top with lemonade.

Suggestions for Serving: Drop a lime slice and cherry in.

BLUE NOTE

Ingredients: 15ml tequila; 15ml white rum; 15ml vodka; 15ml Blue Curacao; 15ml gin; top up with lemonade

Method: Build up.

Suggestions for Serving: Serve in a Zombie glass and garnish with lemon wedge and cherries.

CAIPIRINHA

Ingredients: 60ml vodka; 40ml sugar syrup; 5 lemon wedges.

Method: Muddle in a muddler with crushed ice.

Suggestions for Serving: Serve in a Rock glass.

CAIPIROSKA

Ingredients: 60ml Smirnoff vodka; 3tbsp grain sugar; 15ml cointreau shaved ice; 6 lemon wedges

Method:

- Muddle the lemon wedges in an old-fashioned glass along with sugar.
- Fill glass upto 3/4ths with shaved ice, pour vodka and top up with cointreau.
- Stir gently.

Suggestions for Serving: Serve with a short straw. Create your own flavours by replacing vodka with the spirit of your choice.

CHAMPAGNE MAGIC

Ingredients: 15ml vodka; 90ml champagne; 15ml crème de cassis.
Method: Pour vodka in a flute, top-up with Champagne and add crème de cassis.
Suggestions for Serving: Serve in a Champagne tulip.

COCO KIWI

Ingredients: 60ml mango pulp; 2tsp coconut powder; 30ml kiwi pulp; and a dash of soda.
Method: Blend and add a dash of Blue Curacao.
Suggestions for Serving: Serve in a Cocktail glass.

COOL TOP

Ingredients: 30ml vodka; 10ml lime juice; 15ml cointreau; 15ml crème de menthe. Top-up with 7-Up.
Method:
- Put 4-5 cubes of ice into a Collins glass.
- Add lime juice, vodka, cointreau, top up with 7-Up and crème de menthe.

Suggestions for Serving: Garnish with a slice of lime and cherry.

FLAMING LAMBORGHINI

Ingredients: 20ml Kahlua; 20ml Blue Curacao; 20ml Bailey's, 20ml Sambuca.
Method: Put Sambuca and Kahlua in a glass and flambé the drink.
Suggestions for Serving: As the guest is sipping from the glass, add the Blue Curacao and the Bailey's.

FRUITY FRUIT

Ingredients: 60ml vodka or Bacardi; 30ml mango pulp; 2tsp strawberry tang. Top-up with soda and add a dash of fresh lime.
Method: Build up.
Suggestions for Serving: Serve in a tall glass.
Bartender's Tip: Could use pineapple juice also.

GINGER AWAY

Ingredients: 100ml orange juice; 1tbsp grenadine; 10ml lemon juice; and 30ml ginger ale.
Method: Blend all the ingredients in a blender and top-up with lemonade.
Suggestions for Serving: Serve in a tall glass filled with ice.
Bartender's Tip: Garnish with lemon and drop a ginger slice in the glass.

GINGERY DELIGHT

Ingredients: 60ml ginger syrup; 15ml lime juice; soda.
Method: Fill up a tall Cocktail glass with ice, add ginger syrup, lime juice and finally soda.

Suggestions for Serving: Garnish with a slice of lime and cherry.

GREEN BEAUTY

Ingredients: 45ml vodka; 15ml crème de menthe
Method: Shake well in a shaker.
Suggestions for Serving: Serve in a Cocktail glass filled with ice. Garnish with mint leaves and cherry.
Bartender's Tip: Could use gin instead of vodka.

GREEN CHILLI

Ingredients: 60ml vodka; 1 green chilli; 15ml lime juice; 250ml lemonade; 6 mint leaves.
Method: Muddle crushed ice with mint. Add vodka and lime juice. Add a slit green chilli. Top up with lemonade.
Suggestions for Serving: Garnish with lemon and mint. Makes an excellent evening drink.
Bartender's Tip: For the best presentation, use a crystal-clear hurricane sling glass.

IN THE PINK

Ingredients: 30ml gin; 15ml Malibu; 10ml Blue Curacao; 10ml strawberry crush; lime juice; soda/Sprite; crushed ice.
Method: Build up in a tall, fancy glass. Put in strawberry crush, crushed ice, then spirits, 2 lime wedges, crushed ice, soda/sprite. Add Blue Curacao and the drink turns purple; hence the name.

JUMP AND KISS ME

Ingredients: 60ml white rum; 15ml lemon juice; 15ml galliano; 120ml pineapple juice; 15ml apricot brandy; and 1 egg white.
Method: Shake with lots of ice.
Suggestions for Serving: Serve in a hi-ball glass. Garnish with pineapple slice, cherry apple slice, and strawberry on a cocktail stick.

KHUS DELIGHT

Ingredients: 30ml khus syrup; 120ml cream; ½ glass Sprite
Method: Stir and shake to blend.
Suggestions for Serving: Garnish with pineapple and cherry.

LOVELY LADY

Ingredients: 45ml gin; 5-7ml sugar syrup; 15ml fresh lime juice; 15ml cointreau
Method: Shake well with 3 cubes of ice.
Suggestions for Serving: Serve with sugar rim in a Cocktail glass. Garnish with lemon and orange slice.

MAISON MARTELL

Ingredients: 40ml Martell cognac; 60ml peach juice; 10ml fresh lemon juice; 10ml cranberry juice; and ice.
Method: Fill a tall glass with ice and add the cranberry juice. Combine the other three ingredients and shake. Then strain into the glass.

MARINE COOLER

Ingredients: 45ml vodka; 15ml triple sec; 10ml lime juice; dash of grenadine. Top-up with 7-Up.
Method: Build up.
Suggestions for Serving: Serve in hi-ball glass and garnish with orange slice.

MARTELL COSMOPOLITAN

Ingredients: 40ml Martell cognac; 10ml triple sec; 10ml lemon; 40ml cranberry juice; and ice.
Method: Fill a Martini glass with ice, pour all the above ingredients in a shaker and shake. Strain and pour in a chilled Martini glass.
Suggestions for Serving: Garnish with a lemon slice.

ORANGE SUN

Ingredients: 30ml fresh lime juice; 30ml sugar syrup; orange juice; pinch of salt. Top-up with Limca.
Method: Pour crushed ice, lime juice and sugar syrup into a Collins glass. Add salt, top-up with Limca and float it with orange juice.
Suggestions for Serving: Garnish with orange slice and cherry.

PEPPERMINT DELIGHT

Ingredients: 30ml crème de menthe (green); 2 chocolate biscuits (Hide 'n' Seek); 30ml crème de cacao (brown); and 2 scoops vanilla ice cream.
Method: Put all the ingredients in a mixer and blend with crushed ice.
Suggestions for Serving: Serve in a Parfait glass with chocolate rim inside.

PINK PASSION (MOCKTAIL)

Ingredients: 250ml fresh watermelon; and ½ scoop vanilla ice cream.
Method: Blend with ice cubes.
Suggestions for Serving: Serve in a tall glass garnished with cinnamon powder

SMOOCHIE

Ingredients: 30ml peach apricot syrup; 1 scoop vanilla ice cream; 30ml litchi crush; 1 wedge canned peach; and 90ml orange juice.
Method: Blend all ingredients with crushed ice.

Suggestions for Serving: A wedge of canned peach on the rim of a wineglass.
Bartender's Tip: Could use pineapple juice also.

POLYNESIAN PEPPERPOT

Ingredients: 200ml pineapple juice; 15ml lemon juice; 1tsp almond powder; 5 dashes Tabasco Sauce.
Method: Pour the ingredients in a cocktail shaker and shake with ice cubes.
Suggestions for Serving: Pour in an Old-fashioned glass rimmed with Madras curry powder.

ROSY CHEEKS

Ingredients: 60ml litchi crush; 30ml fresh cream; 15ml strawberry crush; ½ scoop vanilla ice cream; and 120ml pineapple juice.
Method: Blend well.
Suggestions for Serving: Serve in a Brandy Balloon. Chill and garnish with 1 fresh litchi and a cherry on top.

SHARP BITE

Ingredients: 30ml vodka; 5ml lime juice; 15ml triple sec; 5ml sugar syrup; 15ml Blue Curacao. Top-up with 7-Up
Method: Blend all ingredients in a blender.
Suggestions for Serving: Serve in a Champagne saucer glass and garnish with cherries.

SIZZY LIZZY (COCKTAIL)

Ingredients: 45ml vodka; 90ml orange juice; 15ml Peach Schnapps; 10-15ml lemon juice.
Method: Put ice and 10-15ml lemon juice; add orange juice; whip it with vodka and Peach Schnapps.
Suggestions for Serving: Garnish with orange and cherry in a tall glass.

STRAWBERRY SLING (MOCKTAIL)

Ingredients: 2 fresh strawberries; 15ml lemon juice; 10ml strawberry crush; 20ml water.
Method: Put fresh strawberries. Add ice, strawberry crush, lemon juice and water in the blender. Blend it for around 1 minute. Put these juices in a salted rim glass.
Suggestions for Serving: Garnish with fresh strawberry in a Martini glass.

SWEET CHEER

Ingredients: 45ml vodka; 15ml Blue Curacao; a dash of fresh lime; and lemonade.
Method: Put vodka in a Champagne tulip, add Blue Curacao, a dash of fresh lime and top-up with lemonade. Stir well, and garnish with lime and cherry.
Suggestions for Serving: Serve in a champagne tulip.
Bartender's Tip: Could use gin or white rum instead of vodka.

TOASTED ALMOND

Ingredients: 15ml vodka; 15ml amaretto; 15ml Kahlua; 60ml heavy cream.
Method: Shake all ingredients with ice and strain into a chilled Cocktail/Martini glass. Dust with nutmeg powder.

FRENCH 75

It is said that Franco-American World War I flying ace Raoul Lufbery concocted this drink. A connoisseur of Champagne, he mixed cognac with it when he wanted a kick from his drink. Called Soixante Quinze in French, French 75 was popularized in America at the Stork Club.

Ingredients: Two parts gin; 1½ ounces of simple syrup; juice of half a lemon; champagne.

Method: Combine sugar, lemon juice and gin in a shaker full of ice. Shake well, then pour into a tall glass and top with champagne.

Bartender's Tip: If possible, ice the glass ahead of time.

MIMOSA

Often called a Buck's Fizz in the UK, the Mimosa was reportedly invented at the Ritz Hotel in Paris around 1925. Orangina or a tablespoon of Grand Marnier (also known as a Grand Mimosa or a Morning Glory) are sometimes added.

Ingredients: Three parts Champagne; two parts orange juice.

Method: Ensure both ingredients are well chilled; then mix together into the glass. Serve cold.

B-52

Created in the famous Alice's restaurant in Malibu, California, the name refers to the US B-52 Stratofortress long-range bomber. This bomber was also used in the Vietnam War for the release of incendiary bombs, which most likely inspired today's flaming variant of the B-52.

Ingredients: 1/3 shot Kahlua coffee liqueur; 1/3 shot Amaretto almond liqueur; 1/3 shot Bailey's Irish cream

Method: Carefully layer ingredients, in order, into a shot glass: Kahlua, Amaretto, and then Irish cream.

FLATLINER

A layered drink with half sambuca and half tequila with a few dashes of Tabasco makes people pass out just after the second drink. The Tabasco is layered in between the Sambuca and tequila.

Ingredients: 45ml sambuca; 1 shot gold tequila; 3 dashes Tabasco Sauce.

Method: Layer the tequila over sambuca. Add Tabasco Sauce.

KAMIKAZE

Named after the famous Japanese fighter aircraft in World War II, which ravaged US ships off the coast of Japan, this mix of vodka with lime and cointreau is as fatal as its name.

Ingredients: 30ml vodka; 30ml triple sec; 30ml lime juice.

Method: Shake all ingredients with ice, strain into an old-fashioned glass over ice cubes, and serve.

MIND ERASER

This family of drinks is named in Gary Regan's The Joy of Mixology. While there is tremendous variation in the ingredients among the members of this family, the defining feature is that they are sweet due to the liqueur. Irish cream is a commonly used ingredients in this.

Ingredients: 30ml vodka; 30ml coffee liqueur; soda water; lime wedge for garnish.

Method:

- Fill an old-fashioned glass with ice.
- Pour the vodka and coffee liqueur over the ice.
- Fill with soda water.

Suggestions for Serving: Garnish with a lime wedge and serve with a straw.

TEQUILA SLAMMER

A favourite of fictional character Inspector Tequila Yuen of the 1992 action movie Hard Boiled, Tequila Slammers have become recently popular as a late-night indicator of a bar's impending closure in Belgium.

Ingredients: 30ml tequila; 30ml ginger ale or lime soda; soda water; lime wedge for garnish.

Method:

- Pour into a shot glass.
- Cover the glass with a napkin and your hand.
- Slam the glass on the bar counter.

PAIRING INDIAN FOOD WITH WINE

SONAL HOLLAND

An ace wine educator, consultant, writer and commentator, Sonal Holland's passion for wines in unparalleled. She is highly qualified in wines, having pursued wine courses in the UK from the renowned Wine & Spirit Education Trust (WSET). She holds the WSET Diploma in Wines & Spirits from London, and is also the first Indian woman to be enrolled into the Masters of Wine (MW) education programme, the highest academic achievement in wines.

Sonal is the founder of the Sonal Holland Wine Academy, launched in 2009, and is an approved programme provider of WSET (the foremost wine-centric institution in India for the appreciation and education on wines to consumers, hospitality, and the wine trade) wine courses in India. She is the Country Representative in India for the Antique Wine Company. Sonal is passionate about fine wines and her client list is the who's who of India whom she advises on wines... both for consumption as well as for investment purposes. An independent wine consultant, she regularly organizes wine-tasting and has been on the judging panel of several wine competitions. She has also worked closely with the Wine Society of India and writes for several publications.

Having completed her Diploma in Hotel Management from the Institute of Hotel Management, Dadar, an MBA from the University of Mumbai, and also Advanced Certificate Course in Management (XLRI, Jamshedpur), she gained business experience with Kelly Services, a US$6 billion company as the Director of National Sales.

PAIRING WINE WITH INDIAN SPICE

The subject of "Pairing Wines with Indian Spice" is of great relevance today and I chose to write on the subject in this chapter for two main reasons.

Firstly, I believe this topic is of both importance and interest to all wine communities of the global wine industry — wine producers, wine importers, the wine retailers and, most importantly, the wine consumers.

India stands poised among one of the world's top ten fastest-growing wine markets in the world with an annual growth of 25-30 per cent and an estimated 30 million potential future wine-drinkers, which will be instrumental in achieving a per capita annual consumption from the current one tablespoon to half-a-bottle over the next decade.

Therefore, only if we dabble with the subject of matching wine with our national, regional, and local cuisine with much seriousness, can we hope for this fascinating drink to make it to our dinner tables on a daily basis instead of one that celebrates just social or economic status.

Secondly, the realm of matching Indian cuisine to global wines has been surrounded by controversy. Many country experts have been known to advocate whisky over wine (why am I not surprised) as the real partner to Indian food as wine supposedly does not complement the flavours of Indian dishes on the premise that it is too spicy.

Now, contrary to most experts viewing this subject as a challenging task, I consider matching wines to Indian foods as an area of enhanced learning. Where all rules and guidelines have been laid out keeping in mind Western or European/Global cuisine, Indian food takes it to another dimension.

Indian food has loads of personality with a myriad of textures and flavours at work at the same time. A curry dish, Tikka Masala or a Biryani may have close to twenty spices in the blend, and just as each of these lend certain flavours to the dish, each in turn interact differently with the wine. And it is so easy to get it wrong! The margin for error when matching wine to Indian dishes is relatively smaller.

But we must also appreciate that Indian taste buds have been changing over the past few years. We no longer enjoy only those dishes that are laden with chillies and masala, but also enjoy those which have subtle flavours of delicate spices making the food fragrant and rich in flavour, but not necessarily spicy. Like a delicately rich Dum ke Phooley — paneer rolled and filled with fresh vegetables, black cumin and cooked in creamy saffron butter, which I discovered pairs beautifully with the Italian Verdicchio dei Castelli di Jesi DOC, a remarkably elegant and fruity white wine with flavour of peaches, apples, and a freshness that cannot be ignored.

Conventional wisdom of matching Red and White Wines with red and white meats respectively does not apply to Indian cuisine. Spice and flavours are also equally crucial to consider. Deep ruby and tannic Australian Shiraz which seems like a sure shot match for a creamy rich Lamb Korma (matching Red Wine to red meat) will surprise you by pairing better with a white oaked Chardonnay from Australia or Argentina as will a grilled flavourful Pomfret (white meat) with a light red fruity Pinot Noir from New Zealand or Beaujolais Fleurie.

One could draw out an elaborate list of Indian dishes and suggest a unique wine to pair it with, but that would defeat the real purpose of food and wine pairing — enjoyment through experimentation. Indian food, like wines, is varied and diverse with each having its own individual style and it would be grossly unfair to limit the scope to just one wine for each dish. The idea is to try as many wines as possible and find one that suits your individual palate.

Rather than seeking specific wines for specific foods, it is easier to think of Indian cuisine broadly in terms of flavour groups. The emphasis must be on trying to match the overall intensity and strength of flavour of the dish keeping in mind the method of cooking which in turn influences the weight of the dish.

The main flavour groups are:

- Spice and Spicy
- Sour
- Smoky
- Creamy
- Fried/Oily
- Sweet

Let us try and elaborate on some of these flavour groups and wine pairing concepts:

SPICE AND SPICY

Let me first clarify these are two different flavour groups. Spices such as cardamom, cinnamon, cumin, coriander seeds, star anise, cloves, onions, garlic, etc, which are commonly known as Garam Masala make Indian dishes full of rich spice and flavour but not necessarily chilli hot or spicy.

A classic like Biryani is an example of flavourful dish which must be paired with a wine which is equally flavourful. In whites, Australian Riesling, oaked Viognier from Rhone Valley, and oaked Chardonnay from Burgundy in France can be examples of flavoursome wines, whereas in reds, a Barossa Valley Shiraz and New Zealand Pinot Noir will complement flavoursome foods cooked with several Indian spices.

Spicy, on the other hand, as we all know is one that sets your taste buds on fire. This is a difficult flavour to try and pair effectively with wine, the reason being your tasting equipment — i.e., your tongue — is set ablaze making assessment and appreciation, both go out of the window. To make matters worse, pronounced tannins with oak, excessive acidity or alcohol, any or all of these characters in wine increase the intensity of the heat in the dish, producing a not so desirable outcome on the palate.

Remember the proverb — "Sugar and Spice and All things Nice"?

We must reach for ripe fruit forward, off-dry (slightly sweet); un-oaked, refreshing whites with crisp acidity to counter balance the spiciness. Excellent choices of such white wines could be Alsatian Gewurztraminer or Pinot Blanc, German or Australian Riesling, Austrian Gruner Veltliner or an Indian Chenin Blanc. If sparkling wine is preferred, Italian Asti or Prosecco with off-dry notes complements beautifully. In reds, I would recommend a soft-bodied and fruity Pinot Noir which is not heavily oaked with medium alcohol levels. High tannic wines made from Cabernet Sauvignon or a Shiraz are best avoided for this flavour group as the tannins will only aggravate the spice.

SOUR

These are dishes that use a lot of tamarind, vinegar, lemon or tomatoes and the sourness is the predominant flavour. Examples of such dishes are the Goan Sorpotel, Vindaloo, Lemon Rice and other vegetables/meat dishes cooked in a tomato-based gravy. The sourness in these dishes must be balanced off by pairing it with a wine having mouth-watering acidity levels. The high acidity levels of the food will make the high-acidity wine taste sweeter bringing out the fruit and hence will taste better. One must avoid wines which have acid levels lesser than that in the dish so avoid wine made from the Gewurztraminer, Pinot Blanc or a Semillon grape.

Italian wines like a Chianti Classico, Barbera d'Asti as well as the French Champagne, known for their high acidity will complement these dishes very well. I once tried a New Zealand Pinot Noir with Lemon Rice and Curd, and can assure you it worked like magic! But if you are a lover of whites, then a French Sancerre or a Sauvignon Blanc from Marlborough New Zealand is the perfect winner.

SMOKY

Tandoor items like meat tikkas and kebabs are cooked on slow fire in clay oven, and have a smoky flavour which best complements wines with pronounced oak characteristics.

An Australian Shiraz, a Californian Zinfandel or a Reserva/Gran Reserva Rioja from Spain with their ripe fruit and spicy flavours further enhance the smoky food taste, causing a magical combination. Foods in this group can also benefit from some slight sweetness in White Wines found in Rieslings from Germany and Australia, and Chenin Blancs from South Africa or Loire Valley. Smoked Burgundian Chardonnay would also be a classic pairing for such foods.

CREAMY

Where there is a creamy or curry component in a dish, the main food consideration is the texture, flavour, and consistency of the curry and the choice of wine must support this feature. So, where a tomato-based curry falls under sour flavour group, and an onion-garlic-chilli-based curry falls under spicy flavour group, creamy curries have a cashew nut-saffron-onion, coconut or yoghurt-based curries often laced by dollops of butter.

Oaked Australian, Chilean or Argentinean Chardonnay with ripe tropical fruits on palate and buttery, toasty flavours from some oak-ageing complement the creamy textures of the curry best.

Dals, both yellow and black, also have creamy consistency and fall under this flavour group. To enjoy this, you may choose a medium-bodied, soft Red Wine with fruit forward characteristics and crisp acidity like a Merlot from St Emillion, Chile, and Washington State or a Pinot Noir from Burgundy, Oregon, and Central Otago.

FRIED/OILY

How can any chapter on Indian cuisine be complete without a mention of the fried foods? If there are two flavours that could be used by people around the world to describe Indian cuisine, they would be spicy and greasy!

We have already dealt with the spicy flavour group

earlier in this chapter. For food items whose flavours are dominated by their cooking method, ie, foods that are pan-fried or deep-fried must be paired with high-acidity wines making the mouth water that helps cut through the grease and cleanse the palate, thereby making the dish enjoyable. Acidity in wines is the easiest to manipulate at the winery and can be adjusted to the right level by adding tartaric acid so most wines from around the world are refreshing with mouth-watering acidity. In general however, White Wines made from Chenin Blanc, Riesling, Sauvignon Blanc grape and Red Wines made from Pinot Noir and Sangiovese grape are almost always known for producing high-acidity wines, irrespective where they are grown or made.

The only guideline to remember about this flavour group is to never pair it with a wine with high tannins like a Cabernet Sauvignon, Tempranillo (Spanish Rioja) or a Nebbiolo (Barolo), as the oil clashes with tannins to create an awful metallic taste in your mouth which is best avoided.

SWEET

When it comes to standing up to the sweetness of Indian desserts, only one rule applies — the wine must be sweeter than the sweet dish. Indian desserts with their high sweetness levels pose a challenge for the dessert wines that have been traditionally matched with mousse, cake or custard. Many great dessert wines fail to stand up to the intensity of a Jalebi or a Gulab Jamun therefore here is a quick list of pairings for sweet foods.

SWEET WINES TO MATCH WITH INDIAN DESSERTS

- Spanish Pedro Ximenez (PX) Sherry with Gulab Jamun
- French Sauternes with Gajar ka Halwa
- German Trockenbeerenauslese with Rice Pudding/Kheer or Shahi Tukda
- Austrian or Canadian Ice Wine with Jalebis
- Australian Liqueur Muscat Gujia with Khoya filling
- 10-year-old-Tawny-Port with steamed Modak or Karanji

Sweet wines are expensive and also difficult to access in India. The Port is widely available in India at sensible price points where other imported fine dessert wines are going for a killing.

Considering that methods of cooking is important because they in turn influence the level of flavour in the dish, eg, poaching or boiling produces delicate flavours while grilling or tandoor gives us robust flavours.

The general thumb rule is that stronger the flavours of the dish, the more flavour the wine will need to have. Indian food we know does not lack any measure of flavour and hence demand wines in general that are high on fruit flavours.

For whites in general, the preference leans towards aromatic, off-dry to medium-dry, unoaked for spicy and slightly oaked for creamy dishes, with good levels of acidity. This wine style will pair with a vast majority of

Indian dishes.

In reds, light- to medium-bodied with soft tannins, ripe red or black fruit flavours with balanced acidity and little or no oak can work beautifully. In all cases, modest alcohol levels are crucial.

This leads me to conclude that where most of the world wine connoisseurs smirk at any hint of sweetness in whites as "cheap and cheerful" and where their palates and vino-sensibilities lean towards the dry and tannic flavours of the "serious reds" from Bordeaux, India with its cuisine and its people opens its arms to the relatively uncelebrated and unassuming fun, fruity and fascinating wines from around the world.

FINE WINES FOR PROFIT AND PLEASURE — WINE AS AN INVESTMENT

SONAL HOLLAND

MOTIVES FOR INVESTMENT IN FINE WINES?

First, let us take a quick look at some compelling statistics. FTSE 100 is up 6 per cent, Dow Jones is up 7.5 per cent, Indian equity market (SENSEX) is up 19 per cent and gold prices are up 23 per cent, year to date (November 2010). But did you know that Liv-Ex Fine Wine 100 index which represents the price movement of the top 100 most sought-after fine wines globally is up a whopping 32 per cent between January and November 2010? If fine wine investment does not yet form a part of your long-term investment portfolio, maybe it is about time you do so.

Over long term, fine wine investment has consistently out-performed equity, debt as well as gold. An investment in the top fine wines has never lost money in any three-year period, including the sub-prime crises of 2008-09. In fact, during the period Jan. 2004 and Jan. 2009, including the period of the sub-prime crises, an investment in the top hundred fine wines yielded a return of 16.1 per cent per annum whereas a similar investment in BSE 100 returned a 10.2 per cent and the NASDAQ a negative return of -6.5 per cent. Fine wine was one of the last asset classes to fall and was certainly one of the first to rise, continuing to show less volatility and making it a much safer haven for investors.

As an asset, class fine wine is unique. It is a tangible and consumable investment that benefits from a unique supply and demand environment. There are no lock-in periods and investments can be increased or reduced as desired and it is one investment that you can drink for utmost pleasure!

WHY DOES WINE RISE IN VALUE?

Let us understand the fundamental economics of wine investment. On the supply side, Bordeaux Chateaux which produces over 90 per cent of all investment grade wines, cannot increase production or yield — by law. Therefore, the global supply of fine wine is highly limited by law and limited terrain. In fact, over the past few years, the top 5 Chateaux from Bordeaux have actually cut production in an effort to increase quality further. They each produce no more than 15,000 cases a year.

On the demand side, the top-class growths and super seconds of Bordeaux, which have been classified and crowned as the best in class wines over the last 150 years and as such remain unrivalled in value and quality since 1855, have consistently been sought after globally by investors and collectors in traditional markets of the US and Europe. The total global fine wine market is $3 billion annually. In 2009, the US and UK fine wine auctions clocked in a total turnover of $250 million with the UK wholesalers and merchants representing a GBP 400 million share.

However, over the past few years, there has been a demand for this luxury scarce commodity from new Asian markets such as China, Brazil, Hong Kong, and India where increasing number of wealthy buyers continue to put an upward pressure on prices. Hong Kong is already being crowned the next global hub of fine wine auctions with 2010 sales predicted to cross over $100 million, overtaking the US for the first time. Hong Kong government's demonstrated support by abolishing import tax and duty on wines has almost single-handedly been instrumental in carving out this special position for the country.

In a nutshell, the demand for fine wines of finest vintages always outstrips the supply thereby causing an upward price movement. Moreover, as the wine matures and reaches its optimum drinking age, people start to drink it. Each time a bottle of fine wine is opened and consumed, the value and price of the remaining bottles goes up!

ADVANTAGES OF BUYING FINE WINE EARLY

Undoubtedly, these are interesting times for wine investors and collectors. One definite reason behind this has been the 2009 Bordeaux En Primeur campaign which has been the strongest for decades, causing an unsurpassed demand for these wines. En Primeur is the system whereby buyers can purchase or invest in wines prior to bottling and their subsequent release in the market. The prices are released during the spring following the harvest, when the leading wine-makers of Bordeaux release their wines of the previous year's vintage for tasting by merchants and world renowned wine critics. Perfect weather conditions, adequate rainfall followed by unhindered dry summer led grapes to realize their true expression, ripeness, and maturity. As a result, several wine commentators and experts around the world have unanimously declared 2009 as one of the finest vintages that they have tasted in the last thirty years, and in the case of some, the best through their entire lifetime! The wines have been released for buying at eye-popping prices; nearly 30 per cent more expensive than the 2005, another outstanding vintage.

In 2010, the global fine wine market has been very active, thanks largely to the growing demand for fine wines from Asian investors and other emerging markets like Brazil, China, and India. Asian investors are demanding the best of the Bordeaux brands including Chateau Lafite and Petrus, the blue-chip of the blue-chip wines.

Advantages of investing in wines en primeur are the ability to secure stocks of wine that are otherwise difficult to obtain, as well as the opportunity to buy the best wines of the best vintages at their lowest potential price point. Investment grade wines are improving assets. As the wines mature, they develop further in quality and hence the demand and value increases. As the wine approaches maturity, consumption of the wines makes it rarer to find, further causing an upward pressure on the price. Buying more immature blue-chip wines than you will require for your own consumption means that you can trade an excess of mature wines for a handsome return and then re-invest the earnings in younger set of wines or newer vintages for further profit and pleasure. The net result is that you not only make money but also drink the greatest wines in the world at zero cost.

DOS AND DON'TS OF INVESTING

Surely, like any other investment class, there are some parameters to follow to ensure healthy returns. First and foremost, stick to purchasing the best wines from the best vintages. These include the first growths such as Lafite, Latour, Margaux, Haut Brion, and Mouton-Rothschild as well as some of the "Super Seconds" such as Pavie, Palmer, Leoville las Cases, Montrose, and Cos d'Estournel. Merlot lovers should concentrate on chateaux such as Petrus from Pomerol and Cheval Blanc' and Ausone from St Emilion. Burgundy top wine is Domaine de la Romanee Conti. These particular chateaux possess all the required characteristics for investment grade status: history, track record, global demand, quality, longevity, and consistent upward price movement. Best vintages over the last fifty years have been 1959, 1961, 1982, 1986, 1989, 1990, 1996, 2000, 2005 and, certainly the blockbuster, 2009. If you combine a top chateau with a top vintage, then the investment potential can be huge.

It is most important that you buy from reputable wine merchants with long-standing experience and credible track record in the fine wine trading industry. If you are investing in wines for purely speculative purposes, it is best to keep your wines stored in a bonded warehouse maintained in your own account either in France, the UK or Hong Kong, where they remain perfectly stored without attracting any VAT or import duty.

It may be worthwhile to seek professional help from a fine wine investment advisor who can guide you on appropriate wine selections and help you gain access to the right wines with the perfect provenance at the right time for the right price, as well as manage your wine portfolio advising on how long to keep and when to divest once the wines reach the right value for a profit based resale or for your enjoyment on maturity.

Purchase full cases with their original wooden cases — this will make them more tradeable and add to their re-sale value.

Keep all records and documentation pertaining to your wine collection; provenance is such an important factor in the value of your investment. Make sure your wines are fully insured at full replacement value.

Investors should be looking to reap the maximum returns over a period of 10-15 years and avoid short-term trading with wine because frictional costs can be high.

Short-term returns can be interesting by investing in wines that are just a few years ahead of their optimum maturity and readiness for drinking.

In the last twenty years, fine wine has consistently outperformed a number of equity and fixed income indices. My view is that a well-managed portfolio should provide returns of 15 per cent per annum — and possibly even more. That should provide some very tidy profits and some very pleasurable drinking.

Hot Picks from the 2009 vintage

- Château Lafite Rothschild
- Château Latour
- Château Margaux
- Château Mouton-Rothschild
- Château Haut Brion
- Château Angélus
- Château Pavie
- Château Montrose
- Château Cos d'Estournel
- Château Pontet Canet

MUSIC

I admit. I have often wondered why the music in today's nightclubs and bars is monotonously thumping like a factory at work at best or like skeletons on a tin roof at worst. Okay so in some crazy way I enjoy it (whatever happened to the good old Beatles?) and even more because it plugs me to my college-going son and his buddies' generation.I sure have plenty to learn about music in todays night clubs and bars. So I get the help and inputs from singer and song writer Ashu Phatak of the revolutionary, integrated music project BLUE FROG. He is a graduate in Western Classical Music Theory from University of Pennsylvania has been professionally composing music for the last 15 years. He gives inputs to our chapter on MUSIC...Read what follows and Rock away!

PS: Blue Frog, is the collective brainchild of Composers Ashu Phatak and Dhruv Ghanekar, film-maker Mahesh Mathai (Bhopal Express), Simran Mulchandani (ex-JP Morgan investment banker) and Producer Srila Chatterjee (Highlight Films). The founders' shared vision is to break new ground in the creation, production and distribution of music through people, technology, sound and innovation anywhere in the world. It has launched many albums and international and Indian bands have performed here. It consists of the country's premiere live music performance club, four state-of-the-art music recording soundlabs, a music production house comprising top-notch composers, musicians and producers, and an independent record label & artist management service.The Blue Frog Club is Mumbai's premier live music performance space in Lower Parel and serves alcohol, dinner, and a Sunday brunch.

ROCK

Just like the definition of the word rock implies."rock n. Relatively hard, naturally formed mineral or petrified matter; stone". Thus the music, also characterized by its raw nature and spirit, always showcasing elements of raw grit and emotion. The rock songs through the years have been written on guitars and usually rest on that melody. Rock has gone through several morphs from the Progressive Rock of 1970s when bands like Pink Floyd ruled, to the heavily amplified Heavy Metal acts like Led Zeppelin and Deep Purple. There was also Punk Rock, The Sex Pistols and then Post-Punk or New Age when bands like The Police took over. Kurt Cobain and Nirvana took rock into a Grungy phase and then came the Post-Grunge and Post Punk of acts like Greenday. In the mid-90s Alanis Morissette and her Jagged Little Pill album made rock more introspective and confessional; a trend taken up by artists like Jewel, Tori Amos and Avril Lavigne. The latest is Nu Metal, with bands like Linkin Park and Limp Bizkit becoming popular. And Mumbai enjoys rock from every era and in all its avatars; you'll get to hear hits from all rock eras in the city's nightclubs.

HIP HOP

Hip-hop, also called RAP (Rhythm And Poetry) consists of music that gets your hips to hop. Hip-hop was born when New York DJs began isolating the percussion breaks to hit funk, soul, R&B and disco songs. A rapper sings or speaks rhythmic lyrics and is accompanied by an instrumental track termed a 'beat'. The beat may be performed by a DJ or created by a producer or one or more instrumentalists. The beat is often a sample of the percussion break of another funk or soul song. And lately, it may be built up from individual drum samples. In the 1990s, a controversial form of hip hop called "gangsta rap" became popular, with lyrics that were perceived as promoting violence, terrorism, promiscuity, drug use and misogyny. The stars of gangsta rap were artists like The Notorious BIG and Tupac Shakur.

Must hear: Eminem, Jurassic 5, Jay Z.

HOUSE

No not the music you play at your home! But a style of electronic dance music that originated in Chicago, USA, in the mid-80s. House has a prominent beat produced by drum machines or electronically, say with a sampler. House also has a continuous thump layered with bass lines and music samples from genres like jazz, blues, and synth pop as also additional percussion.

House music also includes elements of New Wave, Reggae, Euro-Synth Pop, Industrial, and Punk, and uses electronic gadgetry to produce unreal sound effects. What you usually get by way of house in most nightclubs in the city is pre-recorded Ministry Of Sound offerings.

Must hear: Bob Sinclair, Daft Punk, Sanjay Dutta (Kolkata).

REGGAETON

Taking a Jamaican Bob Marley reggae vibe to the energetic high BPM(beats per minute) dance floor is what reggaeton is all about. Reggaeton is a form of dance music that has its roots in Panama but truly became popular in Puerto Rico. It developed from the music of the post-salsa urban Latino youth of the 80s and early 90s. Once characterized by explicit lyrics about love, sex, poverty, homophobia, drugs, and violence — in short the problems of inner city life, what's now popular is a much cleaned up version sans much of the profanity and sexual explicitness.

However, a reggaeton song might sound innocuous but its lyrics often have multiple interpretations some of which may be far from innocent.

Reggaeton blends Jamaican influences like reggae and dancehall with Latin American influences like bomba, plena, and hip-hop. Its distinctive feature is a driving drum-machine track derived from a popular Jamaican dancehall rhythm called Dem Bow after a Bobby Dixon-produced song of the same title from the early 90s, which was performed by Shabba Ranks. The music is often influenced by genres such as techno, house, bolero, and salsa. Reggaeton singles like Gasolina by Daddy Yankee, a staple of the party scene, have been making their way to India in recent times via enterprising DJs.

UK BHANGRA

Started by a Diaspora starving for a cultural identity, UK BHANGRA started a musical revolution in the British Asian Scene, and then spread like wildfire to the rest of the world. This genre is an import from the British Asian scene. Its current stars are artists like Rishi Rich, Juggy D, Jay Sean, and groups like the Bombay Rockers from Denmark. This is fusion music that mixes traditional Punjabi bhangra with disco, reggae, techno, house, ragga, and now even jungle. However, the most popular tracks are usually a fusion of hip-hop and rap. It's a great hit with the youth of the South Asian diaspora and also Delhi, with all and sundry shaking a leg to songs like Mundian To Bach Ke, born of a collaboration between rapper Jay-Z and Punjabi MC. In fact, such is the popularity of UK Bhangra that it's now being re-exported back to India. Its sub genres are Bhangraton and Bhangraragga. The first fuses bhangra with Reggaeton's Dem Bow beat and has given rise to songs like Push it Up (Ajja Kurieh) by Jay Sean, Juggy D, and Rishi Rich. The second is dancehall reggae inspired and its leading light was Apache Indian who took the nightclub scene by storm in the early 90s with hits like Boom-Shak-A-Lak and Arranged Marriage.

AMBIENT

The music behind the music; focusing more on textures and sound-scapes, this technically superior sound is characterized by the flavour underneath the melodies.This is a loosely defined genre that is influenced by many different styles like Jazz, Electronic, New Age, Classical Music, and World Music. But this genre can most accurately be defined by a prominent example: the Buddha Bar collections.

Ambient music is no longer that popular in nightclubs, this being the hip-hop era but the composition Milky Way from Enigma's new album Posteriori is worth checking out for pure listening pleasure.

RETRO

Retro music is defined by an outdated or aged trend, from the past, but induces nostalgia and superficially makes it the norm once again. When we speak of retro we generally mean music from all genres from the past. Music from the 60s, 70s, 80s, and early 90s is still very popular, so on any night at any nightclub the DJ will get requests for Madonna's La Isla Bonita and Holiday, also for tracks by the Beatles, for Michael Jackson's Billie Jean or Don't Stop Till You Get Enough, for Santana's Black Magic Woman, songs by the Swedish pop group from the 70s, and even for songs from old Hindi movies or for songs like Disco Deewane by Nazia Hasan.

RHYTHM AND BLUES (R&B)

Pioneered by Ray Charles, R&B is popular music that originally combined jazz, gospel and blues influences, to bring you that soulful feeling that most of today's pop music is inspired by. R&B classics like Shake Rattle And Roll performed by Bill Haley and The Comets and a lot from groups like the Rolling Stones (while they were with Decca Records), The Animals and The Who are still staples at many a nightclub and party. But there's a lot of contemporary work by artists in this genre that is also played and partied to like Prince's Purple Rain and songs by Luther Van Dross, Whitney Houston and Janet Jackson. Contemporary R&B is focused more on individual artists than on groups; so while groups like TLC and their album CrazySexyCool and Boys II Men were extremely popular, right now the most successful R&B singers are Usher, Beyonce and Mariah Carey. And R&B cross-pollinates other genres like hip hop and pop. Artists whose work is R&B-influenced include Gwen Stefani, Pink and Christina Aguilera.

R&B is today most often used to define a style of African-American music originating after the demise of disco in the 1980s.

TRANCE

Trance is a style of electronic dance music developed in the 1990s. "Trance" is characterized by, up-tempo melodies, and layers of musical form that build up and down throughout the track. Trance is a combination of many forms of electronic music, such as ambient, techno, and house. Trance music could be described as a pleasant-sounding style of music, with a lot of influence from house music. Based around rifts and sacred songs, this music can either be chilled out or highly energetic. Trance is often described as a fusion of techno and house music and is build up elements like rifts and rolls, short samples of notes, anthems and highly inter-mixed major and minor chords. Trance Music has various sub-genres:

Euro Trance: One of the easiest forms of trance, it's a good choice to listen for those who are new to trance music. It has big rifts and is purely commercial trance.

Psychedelic Trance: This particular genre of trance took off during the 90s and is often referred by some as psy trance. Particularly liked in United Kingdom, it's now popular around the world. Often played with other forms of trance such as Progressive Trance and Goa Trance, it is very fast-paced in comparison to the other forms of trance. In fact, it is often considered to be highly inspired by Goa Trance and is regarded as an offshoot of the same. Astral Projection, Space Tribe, Infected Mushroom, Atmos, Total Eclipse, Cosmosis, and Simon Posford are some of the popular groups that make Psychedelic Trance.

Ambient Trance: The antecedent to progressive trance, this music gets you dreaming and is hypnotic in J15 nature. It utilizes atmospheric pads, epic melodic progressions and occasionally symphonic arrangements. Often regarded as trance from the old school, this genre is highly popular in raves and took trance to a new level. Oliver Lieb is regarded as the god of Ambient Trance who was responsible for the popularity of this form. Today it is somewhat lost though artists like Humate, Salt Tank, Lieb and Paul van Dyk make it, but in a modern setting.

Progressive Trance: Also known as Deep Trance, this form of trance keeps coming into your ear and to your mind. It has moved into deep tribal sounds and involves a lot of variations. It relies more on subtle builds and drops guided by the DJ and as the party goes on the music gets deeper. It is also referred as "Progressive House".

Hard Trance: As the name suggests, it comprises harder elements more evocative of Techno and Acid forms. A lot of bass and increased tempo is used in hard trance for an incomparable clubbing experience.

Your attention, please.... This is for the night owls with cast-iron stomachs and an adventurous spirit! Look here for a taste of food on Mumbai's streets — high in flavour and low in prices. When the party's over, the music dies down and you get to the honeyed, middle-of-the-night moments, come join me on a sojourn of the city, as we go along the taste highway.

Join me as I eat my way into bustling Madanpura, explore the crammed Minara Masjid area, walk into the busy Mahim bylanes, hang out near railway stations and mingle with the midnight Mumbaikars. A true taste of Mumbai by night....

Sab Kuch Milta Hai... Bhurji Pao and Bheja, Grilled Bater and Nalli Nihari, Corn Bhel, 24 types of Shrikhand, Aflatoon, Barahandi, Egg Bhuna and even *garama garam* glass of *doodh* — you get it all in our magnificent city. From street-sides to the 16,000sq ft restaurant in Bhendi Bazaar, I've been to them all and included them here.

Gourmet? Hygiene Freak? Die-hard night birds swear by the food on the streets, calling it more hygienic than whatever is served in restaurants because the turnover is so high and the food is cooked at such high temperatures. I would agree with them up to a point, but consider the buckets full of dirty water into which the plates are dipped, the stacks of raw meats waiting to be skewered! That definitely isn't my idea of hygiene and I'll not send people with the delicatest of stomachs for a taste of streetfood. It would be naive romanticism to pretend that all the streetfood is outstanding, though let me tell you that some of it really is. Every now and then, the sheer flavour and freshness of the food delight me, and make me think that Mumbai's palate lies in its restaurants all right, but its soul is right here.

From "Cutting" to "Tari Maar Ke"... My vocabulary has expanded much and I am now enlightened enough to know that there's a "Jeanie Dosa", a "Maggi Dosa" and even a "Jhanak Jhanak Payal Dosa". When I want half a cup of chai, I would ask for a "Cutting"; service in the car will be "Bonnet Service" and it would always be "double tan maar kedo" or "malai maarke"...

Bollywood's Favourite Too... Shah Rukh Khan, Aamir Khan, Sachin Tendulkar, Ustad Zakir Hussain, Sanjay Dutt, Naved and Jaaved Jaifrey often eat on the streets of Mumbai.

Please Excooz... *Hum police ke saath chor-police khelta hai*, says one of the stall owners, with a big smile on his face. So, it may be here today, gone tomorrow. Even as the book goes to print, I step up with quick rechecks, I notice some places renovating and others lost in oblivion, no one knows where. And many have been towed away by the "Mooncipal" van. I've tried to keep the book as current and as reliable as I could.

Timings? Legally? We are throttling our nightlife and snuffing it out by 1.30am. Some close earlier, but the real late-birds can sniff around and survive happily.

Pricing? Cheap and affordable! Can get a filling meal for less than ₹50!

Finally, I thank God for these eatabouts and am happy to note that the eateries too are equally grateful — many of them display inscriptions from the Quran praising and thanking Allah and I'd also like to join in and say, Allah am *Dullillahi Lazi Atamana*....

Colaba to Haji Ali, Parel

- The hottest and most happening *adda* here is **Ayub's**. It's rock-n-roll time here, always Chicken Roll, to be precise. Slinky cars, slinkier babes and what dudes you'd find outside Ayub's! The aroma of kebabs on coal wafts across the street as *chokra* boys clad in tee-shirts with "Ayub's" written on them weave between parked cars and customers standing around the coal-fired makeshift metal barbecues. The bearded, scruffy and friendly Ayub Sheikh and his two sons, Ashfaq and Ashziaque, are in great demand for their succulent Chicken Tikkas wrapped in Rotis, Boti Kebabs, and even the Veg Paneer Tikkas and Mushroom Tikkas (from ₹65 onwards). It felt so good standing on the street and eating in the cool winter night, even as warm barbecue aromas infused my Chicken Tikka Roll with flavour. Tasty and well-spiced fare here, including Tawa specials like Paneer Bhurji, Mutton Bhuna and more. Ayub takes party orders too. He and his family set up shop at the end of Kala Ghoda, (43, Dr VB Gandhi Marg, Shop No.5, Near Rhythm House, Fort, Ph: 9821199147). Go rock-n-roll (6.30pm to 1.30am; outdoor seating, car service)!
- A lot of the street-side action centres around the legendary Bade Miya (the lane behind Taj Mahal Hotel) where you'd find plenty of kebabs (₹100 onwards) and rotis to eat (7pm to 1.30am; outdoor seating). Tulloch Road, Apollo Bunder, Behind Taj Mahal Hotel, Mumbai, Ph: 22848038, 22848038. Now they have an elegant new restaurant too at Horniman Circle (Shop No.6, Botawala Bldg., Near State Central Library, Horniman Circle, Fort, Mumbai, Ph: 22655657, 22655658, 22655659)
- The other hot favourite is Café Noorani for biryani, kebabs and Butter Chicken; ₹90 onwards at Haji Ali. (10am to midnight; indoor and outdoor seating; 5-D, Tardeo Road, Haji Ali Circle, Mumbai, Ph: 23534753/3054).

  Visit the Haji Ali Juice Centre for juices and veg sandwiches, pizzas, etc. sold off their narrow shop at the street corner of Haji Ali (Lala Lajpat Rai Road, Haji Ali Circle, Haji Ali, Mumbai, Ph: 23510957, 23517632), (6am to 1 am; Car service; accepts credit cards too)!
- Koyla and Basilico remain crowded in the wee hours too, despite the fact that they don't serve alcohol. Koyla (Gulf Hotel, HNA Azmi Marg, Colaba, Ph: 66369999) is open from 1pm to 1.30am, closed on Mondays and has indoor/rooftop seating. Basilico (Sentinel House, Arthur Bunder Road, Colaba, Near Radio Club, Ph: 66345670, 66345671) is open from 9am to 1am and has indoor seating).

Maroush at High Street Phoenix serves up VFM shawarmas (11am to midnight).

- Golden Crown at Gowalia Tank, a large bustling eatery, is a good bet to drop in for a drink and a late Mughlai meal. This one rocks late into the night 11am to 1.30am; Indoor Seating; 29/33 August Kranti Marg, Gowalia Tank, Nana Chowk, Kemps Corner, Cumballa Hill, Phone: 23805247, 23805886

Grant Road, Crawford Market, Mohammedali road, VT Byculla

Late-night kebabs and more on the street? Zero in on Crawford Market, Bhendi Bazaar, Minara Masjid. Hospital and the Agripada and Nagpada areas. The counters and gadis are nameless and are always on the move - cruise around and you'll find them scattered all over. A few tips:

- For grilled to perfection Khiri and Kaleji, go behind Crawford Market to hunt for Nagdevi Street's handcart-driven delicacies.
- Zaffran (B Block, Dr DN Road, Sitaram Bldg., Crawford Market, Chhatrapati Shivaji Terminus, Ph: 23442690) is an air-conditioned restaurant serving above-average food (refer to the "Restaurant" section in the "Food Guide") remains open up to 4am, and home delivers too. Open from 7pm to 4am with indoor seating.
- The Naan-Chaanp-*wallah* opposite Pydhonie police station is worth checking out. Mind-blowing nightlife here — it's like midday at midnight! Brisk business carries on, children run around, medical stores remain open and juicewallahs (with mixies on their handcarts) bustle around. There's a lane here known for its Naan-Chaanp. Large tawas are piled with Boti, and parathas are rolled on the side. Rickety plastic buckets, large gas cylinders and fast-and-furious cooking - that's the scene. Makeshift tables and red plastic chairs laid out under a corrugated covering make for a small, no-frills, indoor seating area. Three basic, similar eateries stand cheek-by-jowl, serving parathas, Mutton Boti, Nalli and Liver. You could even shop for veggies (like I did) well past midnight and get some really fresh, unusual varieties.

  Sayeed's Sheekh Kebab at Bachu Seth Ki Wadi serves plump Seekh Kebabs with fistfuls of pudina and rotis on battered steel plates in a shed and has been a long-time favourite with nightowls on the prowl (Bacchubhai Ni Wadi, Shop No. 7, Grant Road, Near Kamathipura, Ph: 65590646, 65590646). Open from 6pm to 5am; it offers outdoor seating.
- Light of Asia (opposite VT) is a great late-night option for usual Mughlai fare, says Dilip Joshi (Kothari Mansion, Mint Road, Fort, Opp. GPO, Ph: 65537626). Open 24 hours with outdoor seating.
- "Nawab Seekh" at Do Taki, Maulana Shaukat Ali Road, near ii. Hospital makes luscious, long Seekh Kebabs and serves them with onion rings, pudina leaves and nimbu. Right next to this "kebab factory" lie stacks of large, white parathas.

Dadar, Shivaji Park, King's Circle, Matunga

- Pao Bhaji, Pulao and more are sold off handcarts near Sena Bhavan. Hunt for superb-fresh idlis, Upma and Sheera early in the morning at Ramashreya, Matunga. At Dadar Station (E), there's plenty of food to be had, especially the Bhurji Amlait Pay. This is where the night birds flock when the hunger pangs strike for omelette and Bhurji. The Rajus from Bihar and the Amars from UP whip up a mean *amlait* (omelette) by the railway tracks, amid folding chairs, plastic stools, egg-racks piled on handcarts and scattered, messy plastic buckets holding dirty plates. The full-bodied two-egg amlait with garlic and garam masala will set you back by ₹25 and the vegetarian rice plate by ₹30. Guess what? You get Chinese Manchow soup too! There's Baban Chaiwala at Dadar Station (W). Chocolate Chai for you? "Cutting" or a full glass? For ₹8 (give me "Cutting" any day), I enjoy a small glass of heavily-brewed, strongly-flavoured sweet tea. I stand alongside the small gadi and drink it as millions mill past under the grotty bridge. Small brass kettles hum busily and there are at least two more *gaadis* offering the same Chocolate Chai — they've been doing so since 1966.
- Next to Aurora Theatre and the Gujarat Club, you can get yourself some really delicious Pao Bhaji.

Mahim

- Walk down U 2nd Cross Road and you'd find many kebab-wallahs briskly frying kebabs, Khiri and more. Check out the Ragda and Chana Batata served in a pyali. A delightful, if somewhat messy and cluttered street. Right next to the brightly-lit Baba Falooda stands the young, smiling Mubarak Husain with his large brass vessel. He dishes out the most delicious Khichda. Freak out on this unique Muslim dish of wheat and meat, and don't forget the nimbu. Do go early, because he runs out of Khichda really fast. He can also come home and cook for you, on request.

Sion Koliwada

- Go below the flyover adjoining the bus depot if you're looking for some good Bhurji Pay. At the Sion Station-Highway Junction Rickshaw Stand, opposite Chhagan Mitha Petrol Pump, you'll find Tambi Idliwalla. This native of Chennai creates the hot flavour of Sion's sidewalks, catering to the nightlife of the city. Through the night, South Indian specialities are served — recommended are the idlis and dosas at ₹6. The service is swift, and the food is quite good too.

Bandra (East and West)

- Dilip Joshi's insider's tip is to go to (or order from) U Turn (Near Khar Station, Ph: 26460441; 11am to 1.30am) which serves up superb Biryani, Mutton Rogan Josh and Butter Chicken, all of which is swiftly home delivered.

- Go to Janata (78-A, Dr Ambedkar Road, Pali Naka, Bandra (W), Opp. Five Spice; Ph: 26005180; Noon to 1am with indoor seating) for fuelling yourself up with beer. Go opposite Bandra Station (the road which connects the station to Lucky's) for kebabs from the kebabwallahs lined up there.

Andheri (East and West)

- A well-known mecca for night birds, the Cooper Hospital area boasts Bhurji Pao-wallahs serving piping hot Pay Bhaji and Veg Biryani. Each time I've been there, Zakir Bhurjiwala goes taka-tak with his Bhurji Pay and Veg Biryani and his handcart is always surrounded by eager customers. Just outside Andheri Station (W) is an "Irani" joint which is a great place to visit for a very early breakfast. It's a functional, no-frills eatery where you can ask for Kheema Pay, Brun Malal and eggs-to-order.
- At the Terminal 1B (Terminal 1/B, Domestic Airport, Andheri (E), Ph: 26164798, 26164799; 24 hours and indoor seating;) at the domestic airport in Andheri (E), is a VFM 24-hour eatery called "Balaji" that serves up pure-veggie stuff including Bhel Puris, pizzas and burgers.

Jogeshwari

- Behind the spare-parts market in Behram Baug at Jogeshwari, Fareed Sayyed serves up some great kebabs and Tandoori fare, including Tandoori Chicken.

Malad

- Go to Raju Kabab and Chinese Corner (opposite Orlem Church, Marve Road, Malad West, Ph: 28793345; noon to midnight with outdoor seating) for variety fare like Bheja Fry and Chicken Tandoori. Check out Dial-a-Biryani too (see listings).

  Chincholi junction (Malad Link Road) just before Toyota showroom is a haven for late birds and those working in the various BPOs, KPOs etc. in MINDSPACE Corporate Park. The variety of food is unlimited. A Shetty place has pav bhaji, pizzas, grilled sandwhiches, hot dosas, idlis, medu wadas, tava pulao, wraps etc served 24 hours. Yes, its true this place has eateries which are operational thru day and night. They also have a Smokin Joe's which is open till 4am in the morning. There are lots of other options like chinese food stalls, complete home made khana stalls which looks very unhygenic and lots of chai wallas. But the actual hero of the street is a Brun Maska place which serves various types of biryani till wee hours of the night but from dawn onwards they get these fresh "laadis" of brun paos and sweet buns and serve with a generous helping of butter. Perfect combo with Masala Chai to start your day. He has all sorts of add ons available with him like jams, cheese etc. This lane does good business through out the day as it has a Jumbo Vada Pao shop, frankie stalls and lot of small drinking bars lined up. All are economically priced and attract people who frequent the place often.

Chembur, Ghatkopar

- Sindhi food is served at Chembur Camp and Achija at Ghatkopar (the latter being especially known its for Pao Bhaji). These are well-known options for eating out late at night. At Achija, *makkhan lagaana* takes on a whole new meaning as I bite into the Pao glistening with butter, and watch blobs of it swimming in full-bodied, spiced-up Bhaji. I enjoy the classic preparation and even the one with grated cheese in it. They have quite a range here, including the cheese-and-dry-fruit Achija special. This is the Ghatkoparites' mecca for Pao Bhaji. The pure-veg, functional eatery also serves, with lightning swiftness, the usual pizzas, noodles, idlis, dosas and what-not, all priced between ₹12–50 (Vasant Niwas, Tilak Road Naka, Ghatkopar East).

OPEN 24 HOURS

022
Trident Bandra-Kurla, C-56, G-Block, Bandra-Kurla Complex, Mumbai, Ph: 66727610, 66727606/07

180 Degrees
Grand Sarovar Premiere, AK Plaza, Goregaon (W), Mumbai, Ph: 28718000, 421580000

24/7
The Lalit – Mumbai, Sahar Airport Road, Andheri (E), Mumbai, Ph: 66992222, 30673123

Aqua
Sun-n-Sand Hotel, 39, Juhu Beach, Mumbai, Ph: 66938888

Bayview
Hotel Marine Plaza, 29, Marine Drive, Mumbai, Ph: 22851212

Baywatch
The Resort, Aksa Beach, Madh–Marve Road, Malad (W), Mumbai, Ph: 28808888 284477715

Blue Flame
Hotel United 21, 29, LBS Marg, Near Castle Mill Circle, Gokul Nagar, Thane (W), Ph: 41579999, 61165999

Boulevard
The Orchid, 70-C, Nehru Road, Vile Parle (E), Mumbai, Ph: 26164040 (Extn. 4010/4011)

Café Oregano
Ramee Guestline Hotel, 462, Abnair Road, Juhu, Mumbai, Ph: 6,693,555,567,159,200

Café Prato
Four Seasons Hotel, 114, Dr E Moses Road, Worli, Mumbai, Ph: 24818000

Carafe
The Peninsula Grand Hotel, Saki Naka Junction, Andheri (E), Mumbai, Ph: 28519191, 28531110

Citrus
The Leela Kempinski Mumbai, Sahar, Andheri (E), Mumbai, Ph: 66911359

The Earth Plate
Sahara Star, Near the Domestic Airport, Santacruz, Mumbai, Ph: 39895000 (Extn.7163/65)

Flavors
The Ambassador Hotel, Ground Floor, Nariman Road, Churchgate, Mumbai, Ph: 22041131

The Glasshouse
Hyatt Regency Mumbai, Sahar Airport Road, Andheri (E), Mumbai, Ph: 66961621/24

Hornby's Pavilion
ITC Grand Central, 287, Dr Ambedkar Road, Parel, Mumbai, Ph: 24101010 (Extn. 5121-22)

La Brasserie
Hilton, Sahar Airport Road, Andheri (E), Mumbai, Ph: 28380000, 29262731

Lakeview Café
Renaissance Hotel & Convention Centre, 2&3B, Powai, Mumbai, Ph: 66927550

Lotus Café
JW Marriott Hotel, Juhu Tara Road, Mumbai, Ph: 66933276-77

Momo Café
Courtyard By Marriott, CTS No. 215, Andheri–Kurla Road, Andheri (E), Mumbai, Ph: 61369999

The Peshwa Pavilion
ITC Maratha, Sahar, Andheri, Mumbai, Ph: 28303030

Pondichery Café
Sofitel Mumbai BKC, C-57, Block G, Bandra Kurla Complex, Bandra (E), Mumbai, Ph: 61175000-01

Poolside
VITS Business Hotel, International Airport Zone, Andheri–Kurla Road, Andheri (E), Mumbai, Ph: 61517555

Princess Lounge
Hotel Sea Princess, Juhu Beach, Mumbai, Ph: 26611111, 66924455

Seasonal Tastes
The Westin Mumbai Garden City, International Business Park, Oberoi Garden City, Goregaon (E), Mumbai, Ph: 61470000, 67361050, 67361801, 67361803

Seven
Palladium Hotel, 462, Senapati Bapat Marg, Lower Parel, Mumbai, Ph: 61628000

Shamiana
The Taj Mahal Palace, Lobby Level, Apollo Bunder, Mumbai, Ph: 66653366 (Extn. 3271)

Spice It
IBIS Hotel Mumbai, Plot No. F-77, Junction of Nehru Road, Western Express Highway, Vile Parle (E), Mumbai, Ph: 67087777

The Square
Novotel Mumbai Juhu Beach, Balraj Sahani Marg, Juhu Beach, Mumbai, Ph: 66934444/4343

Tangerine
Ramada Plaza Palm Grove, Juhu Tara Road, Juhu, Mumbai, Ph: 26112323

Tangerine Café
The Retreat, Erangal Beach, Madh–Marve Road, Malad (W), Mumbai, Ph: 28813500/6379/6383

Trattoria
Vivanta by Taj – President, Mumbai, 90, Cuffe Parade, Mumbai, Ph: 66650808 (Extn. 3271), 66650971

Verandah
The Trident, Nariman Point, Mumbai, Ph: 66326326

Vista
Taj Lands End, Band Stand, Bandra (W), Mumbai, Ph: 66681234

West 1
The Park, No. 1, Sector-10, CBD Belapur, Navi Mumbai, Ph: 27589000

Wrapped
Four Points by Sheraton, Plot 39/1, 6 to 15, Sector-30A, Vashi, Navi Mumbai, Ph: 27817777

LATE-NIGHT EATABOUTS

210 Degree Celcius
Matru Ashish Bldg., Ground Floor, Napean Sea Road, Mumbai, Ph: 65249279

Prem Court, Jamshedji Tata Road, Near Eros Cinema, Churchgate, Mumbai, Ph: 42135407

Rushabh Tower, Shop no. 15, Prathana Samaj, Near Girgaon Court, Mumbai, Ph: 23883838

5 Spice
3/4, Dheeraj Pali Arcade, Dr Ambedkar Road, Pali Naka, Bandra (W), Mumbai, Ph: 26421941

Swati Apts., Anand Nagar, Oshiwara, Andheri (W), Mumbai, Ph: 26335550

Shiva Industrial Estate, Andheri–Kurla Road, Mumbai, Ph: 28562186–88

296/A, Sangli Bank Bldg., Behind Old Reserve Bank of India Bldg., Perin Nariman Street, Mumbai, Ph: 22691257, 22666434/4543

Renis Apts., Lane Opp. Green Hotel, Near Inorbit Mall, Off Link Road, Malad (W), Mumbai, Ph: 28760172, 28760173, 28760170

91, Shalimar Bldg., Near Everest Bldg., G Road, Marine Lines, Mumbai, Ph: 22817156-58

Virajdeep Apts., Chandavarkar Road, Borivali (W), Mumbai, Ph: 28338311-14, 9820780846

5 The Restaurant
25/D, Willingdon, Catholic Colony, SV Road, Santacruz (W), Mumbai, Ph: 26000367, 66939919

Aafrein
Sahara Star, Opp. Domestic Airport, Vile Parle, Mumbai, Ph: 39895000, 39807170

Achija Juice Centre
13, Vasant Niwas, Tilak Road Naka, Ghatkopar (E), Mumbai, Ph: 21025982, 21027359, 21024909, 9820902736

Akarshan
Station Road, Vikhroli (W), Mumbai, Ph: 25791964, 25779470

Alfredo's
King's International, Opp. Juhu Bus Depot, 5, Juhu Tara Road, Mumbai, Ph: 66922222, 26184381

All Stir Fry
The Gordon House Hotel, 5, Battery Street, Apollo Bunder, Colaba, Mumbai, Ph: 22871122, 22894451-52

Almond Flower
461, Adarsh Nagar, Oshiwara, Andheri (W), Mumbai, Ph: 26316888, 26316999, 9870856691

Amadeus
NCPA, Nariman Point, Mumbai, Ph: 22821212, 67230234/02222

Amantran
Minerva Chambers, JN Road, Mulund (W), Mumbai, Ph: 25640122, 25617467, 25900122

Ankur
Meadows House, Tamarind Lane, Fort, Mumbai, Ph: 22654194, 22630393

Apoorva Restaurant & Bar
Vasta House, Noble Chambers, SA Brelvi Marg, Fort, Mumbai, Ph: 22870335, 22881457

Appetite
Plot No. 8, Sector-24, Sion–Panvel Highway, Turbhe, Navi Mumbai, Ph: 27830069/5857/1083

Aroma
97, Dadasaheb Phalke Road, Dadar (E), Mumbai, Ph: 24147888, 24181788

Arsalan
Sapphire Bldg., SV Road Corner, Khar (W), Mumbai, Ph: 26045171

Asia 7
3rd Floor, Palladium Mall, High Street Phoenix, Mumbai, Ph: 43473901/02

Atrium Lounge
Taj Lands End, Bandstand, Bandra (W), Mumbai, Ph: 66681234, 66687420

Aurus
Ground Floor, Nichani Kutir, Beside Reid & Taylor Showroom, 12th Juhu Tara Road, Mumbai, Ph: 67106666-67

The Avenue
The Avenue Hotels Pvt. Ltd., Western Express Highway, Thakur Complex, Kandivali (E), Mumbai, Ph: 28540888, 28700000/9999

Ayub's
Shop No. 5, 43, Dr VB Gandhi Marg, Near Rhythm House, Fort, Mumbai, Ph: 65618000, 9821199147

Bachu Seth Ki Wadi
Shop No. 7, Sayeed Seekh Kabab Centre, RS Nimkar Marg, Bachu Wadi, Mumbai

Bade Miya
Tulloch Road, Apollo Bunder, Behind Taj Mahal Hotel, Mumbai, Ph: 22848038

Shop No. 6, Botawala Bldg., Near State Central Library, Horniman Circle, Fort, Mumbai, Ph: 22655657–59, 22021447

Badshah
152/156, LT Marg, Near Churchgate, Mumbai, Ph: 23425950, 23449316

Bagdadi Restaurant
11, Tulloch Road, Apollo Bunder, Mumbai, Ph: 22028027

Balthazar
Juhu Tara Road, Adjacent to SNDT, Mumbai, Ph: 26609292, 26603947, 9930999930

Bamboo
The Park, No. 1, Sector-10, CBD Belapur, Navi Mumbai, Ph: 27589000

Banana Leaf
Shubham CHS, Juhu–Versova Link Road, Andheri (W), Mumbai, Ph: 26709999, 26239999

Gayatri Satsang Bldg., Behind Vishnu Shivam Mall, Thakur Village, Kandivali (E), Mumbai, Ph: 28862887, 28862889

3rd Floor, R City Mall, Ghatkopar (W), Mumbai, Ph: 9930756127

3rd Floor, Neptune Magnet Mall, Bhandup, Mumbai, Ph: 26239999

3rd Floor, Korum Mall, Near Cadbury Compound, Panch Pakhadi, Mumbai, Ph: 65612791, 65612790

Barbeque Nation
Ground Floor, Greensquares, Near Fun Republic Mall, Lokhandwala, Andheri (W), Mumbai, Ph: 9320005614

Shop No. 403, Ground Floor, Om Palace, Dr Ambedkar Road, Junction Pali Hill, Khar, Mumbai, Ph: 60600000, 65934343, 9323905592

Sun Magnetica Bldg., Greens Road, Near LIC Bldg., Eastern Express Highway, Louiswadi, Thane (W), Ph: 32162333/444

Plot No. 20, 1st Floor Beverley Park, Sector 6, Above ICICI Bank, Palam Beach Road, Nerul,

Navi Mumbai,
Ph: 9321201040

Tower A, 1st Floor, Timesquare, Opp. Mittal Industrial, Kurla Road, Narol, Andheri (E), Saki Naka, Mumbai, Ph: 9320001619

Atria Mall, 4th Floor, Opp. Poonam Chambers, Worli, Mumbai, Ph: 9022011888

Bhagat Tarachand

51/53, Mumbadevi Commercial Centre, Zaveri Bazaar, Kalbadevi, Mumbai, Ph: 22426167, 22420215

Shop No. 6/6A, Shatrugan Tower, Near Mafco Market, Sector-18, Vashi, Navi Mumbai, Ph: 27888126, 65116242

Bharat Lunch Home

317, Bharat House, Shaheed Bhagat Singh Road, Mumbai, Ph: 22618991, 22672677

Bhojohori Manna

3&4, Reliable Buisness Centre, Near Om Heera Panna Mall, Oshiwara, Off Link Road, Andheri (W), Mumbai, Ph: 65993385

Big Daddy

Hotel Unicontinental, Next to Khar Station, Mumbai, Ph: 9819930930, 9819930830, 65819996/7

Third Road, Khar, Mumbai, Ph: 65819996-97

shop No. 235, Bharat Nagar Society Andheri Versova Link Road, Andheri, Mumbai, Ph: 9819830280, 9819800000

Blend n Brew

70 (0), Central Avenue Road, Chembur (E), Mumbai, Ph: 25280014, 67692222

The Blue Frog Club

D-2, Todi Industrial Estate, Opp. Kamala Mills Compound, Mathuradas Mill Compound, NM Joshi Marg, Lower Parel, Mumbai, Ph: 65251716, 65251718, 61586158

Blue Waters

Opp. Tata Power House, Andheri New Link Road, Andheri (W), Mumbai, Ph: 26743615/4805

Bombay Blue

Shoppers' Stop Premise, SV Road, Andheri (W), Mumbai, Ph: 26232222/7000

18, Har Govindas Bldg., K Dubhash Marg, Kala Ghoda, Mumbai, Ph: 22041661

High Street Phoenix, 462, Senapati Bapat Marg, Lower Parel, Mumbai, Ph: 24961999

Summerville, Junction of 14th & 33rd Road, Linking Road, Khar (W), Mumbai, Ph: 26000444/888

Bombay Blue Express, Plot No. 5-6, 2nd Floor, InOrbit Mall, MindSpace, Malad (W), Link Road, Mumbai, Ph: 32911802

Busaba

4, Mandlik Road, Colaba, Mumbai, Ph: 22043769/72/79

Mathura Das Mill Compound, NN Joshi Marg, Opp. Blue Frog, Lower Parel, Mumbai, Ph: 67478971–74

Café Basilico Bistro & Deli

St. John Road, Opp. Gold's Gym, Pali Naka, Bandra (W), Mumbai, Ph: 67039999, 67100000

Sentinel House, Arthur Bunder Road, Near Radio Club, Colaba, Mumbai, Ph: 66345670-71

Café Churchill

103-B, East West Court Bldg., Shaheed Bhagat

Singh Road, Mumbai, Ph: 22844689, 22042604

Café Ideal
Shop No. 5, Fulchand Nivas, Chowpatty, Mumbai, Ph: 23630943

Café Mangii
14th Road, Off Linking Road, Khar (W), Mumbai, Ph: 26498100, 65268100, 26498200

Ground Floor, 3, Transocean Garden, Hiranandani Garden Lane, Opp. Powai Lake, Powai, Mumbai, Ph: 25705136–39

Shop No. 28, Aram Nagar 1, Versova, Andheri (W), Mumbai, Ph: 26316100-02

Junction of Khar Pali and 14th Road, Off Linking Road, Inside Nike Showroom Lane, Khar, Mumbai

Café Mangii
R City Mall, LBS Marg, Ghatkopar (W), Mumbai

Café Mondegar
Metro House, Shaheed Bhagat Singh Road, Colaba, Mumbai, Ph: 22020591

Café Noorani
5-D, Tardeo Road, Haji Ali Circle, Mumbai, Ph: 23534753/3054

Café Zoe
Todi Mathuradas Mill Compound, 126, NM Joshi Marg, Lower Parel, Mumbai, Ph: 24902065

California Pizza Kitchen
North Avenue, Maker Maxity, Bandra–Kurla Complex,Bandra (E), Mumbai, Ph: 65588888, 65606560

California Pizza Kitchen
Courtyard, phoenix Mills, Lower Parel, Mumbai, Ph: 66366636, 65588880

3rd Floor, Food Court, Infinite 2, Next to Goregon, Sports Club, Link Road, Malad (W), Mumbai, Ph: 65848888, 67656600

Cannon Pav Bhaji
Opp. CST, Chhatrapati Shivaji Terminus, Churchgate, Mumbai, Ph: 22074205

Canvas
Palladium Mall, 4th Floor, Senapati Bapat Marg, Lower Parel, Mumbai, Ph: 43485050, 43485010/5020

Canvas Laugh Factory
3rd Floor, Palladium Mall, High Street Phoenix, Mumbai, Ph: 43485000, 43485010, 43485020

Celebrations
Sunny Estate, 1, Sion–Trombay Road, Chembur, Mumbai, Ph: 25224446-47

Days Inn Hotel, Sector-19, Plot No. L-1, Near St Lawrence School, Vashi, Navi Mumbai, Ph: 27800403–05

Central Peninsula
88, Satyam Shivam Sunderam Apts., Sion Circle, Mumbai, Ph: 24031133/77, 24041144

Chakra
Saki Naka Junction, Kurla Road, Andheri (E), Mumbai, Ph: 28513331/5205/2463

Chandragupta
Vidya Bhavan Cooperative Society, Opp. Sena Bhavan, Dadar, Mumbai, Ph: 24446405-06

Chef's Studio
The Taj Mahal Palace, Apollo Bunder, Mumbai, Ph: 66653366 (Extn. 6268)

Chenab
Plot No. 133/ A, Sector-8, Next to Sagar Vihar, Vashi, Navi Mumbai, Ph: 27821722/26, 9820136471

Chili's

Ventura Bldg., Ground Floor, Opp. Wipro Company, Hirandani Gardens, Powai, Mumbai, Ph: 67419002-04

China Garden

Gabbana House, 15th Road, Khar (W), Mumbai, Ph: 26002626/11, 26512828

China Gate

Royal Plaza, Near Citi Mall, New Link Road, Andheri (W), Mumbai, Ph: 2639001–05, 42631000

Atria Mall, Dr Annie Besant Road, Worli, Mumbai, Ph: 24813313/23/32/39, 9969258217

150, Waterfield Road, Bandra (W), Mumbai, Ph: 26452600

Grand Hyatt Mumbai, Off Western Express Highway, Santacruz (E), Mumbai, Ph: 66761234

Chinese Room

Kwality House, Kemp's Corner, Mumbai, Ph: 23806771/5268, 23864991

Copper Chimney

18, Har Govindas, K Dubhash Marg, Kala Ghoda, Mumbai, Ph: 22041661, 22022555/444

Phoenix Mills Coumpound, 262, Senapati Bapat Marg, Lower Parel, Mumbai, Ph: 24963333

12/A, Lotus Court, Near Nehru Planetarium, Dr Annie Besant Road, Worli, Mumbai, Ph: 24925353

3rd Floor, Oberoi Mall, Goregaon (E), Mumbai, Ph: 67105967, 67105968

Above Toyota Showroom, KharDanda Road, khar (W), Mumbai, Ph: 67412400

101, 1st Floor, Fortune Classic, Junction Off 15th Road, Opp. Gabana Showroom, CD Marg, Khar, Mumbai, Ph: 67412401, 67256250

Corleone

InterContinental Marine Drive, Level 1, 135, Marine Drive, Mumbai, Ph: 39879999

Corniche

B-15 Gagangiri Society, Next to Café Coffee Day, Carter Road, Khar (W), Mumbai, Ph: 26460147, 9819800239

The Creek

Abbott Hotel, Sector-2, Vashi, Navi Mumbai, Ph: 27826677, 40854560

Dakshin Culture Curry

TH Kataria Road, Near Hinduja Hospital, Mumbai, Ph: 24440202/0707, 24468262

Lokhandwala Road, Nr Versova Telephone Exchange, Andheri (W), Mumbai, Ph: 26313222-777-999, 9619961818

Dara's Dhaba

Western Express Highway, Post Mira, Thane, Ph: 28456119, 32970818

Delhi Darbar

10/14, Holland House, Shaheed Bhagat Singh Road, Near Regal Cinema, Colaba, Mumbai, Ph: 22020235/5656, 22825858, 22845152

Destiny Dining Bar

Hotel Tunga Paradise, P-16, MIDC Central Road, Andheri (E), Mumbai, Ph: 28217272–77

Di Bella

Title Waves, Ground Floor, St Paul's Media Complex, 24th Road, TPS III, Bandra (W), Mumbai, Ph: 65140333

Diva Maharashtracha

TH Kataria Marg, Near Hinduja Hospital, Shivaji Park, Mahim,

Mumbai, Ph: 24454433, 24440202

SVP Nagar, Lokhandwala Road, 4 Bungalows, Andheri (W), Mumbai, Ph: 26313222, 26313770

DP's Wok Hei

Khimji Nagji Bldg., Senapati Bapat Marg, Opp. Phoenix Towers, Lower Parel, Mumbai, Ph: 24954627

Dum Pukht

ITC Maratha, Sahar Road, Andheri, Mumbai, Ph: 28303030

Dynasty

Geetika Cooperative Housing Society, 85, SV Road, Santacruz (W), Mumbai, Ph: 26487436, 26054741

Eat Around the Corner

Junction of 24th & 30th Road, TPS III, Bandra (W), Mumbai, Ph: 26006717/2665

Elbo Room

Plot No. 500, Sant Kutir Apts., Khar Linking Road, Behind Levi's Showroom, Khar (W), Mumbai, Ph: 26483316

Elco Caterers

46, Hill Road, Opp. Elco Market, Bandra (W), Mumbai, Ph: 26437206, 26457677,65877171

Emperor's Court

Renaissance Hotel & Convention Centre, 2&3-B, Powai, Mumbai, Ph: 66927561/8888

Esplanade Canteen

Azad Maidan Police Club, Behind Esplanade Quilla Court, Fort, Mumbai, Ph: 9702838666

Roopam, Near Crawford Market, DN Road, Mumbai, Ph: 9702828666

The Excellensea

317, Bharat House, Opp. Fort Market, SBS Road, Mumbai, Ph: 22618991, 66359945

Fifty Five East

Grand Hyatt Mumbai, Off Western Express Highway, Santacruz (E), Mumbai, Ph: 66761234

Firangi Paani

Fun Republic, Level 3, Link Road, Andheri (W), Mumbai, Ph: 26744144, 26734730

Fire Bowl

A/1, Mangal Orchid, Off Yari Road, Versova, Mumbai

Shop No. 1, Mangal Nagar, Mangal Orchid Bldg., Yari Road, Versova, Andheri, Mumbai, Ph: 65742005

Shop No. 17, Link Plaza, New Link Road, Near Shreeji Restaurant, Oshiwara, Mumbai, Ph: 65226060

Flags

Asiad Co. Housing Society Ltd., BJ Patel Road, Malad (W), Mumbai, Ph: 28832222, 28821111

Flamboyante

Fountain Hospitality Pvt. Ltd., World Trade Centre, Cuffe Parade, Colaba, Mumbai, Ph: 22180433-34, 40647700

Flames

Hilton, Sahara Airport Road, Andheri (E), Mumbai, Ph: 28380000

Fountain Sizzlers

57, MG Road, Opp. HSBC Bank, Fort, Mumbai, Ph: 22675315/0920, 40647777, 9773565798

Frangipani

The Trident, Nariman Point, Mumbai, Ph: 66326310/4343

Fratelli Fresh

Renaissance Hotel & Convention Centre, 2&3-B, Powai, Mumbai, Ph: 66927540/7777/8888

Fredrick's Lounge
ITC Grand Central, 287, Dr Ambedkar Road, Parel, Mumbai, Ph: 24101010, 40175117

Fusion Dhaba
Road No. 16, Near Wagle Estate Fire Brigade, Wagle Estate, Thane (W), Ph: 25825166/0134/, 9619719944

Gajalee Coastal Food
Amrapali Shopping Centre, VL Mehta Marg, Vile Parle, Juhu, Mumbai, Ph: 26107040, 66960902

Akshaye Villa, Plot No. 24, Seven Bungalows, Andheri (W), Mumbai, Ph: 26341614-15

Annexe E-3, Udyog Sadan No. 2, MIDC, Andheri (E), Mumbai, Ph: 28227272/7373

Kadambari Complex, Hanuman Road, Vile Parle (E), Mumbai, Ph: 26166470, 26114093

High Street Phoenix Mills Compound, Unit 2, Block 3, Lower Parel, Mumbai, Ph: 24950667-68

Gallops
Mahalaxmi Race Course, Mahalaxmi, Mumbai, Ph: 23071448/1453/1258

Garden Court Restaurant
Neelyog Square Mall, Ghatkopar (E), Mumbai, Ph: 25010379/52

167, Marve Road, Malad (W), Mumbai, Ph: 28072973/8342

JP Road, Near Sports Complex, Andheri (W), Mumbai, Ph: 26770318/0253

InOrbit Mall, 2nd Floor, Vashi, Mumbai, Ph: 27810290-91

Gary's Menu
Shop No. 1, Daffodil Bldg., Hiranandani Gardens, Powai, Mumbai, Ph: 25706159/1786

Gaylord
Mayfair, Veer Nariman Road, Churchgate, Mumbai, Ph: 22821259, 22044693, 22848076

Global Fusion China Gate
3rd Floor, Link Square Mall, Linking Road, Bandra (W), Mumbai, Ph: 26469001-02/111/222, 42633000

Gloria Jean's
Carlton Court, Junction of Pali Hill and Turner Road, Pali Hill, Bandra (W), Mumbai, Ph: 26426053

G-3 Ground Floor, CitiPark Bldg., Hiranandani Business Park, Hiranandani Gardens, Powai, Mumbai, Ph: 40156262

Oberoi Mall, International Business Park, Oberoi Garden City, Off Western Express Highway, Goregaon (E), Mumbai, Ph: 40034754

Janaki Kutir, Next to Pithvi Theatre, Juhu, Mumbai, Ph: 67981621

Floor, Infinity 2 Mall, Malad (W), Mumbai, Ph: 67656634, 8796477097

Goa Portuguesa
Near Hinduja Hospital, TH Kataria Road, Opp. Head Post Mahim, Shivaji Park, Mumbai, Ph: 24440202/0707, 24468262/8515

Andheri (W), Lokhandwala Road, Near versova Telephone Exchange, Mumbai, Ph: 26313222, 9167096000

Next to R Mall, Ghodbandar Road, Opp. Lawkim Godrej, Thane (W), Ph: 25890184, 9769919581

Gokul Restaurant & Bar
10, Tulloch Road, Nawaz Bldg., Behind Taj Mahal Palace, Apollo Bunder, Colaba, Mumbai, Ph: 22848248, 22848206

Golden Chariot

Evershine City, Vasai (E), Ph: 02502463070, 9881185604

Girnar Tower, Opp. New Petrol Pump, Mira Byander Road, Mira Road (E), Ph: 28106066, 28100948, 28106350

V-Mall, Asha Nagar, W.E. Highway, Kandivali (E), Mumbai, Ph: 28547259

Growel, 101, Akurli Road, Kandivali (E), Mumbai, Ph: 28461414

Hub Mall, 2nd Floor, Western Express Highway, Goregaon (E), Mumbai, Ph: 67988777, 67988790

Golden Dragon

The Taj Mahal Palace, Apollo Bunder, Mumbai, Ph: 66653366

Golden Lawn

Krishna Baug, RC Marg, Near Fine Arts Society, Chembur, Mumbai, Ph: 25286850/4441/2290

Gondola

4, Silver Croft, Opp. Pali Market, Pali Mala Road, Bandra (W), Mumbai, Ph: 26040294/0046, 26055826, 65552152

Grain & Bagel

Interface 11, Raheja Complex, Behind Infiniti Mall, Off Link Road, Malad (W), Mumbai, Ph: 65610291

Grasshopper

Rinku Apts., VP Road, Vile Parle (W), Mumbai, Ph: 26183920, 26130840

Great Punjab Restaurant & Bar

Opp. Fire Brigade, Dr Ambedkar Road, Dadar (Central), Mumbai, Ph: 24114946/4713

266, Linking Road, Next to Shoppers' Stop, Bandra (W), Mumbai, Ph: 26429846, 26408036, 26413978

The Great Wall

Hotel Avenue, Thakur Complex, Western Express Highway, Kandivali (E), Mumbai, Ph: 28708888/9999/0000

Gulmurg

Shalimar Hotel, August Kranti Marg, Mumbai, Ph: 66641000

Gypsy Chinese

121, Maryland Corner, Keluskar Marg, Shivaji Park, Dadar, Mumbai, Ph: 24455965, 24467518, 65006855

Hard Rock Café

Bombay Dyeing Mills Compound, Pandurang Budhkar Marg, Worli, Mumbai, Ph: 24382888, 66511209

Home Town Café

Opp. Ramada Palm Grove, Juhu Tara Road, Mumbai, Ph: 26112211, 26112212

Oberoi Chambers Opp. Tanishq Showroom, Link Road, Andheri (W), Mumbai, Ph: 26748702-03

Caravan Serial Building 155, Water Fill Road, Bandra (W), Mumbai, Ph: 42636000/1000, 42636060-61

Horn Ok Please – The Indian Dhaba

Plot No. 47, Gulmohar Road, JVPD Scheme, Vile Parle (W), Mumbai, Ph: 26712598, 26707011

Hotel Purva Pangat

Shree Dutta Boarding House, Narayan Ashram Bldg. No. 7, Dr Ambedkar Road, Ganesh Gali, Lalbaug, Near Bharat Mata Cinema, Mumbai, Ph: 24710830

Hotel Purva Pangat

Shop No. 8, 301, Miranda Chawl, NC Kelkar Marg, Dadar, Mumbai, Ph: 24386504

Howrah

Hotel New Bengal, 'B' Shalimar Estates, Dr DN Road, Near Crawford Market, Mumbai, Ph: 23401951–56

Imperial China

Hilton, Sahar Airport Road, Escort Centre, Andheri (E), Mumbai, Ph: 28380000

India & Beyond

Ground Floor, Mahapalika Nagar, KAG Khan Road, Worli, Mumbai, Ph: 24920033/55

India Jones

The Trident, Nariman Point, Mumbai, Ph: 66326330

Indian Summer

Parekh Mahal, 80, Veer Nariman Road, Churchgate, Mumbai, Ph: 22835445/5650

Indigo

4, Mandlik Road, Colaba, Mumbai, Ph: 23549888, 23536262

Indigo Deli

Palladium Mall, Level 1, Phoenix High Street, Lower Parel, Mumbai, Ph: 24986262

5, Ground Floor, Pheroza Bldg., Chhatrapati Shivaji Marg, Apollo Bunder, Mumbai, Ph: 66551010

8, Fatima Villa, 29th Road, Pali Naka, Mumbai, Ph: 26426262

Indus

Hotel Diplomat, Ground Floor, BK Boman Behram Marg, Apollo Bunder, Colaba, Mumbai, Ph: 22021661

The Irish House

Phoenix Mills, Senapati Bapat Marg, Lower Parel, Above Gajalee, Ph: 43471111

30, K Dubhash Marg, Kala Ghoda, Fort, Mumbai, Ph: 49150000-02

Ivy Wine Cafe & Bistro

Indage House, 82, Dr Annie Besant Road, Opp. RBI, Worli, Mumbai, Ph: 66547939

7 Bungalows, Picnic Cottage, Opp. Beach Tower Classic, Aram Nagar, 1, JP Road, Mumbai, Ph: 26395995

Shop No. 6, Mangal Bhavan, Corner Of Khar Pali Road, 14th Road, Khar (W), Ph: 65347788

Jaffer Bhai's Delhi Darbar

18, Lady Jamshedji Road, Opp. St Michael Church, Mahim (W), Mumbai, Ph: 24465651/52/54

1st Marine Street, Near Round Masjid, Dhobi Talao, Mumbai, Ph: 22084613, 22016363

197, Corner of PB Marg, Opp. New Roshan Cinema, Grant Road (E), Mumbai, Ph: 23875656/97/98

13-15-17, Dr Meishwari Road, Next to Dongri Police Station, Noor Baug, Mumbai, Ph: 23715656/4242

Shop Nos. 6&7, Rendezvous Bldg., Ravi Raj Oberoi Complex, Off New Link Road, SAB TV Lane, Andheri (W), Mumbai, Ph: 26321370-71

151/153, Abdulla Mansion, SVP Road, Charnul, Dongri, Mumbai, Ph: 23433339

1/4 Plot No. 4, Sector 5, 18 Mafco Road, Next to APM E Market Ram Laxman Tower, New Mumbai, Vashi,

Jai Hind Lunch Home

6, Mantri Corner Bldg., Gokhale Road, Dadar, Mumbai, Ph: 24314256, 32951480

Madhav Bhuvan, B-Block, SB Marg, Opp. Kamla City, Lower Parel, Mumbai, Ph: 24902213, 32951481

Rizvi House, Ramdas Nayak Road, Hill Road, Bandra (W), Near Police Station, Mumbai, Ph: 26422974, 26512821

Shop No. 6, Thuru Apartments, Near Sangam Bar, VS Road, Dadar, Ph: 24308033

Pali Naka, Bandra (W), Mumbai, Ph: 32951482, 26483381/83

Jamavar

The Leela, Mumbai, Sahar, Andheri (E), Mumbai, Ph: 66911350, 66911351

Jewel of India

Nehru Centre, Dr Annie Besant Road, Worli, Mumbai, Ph: 24949214/9435 /9204/9219

Jugheads – The Unrestaurant

1st Floor, Jheel Darshan, Opp. Powai Lake, Mumbai, Ph: 25705222/5333

G-2, Thakur Mall, Next to Fame Box Office, Dahisar (E), Mumbai, Ph: 28456869, 28456860

Jagdamba Complex, Behind Movie Time Cinema, Malad (W), Mumbai, Ph: 28445514-15

Mishra House, Near Khar Station, Khar (W), Mumbai, Ph: 26059401-02

D-mall, First Floor, Off Veera Desai Road Andheri (W), Ph: 26731761

Jumjoji

Ankleshwar Bldg., ONGC Colony, Bandra Reclamation, Bandra (W), Mumbai, Ph: 26516156

Jyran

Sofitel Mumbai BKC, C-57, Block G, Bandra Kurla Complex, Bandra (E), Mumbai, Ph: 61175000-01

Kabab Hut

Sun-n-Sand Hotel, 39, Juhu Beach, Mumbai, Ph: 66938888, 26201811

Kailash Parbat Restaurant

1st Pasta Lane, Sheela Mahal, Colaba, Mumbai, Ph: 22874823, 22045281, 22812112

Inorbit Mall, Vashi, Mumbai, Ph: 9820355355

Oberoi Mall, Goregaon (E), Mumbai, Ph: 9320843700, 9820063365

InOrbit Mall, Malad (W), Mumbai, Ph: 9773616364

R City Mall, Ghatkopar (W), Mumbai, Ph: 9960069000, 9820330800

7/8, A Wing, Crystal Plaza, Opp. Infinity Mall, Andheri (W), Mumbai, Ph: 226743810, 67023300

Infinity 2 Mall, Malad (W), Mumbai, Ph: 9960069000, 9820330800

Growel's Mall, Kandivali (E), Mumbai, Ph: 9960069000, 9820330800

Phoenix Market City, Kurla, Mumbai, Ph: 9960069000, 9820330800

Opp. Mc Donalds Restaurant, Next to Honda Showroom, Saki Naka Junction, Saki Naka, Ph: 22612709, 27226120

Kakori House

Link Way Housing Coop Society, Bldg. 25, Shop No. 4&5, Opp. Meera Tower, New Linkway Road, Oshiwara, Andheri (W), Mumbai, Ph: 64539950-54

10-A, Shiv Sagar Housing Society, LJ Road, Opp. Paradise Cinema, Mahim, Mumbai, Ph: 65259211, 65269211, 65129211, 65229211

5, Dunhill Apts., 26, Waroda Road, Bandra (W), Mumbai, Ph: 65149211, 65159211, 65149211, 65159211

Shop No. 3, Sage Baug, Saki Naka, Near Mitthal Industries, Opp. Mahalaxmi Garden Restaurant, Andheri

Kurla Road, Andheri (E), Mumbai, Ph: 28520990–92

Kala Ghoda Café

10, Ropewalk Lane, Kala Ghoda, Fort, Mumbai, Ph: 22633866

Kangan

Level 18, The Westin Mumbai Garden City, International Business Park, Oberoi Garden City, Goregaon (E), Mumbai, Ph: 61470000, 67361050

Kareem's

134, Galleria Shopping Mall, Opp. Mocha, Hiranandani Garden, Powai, Mumbai, Ph: 40051400, 40051600

5, Jagdamba Complex, Movietimes Compound, Malad Link Road, Malad (W), Mumbai, Ph: 228888807/08/09

Shop No. 20, Juhu Ekta Bldg Juhu-Versova Link Road, Andheri (W), Mumbai, Ph: 26280674-75

Rita Apartments, 16th Road, Bandra West, Mumbai, Ph: 26463501, 66760718, 9619176543

B8, Shiv Sagar Bldg., Near Surbhi Life Care Hospital, Thakur Complex, 90 Feet Road, Kandivali (E), Mumbai, Ph: 65110391, 65110392

148-A, Colaba Estate, 3&4, Near Sasoon Dock, Colaba Road, Colaba, Mumbai, Ph: 22152206–08

120, Arcadia Shopping Centre, Hiranandani Estate, Thane West, Mumbai, Ph: 25316288, 25316299

1, Varsha, Bank of Maharashtra Lane, 7 Bungalows, Andheri, Mumbai, Ph: 7738987860, 9867600955

Karma

534, SVP Road, Hughes Road, Opera House, Mumbai, Ph: 40287119, 40287116

Oberoi Chamber, Bldg. No. 1, Link Road, Andheri (W), Mumbai, Ph: 26748704

Kebab Korner

InterContinental Marine Drive, Level 1, 135, Marine Drive, Mumbai, Ph: 39879999

Khane Khas

Shop No. 4, Silver Croft Bldg., Junction of 16th & 33rd Road, TPS III, Bandra (W), Mumbai, Ph: 26006970/4605, 26054605

Khau Galli

near Vijay Industrial Estate, Chincholi bazar, Link Road, Malad (W), Mumbai, Ph: 9867029427, 993020000

Khyber Restaurant

145, Mahatma Gandhi Road, Kala Ghoda, Fort, Mumbai, Ph: 40396666

Kofuku

Second Floor, Kenilworth Shopping Arcade, Linking Road, Bandra (W), Mumbai, Ph: 67101101, 67105105

Koh

InterContinental Marine Drive, 135, Marine Drive, Mumbai, Ph: 39879999

The Konkan Café

Vivanta by Taj – President, 90, Cuffe Parade, Mumbai, Ph: 66650808 (Extn. 3276, 3278)

Kung Food

Government Colony, Next to Chetna College, Bandra (E), Mumbai, Ph: 26452484, 32912484, 65592484

Kushal

5/6, Dattani Centre, Akurli Road, Kandivali (E), Mumbai, Ph: 28877418, 28864950

Lagerbay

183, Waterfield Road, Bandra (W), Mumbai, Ph: 67369900

Lamba

16, Chhadva Apts., Near Diamond Garden, Chembur, Mumbai, Ph: 25222878, 8652865000

Laughing Cavalier

Fobeoz Tower, Ramchandra Lane, Kanchpada, Malad (W), Mumbai, Ph: 28803411–13, 9821253581, 9930760518

Le Pain Quotidien

Dhanraj Mahal, Apollo Bunder, Colaba, Mumbai, Ph: 66150202

Maker Maxx City, 3rd North Avenue, Next to California Pizza Kitchen, BKC Complex, Mumbai, Ph: 66431617

Lebanese Point

Deccan Court Bldg., Shop No. 9, SV Road, Opposite Movietime Theatre and Shopper's Shop, Bandra (W), Mumbai, Ph: 65290303/0404, 30633290-91

19B, Sunshine Bldg., 1st Cross, Lokhandwala Complex, Andheri (W), Mumbai, Ph: 26333370

Legacy of China

Tirupati Towers, JP Road, Versova, Andheri (W), Mumbai, Ph: 26368223, 26311332/2061

The Leisure Point

Chandavarkar Cross Road, Opp. Raj Mahal Hotel, Borivali (W), Mumbai, Ph: 28951433, 28926595

Lemon Grass Café

106, 1st Floor, Palm Spring Mall, Link Road, Malad (W), Mumbai, Ph: 28817444, 28817888

Shop No. 4, Carlton Court, Turner–Pali Road Junction, Opp. Axis Bank, Bandra (W), Mumbai, Ph: 26429193

Leopold Café & Bar

Shaheed Bhagat Singh Road, Colaba, Mumbai, Ph: 22020131, 22828185

The Little Door

Unit A-17, Ground Floor, Plot No. 31, Shree Siddhivinayak Plaza, New Link Road, Andheri (W), Mumbai

Little Italy

102, Palm Spring, Above Croma, Link Road, Malad (W), Next to D'Mart, Mumbai, Ph: 66716205-06

18-B, Hotel Atlantic, Near Maneckji Cooper School, Juhu Tara Road, Juhu, Mumbai, Ph: 26608815, 26608885, 66923266

302&303, Destination Bldg., DM Road, MG Road, Amar Mahal, Ghatkopar, Mumbai, Ph: 25260125

Shop No. 5, Shalimar Bldg., Ground Floor, 91-G Road, Marine Drive, Mumbai, Ph: 66153322, 66153555

Raja Ram Mohan Rai Road, Next to Central Plaza Theater, Mumbai, Ph: 23870052

Love and Latte

4, Humkund CHS, Waterfield Road, Near Stomach Restaurant, Bandra (W), Mumbai, Ph: 26416661

38/39, Aviour Bldg., Nirmail Galaxy, LBS Marg, Mulund (W), Mumbai

Love and Latte

Shop No. 1, Samarth Vaibhav CHS, Off New Link Road, Andheri Lokhandwala Complex, Andheri (W), Mumbai

Ground Floor, Interface 11, Near ICICI Lombard, Malad (W), Mumbai

Lucky

Next to Goregaon Flyover (E), Near Durian Estate, Goregaon (E), Mumbai, Ph: 61426261, 28761977/5599

Junction of Hill Road & SV Road, Bandra (W), Mumbai, Ph: 26442973-74, 26516019

Mabruk
Sahara Star, Opp. Domestic Airport, Vile Parle (E), Mumbai, Ph: 39895000

Mah Jong
Hotel Ramee Guestline, 757, SV Road, Khar (W), Mumbai, Ph: 61506660/1, 9920070022

Mahesh Lunch Home
Andheri Kurla Road, Saki Naka, Opp Mc. Donald's Andheri (E), Mumbai, Ph: 28565560/61/62

8-B, Cawasji Patel Street, Fort, Mumbai, Ph: 22870938

Juhu Tara Road, Near JW Marriott Hotel, Santacruz (W), Mumbai, Ph: 66955554/59, 66978966

Vihang Palm Club, Pokhran Road No. 1, Opp. Rehman's, Thane (W), Ph: 25441616/1882/5080

Majestic Deluxe Family Restaurant
Parivar Hotels Pvt. Ltd, Neelangi Apts., BP Road, Dahisar (W), Mumbai, Ph: 28954838, 28914746, 9892031244, 8879211097

LIC Colony, Opp. Karnataka Bank, Borivali (W), Mumbai

Malwan
Shripal Apts., Near Aradhana Theatre, Panch Pakhadi, Thane (W), Ph: 25368668, 25438752

Mangi Ferra
Gulmohar Cross Road No. 7, JVPD Scheme, Vile Parle (W), Mumbai, Ph: 66751728-29

Mangii Café
Junction of Khar Pali & 14th Road, Off Linking Road, Khar (W), Mumbai, Ph: 26498100, 26498000, 26498200,

Maratha Darbar
Bandra Nishigandha Cooperative Housing Society, MHB Colony, MIG Club Samor, Gandhi Nagar, Bandra (E), Mumbai, Ph: 26511004/3211, 26451390

Maroosh
13, Meera CHS Ltd., New Link Road, Oshiwara, Andheri (W), Mumbai, Ph: 26333344/45

Phoenix Mills Compound, Lower Parel, Mumbai, Ph: 66101000, 9833397060

A/6, Gagangiri Apts., Carter Road, Khar (W), Mumbai, Ph: 26005584

Masala Bay
Taj Lands End, Band Stand, Bandra (W), Mumbai, Ph: 66681234, 66687470

Masala Craft Bar & Kitchen
289, kadell Road, Next to Dadar Catering College, Shivaji Park, Dadar(W), Mumbai, Ph: 65658111/222

21-B, Santhal, ONGC Complex, Opp. Lilavati Hospital, Bandra (W), Mumbai, Ph: 26452031

Masala Kraft
The Taj Mahal Palace , Apollo Bunder, Mumbai, Ph: 66653366 (Extn. 3278)

Maya
Trident Bandra–Kurla, C-56, G-Block, Bandra–Kurla Complex, Mumbai, Ph: 66727651

Melting Pot
Juhu Residency Hotel, J49, Juhu Tara Road, Near Marriott Hotel, Juhu, Mumbai, Ph: 26134949

Mesa Bistro
Svenska Design Hotel, Off Link Road, Near SAB TV Office, Andheri (W), Mumbai, Ph: 44310000

Mezzo Mezzo

JW Marriott Hotel, Juhu Tara Road, Juhu, Mumbai, Ph: 66933220/3000

Mia Cucina

Gasper Enclave, 16/17, St John Street, Pali Naka, Bandra (W), Mumbai, Ph: 67104000

12, Jewel Mahal Shopping Center, JP Road, Versova, Andheri (W), Mumbai, Ph: 42414000

G-3, Transocean House, Lake Boulevard Street, Hiranandani Business Park, Powai, Mumbai, Ph: 67094000

Ming Yang

Taj Lands End, Band Stand, Bandra (W), Mumbai, Ph: 66681234 (Extn. 7474)

Mini Punjab

Punjabi Colony, GTB Nagar, Sion Koliwada, Mumbai, Ph: 24013232/5103

Mini Punjab

Shop No. 3, Corner of 33rd & 16th Road, Bandra (W), Mumbai, Ph: 26002164/5206/6164

Adi Sankracharya Marg, Near Panch-Kutir Bus Stop, JVLR, Powai, Mumbai, Ph: 25708688-89

Miro

Svenska Design Hotel, F/73-74, Level 1, Oberoi Complex, Opp. Laxmi Industrial Estate, Lokhandwala, Andheri, Mumbai, Ph: 44310000

Mocambo Café & Beer Bar

23/A, Sir Pherozeshah Mehta Road, Fort, Mumbai, Ph: 22870458, 65065264

Mocha

82, Nagin Mahal, Veer Nariman Point, Opp. Gaylords, Churchgate, Mumbai, Ph: 66336070

1st Floor, Phast 1, R City Mall, Amrut Nagar, LBS Marg, Ghatkopar (W), Mumbai, Ph: 25181259

Mocha Mojo

Classic Corner Bldg., Next to Holy Family Hospital, Hill Road, Bandra, Mumbai, Ph: 26421484, 26433098, 9167727782

Modern Lunch Home

Hussaini Chamber, AD Marg, Near Wadia Children, Parel (E), Mumbai, Ph: 24149782

184, Lamington Road, Next to Minerva Cinema, Grant Road, Mumbai, Ph: 23098708

Hotel Modern, Harak Nivas, Near Railway Station, Sion (E), Mumbai, Ph: 24097942, 24023766

Moshe's

7, Minoo Manor, Cuffe Parade, Mumbai, Ph: 22161226, 22161266

133, Gazebo House, 1st Floor, Above Godrej's Nature's Basket, Hill Road, Bandra (W), Mumbai, Ph: 26415555, 26425555

Jeroo Bldg., 137, MG Road, Kala Ghoda, Fort, Mumbai, Ph: 22623552-53

3, Feroz Bldg., Chhatrapati Shivaji Marg, Apollo Bunder, Gateway of India, Colaba, Mumbai, Ph: 22020934, 22021205

Crosswords, Mohammedbhai Mansion, Below Kemps Corner Flyover, NSP Marg, Mumbai, Ph: 23862799/95

Janki Kutil, Juhu Church Road, Opp St. Joseph's High School, En Route to Prithvi Theatre, Juhu, Ph: 65345455

Infinity Mall, 1st floor, Malad (W), Ph: 28896555

Ground Floor, Palladium Mall, High Street Phoenix, Lower Parel, Ph: 24912210/11

R City Mall, Ghatkopar (W), Mumbai, Ph: 25171272

Mostly Grills

The Orchid, 70-C, Nehru Road, Vile Parle (E), Mumbai, Ph: 26164040 (Extn. 4020-21)

Moti Mahal

116, Junction of Guru Nanak and Waterfield Road, Bandra (W), Mumbai, Ph: 26408577, 65138800

Moti Mahal Delux

Phoenix Mall, Kurla, Mumbai

R-2, 3rd Floor, Neptune Magnet Mall, Living Point, LBS Marg, Bhandup (W), Mumbai

102, Level 1, CR-2 Mall (Inox), Nariman Point, Mumbai, Ph: 66546454

Shop No. 21-A, 2nd Floor, InOrbit Mall, Link Road, Malad (W), Mumbai, Ph: 32902945

Shop No. 11, Oberoi Mall, 3rd Floor, Goregaon (W), Mumbai, Ph: 32902946

Mukkam Post Malwan

30/31, Dr Annie Besant Road, Opp. Charity Trust Office, Worli Naka, Mumbai, Ph: 24929369, 8080889000

5-296, Nafa Junction, Opposite Raheja Centre Point, Kalina, Santacruze, Mumbai, Ph: 6664078, 9619989897

Mumbai Masala

Hotel Parkway, Shivaji Park, Ranade Road, Dadar (W), Mumbai, Ph: 24453362–63

Namak

Sahara Star, Opp. Domestic Airport, Vile Parle (E), Mumbai, Ph: 39895000, 39897170

Namyasheth Bhejawala

Bhavani Shankar Road, Patil House, Near SS Shakha No. 16 & Kabutar Khana, Dadar (W), Mumbai, Ph: 24331000, 9869400874

Nawab Saheb

Renaissance Hotel & Convention Centre,Hotel, 2&3-B, Near Chinmayanand Ashram, Powai, Mumbai, Ph: 66927777/7558

Neel on the Turf

Mahalaxmi Race Course, Keshva Rao Khadye Marg, Mahalaxmi, Mumbai, Ph: 61577777

Neelam Pride

LT Road, Gorai Creek, Borivali (W), Mumbai, Ph: 28698076, 28680930

New Yorker

25, Fulchand Niwas, Chowpatty Seaface, Mumbai, Ph: 23677500/02

NH-1 Kitchen & Bar

Kajuwadi, Cardinal Gracious Road, Chakala, Andheri (E), Mumbai, Ph: 28227922, 28257922

Nom Nom

3, Shubham Housing Society, Juhu Versova Link Road, 7 Bungalows, Mumbai, Ph: 26244280, 26244371

Nom Nom

Ground Floor, Deluxe Mahal Bldg., Opp. Mini Punjab, 16th Road, Bandra (W), Mumbai, Ph: 26057766

Noor Mohammadi Hotel

179, Wazir Bldg., Abdul Hakim Noor Mohammadi Chowk, Bhendi Bazaar, Mumbai, Ph: 23456008, 23476188

Northern Tadka

1st Floor, Jagdamba Complex, Behind Movie Time Cinema, Malad (W), Mumbai, Ph: 28811717, 28803939

Northern Tadka

F-1, Thakur Mall, Near Fame Box Office, Dahisar (E), Mumbai, Ph: 28455777/8699

Northern Tadka

New Chandra Co-op Society, Above Skoda Showroom, Off Veera Desai Road, Lokhandwalla, Andheri (W), Mumbai, Ph: 26731764

Oasis

211-D, SV Road, Next to Shopper's Stop, Andheri (W), Mumbai, Ph: 26205205/9471, 26284213

Ocean – The Aquarium Restaurant

Sahara Star, Opp. Domestic Airport, Vile Parle, Mumbai, Ph: 39895000, 39807440

Sahara Star, Opp. Domestic Airport, Vile Parle, Mumbai, Ph: 39895000, 38904440

Oceanic

Bal Krishna Center, NG Acharya Marg, Chembur (E), Mumbai, Ph: 25214766, 25216765/4266

Olive Bar & Kitchen

Pali Hill Tourist Hotel, 14, Union Park, Pali Hill, Khar (W), Mumbai, Ph: 26058228-29

Olympia Coffee House

Rahim Mansion, 1, Shaheed Bhagat Singh Road, Colaba, Mumbai, Ph: 22021043, 22045220

On Toes

7, Mithila Shopping Centre, V Mehta Road, JVPD Scheme, Juhu, Mumbai, Ph: 26144274, 9819306193

1st Floor, Palm Spring, Croma, Next To D'Mart, Malad Link Road, Malad (W), Mumbai, Ph: 66710679/90

One Above On Toes

VN Sphere, Above VN Jewellers, Junction of Turner & Linking Road, Linking Road, Bandra (W), Mumbai, Ph: 26425411-12

Only Parathas

471 Radha Bhavan, Opp. Maheshwari Udyan, King's Circle, Mumbai, Ph: 65758118, 65758228

355, Linking Road, Khar (W), Mumbai, Ph: 66964198-99

The Oriental Blossom

Hotel Marine Plaza, 29, Marine Drive, Mumbai, Ph: 22851212

Ornament

Hotel Rajhans, Opp. Chembur Railway Station, Chembur, Mumbai, Ph: 25280987/1055, 67856600/66

Otto Infinto

Raheja Tower Bandra Kurla Complex, Take a right at the signal at the ILFS Building Bandra (E), Mumbai, Ph: 26567777

Out of the Blue

Hotel Pali Hills, 14, Union Park, Off Carter Road, Khar (W), Mumbai, Ph: 26003000, 26058227, 9324839393

Level 1, Haiko Mall, Hiranandani Gardens, Powai, Mumbai, Ph: 8879366202-03

Pali Village Café

Next to Janata Bar, Pali Naka, Bandra (W), Mumbai, Ph: 26050401

Pal's Fish Corner

Shop No. 8, Kailash Shopping Centre, Corner of 16th Road, Khar, Mumbai, Ph: 26002995/4318

Pan Asian

ITC Maratha, Sahar, Andheri, Mumbai, Ph: 28303030

Pancham Puriwala

8/10, Bazaar Gate Street, Fort, Mumbai, Ph: 9004188052

Papa John's

Shop No. 20, Greenvilla Apts, Lokhandwala Circle, Next to Pizza Hut, Lokhandwala, Anderi (W), Mumbai, Ph: 42957676

Shop No. 10–12, Ground Floor, City Park, Hiranandani Business Park, Powai, Mumbai, Ph: 25707373

Pebbles

Juhu Residency Hotel, 148-B, Juhu Tara Road, Juhu, Vile Parle (W), Mumbai, Ph: 67834949

Peking Tom

Jagdamba Complex, Behind Movie Time, Malad (W), Mumbai, Ph: 65027789-90, 28808886

Peninsula

117, Peace Heaven, Opp. Cinemax Planet, Sion (E), Mumbai, Ph: 24078200, 24073611

Peninsula Next

117, Peace Heaven, Opp. Cinemax Planet, Sion (E), Mumbai, Ph: 24070150

Persian Darbar

Alexandra Terrace, Dr Babasaheb Ambedkar Road, Opp. Palace Cinema, Byculla, Mumbai, Ph: 23724525, 23791112-9

Persian Darbar

Moray Mahal, Next to Shoppers Stop, Linking Road, Bandra (W), Mumbai, Ph: 26401326, 26431741

Peshawri

ITC Maratha, Sahar, Andheri, Mumbai, Ph: 28303030

Picasso

New Link Road, Opp. Bangur Nagar, Goregaon (W), Mumbai, Ph: 28741122, 28723355

Pico Express

Shop No. 7, Ground Floor, Janata Industrial Estate, Senapati Bapat Marg, Opp. Phoenix Mills, Lower Parel, Mumbai, Ph: 24950380, 9167972009

Shop No. 7, Ground Floor, Pearl Heaven CHS Ltd., Chapel Road, Behind Lilawati Hospital, Bandra (W), Mumbai, Ph: 26550544, 9619420003

Shop No. 16, Ground Floor, New Link Palace CHS Ltd., Lokhandwala Complex, Near Infinity Mall, Andheri (W), Mumbai, Ph: 26323209, 9769792009

The Cooling Tower, Nirlon Knowledge Park, Near Hub Mall, Western Express Highway, Goregaon (E), Mumbai, Ph: 26858387

G-50, G-51, R City Phase 2, LBS Marg, Ghatkopar (W), Mumbai, Ph: 67702306, 8879489952

Pizza By the Bay

Soona Mahal, 143, Marine Drive, Mumbai, Ph: 22851876

Poco Loco

5 , Lourdes Heaven, Next to Toto's Garage, Off Pali Naka, Bandra (W), Mumbai

Polpo

Shatranj Napoli, Ground Floor, 12, Union Park, Off Carter Road, Bandra (W), Mumbai, Ph: 26499844, 26498458

Pop Tate's

3rd Floor, R Mall, LBS Marg, Mulund Check Naka, Mulund (W), Mumbai, Ph: 22929456

C/13, Mayfair Sonata Green, Godrej Hiranandani Link Road, Vikhroli, Mumbai, Ph: 40110946-47/49

1st Floor, Sagar Palaazio, Saki Naka Junction, Next to Bank of India, Andheri (E), Mumbai, Ph: 28591277-78

Shiv Shopping Centre, Five and a Half Bungalows,

Versova, Andheri (W), Mumbai, Ph: 26345664/6/2890

G2, 104, Ground Floor, Morya Classic, Opp Infinity Mall, Off New Link Road, Andheri (W), Mumbai, Ph: 26730601

T28, 3rd Floor, Center One Mall, Vashi, Navi Mumbai, Ph: 27815478, 27815479

4th Floor, Korum Mall, Mangal Pandey Road, Near Cadbury Junction, Thane (W), Mumbai, Ph: 66737988, 66737987

Pop Tate's, Lower Ground Floor, R Mall, Ghodbunder Road, Mumbai, Ph: 9167870783

7th Floor, Parth Business Plaza, Link Road, Mith Chawk, Malad (W), Mumbai, Ph: 28890736-37

Poush – Essence of Kashmir

Krishna Garden Resort, Maljipada, Mumbai–Ahmedabad Highway, Vasai, Thane, Ph: 9821213232, 9221779384

S-25, 2nd Floor, Phoenix Market City, LBS Road, Kurla, Mumbai, Ph: 9821213232

17, May Fair, Oberoi Complex, Off New Link Road, Andheri (W), Mumbai, Ph: 66994553

Prangan

Golden Gate, Laram Centre, SV Road, Andheri (W), Mumbai, Ph: 26208088-89

Pratap Lunch Home

79, MB House, Janmabhoomi Marg, Mumbai, Ph: 22871101, 22871818, 40021101

Pratap's Wild Dining

Om Heera Panna Shopping Arcade, 3rd Floor, Oshiwara, Andheri (W), Mumbai, Ph: 26362020/3030, 9029093636

Pratap's – The Dhaba

Shop No. 30/31, Link Plaza, MHADA Shopping Complex, Oshiwara, Andheri (W), Mumbai, Ph: 26322323, 26342323, 9023072323

Prego

The Westin Hotel Mumbai Garden City, International Business Park, Oberoi Garden City, Goregaon (E), Mumbai, Ph: 61470000, 67361064-65

Pritam Da Dhaba

32 Dharamputra, Pritam Estates, Dadar (E), Near Swami Narayan Mandir, Mumbai, Ph: 24143311/5555/3817

Pritam Restaurant & Bar

32, Dharamputra, Pritam Estates, Dadar (E), Mumbai, Ph: 24145555/3311/3817

Punjab Grill

T-17, 3rd Floor, Palladium Mall, High Street Phoenix, 462, Senapati Bapat Marg, Lower Parel, Mumbai, Ph: 43473980

R City Mall, Ghatkopar (W), Mumbai, Ph: 25180211/12, 9619790348

Juhu Shopping Center, Opp. Criticare Hospital, 9th Gulmohar Road, JVPD, Vile Parle (W), Mumbai, Ph: 42433100-01

Quiznos

1, Gaspar Enclave, Pali Naka, Next to Café Basilico, Bandra (W), Mumbai, Ph: 26555588

Rainforest Restobar

T-20, 3rd Floor, R-City Mall, LBS Marg, Ghatkopar (W), Mumbai, Ph: 65176566, 9821196270

17-21, Kukreja Centre, Palm Beach Road, Sector-11, CBD Belapur, Navi Mumbai, Ph: 65176565, 9223395004

Phoenix Market City, LBS Road, Kurla (W), Mumbai, Ph: 9223394915

Rajbhog

The Avenue, Thakur Complex, Western Express Highway, Kandivali (E), Mumbai, Ph: 28542791, 28700000/8888/9999

Rangoli

Opp. SIES College, Sector-3, Nerul, Navi Mumbai, Ph: 27707582, 27707547, 27711888

Red Box Café

891 Notan Classic, Behind Taava Restaurant, Off Turner Road, Bandra (W), Ph: 26557577-78, 42588000-99

Royal Plaza, Near City Mall, Andheri Link Road, Andheri (W), Mumbai, Ph: 42634000

Regency

Vasant Bldg., Professor Phadke Road, Opp. Poonam Plaza, Near Western Express Highway, Near Bisleri Factory, Andheri (E), Mumbai, Ph: 26824711/1423

Hotel Silver Inn, Near SBI Bank, Marol–Maroshi Road, Marol, Andheri (E), Mumbai, Ph: 42359999

Ristorante Don Giovanni

5, King International House, Opp. Juhu Church, Juhu Tara Road, Mumbai, Ph: 67426771, 67426772, 67426770

Roti

Hotel Imperial Palace, 45, Telly Park Road, Andheri (E), Mumbai, Ph: 26833342/5235

Royal Challenge

Empire Wing, Opp. Nitin Casting, Eastern Express Highway, Thane, Ph: 25406689, 25372072

Royal Challenge Complex, Film City Road, Goregaon (E), Mumbai, Ph: 28400208/1982/7757

Royal China

192, Turner Road, Bandra (W), Mumbai, Ph: 26425533, 67049553, 67049555

192, Turner Road, Bandra (W), Mumbai, Ph: 26425533, 67049553, 67049555

Saayba

Shop Nos. 1&2, Zarina Cooperative Society, SV Road, Bandra (W), Mumbai, Ph: 26436620, 26424949

Saffron

JW Marriott Hotel, Juhu Tara Road, Juhu, Mumbai, Ph: 66933225

Saibini Gomantak

Shivaji Park House, LJ Toad, Mumbai, Ph: 24328065, 24385429

Salt Water Café

Rose Minar Annexe, 87, Chapel Road, Bandra Reclamation, Bandra (W), Mumbai, Ph: 26434441

Salt 'n' Pepper

A/5, Royal Classic, Next to Fame Adlabs, Link Road, Andheri (W), Mumbai, Ph: 26372637/1234, 65720057

Opp. Tulip Star Hotel, Juhu Tara Road, Santacruz (W), Mumbai, Ph: 26178262, 26191452-53, 26109831

Fish island, Kamal Rubber Compound, Near Maroli Church, opp. Ashish Cinema, RC Marg, Mahul Road, Chembur (E), Mumbai, Ph: 61611180, 25531166, 9870085050

The Salute

Dhaneshwar Apts., Shimpoli Road, Near Gokhale School, Borivali (W), Mumbai, Ph: 28988559, 32632398, 9920803247

Sammy Sosa
Shop No. 18, Mira Housing Society, Oshiwara, Andheri (W), Mumbai, Ph: 65278722/44

San Churro
Shop No. 11, Silver Pearl, Waterfield Road, Bandra (W), Mumbai, Ph: 26400044

Next to Citi Mall, New Link Road, Andheri Lokhandwala, Mumbai, Ph: 26355725

San-Qi
Four Seasons Hotel, 114, Dr E Moses Road, Worli, Mumbai, Ph: 24818000

Sancho's
Pinnacle House, Plot No. 604, Ground Floor, PD Hinduja Road, 15th Road, Bandra (W), Mumbai, Ph: 67094455

Santoor
Maker Arcade, Near World Trade Centre, Cuffe Parade, Mumbai, Ph: 22182262/5449

Santosh Sagar
Shop No. 6, Matru Ashish, Nepean Sea Road, Mumbai, Ph: 23631199, 23640099

Sapphire
The Emerald, Juhu Tara Road, Juhu, Mumbai, Ph: 26611150, 67144000

Sardar Refreshment
166-A, Tardeo Road Junction, Opp. Tardeo Bus Depot, Tardeo, Mumbai, Ph: 23530208

Sarovar
Payyade International, VL Road, Kandivali (W), Mumbai, Ph: 28011468/ 0732/2876/2877, 28082649-50

Sarvi
184/196, Dimtimkar Road, Opp. Nagpada Police Station, Mumbai, Ph: 65177786

Sasural
Lokhandwala Complex, Andheri (W), Mumbai, Ph: 26368222, 26338906, 26324895

Satkar Rice Plate House
15, Dreamland Bldg., 1st Floor, Railway Station, Goregaon (E), Mumbai, Ph: 65729257

Serafina
Level 3, Palladium Mall, Senapati Bapat Marg, Lower Parel, Mumbai, Ph: 40237711–14

Sernyaa
185, Palm Spring Complex, Shop No. 8, Adarsh Nagar, Oshiwara Link Road, Andheri (W), Mumbai, Ph: 66784645, 65741005

Shop no. 8, Ashok Enclave, Chincholi Bunder Junction, Link Road, Malad (W), Mumbai, Ph: 28765105, 9920274261

Shagun
Hotel Sea Princess, Juhu Tara Road, Mumbai, Ph: 26611111, 66924455

Shahi Dawat
Orchid City Center Mall, Ground Floor, Next to KFC, Bellasis Road, Mumbai Central (E), Mumbai, Ph: 65667666, 9967802220

Shalimar
Vazir Bldg., Bhendi Bazaar, Mumbai, Ph: 23456630–34, 23455035

Apna Bazaar, JP Road, Andheri (W), Mumbai, Ph: 26719910–12

Sector No. 19C, Agarwal Chamber, ATMT Market Road, Vashi New, Mumbai, Ph: 27836767–69

Shanghai Club
ITC Grand Central, 287, Dr Ambedkar Road, Parel, Mumbai, Ph: 24101010

Shao Lin

Shop Nos. 192&193, Galleria Shopping Centre, Powai, Mumbai, Ph: 25797565, 9819959000

Shatranj Napoli

Ground Floor, 21, Union Park, Jashani House, Union Park Road, Khar (W), Mumbai, Ph: 26499844, 26498458

Sheetal

648, Rajasthan Bldg., Khar–Pali Road, Mumbai, Ph: 26497938, 26460643

Sheetal Bukhara

Royal Inn, Opp. Khar (W) Telephone Exchange, Off Linking Road, Khar (W), Mumbai, Ph: 26487627-28

Shikara

Hotel Highway View, Opp. Railway Station, Mumbai-Pune Road, Sanpada, Mumbai, Ph: 27832203, 27832196, 27831195

Shiv Sagar

Opp. Ramada Hotel Palm Grove, Juhu Beach, Mumbai, Ph: 26183585, 26120370

Dharam Prem Bldg., Ground Floor, Nehru Road, Vile Parle (E), Mumbai, Ph: 26153258

82, Nagin Mahal, Veer Nariman Road, Churchgate, Mumbai, Ph: 22824862, 22045829, 22848807

97-98A, Marshall Apts., August Kranti Marg, Gowalia Tank, Mumbai, Ph: 23804541/3267, 9167617281

Shyam Kunj, Pali Naka, 16th Road, Bandra (W), Mumbai, Ph: 26006318/2666/6894

Shivala

117/119, Walchand Hirachand Marg, Bhatia Baug, CST, Fort, Mumbai, Ph: 22626764, 22701342

Shree Krishna

SV Road, Opera House, Mumbai, Ph: 23865798, 23859822, 23821117

Motasha Bldg., 1st Road, Khar (W), Mumbai, Ph: 26052656, 26052655, 26051910

New Municipal Bldg., Jobanputra Compound, Nana Chowk, Mumbai, Ph: 23867544, 23827326

Silk Route

38, K Dubash Marg, Kala Ghoda, Fort, Mumbai, Ph: 22844324, 22818572

Silver Beach Café

Jaldarshan Bldg., Near Hare Rama Hare Krishna Temple, Gandhigram Road, Juhu, Mumbai, Ph: 26208930

Sindhudurg

Sita Bldg., RK Vaidya Road, Near Shivaji Park Police Station, Dadar (W), Mumbai, Ph: 24301610, 24301849

Sitara

Dhiraj Annexe, Sarojini Naidu Road, Mulund (W), Mumbai, Ph: 25618758, 25641242

Smoke House Deli

Unit 9G, Block 3, High Street Phoenix, Lower Parel, Mumbai, Ph: 24933222, 9320098621

Soam

Sadguru Sadan, Ground Floor, Opp. Babulnath Mandir, Chowpatty, Mumbai, Ph: 23698080, 23698089

Soda

Shop 9, Rustomji O-zone Tower 3, Goregaon Link Road, Malad (W), Ph: 9833025645

JP Road, Seven Bungalows, Andheri (W), Mumbai, Ph: 26364467, 9867601196, 8655870520

Soma
Grand Hyatt Mumbai, Off Western Express Highway, Santacruz (E), Mumbai, Ph: 66761080, 66761234

Souk
The Taj Mahal Palace, Rooftop, Apollo Bunder, Mumbai, Ph: 66653366

Soul Fry
Silver Craft, Pali Mala Road, Opp. Pali Market, Bandra (W), Mumbai, Ph: 26046892

Soul Fry Casa
Opp. Mumbai University, MG Road, Next to Rasraj, Fountain, Fort, Mumbai, Ph: 22671421

Spaghetti Kitchen
CR2 Mall, 1st Floor, Opp. Bajaj Bhavan, Nariman Point, Mumbai, Ph: 67439429, 67439430

Phoenix Mills Compound, 462, Senapati Bapat Marg, Lower Parel, Mumbai, Ph: 24963333/4333

1st Floor, Ventura Bldg., B Wing, Opp. D'Mart, Central Avenue, Hiranandani Garden, Powai, Mumbai, Ph: 66718800

2nd Floor, Inorbit Mall, Malad Link Road, Malad (W), Mumbai, Ph: 65344660, 9619439112

15th Road, Opposite Gabbana, Above Toyota showroom, Khar Danda Road, Khar (W), Mumbai, Ph: 67412402–04

Spice Tree
Fernandez Villa, 95, Hill Road, Bandra (W), Mumbai, Ph: 26405161/5053, 26424308

Spices
JW Marriott Hotel, Juhu Tara Road, Juhu, Mumbai, Ph: 66933290/3000

The Square
Novotel Mumbai Juhu Beach, Balraj Sahani Marg, Juhu Beach, Mumbai, Ph: 66934444/4343

Starbucks
Ground Floor, Oberoi Mall, Off Western Express Highway, Goregaon (E), Mumbai

Ground Floor, Taj Mahal Palace Hotel, Apollo Bunder, Colaba, Mumbai

The Elphinstone Bldg., Veer Nariman Road, Horniman Circle, Mumbai, Ph: 66551927, 66551928

Star's Parade
Swami Jairamdas Shopping Centre, Opp. Basant Park, Chembur, Mumbai, Ph: 25270307/1787

Stax
Hyatt Regency Mumbai, Sahar Airport Road, Andheri (E), Mumbai, Ph: 66961234

Stella
The Leela Kempinski Mumbai, Sahar Airport Road, Andheri (E), Mumbai, Ph: 66911234/1219-20

Stomach
117, Waterfield Road, Bandra (W), Mumbai, Ph: 26431236, 66960738-39

Sudama
Hotel Krishna Palace Residency Pvt. Ltd., 96/98, Slater Road, Nana Chowk, Mumbai, Ph: 23873311, 66293333

Suhail's China Blue
Shop No. 8/9, Ray's CHS, New Kantwadi, Off Perry Road, Bandra (W), Mumbai, Ph: 26451786, 26452786, 26422786

Sukh Sagar
Sukh Sagar Bldg., SVP Road, Chowpatty, Mumbai,

Ph: 23640088, 23636856, 23633523

Sun, Moon & Potatoes
Shop No. 11/12, Pleasant Park Bldg., Evershine Link Road, Malad (W), Mumbai, Ph: 65752866

Sundeep
Opp. Railway Station, Above Bharat Café, Ghatkopar (W), Mumbai, Ph: 25158380

Sunset Room
Sun-n-Sand Hotel, 39, Juhu Beach, Mumbai, Ph: 66938888

Surbhi
Shiv Sagar Bldg., 90 Feet Road, Asha Nagar, Kandivali (E), Mumbai, Ph: 28540000 /3333 /8464/1011

The Table
Kalatehi Trust Bldg., Behind Regal Cinema, Appollo Bunder Marg, Colaba, Mumbai, Ph: 22825000

Tamnak Thai
274, VS Marg, Near Natural Ice Cream, Shivaji Park, Dadar (W), Mumbai, Ph: 24474949/4646

Tao
Tunga Regale, Plot No. 31, Phase 2, Central Road, MIDC, Andheri (E), Mumbai, Ph: 66726672, 66726668

Tasting Room
Good Earth, Raghuvanshi Mills, Next to High Street Phoenix, Senapati Bapat Marg, Lower Parel, Mumbai, Ph: 24951954, 65285284

Tavaa
Saquib Bldg., Corner of 24th & Turner Road, Bandra (W), Ph: 26510222, 26406351

TGI Fridays
R City Mall, G-73, Ground Floor, Phase-2, LBS Marg, Ghatkopar (W), Mumbai, Ph: 61273971

2nd Floor, Infinity Mall, Oshiwara, New Linking Road, Andheri (W), Ph: 26367047, 67032063/65,

F-11–13, 1st Floor, Palladium Mall, Phoenix Mills Compound, 462, Senapati Bapat Marg, Lower Parel (W), Ph: 6615568, 66155687

Thai Ban
Shop No. 8, Gaspar Enclave, Pali Naka, Bandra (W), Ph: 26459775/8176

Tiara
Meluha The Fern – An Ecotel Hotel, Central Avenue, Hiranandani Gardens, Powai, Mumbai, Ph: 25755555, 42611111

Time and Again
9, Raheja Classique, Oshiwara Link Road, Lokhandwala, Andheri (W), Mumbai, Ph: 26351119–21, 9819997555

Trikaya
7/11, Mera Apts., Juhu–Versova Link Road, 7 Bungalows, Andheri (W), Mumbai, Ph: 65021389, 65047177

Trishna
7, Saibaba Marg, Kala Ghoda, Fort, Mumbai, Ph: 22672176, 22614991, 22703213-15

Tuskers
Sofitel, Bandra Kurla Complex, Bandra (E), Mumbai, Ph: 61175000

Two One Two Bar and Grill
12-A, Hornby Vellard Estate, Next to BMW Showroom, Worli, Mumbai, Ph: 24901994, 24901992, 24901993

Umame
1st Floor, Eros Theatre Bldg., East Wing, Maharshi Karve Road, Churchgate, Mumbai, Ph: 61110303

Uncle's Kitchen
Behind Orlem Church, Sunder Lane, Malad (W), Mumbai, Ph: 28881752, 28816204

Urban Tadka
Juhu-Versova Link Road, JP Road, Seven Bungalows, Junction of Bon Bon Lane, Andheri (W), Mumbai, Ph: 26392413,26397017, 26328172/73

3rd Floor, R Mall, Mulund Check Naka, LBS Road, Mulund (W), Mumbai, Ph: 25614473-75, 21644473, 21644475, 22929457

1st Floor, Sagar Palazzio, Saki Naka Junction, Andheri (E), Mumbai, Ph: 28512532/35, 22945895

Shop T-17, 3rd Floor, R City Mall, Level 3, LBS Road, Ghatkopar (W), Mumbai, Ph: 9769005769/70

4th Floor, Korum Mall, Near Cadbury Junction, Mangal Pandey Road, Thane (W), Mumbai, Ph: 66739586, 8879789643

Vaishali Garden
Navketan Bldg., 1st Floor, Opp. Railway Station, Chembur, Mumbai, Ph: 25214294, 25217881

Veda
2nd Floor, Palladium Mall, Senapati Bapat Marg, High Street Phoenix, Lower Parel, Mumbai, Ph: 24900055, 9873655216,43326666, 8879170164

Vetro
The Oberoi, Nariman Point, Mumbai, Ph: 66326215

Vindhyas
The Orchid, 70-C, Nehru Road, Vile Parle (E), Mumbai, Ph: 26164040 (Extn. 4060-61)

Vinoteca by Sula
Ground Floor, Sunville Bldg., 9, Dr Annie Besant Road, Worli, Mumbai, Ph: 40046234

Vishwa Bharati
Opp. Railway Station, Mulund (W), Mumbai, Ph: 25683438, 25610193

Vividh
The Peninsula Grand Hotel, Saki Naka Junction, Andheri (E), Mumbai, Ph: 28519191, 28531188

Vongwong
1st Floor, Express Towers, Nariman Point, Mumbai, Ph: 22875633, 67305592

Wah! Bollywood
B-2 Gagangiri Premises CHS, Carter Road, Khar (W), Mumbai, Ph: 26054716, 32229931, 32229932

Wasabi by Morimoto
The Taj Mahal Palace, Apollo Bunder, Mumbai, Ph: 66653366 (Extn 3202–04)

Waterstone Bar & Grill
Waterstones Hotel, Near InterContinental – The Lalit, Sahar Airport Road, Andheri (E), Mumbai, Ph: 40906633,M4 80

White
The Ozone Club, Rang Sabade Marg, Siddharth Nagar, Goregaon (W), Mumbai, Ph: 28735645, 28735648, 28735646

Wich Latte
Shop No. 4, Ground Floor, Western Breeze Bldg., Colaba, Mumbai, Ph: 65254827

Shop No 64, Thakur Village, Kandivali (E), Mumbai, Ph: 61371818

Shop No. 47, Raj Arcade, G Wing, Mahavir Nagar, 90 Feet Road, Kandivali (W), Mumbai, Ph: 61371818

La Festa Food Junction, IRCTC Food Plaza, Nagardas Road, Andheri (E), Mumbai, Ph: 61371818

Wonton House

Shams Palace, 98, Hill Road, Bandra (W), Mumbai, Ph: 26516314

Woodside Inn

Indian Mercantile Mansion, Wodehouse Road, Opp. Regal, Colaba, Mumbai, Ph: 22875752

Woodside – All Day Bar & Eatery

New Link Plaza, Next to Oshiwara Police Station, Oshiwara Link Road, Andheri (W), Mumbai, Ph: 26328963, 26336549

Woodstock

Rajawadi, MG Road, Ghatkopar (E), Mumbai, Ph: 32639692, 21027136, 9892929366

Yauatcha

Unit No. 10, Block G, Raheja Tower, Opp. Bank of Baroda & ING Vysya Bank, Bandra–Kurla Complex, Bandra (E), Mumbai, Ph: 26566060

The Yellow Chilli

2nd Level, Citipark Bldg., Near D'Mart, Hiranandani Gardens, Powai, Mumbai, Ph: 40156161

Yellow Tree Café

33rd Street, Ambedkar Road Junction, Bandra (W), Mumbai, Ph: 26487800, 65287800

Yogi

403-K, Sion–Trombay Road, Diamond Garden, Chembur, Mumbai, Ph: 25280289/0011/6826

Yoko Sizzlers

10/11, West View, 309, SV Road, Near Akbarally's, Santacruz (W), Mumbai, Ph: 26492313/1528

8/9, Oshiwara Link Plaza, Near Oshiwara Police Station, Link Road, Oshiwara, Jogeshwari, Mumbai, Ph: 26395851-52

Shahzan Rizwi House, 34, Hill Road, Bandra (W), Mumbai, Ph: 66779290, 26423105, 26401746

C/O Star of Asia Restaurant, Junction of Cowasji Patel Street & Rustom Sidhwa Marg, Fort, Mumbai, Ph: 66364607, 66364606

16–20, Gayatri Sadan, Behind Shivam Mall, Thakur Village, Kandivali (E), Mumbai, Ph: 65250130/55

China Link, Opp. Goregaon Sports Club, New Link Road, Malad (W), Mumbai, Ph: 28443077, 32665997

R City Mall, Unit G/66, Ground Floor, C-1 Block, LBS Marg, Ghatkopar (W), Mumbai, Ph: 25175180, 25185180

C/O Hotel Bahri Residency, 1st Floor, Plot No.1, Opp. Diamond Garden, Next To Barista, Sion Trombay Road, Chembur (E), Mumbai, Ph: 25200028, 9769991795

136 Galleria, Next to Mocha Hiranandani Gardens, Powai, Mumbai, Ph: 25703674, 25701800, 40054100

R Mall, Lal Bahadur Shastri Road, Mulund (W), Mumbai

Zaffran

B-Block, Sitaram Bldg., Dr DN Road, Mumbai, Ph: 23442690, 23401976

R City Mall, Off LBS Marg, Ghatkopar, Mumbai, Ph: 65567638, 65567647

Growel 101 Mall, Off Western Express Highway, Kandivali (E), Mumbai

Infinity 2 Mall, Link Road, Malad (W), Mumbai, Ph: 64502828, 64502929

Zing

The Ozone Club, Rang Sabade Marg, Siddharth Nagar, Goregaon (W), Mumbai, Ph: 28735645–48

Zitar

G1–G3, Ventura House, Opp. D-mart, Hiranandani Gardens, Powai, Mumbai, Ph: 40157888

Zodiac

15, Brindaban, Poonam Nagar, Off Mahakali Caves Road, Andheri (E), Mumbai, Ph: 28346143/1708, 9920289300

Zodiac Grill

The Taj Mahal Palace, Apollo Bunder, Mumbai, Ph: 66653366 (Extn.3111)

BARS – ALPHABETICAL

#

3 Wise Monkeys...17
6 Degrees...17
72...18

A

A Bar...18
Adarsh Bar & Restaurant...19
Aer...19
Alfredo's...20
Alfresco Nights...20
Amadeus...20
Apicius...21
The Ark Bar...21
Arola...21
Asia 7...22
Asilo...22
Aurus...23

B

The Bar & Verandah...23
The Bar...24
The Barking Deer...24
Bayview Café...25
The Beachcomber...25
Beluga – The Bar...25
The Beryl Club...26
Big Bang Bar Café...26
The Big Nasty...26
Blend N Brew...27
The Blu Balcony...27
The Blue Frog Club...27
Blue Waters...28
Bombay High...28
Bonobo...29
Bora Bora...29
Botticino...30
Bottle Bar...30
Boveda...31
Brass Monkey...31
Busaba...31

C

Café Ideal...32
Café Mangii...32
Café Oval...33
Café Sundance...33
Café Universal...33
Canvas...34
Captains Bar...34
Cerveza...35
Champagne Lounge...35
Cheval Bar & Restaurant...36
Cheznous...36
China House...36
Clove Bar...37
Club Alibii...37
Club Escape...38
Copa...38

D

The Daily...39
Dara's Dhaba...39
Deccan Bar...40
The Den...40
Dhanraj...41
Divyasagar Bar & Rest...41
Diwine...41
Dome...41
Dublin...42
Dusk...42
D'Bell...43

E

The Eau Bar...43
Eighteen Lounge & Bar...44
Elbo Room...44
Ellipsis...45
Enigma...45
Enigma – The Lounge...45
Escobar...46
Exo...46

F

F Bar...46
Fever – The Night Club...47
Finger Cross...47
Firangi Paani...48
Flamboyante...48
Flute – Champagne Lounge...49
Frederick's Lounge...49
Fuel — The Lounge...49
Fusion...50

G

Gadda Da Vida...50
Gallops...51
Garden Bar...51
Garden Court...51
Gaylord...52
Geoffrey's...52
The Ghetto...53
Ghost...53
Goa Portuguesa...53
Gokul Rest & Bar...54
Golden Chariot...54
Golden Wok...54
Grand Centre...55
Green Jade Oriental Lounge & Bar...55

H

H2O – The Liquid Lounge...56
Hakkasan...56
Harbour Bar...57
Hard Rock Café...57
Harry's...58
Hawaiian Shack...58
The High Stake...58
HQ's – City's 1st All Day Pub...59
The Hub...59
Hype...60

I

I-Bar...60
Image...61
Indigo...61
Indus – Cocktail Bar & Tandoor...61
Irish House...62
Irish Pub...62
Ivy Bar & Bistro...63

J

Jalsa...63
Jam Jar Diner...64
Janata Lunch Home Restaurant & Bar...64
Jewel of India...64

K

Karma...65
Kino 108...65
Koh...66
Kolonials...66

L

The Lazy Dog...67
Leopold Café...67
Levo Restaurant & Lounge...68
Li Bai...68
Lido Bar...69
Liquid Lounge – The Bar...69
LIV...69
The Lobby Lounge...70
Loca Loca...70
The Local...71
Long & Short – The Gastro Bar...72
Lounge Bar...72

M

Madness...72
Manchester United...73
Mangi Fuori...73
Merlin's...74
Mesa Bistro...74
Mezzo Mezzo...75
Midland Bar & Restaurant...75
Miro Lounge...75
Mocambo Café...76
Mocha Bar...76

Mocha Mojo...77
Mumbai Masala...77

N

New Yazdani & Co....78
Nonsense...78

O

O 15 Café...78
Oasis Restaurant & Bar...79
Olive Bar & Kitchen...79
On Toes...80
One Above On Toes...80
Opa...80
Open House Café & Bar...81
Opium Den...81
Or-G...81
Orbits...82
Otto Infinito...82

P

Pali Bhawan...83
Pali Village Café...83
Pan Asian...83
Panchratna Restaurant & Bar...84
Peninsula Next...84
Penne...84
Piano Lounge...85
The Pier...85
Pint Room...85
Polpo Bar & Café...85
Pop Tate's...86
Punjab Grill...86

Q

Quench...87

R

Raga...87
Railway Bar...87
Red Ant...88
Reflections...88
Ren by China Garden...89
Ristorante Don Giovanni...89
Rock Bottom...89
Roof top Bar...90
Royal Challenge...90
Royalty...90
Ruby's Bar & Grill...91
Rude Lounge...91

S

Saffron Bay...92
Salt Water Café...92
Sancho's...92
Sassy Spoon...93
Score Sports Bar & Grill...93
Shankari...94
Sheesha Moroccan...94
Shiro...94
Shockk...95
Shooters...95
Sigree Global Grill...96
Skky...96
Slice of Lime...96
Smoke House Deli...97
Smooth...97
Soul Fry...97
The Spare Kitchen...98
Splash...98
Sports Bar Express...98
Starboard...99
Stax...99
Stella...99
Step lin Bar & Kitchen...100
Sutra – The Night Lounge...100
Suyog Rest. & Bar...100

T

The Table...101
Tamarind...101
Tamnak Thai...101
The Tavern...102
Temptation...102
TGI Fridays...102
Three Wise Men...103
Tippler's Lounge...103
Tote Bar...104
Toto's Garage...104
Town House Café...105
Trader Vic's Mai Tai...105
Trilogy...106
Tryst...106
Two One Two Bar & Grill...107

U

Unplugg Wine & Dine...107
Upper Deck...108

V

Veda...108
Velvet Lounge...109
Vicinia Café & Bar...109
Vie Lounge & Deck...109
Vinoteca by Sula...109

W

Waves...110
The White Owl...110
Wink...111
Woodside Inn...111
Woodside – All Day Bar & Eatery...112
WTF...112

Y

Yauatcha...113

Z

Zenith Party Suite...113

BAR TYPES

BAR

6 Degrees...17
The Ark Bar...21
The Barking Deer...24
The Beachcomber...25
Beluga – The Bar...25
The Beryl Club...26
Big Bang Bar Café...26
The Big Nasty...26
Bombay High...28
Bottle Bar...30
Boveda...31
Captains Bar...34
China House...36
Clove Bar...37
The Daily...39
Deccan Bar...40
Dublin...42
Elbo Room...44
Ellipsis...45
Exo...46
Geoffrey's...52
Harbour Bar...57
The High Stake...58
I-Bar...60
Ivy Bar & Bistro...63
The Lazy Dog...67
Liquid Lounge – The Bar...69
The Lobby Lounge...70
Loca Loca...70
Lounge Bar...72
Mocha Mojo...77
New Yazdani & Co....78
Opium Den...81
Railway Bar...87
Red Ant...88
Ristorante Don Giovanni...89
Shankari...94
Sheesha Moroccan...94
Shockk...95
Shooters...95
Slice of Lime...96

Smooth...97
Stax...99
The Tavern...102
Temptation...102
Tote Bar...104
Toto's Garage...104
Upper Deck...108
Veda...108
Vicinia Café & Bar...109
Wink...111
WTF...112

BAR WITH LIVE MUSIC

The Eau Bar...43
Flamboyante...48
Merlin's...74
Starboard...99

BEER BAR

Cerveza...35
Quench...87

CHAMPAGNE LOUNGE

Flute – Champagne Lounge...49

DISCOTHEQUE/ NIGHTCLUB

Alfresco Nights...20
Canvas...34
China House...36
Club Alibii...37
Club Escape...38
H2O – The Liquid Lounge...56
Hype...60
Kino 108...65
Madness...72
Orbits...82
Rock Bottom...89
Royalty...90
Sutra – The Night Lounge...100
Trilogy...106
Tryst...106
Velvet Lounge...109
Vie Lounge & Deck...109

LOBBY BAR

A Bar...18
Reflections...88

LOUNGE BAR

3 Wise Monkeys...17
72...18
Aer...19
Arola...21
The Bar & Verandah...23
The Bar...24
Blend N Brew...27
Brass Monkey...31
Champagne Lounge...35
The Den...40
Dusk...42
D'Bell...43
Eighteen Lounge & Bar...44
Enigma – The Lounge...45
Escobar...46
F Bar...46
Frederick's Lounge...49
Fuel — The Lounge...49
Gadda Da Vida...50
Ghost...53
Green Jade Oriental Lounge & Bar...55
Irish House...62
Koh...66
Or-G...81
Piano Lounge...85
Tippler's Lounge...103
Waves...110

POOLSIDE BAR

Splash...98

PUB

3 Wise Monkeys...17
Bora Bora...29
Fever – The Night Club...47
Finger Cross...47
The Ghetto...53
Ghost...53
Harry's...58
HQ's – City's 1st All Day Pub...59
Irish Pub...62
LIV...69
On Toes...80
Red Ant...88
Sheesha Moroccan...94

RESTO-BAR

Adarsh Bar & Restaurant...19
Alfredo's...20
Amadeus...20
Asia 7...22
Aurus...23
Bayview Café...25
The Blu Balcony...27
The Blue Frog Club...27
Blue Waters...28
Bonobo...29
Botticino...30
Busaba...31
Café Ideal...32
Café Mangii...32
Café Oval...33
Café Sundance...33
Café Universal...33
Cheval Bar & Restaurant...36
Cheznous...36
Dara's Dhaba...39
Dhanraj...41
Divyasagar Bar & Rest...41
Dome...41
Fusion...50
Gallops...51
Garden Bar...51
Garden Court...51
Gaylord...52
Goa Portuguesa...53
Gokul Rest & Bar...54
Golden Chariot...54
Golden Wok...54
Grand Centre...55
Hakkasan...56
Hawaiian Shack...58
Image...61
Indigo...61
Indus – Cocktail Bar & Tandoor...61
Jalsa...63
Jam Jar Diner...64
Janata Lunch Home Restaurant & Bar...64
Jewel of India...64
Karma...65
Kolonials...66
Leopold Café...67
Levo Restaurant & Lounge...68
Lido Bar...69
The Local...71
Long & Short – The Gastro Bar...72
Mangi Fuori...73
Mesa Bistro...74
Mezzo Mezzo...75
Midland Bar & Restaurant...75
Miro Lounge...75
Mocambo Café...76
Mocha Bar...76
Mumbai Masala...77
Nonsense...78
O 15 Café...78
Oasis Restaurant & Bar...79
Olive Bar & Kitchen...79
One Above On Toes...80
Opa...80
Open House Café & Bar...81
Otto Infinito...82
Pali Bhawan...83
Pan Asian...83
Panchratna Restaurant & Bar...84
Peninsula Next...84
Penne...84
Polpo Bar & Café...85
Punjab Grill...86

Raga...87
Ren by China Garden...89
Royal Challenge...90
Ruby's Bar & Grill...91
Saffron Bay...92
Salt Water Café...92
Sancho's...92
Sassy Spoon...93
Shiro...94
Sigree Global Grill...96
Skky...96
Smoke House Deli...97
Soul Fry...97
The Spare Kitchen...98
Stella...99
Step Iin Bar & Kitchen...100
Suyog Rest. & Bar...100
The Table...101
Tamarind...101
Tamnak Thai...101
TGI Fridays...102
Three Wise Men...103
Town House Café...105
Trader Vic's Mai Tai...105
Two One Two Bar & Grill...107
Unplugg Wine & Dine...107
Vinoteca by Sula...109
The White Owl...110
Woodside Inn...111
Woodside – All Day Bar & Eatery...112
Yauatcha...113

RESTO-BAR WITH LIVE MUSIC

Firangi Paani...48
Hard Rock Café...57
Pop Tate's...86
Rude Lounge...91

ROOFTOP BAR

Aer...19
Asilo...22
Roof top Bar...90

SPORTS BAR

72...18
Blend N Brew...27
Manchester United...73
Score Sports Bar & Grill...93
Sports Bar Express...98

WINE BAR

The Den...40
Diwine...41
Flamboyante...48
Ivy Bar & Bistro...63
Pali Village Café...83
Zenith Party Suite...113

BARS — AREA-WISE INDEX

ANDHERI

6 Degrees...17
72...18
Apicius...21
Beluga – The Bar...25
The Beryl Club...26
The Blu Balcony...27
Blue Waters...28
Bombay High...28
Bora Bora...29
Boveda...31
Café Mangii...32
Club Escape...38
Divyasagar Bar & Rest...41
Finger Cross...47
Firangi Paani...48
Garden Bar...51
Garden Court...51
Green Jade Oriental Lounge & Bar...55
Ivy Bar & Bistro...63
Jalsa...63
Levo Restaurant & Lounge...68
The Lobby Lounge...70
Lounge Bar...72
Mesa Bistro...74
Miro Lounge...75
Mocha Bar...76
Nonsense...78
Oasis Restaurant & Bar...79
Pan Asian...83
Pop Tate's...86
Red Ant...88
Shankari...94
Stax...99
Stella...99
Sutra – The Night Lounge...100
TGI Fridays...102
Woodside – All Day Bar & Eatery...112
WTF...112

APOLLO BUNDER

Harbour Bar...57
Indus – Cocktail Bar & Tandoor...61
Starboard...99
The Table...101

BANDRA

Big Bang Bar Café...26
The Big Nasty...26
Bonobo...29
Bora Bora...29
Botticino...30
Captains Bar...34
The Daily...39
Dhanraj...41
Escobar...46
Hakkasan...56
Hawaiian Shack...58
I-Bar...60
Janata Lunch Home Restaurant & Bar...64
Mocha Mojo...77
One Above On Toes...80
Or-G...81
Otto Infinito...82
Pali Bhawan...83
Pali Village Café...83
Pint Room...85
Polpo Bar & Café...85
Quench...87
Red Ant...88
Royalty...90
Rude Lounge...91
Salt Water Café...92
Sancho's...92
Shockk...95
Soul Fry...97
Temptation...102
Toto's Garage...104
Trader Vic's Mai Tai...105

BELAPUR

Dusk...42
Rude Lounge...91

BYCULLA

Deccan Bar...40

CHEMBUR

Adarsh Bar & Restaurant...19
Blend N Brew...27
Golden Wok...54

CHURCHGATE

Café Oval...33
Café Sundance...33
Gaylord...52
Lido Bar...69

COLABA

Bayview Café...25
Busaba...31
Club Alibii...37

Ellipsis...45
Ghost...53
Gokul Rest & Bar...54
HQ's – City's 1st All Day Pub...59
Indigo...61
Leopold Café...67
The Pier...85
Sports Bar Express...98
Tamarind...101
The Tavern...102
Wink...111
Woodside Inn...111

CUFFE PARADE

Flamboyante...48

DADAR

Mumbai Masala...77
Open House Café & Bar...81
Tamnak Thai...101

DHOBI TALAO

Panchratna Restaurant & Bar...84

FORT

Bottle Bar...30
Café Universal...33
Cerveza...35
Cheval Bar & Restaurant...36
The Lazy Dog...67
LIV...69
The Local...71
Mocambo Café...76
Town House Café...105

GHATKOPAR

Garden Court...51
TGI Fridays...102

GIRGAON

Café Ideal...32
New Yazdani & Co....78

GOREGAON

Alfresco Nights...20
Brass Monkey...31
Eighteen Lounge & Bar...44
Golden Chariot...54
Image...61
Liquid Lounge – The Bar...69
Raga...87
Royal Challenge...90
Splash...98

GOWALIA TANK

Grand Centre...55

GRANT ROAD

Railway Bar...87

HUGHES ROAD

Karma...65

JUHU

Alfredo's...20
The Ark Bar...21
Arola...21
Aurus...23
The Beachcomber...25
Bora Bora...29
Copa...38
Enigma...45
Gadda Da Vida...50
Hawaiian Shack...58
Mezzo Mezzo...75
Mocha Bar...76
Opa...80
Penne...84
Reflections...88
Ristorante Don Giovanni...89
Rock Bottom...89
Rude Lounge...91
Shooters...95
The Spare Kitchen...98
Trilogy...106

KANDIVALI

Golden Chariot...54

KEMPS CORNER

Smooth...97

KHAR

3 Wise Monkeys...17
Café Mangii...32
The Den...40
Elbo Room...44
H2O – The Liquid Lounge...56
Irish Pub...62
Ivy Bar & Bistro...63
Loca Loca...70
Madness...72
Olive Bar & Kitchen...79
Ren by China Garden...89
Sheesha Moroccan...94

LOWER PAREL

Asia 7...22
Asilo...22
The Barking Deer...24
The Blue Frog Club...27
Busaba...31
Canvas...34
D'Bell...43
Exo...46
F Bar...46
Irish House...62
The Lazy Dog...67
Manchester United...73
Piano Lounge...85
Punjab Grill...86
Roof top Bar...90
Smoke House Deli...97
TGI Fridays...102
Trader Vic's Mai Tai...105
Tryst...106
Veda...108
The White Owl...110
Zenith Party Suite...113

MAHALAKSHMI

Gallops...51
The Ghetto...53
Olive Bar & Kitchen...79
Tote Bar...104

MAHIM

Goa Portuguesa...53
Midland Bar & Restaurant...75
Step Iin Bar & Kitchen...100

MALAD

Fever – The Night Club...47
Garden Court...51
Manchester United...73
O 15 Café...78
On Toes...80
Pop Tate's...86
Rude Lounge...91
Score Sports Bar & Grill...93
Slice of Lime...96
Unplugg Wine & Dine...107
Upper Deck...108

MARINE DRIVE

Cheznous...36
Dome...41
Geoffrey's...52
Koh...66
Long & Short – The Gastro Bar...72
Saffron Bay...92

MULUND

Manchester United...73
Mocha Bar...76
Pop Tate's...86

NARIMAN POINT

Amadeus...20
Champagne Lounge...35
The Eau Bar...43
Opium Den...81
Ruby's Bar & Grill...91
Sassy Spoon...93

NAVI MUMBAI

Pop Tate's...86

PANCHGHANI

Pop Tate's...86

PAREL

Dublin...42
Frederick's Lounge...49

POWAI

A Bar...18
Café Mangii...32
Clove Bar...37
Fuel — The Lounge...49
Fusion...50
Harry's...58
Rude Lounge...91
Sigree Global Grill...96
Skky...96
Velvet Lounge...109

SANTACRUZ

The Bar...24
China House...36
Three Wise Men...103
Vie Lounge & Deck...109

SENAPATI BAPAT MARG

The Lazy Dog...67

SION

Peninsula Next...84

THANE

Dara's Dhaba...39
Golden Chariot...54
Orbits...82
Pop Tate's...86
Royal Challenge...90
Rude Lounge...91
Waves...110

VASHI

Garden Court...51
Rude Lounge...91
Tippler's Lounge...103

VERSOVA

Enigma – The Lounge...45
Kino 108...65
Pop Tate's...86

VIKHROLI

Pop Tate's...86

VILE PARLE

Diwine...41
Flute – Champagne Lounge...49
The High Stake...58
The Hub...59
Mangi Fuori...73
Merlin's...74
On Toes...80
Punjab Grill...86

WADALA

Suyog Rest. & Bar...100

WORLI

Aer...19
The Bar & Verandah...23
Hard Rock Café...57
Hype...60
Ivy Bar & Bistro...63
Jewel of India...64
Kolonials...66
Shiro...94
Two One Two Bar & Grill...107
Vinoteca by Sula...109

BARS — PRICE-WISE

HIGH

Nightout for 2- ₹2001 & Above

3 Wise Monkeys...17
6 Degrees...17
72...18
A Bar...18
Aer...19
Amadeus...20
Apicius...21
Arola...21
Asia 7...22
Aurus...23
The Bar & Verandah...23
The Bar...24
The Barking Deer...24
The Beachcomber...25
Beluga – The Bar...25
The Beryl Club...26
The Big Nasty...26
The Blu Balcony...27
The Blue Frog Club...27
Blue Waters...28
Bombay High...28
Bonobo...29
Bora Bora...29
Botticino...30
Brass Monkey...31
Café Sundance...33
Canvas...34
Cerveza...35
Champagne Lounge...35
Cheval Bar & Restaurant...36
China House...36
Clove Bar...37
Club Escape...38
Copa...38
The Daily...39
Deccan Bar...40
Dome...41
Dublin...42
Dusk...42
The Eau Bar...43
Eighteen Lounge & Bar...44
Ellipsis...45
Escobar...46
F Bar...46
Fever – The Night Club...47
Flute – Champagne Lounge...49
Frederick's Lounge...49
Gadda Da Vida...50
Gallops...51
Garden Court...51
Gaylord...52
Geoffrey's...52
Ghost...53
Hakkasan...56
Harbour Bar...57
Hard Rock Café...57
The High Stake...58
Hype...60
Indigo...61
Irish House...62
Irish Pub...62
Kino 108...65
Koh...66
The Lazy Dog...67
Levo Restaurant & Lounge...68
Li Bai...68
Liquid Lounge – The Bar...69
LIV...69
The Lobby Lounge...70
Long & Short – The Gastro Bar...72
Lounge Bar...72
Madness...72
Manchester United...73
Mangi Fuori...73
Merlin's...74
Mesa Bistro...74
Mezzo Mezzo...75
Miro Lounge...75
Mocha Bar...76
Mocha Mojo...77
Mumbai Masala...77
Oasis Restaurant & Bar...79

Olive Bar & Kitchen...79
One Above On Toes...80
Opa...80
Opium Den...81
Or-G...81
Otto Infinito...82
Pali Bhawan...83
Pali Village Café...83
Pan Asian...83
Peninsula Next...84
Penne...84
Polpo Bar & Café...85
Pop Tate's...86
Quench...87
Red Ant...88
Reflections...88
Ren by China Garden...89
Rock Bottom...89
Royalty...90
Ruby's Bar & Grill...91
Rude Lounge...91
Saffron Bay...92
Salt Water Café...92
Sancho's...92
Sassy Spoon...93
Shiro...94
Shockk...95
Shooters...95
Sigree Global Grill...96
Slice of Lime...96
Smoke House Deli...97
Smooth...97
Soul Fry...97
Splash...98
Starboard...99
Stax...99
Stella...99
Step Iin Bar & Kitchen...100
Sutra – The Night Lounge...100
The Table...101
Tamarind...101
Tamnak Thai...101
The Tavern...102
Temptation...102
TGI Fridays...102
Three Wise Men...103
Tote Bar...104
Toto's Garage...104
Town House Café...105
Trilogy...106
Tryst...106
Two One Two Bar & Grill...107
Upper Deck...108
Veda...108
Velvet Lounge...109
Vicinia Café & Bar...109
Vie Lounge & Deck...109
Vinoteca by Sula...109
Wink...111
Woodside – All Day Bar & Eatery...112
WTF...112
Yauatcha...113

MEDIUM

Nightout for 2- ₹1001 to ₹2000

Alfredo's...20
The Ark Bar...21
Bayview Café...25
Busaba...31
Café Mangii...32
Captains Bar...34
Cheznous...36
The Den...40
Dhanraj...41
Elbo Room...44
Finger Cross...47
Firangi Paani...48
Flamboyante...48
Fuel — The Lounge...49
Fusion...50
Garden Bar...51
The Ghetto...53
Goa Portuguesa...53
Golden Chariot...54
Golden Wok...54
Green Jade Oriental Lounge & Bar...55
H2O – The Liquid Lounge...56
Hawaiian Shack...58
HQ's – City's 1st All Day Pub...59
I-Bar...60
Indus – Cocktail Bar & Tandoor...61
Jalsa...63
Jam Jar Diner...64
Jewel of India...64
Karma...65
Kolonials...66
Leopold Café...67
The Local...71
Midland Bar & Restaurant...75
Mocambo Café...76
Nonsense...78
On Toes...80
Panchratna Restaurant & Bar...84
Pint Room...85
Punjab Grill...86
Royal Challenge...90
Score Sports Bar & Grill...93
Sheesha Moroccan...94
Suyog Rest. & Bar...100
Tippler's Lounge...103
Unplugg Wine & Dine...107
Woodside Inn...111

LOW

Nightout for 2- Upto ₹1000

Adarsh Bar & Restaurant...19
Café Ideal...32
Café Oval...33
Café Universal...33
Dara's Dhaba...39
Divyasagar Bar & Rest...41
Gokul Rest & Bar...54
Grand Centre...55
Janata Lunch Home Restaurant & Bar...64
New Yazdani & Co....78
Raga...87
Railway Bar...87
Shankari...94
Sports Bar Express...98

BARS IN LEADING HOTELS

FOUR POINTS BY SHERATON

Tippler's Lounge...103

FOUR SEASONS HOTEL

Aer...19
The Bar & Verandah...23

GRAND HYATT MUMBAI

The Bar...24
China House...36

GRAND SAROVAR PREMIERE

Liquid Lounge – The Bar...69

HOLIDAY INN

72...18

HOTEL MARINE PLAZA

Geoffrey's...52

HOTEL METRO PALACE

Temptation...102

HOTEL ROYAL GARDEN

Opa...80

HOTEL SEA PRINCESS

The Ark Bar...21

HYATT REGENCY MUMBAI

Stax...99

IBIS HOTEL

The Hub...59

INTERCONTINENTAL MARINE DRIVE

Dome...41
Koh...66
Long & Short – The Gastro Bar...72

INTERCONTINENTAL THE LALIT

Beluga – The Bar...25
Sutra – The Night Lounge...100

ITC GRAND CENTRAL

Dublin...42
Frederick's Lounge...49

ITC MARATHA

Bombay High...28
Pan Asian...83

JW MARRIOTT HOTEL

Arola...21
Enigma...45
Mezzo Mezzo...75
Reflections...88

NOVOTEL HOTEL

Gadda Da Vida...50

PALLADIUM HOTEL, MUMBAI

Exo...46
Li Bai...68
Piano Lounge...85
Rooftop Bar...90
Zenith Party Suite...113

RAMADA PLAZA PALM GROVE

Shooters...95

RENAISSANCE HOTEL & CONVENTION CENTRE

A Bar...18
Velvet Lounge...109

SAHARA STAR

Flute – Champagne Lounge...49

SUN-N-SAND HOTEL

The Beachcomber...25

THE LEELA KEMPINSKI MUMBAI

6 Degrees...17
The Lobby Lounge...70
Stella...99

THE OBEROI

Champagne Lounge...35
The Eau Bar...43

THE ORCHID

Merlin's...74

THE PARK

Dusk...42

THE RESORT

Upper Deck...108

THE TAJ MAHAL PALACE

Harbour Bar...57
Starboard...99

THE TRIDENT

Botticino...30
Opium Den...81

THE WESTIN MUMBAI GARDEN CITY

Eighteen Lounge & Bar...44
Splash...98

VIVANTA BY TAJ – PRESIDENT

Wink...111

ICE CREAM — ALPHABETICAL

A–Z

Achija Juice Centre...114
Amar Fast Food & Restaurant...114
Amar Juice Centre...114
Amore...115
Anando...116
Apsara Ice Creams...116
Baba Falooda...116
Bachelorr's Juice House...117
Badshah...117
Baskin Robbins...117
Bharat Dairy and Juice Centre...118
Broadway Juice Centre...118
Café Chokolade (Formerly Cad-B)...118
Cocoberry...119
Das Fast Food and Juice Centre...120
Dinshaw's Express...120
FroYo...120
Froot Café...121
Gelato Italiano...121
Gogola...121
Gokul Ice Cream...122
Gupta Sugarcane...122
Häagen Dazs...122
Haji Ali Juice Centre...123
Hokey Pokey...123
Ice Cream Works...124
K Rustom Ice Cream Parlour...124
Kalpana's Tastee...125
Kulfi Centre...125
Mafco Farm Fair...125
Melting Munch...125
Microwave Snacks & Juice Centre...125
Natural Ice Cream...126
Noorani Milk Centre...126
Pankaj Juice Centre...126
Park Malai Gola...127
Pinkberry...127
Rasana Juice Centre...127
Right Place...127
Sancha Ice Creams...128
Sanjay Ice Cream...128
Snow Bite Natural Ice-cream...128
Sukh Sagar Juice Centre...128
Tastings...129
Temptation...129
Temptation Ice Cream Parlour...130
Top 'n' Town...130
Yogurtbay...130
Yogos Ice Cream...131
Zelos and Zest...131

ICE CREAM — AREA-WISE

ANDHERI

Amore...115
Café Chokolade (Formerly Cad-B)...118
Cocoberry...119
Dinshaw's Express...120
FroYo...120
Sancha Ice Creams...128
Temptation...129
Top 'n' Town ...130
Yogos Ice Cream...131

BANDRA

Cocoberry...119
FroYo...120
Hokey Pokey...123
Pinkberry...127
Snow Bite Natural Ice-cream ...128
Yogurtbay...130

BORIVALI

Froot Café...121
Hokey Pokey...123
Temptation...129
Top 'n' Town ...130

BREACH CANDY

Right Place...127
Yogurtbay...130

CHEMBUR

Tastings...129

CHOWPATTY

Bachelorr's Juice House...117
Bharat Dairy and Juice Centre...118
Ice Cream Works...124
Kulfi Centre...125
Mafco Farm Fair...125
Sukh Sagar Juice Centre...128

CHURCHGATE

K Rustom Ice Cream Parlour ...124

CRAWFORD MARKET

Badshah...117

DADAR

Broadway Juice Centre...118
Melting Munch...125
Park Malai Gola...127
Zelos and Zest...131

DAHISAR

Gokul Ice Cream...122

GATEWAY OF INDIA

Gupta Sugarcane...122

GHATKOPAR

Achija Juice Centre...114
Amore...115

GIRGAON

Anando...116

GOREGAON

Häagen Dazs ...122

HAJI ALI

Haji Ali Juice Centre...123

JOGESHWARI

Das Fast Food and Juice Centre ...120
Snow Bite Natural Ice-cream ...128

JUHU

Cocoberry...119
Natural Ice Cream...126

KANDIVALI

Hokey Pokey...123
FroYo...120
Sanjay Ice Cream...128

KHAR

Amore...115
Café Chokolade (Formerly Cad-B)...118
Cocoberry...119
Hokey Pokey...123

LOWER PAREL

Haagen Dazs...122

LOWER PAREL

Ice Cream Works...124

MAHIM

Baba Falooda...116

MALAD

Amore...115
Café Chokolade (Formerly Cad-B)...118
Cocoberry...119
Gokul Ice Cream...122
Hokey Pokey...123
Sanjay Ice Cream...128

MATUNGA

Hokey Pokey...123
Pankaj Juice Centre...126

METRO ADLABS

Amore...115

MINARA MASJID

Noorani Milk Centre...126

MULUND

Rasana Juice Centre...127

POWAI

Amore...115

SANTACRUZ

Gokul Ice Cream...122

SHIVAJI PARK

Ice Cream Works...124

TARDEO

Cocoberry...119

THANE

Amore...115
Café Chokolade (Formerly Cad-B)...118
Hokey Pokey...123
Temptation Ice Cream Parlour...130

VASHI

Amar Fast Food & Restaurant ...114
Hokey Pokey...123

VERSOVA

Amore...115

VILE PARLE

Apsara Ice Creams...116
Amar Juice Centre...114
Gogola...121
Gokul Ice Cream...122
Temptation...129

WADALA

Amore...115

WALKESHWAR ROAD

Apsara Ice Creams...116

WORLI

Apsara Ice Creams...116
Kalpana's Tastee...125
Microwave Snacks & Juice Centre...125

PARTY MAKERS — ALPHABETICAL

A–Z

2DAY-IS-4EVER...141
3 Charlie...134
A to Z Entertainment...143
Akshmey Universal Magical Entertainer...145
All Things Nice...151
Apex Entertainment...134
Art Loft...152
Barwings Hospitality...152
Bhagwati Fruit Juice...149
Candy Floss...145
Catalyst – Event & Design Solutions...135
Charlie Entertainment...145
Classic Concepts...141
Creative Awards & Rewards...149
Creative Chase...150
Cupid...135
Digital Fantasty Birthday World Foundation...150
Entertainment Design Co....141
Ernie...143
Flaming Trio...152
Fratelli Wines...153
Fun 4 U...132
Fun Magic Show...146
Fun Time...135
G Stringz (Groove)...144
Gurleen Manchanda & Geeta Samuel...139
Inflates...142
Joyride...146
Just Smile...146
Karishma Party Organiser...132
Klass Entertainment...136
Learning Ladder Comet Media Foundation...150
Leolans International...136
Maido Enterprises Pvt. Ltd....149
Marigold & Jaygold...147
Mehendi Art (Usha Shah & Ekta)...147
Morani Fireworks...142
National Institute of Event Management...136
Novalis Rodricks...144
Omega Event Management...136
Party Cruisers Pvt. Ltd....137
Party Hard Drivers...154
Party Hites...137
Party Hunterz...139
Party Planet...133
Party Time...147
Party Time Ice Pvt. Ltd....149
Party Warty...142
Payal Bhattacharya...147
Percussionist & Djembe Drum Player...144
Pleasure Group...148
Radhika Events Service...133
Ramesh Magician...148
Red Om Entertainment (ROE)...137
Safe T Drive...154
Satwant Singh Bhatti...142
SG Imani & Sons...140
Showtime Events India Pvt. Ltd....138
Shradha Charitable Trust...140
Shylite Creations Inc....145
Sona Stores...140
South Indian Flower Shop...143
SPK Engineering...140

STIR Academy of Bartending...153
Sunil, the Magician...148
Wanna Party...133
Wasted Fish...153
Wine Warehouse...154
Witty Gift...151
Wizcraft International Entertainment...138
Zara Hatke — The Party Managers...139

PARTY MAKERS — CATEGORY-WISE

PARTY PLANNERS

Fun 4 U...132
Karishma Party Organiser...132
Party Planet...133
Radhika Events Service...133
Wanna Party...133

EVENT MANAGEMENT

3 Charlie...134
Apex Entertainment...134
Catalyst – Event & Design Solutions...135
Cupid...135
Fun Time...135
Klass Entertainment...136
Leolans International...136
National Institute of Event Management...136
Omega Event Management...136
Party Cruisers Pvt. Ltd....137
Party Hites...137
Red Om Entertainment (ROE)...137
Showtime Events India Pvt. Ltd....138
Wizcraft International Entertainment...138
Zara Hatke — The Party Managers...139

WEDDING PLANNERS

Gurleen Manchanda & Geeta Samuel...139

PARTY SUPPLY STORES

Shradha Charitable Trust...140
Party Hunterz...139
SG Imani & Sons...140
Sona Stores...140
SPK Engineering...140

INVITATIONS, DECORATIONS AND FIREWORKS

2DAY-IS-4EVER...141
Classic Concepts...141
Entertainment Design Co....141
Inflates...142
Morani Fireworks...142
Party Warty...142
Satwant Singh Bhatti...142
South Indian Flower Shop...143

MUSIC

A to Z Entertainment...143
Ernie...143
G Stringz (Groove)...144
Novalis Rodricks...144
Percussionist & Djembe Drum Player...144
Shylite Creations Inc....145

ENTERTAINMENT ACTS (MAGIC, JUGGLING, CLOWNS, RIDES), MEHENDI ART AND CALLIGRAPHY

Akshmey Universal Magical Entertainer...145
Candy Floss...145
Charlie Entertainment...145
Fun Magic Show...146
Just Smile...146
Joyride...146
Marigold & Jaygold...147
Mehendi Art (Usha Shah & Ekta)...147
Party Time...147
Payal Bhattacharya...147
Pleasure Group...148
Ramesh Magician...148
Sunil, the Magician...148

FOOD

Bhagwati Fruit Juice...149
Maido Enterprises Pvt. Ltd....149
Party Time Ice Pvt. Ltd....149
Creative Awards & Rewards...149
Creative Chase...150
Digital Fantasty Birthday World Foundation...150
Learning Ladder Comet Media Foundation...150
Witty Gift...151

BARTENDING SERVICES/WORK SHOPS, WINE TASTING/TOURS

All Things Nice...151
Art Loft...152
Barwings Hospitality...152
Flaming Trio...152
Fratelli Wines...153
STIR Academy of Bartending...153
Wasted Fish...153
Wine Warehouse...154

PARTY SAFE

Party Hard Drivers...154
Safe T drive...154
24-hour Cab Services...155

PARTY HALLS — ALPHABETICAL

A-Z

Abott Hotel...156
Ajanta Restaurant...156
The Ambassador...156
Astoria Hotel Banquet Hall...156
Bageecha...156
Bawa International...157
Bhasin Resort...157
Blue Grotto...157
Blue Sea Banquet...157
The Club...157
Courtyard By Marriott...158
CT Chatwani Hall...159
Dios...159
Diplomat...159
Dragon Fly...159
Executive Enclave...159
Fortune Select Exotica...159
Four Points by Sheraton...160
Four Seasons Hotel...160
Gateway Rooms...161
Golden Orchid...161
The Gordon House Hotel...161
Grand Central...161
Grand Hyatt Mumbai...161
Grand Sarovar Premiere...161
Green House...162
Hilton Mumbai International...162
Holiday Inn...162
Hotel Bawa International Private Limited...162
Hotel Marine Plaza...163
Hotel Royal Gardens...163
Hotel Sea Princess...163
Hyatt Regency Mumbai...163
Ikxia...163
Image...164
Imperial Banquets...164
Intercontinental Marine Drive...164
Intercontinental, The Lalit...164
ITC Grand Central...164
ITC Maratha...165
Juhu Hotel Pvt. Ltd....165
JW Marriott Hotel...165
Kohinoor Hall and Banquet...165
Krishna Palace Residency...165
The Leela Kempinski Mumbai...166
The Liquid Lounge...166
Mayfair Rooms...166
Mirador...166
Natraj Lawns...166
Novotel...167
The Orchid...167
Pali Presidency...167
Pan Street...167
The Park...168
Peninsula Next...168
Pritam da Dhaba...168
Puranmal...168
Quality Inn parle International...168
Rajhans Hotel...169
Ramada Plaza Palm Grove...169
Ramada Powai Hotel & Convention Centre...169
Ramee Guestline...169
Ramee Guestline...170
Rangsharda...170
Renaissance...170
The Residence Hotel...170
The Resort...171
Retreat...171
Ritz Hotel...171
Rodas Ecotel Hotel...171
Sahara Star...171
Samrat...172
Sannidhi...172
Shabri...172
Shagun...172
Shatranj Napoli (formerly Attic Lounge)...172
Shiv Krishna...172
Siddhartha...173
Silk Route...173
Silver Coin...173
Sitara...173
Sun n Sand...173
Sunville...173
Svenska Design Hotel...173
Symphony...174
Taj Lands End...174
Taj Mahal Hotel...174
Tamarind...174
Time and Again...175
Tote on the Turf...175
Trident Hotel...175
Trident Hotel (Bandra-Kurla)...175
Tunga International...176
Turf Club...176
Untitled21...176
VITS Business Hotels...177
Vivanta by Taj-President...177
Westin...177
Woodland Retreat...178
Zodiac...178

PARTY HALLS — AREA-WISE

ANDHERI

The Club...157
Courtyard By Marriott...158
CT Chatwani Hall...159
Holiday Inn...162
Hyatt Regency Mumbai...163
ITC Maratha...165
The Leela Kempinski Mumbai...166
Mirador...166
Pan Street...167
Tunga International...176
VITS Business Hotels...177
Zodiac...178
Svenska Design Hotel...173
Time and Again...175
Hilton Mumbai International...162

APOLLO BUNDER

Diplomat...159

AUGUST KRANTI MARG

Symphony...174

BANDRA

Trident Hotel (Bandra-Kurla)...175
Executive Enclave...159
Golden Orchid...161

Pali Presidency...167
Rangsharda...170
Siddhartha...173
Taj Lands End...174

BORIVALI

Ajanta Restaurant ...156
Silver Coin...173

CBD BELAPUR

The Park...168

CHEMBUR

Grand Central...161
Natraj Lawns...166
Rajhans Hotel...169

CHOWPATTY SEAFACE

Ikxia...163

CHURCHGATE

The Ambassador...156
Astoria Hotel Banquet Hall...156
Ritz Hotel...171
Samrat...172

COLABA

Gateway Rooms...161
The Gordon House Hotel...161
Taj Mahal Hotel...174
Tamarind...174

CUFFE PARADE

Vivanta by Taj-President...177

DADAR

Pritam da Dhaba...168
Ramee Guestline...169

FORT

Silk Route...173

GOREGAON (E)

Westin...177
Grand Sarovar Premiere...161
Image...164

JUHU

Hotel Royal Gardens...163
Juhu Hotel Pvt. Ltd....165
JW Marriott Hotel...165
Sun n Sand...173

JUHU BEACH

Hotel Sea Princess...163
Novotel...167

Ramada Plaza Palm Grove...169

KANDIVALI

Imperial Banquets...164
Sannidhi...172

KHAR

Ramee Guestline...170
Shatranj Napoli (formerly Attic Lounge)...172

MADH ISLAND

Bhasin Resort...157

MAHALAXMI

Tote on the Turf...175
Turf Club...176

MALAD

Bageecha...156
The Resort...171
Retreat...171

MARINE DRIVE

Hotel Marine Plaza...163
Intercontinental Marine Drive...164

MULUND

Sitara...173

MUMBAI CENTRAL

Hotel Bawa International Private Limited...162
Shagun...172

NANA CHOWK

Krishna Palace Residency...165

NARIMAN POINT

Dragon Fly...159
Trident Hotel...175

OPERA HOUSE

The Liquid Lounge...166
Shiv Krishna...172

PAREL

ITC Grand Central...164

POWAI

Ramada Powai Hotel & Convention Centre...169
The Renaissance...170
Residence Hotel...170
Rodas Ecotel Hotel...171

PRABHADEVI

Kohinoor Hall and Banquet...165

SAHAR AIRPORT ROAD

Intercontinental, The Lalit...164

SANTACRUZ

Grand Hyatt Mumbai...161
Sahara Star...171

SION

Peninsula Next...168

TARDEO

Dios...159

THANE

Untitled21...176
Woodland Retreat...178

VASHI

Abott Hotel...156
Fortune Select Exotica...159
Four Points by Sheraton...160

VERSOVA

Blue Grotto...157

VILE PARLE

Bawa International...157
Quality Inn parle International...168
Green House...162
The Orchid...167
Shabri...172
Puranmal...168

WORLI

Blue Sea Banquet...157
Four Seasons Hotel...160
Mayfair Rooms...166
Sunville...173

NOTES

Times Group Books

Dear Reader,

In our endeavour to give you the best, we have ensured that the information given in this book is accurate and up to date. But then, as they say, the only thing constant in this world is change. Shops and hotels close down, restaurants go through innumerable avatars and the government decides to change rules – all these are beyond our control. And dear reader, this is where we want your help. If you find something grossly wrong or think we've given some place a complete miss, please tell us about it by giving the name, address, timings etc of the place.

Please use the form given below to send your comments, suggestions, or requests. We want to make our City/Food guides better each year and would really want to know how we can improve things more to give you just the things you've always been looking for. Please take some time to fill as much of this form as you feel comfortable to. Individual information will be treated as strictly confidential and for the sole use of Times Group Books to improve our guides.

Times Group Books

About You:

Title (Mr, Mrs, Miss, Mrs, Dr, Prof): ....

First Name: ....

Surname: ....

Postal Address: ....

Telephone: ....

E-mail: ....

Profession: ....

Other interest areas: ....

Your Feedback: ....

....

You can also send your feedback to **editor.tgb@timesgroup.com** and get our next destination city free.

Times Group Books, Times Annexe (2nd floor), 9-10, Bahadur Shah Zafar, New Delhi – 110 002, INDIA. Phone: 42512162, 43505427

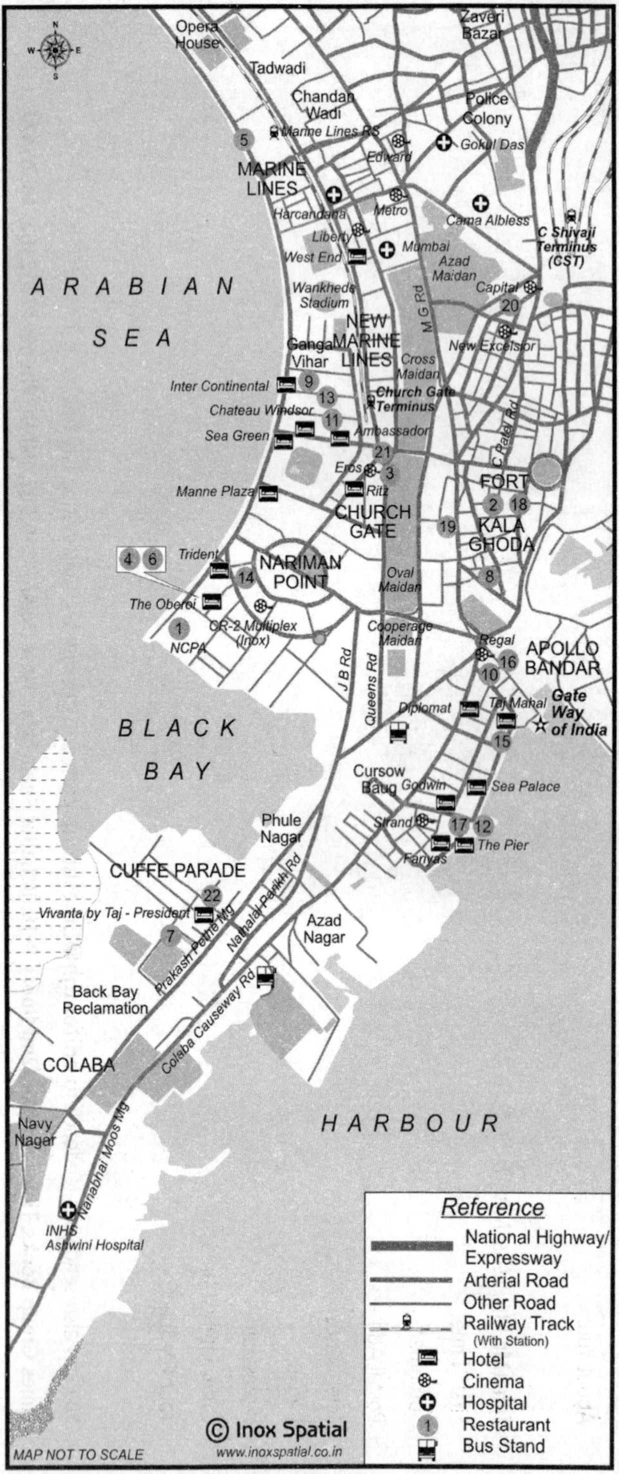
N
S
E
W
Opera House
Zaveri Bazar
Tadwadi
Chandan Wadi
Police Colony
Marine Lines RS
Edward
Gokul Das
MARINE LINES
Harcandana
Metro
Cama Albless
C Shivaji Terminus (CST)
Liberty
West End
Mumbai
Azad Maidan
ARABIAN
SEA
Wankhede Stadium
Capital
20
M G Rd
NEW MARINE LINES
New Excelsior
Ganga Vihar
Cross Maidan
Inter Continental
9
13
Church Gate Terminus
Chateau Windsor
11
Sea Green
Ambassador
C Patel Rd
21
Eros
3
FORT
Manne Plaza
Ritz
2
18
CHURCH GATE
19
KALA GHODA
4
6
Trident
NARIMAN POINT
14
Oval Maidan
8
The Oberoi
1
CR-2 Multiplex (Inox)
Cooperage Maidan
NCPA
Regal
APOLLO BANDAR
16
10
J B Rd
Queens Rd
Diplomat
Taj Mahal
Gate Way of India
BLACK
BAY
15
Cursow Baug
Godwin
Sea Palace
Phule Nagar
Strand
17
12
The Pier
Fariyas
CUFFE PARADE
22
Nathalal Parikh Rd
Vivanta by Taj - President
Prakash Pethe Mg
7
Azad Nagar
Back Bay Reclamation
Colaba Causeway Rd
COLABA
HARBOUR
Navy Nagar
Nanabhai Moos Mg
INHS Ashwini Hospital
Reference
National Highway/ Expressway
Arterial Road
Other Road
Railway Track (With Station)
Hotel
Cinema
Hospital
Restaurant
Bus Stand
© Inox Spatial
www.inoxspatial.co.in
MAP NOT TO SCALE

MAP 2

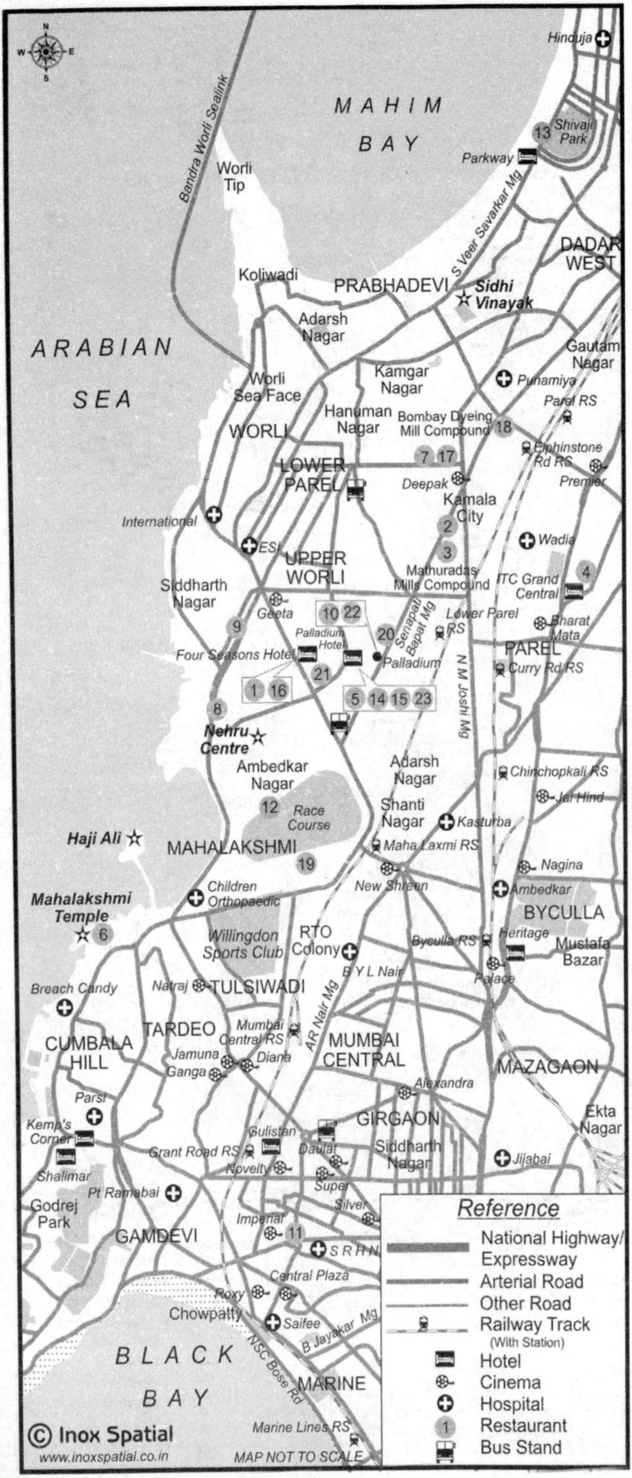

Hinduja
MAHIM
BAY
Shivaji Park
13
Parkway
Bandra Worli Sealink
Worli Tip
S Veer Savarkar Mg
DADAR WEST
Koliwadi
PRABHADEVI
Sidhi Vinayak
Adarsh Nagar
ARABIAN
SEA
Gautam Nagar
Kamgar Nagar
Punamiya
Worli Sea Face
Parel RS
Hanuman Nagar
Bombay Dyeing Mill Compound
18
WORLI
Elphinstone Rd RS
7 17
LOWER PAREL
Premier
Deepak
Kamala City
International
2
Wadia
ESI
3
UPPER WORLI
4
Mathuradas Mills Compound
ITC Grand Central
Siddharth Nagar
Geeta
10 22
Senapati Bapat Mg
Lower Parel RS
Bharat Mata
9
Palladium Hotel
20
PAREL
Four Seasons Hotel
Palladium
Curry Rd RS
21
N M Joshi Mg
1 16
5 14 15 23
8
Nehru Centre
Adarsh Nagar
Chinchpokali RS
Ambedkar Nagar
Jai Hind
12
Race Course
Shanti Nagar
Kasturba
Haji Ali
MAHALAKSHMI
Maha Laxmi RS
19
Nagina
New Shreen
Children Orthopaedic
Ambedkar
Mahalakshmi Temple
6
BYCULLA
Willingdon Sports Club
RTO Colony
Byculla RS
Heritage
Mustafa Bazar
B Y L Nair
Palace
Breach Candy
Natraj
TULSIWADI
AR Nair Mg
TARDEO
Mumbai Central RS
MUMBAI CENTRAL
CUMBALA HILL
Jamuna
Diana
Ganga
MAZAGAON
Alexandra
Parsi
Ekta Nagar
Kemp's Corner
GIRGAON
Gulistan
Siddharth Nagar
Grant Road RS
Daulat
Jijabai
Shalimar
Novelty
Super
Pt Ramabai
Silver
Godrej Park
Imperial
GAMDEVI
11
S R H N
Central Plaza
Roxy
Chowpatty
Saifee
B Jayakar Mg
NSC Bose Rd
BLACK
BAY
MARINE
Marine Lines RS
© Inox Spatial
www.inoxspatial.co.in
MAP NOT TO SCALE
Reference
National Highway/ Expressway
Arterial Road
Other Road
Railway Track (With Station)
Hotel
Cinema
Hospital
Restaurant
Bus Stand

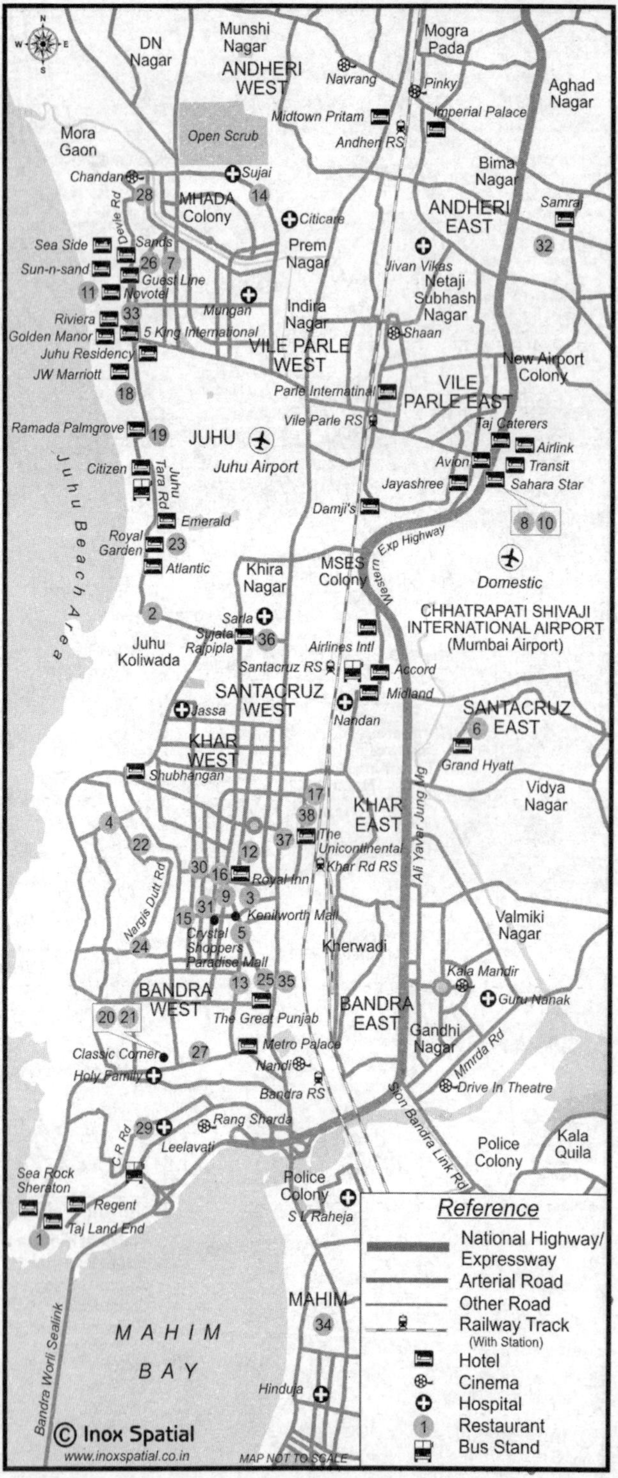
Munshi Nagar
DN Nagar
ANDHERI WEST
Mogra Pada
Navrang
Pinky
Aghad Nagar
Midtown Pritam
Imperial Palace
Andheri RS
Open Scrub
Mora Gaon
Chandan
Sujai
Bima Nagar
28
MHADA Colony
14
Devle Rd
Citicare
ANDHERI EAST
Samraj
Sea Side
Sands
Prem Nagar
32
Sun-n-sand
26
7
Jivan Vikas
Guest Line
Netaji Subhash Nagar
11
Novotel
Mungan
Indira Nagar
33
Riviera
Golden Manor
5 King International
Shaan
Juhu Residency
VILE PARLE WEST
New Airport Colony
JW Marriott
Parle Internatinal
VILE PARLE EAST
18
Vile Parle RS
Taj Caterers
Ramada Palmgrove
19
JUHU
Airlink
Avion
Transit
Citizen
Juhu Airport
Juhu Tara Rd
Jayashree
Sahara Star
Damji's
8
10
Emerald
Western Exp Highway
Royal Garden
23
Domestic
Atlantic
Khira Nagar
MSES Colony
Juhu Beach Area
2
Sarla
CHHATRAPATI SHIVAJI INTERNATIONAL AIRPORT (Mumbai Airport)
Juhu Koliwada
Sujata
Rajpipla
36
Airlines Intl
Santacruz RS
Accord
Midland
SANTACRUZ WEST
Jassa
Nandan
SANTACRUZ EAST
6
KHAR WEST
Grand Hyatt
Shubhangan
Vidya Nagar
17
38
KHAR EAST
4
37
The Unicontinental
22
12
Ali Yaver Jung Mg
30
16
Royal Inn
Khar Rd RS
Nargis Dutt Rd
9
3
31
Kenilworth Mall
Valmiki Nagar
15
Crystal
5
Shoppers Paradise Mall
24
Kherwadi
Kala Mandir
13
25
35
BANDRA WEST
Guru Nanak
BANDRA EAST
20
21
The Great Punjab
Gandhi Nagar
Mmrda Rd
Classic Corner
27
Metro Palace
Holy Family
Nandi
Drive In Theatre
Bandra RS
Sion Bandra Link Rd
29
Rang Sharda
C R Rd
Leelavati
Police Colony
Kala Quila
Sea Rock Sheraton
Police Colony
S L Raheja
Regent
Taj Land End
1
MAHIM
34
MAHIM BAY
Bandra Worli Sealink
Hinduja
© Inox Spatial
www.inoxspatial.co.in
MAP NOT TO SCALE
Reference
National Highway/ Expressway
Arterial Road
Other Road
Railway Track (With Station)
Hotel
Cinema
Hospital
Restaurant
Bus Stand

MAP 4

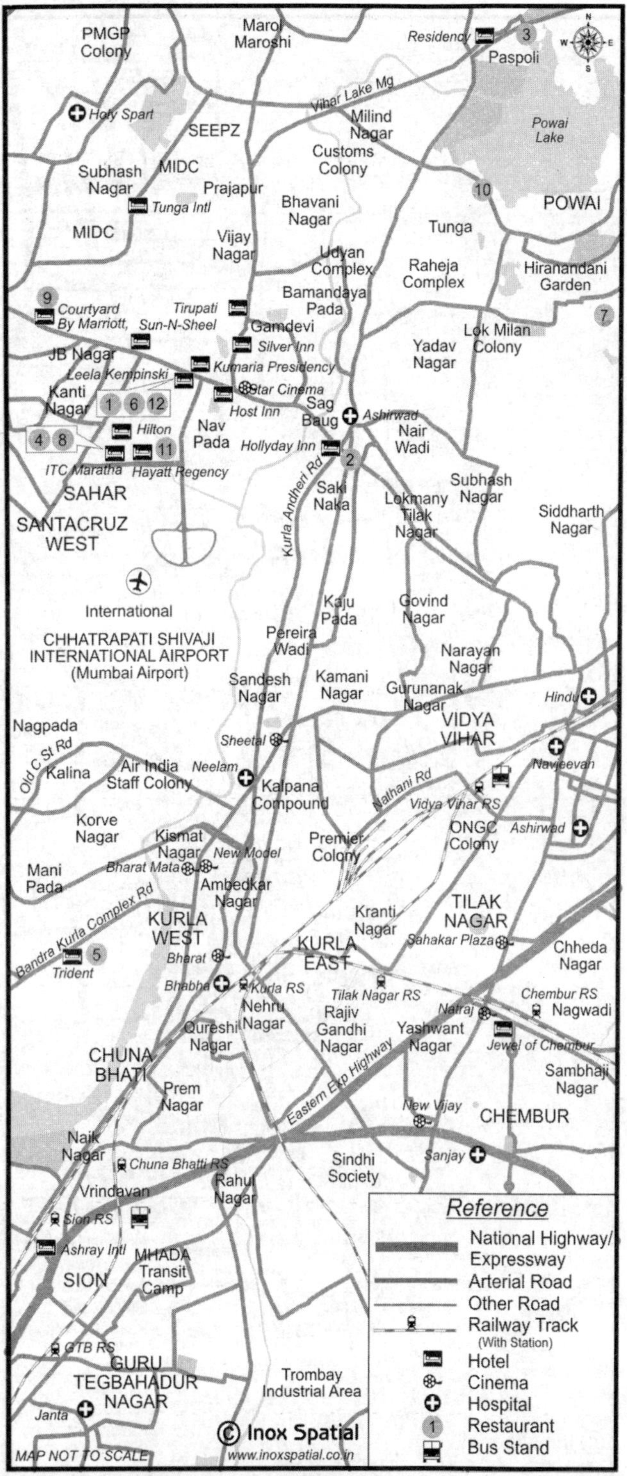

PMGP Colony
Marol Maroshi
Residency
3
Paspoli
Vihar Lake Mg
Holy Spart
SEEPZ
Milind Nagar
Powai Lake
Customs Colony
Subhash Nagar
MIDC
Prajapur
Tunga Intl
Bhavani Nagar
10
POWAI
MIDC
Vijay Nagar
Tunga
Udyan Complex
Raheja Complex
Hiranandani Garden
9
Courtyard By Marriott,
Tirupati
Bamandaya Pada
Sun-N-Sheel
Gamdevi
7
Lok Milan Colony
JB Nagar
Silver Inn
Yadav Nagar
Leela Kempinski
Kumaria Presidency
Kanti Nagar
Star Cinema
1 6 12
Host Inn
Sag Baug
Ashirwad
Nav Pada
Hilton
Nair Wadi
4 8
Hollyday Inn
11
2
ITC Maratha
Hayatt Regency
Saki Naka
Subhash Nagar
SAHAR
Kurla Andheri Rd
Lokmany Tilak Nagar
Siddharth Nagar
SANTACRUZ WEST
Kaju Pada
Govind Nagar
International
CHHATRAPATI SHIVAJI INTERNATIONAL AIRPORT (Mumbai Airport)
Pereira Wadi
Narayan Nagar
Sandesh Nagar
Kamani Nagar
Gurunanak Nagar
Hindu
Nagpada
VIDYA VIHAR
Sheetal
Old C St Rd
Kalina
Air India Staff Colony
Neelam
Navjeevan
Kalpana Compound
Nathani Rd
Vidya Vihar RS
Korve Nagar
Kismat Nagar
New Model
Premier Colony
ONGC Colony
Ashirwad
Bharat Mata
Mani Pada
Ambedkar Nagar
Bandra Kurla Complex Rd
TILAK NAGAR
KURLA WEST
Kranti Nagar
KURLA EAST
Sahakar Plaza
Chheda Nagar
5
Trident
Bharat
Bhabha
Kurla RS
Tilak Nagar RS
Chembur RS
Nagwadi
Nehru Nagar
Rajiv Gandhi Nagar
Natraj
Qureshi Nagar
Yashwant Nagar
Jewel of Chembur
CHUNA BHATI
Eastern Exp Highway
Sambhaji Nagar
Prem Nagar
New Vijay
CHEMBUR
Naik Nagar
Chuna Bhatti RS
Sindhi Society
Sanjay
Rahul Nagar
Vrindavan
Sion RS
Ashray Intl
MHADA Transit Camp
SION
GTB RS
GURU TEGBAHADUR NAGAR
Trombay Industrial Area
Janta
© Inox Spatial
www.inoxspatial.co.in
MAP NOT TO SCALE
Reference
National Highway/ Expressway
Arterial Road
Other Road
Railway Track (With Station)
Hotel
Cinema
Hospital
1 Restaurant
Bus Stand

MAP 5

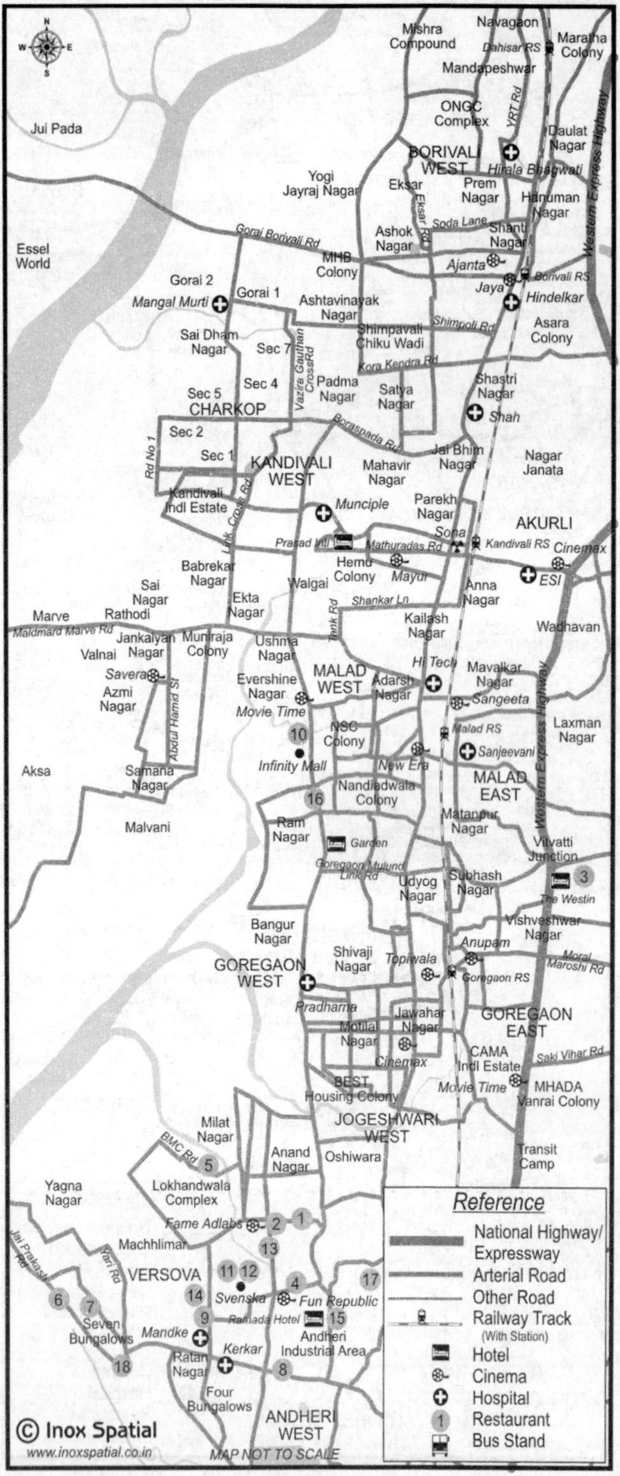
N
S
E
W
Jui Pada
Mishra Compound
Navagaon
Dahisar RS
Maratha Colony
Mandapeshwar
ONGC Complex
YRT Rd
Daulat Nagar
BORIVALI WEST
Hirala Bhagwati
Western Express Highway
Yogi Jayraj Nagar
Eksar
Eksar Rd
Prem Nagar
Hanuman Nagar
Soda Lane
Shanti Nagar
Ashok Nagar
Gorai Borivali Rd
Essel World
MHB Colony
Ajanta
Jaya
Borivali RS
Gorai 2
Gorai 1
Mangal Murti
Hindelkar
Ashtavinayak Nagar
Shimpavali Chiku Wadi
Shimpoli Rd
Asara Colony
Sai Dham Nagar
Sec 7
Vazire Gauthan CrossRd
Kora Kendra Rd
Sec 4
Padma Nagar
Satya Nagar
Shastri Nagar
Sec 5
CHARKOP
Shah
Sec 2
Boraspada Rd
Jai Bhim Nagar
Sec 1
KANDIVALI WEST
Mahavir Nagar
Nagar Janata
Rd No 1
Kandivali Indl Estate
Link Cross Rd
Munciple
Parekh Nagar
AKURLI
Prasad Intl
Mathuradas Rd
Sona
Kandivali RS
Cinemax
Babrekar Nagar
Hemu Colony
Mayur
ESI
Sai Nagar
Walgai
Anna Nagar
Ekta Nagar
Shankar Ln
Marve
Rathodi
Maldmard Marve Rd
Tank Rd
Kailash Nagar
Wadhavan
Jankalyan Nagar
Muniraja Colony
Ushma Nagar
Valnai
Savera
Evershine Nagar
MALAD WEST
Hi Tech
Mavalkar Nagar
Azmi Nagar
Abdul Hamid St
Adarsh Nagar
Movie Time
Sangeeta
Laxman Nagar
10
NSC Colony
Malad RS
Sanjeevani
Aksa
Infinity Mall
New Era
Samana Nagar
16
Nandiadwala Colony
MALAD EAST
Malvani
Ram Nagar
Matanpur Nagar
Garden
Vitvatti Junction
Goregaon Mulund Link Rd
Udyog Nagar
Subhash Nagar
3
The Westin
Bangur Nagar
Vishveshwar Nagar
Anupam
Shivaji Nagar
Topiwala
Moral Maroshi Rd
GOREGAON WEST
Goregaon RS
Pradhama
Jawahar Nagar
GOREGAON EAST
Motilal Nagar
CAMA Indl Estate
Saki Vihar Rd
Cinemax
BEST Housing Colony
Movie Time
MHADA Vanrai Colony
JOGESHWARI WEST
Milat Nagar
BMC Rd
5
Anand Nagar
Oshiwara
Transit Camp
Yagna Nagar
Lokhandwala Complex
Fame Adlabs
2
1
13
Jai Prakash Rd
Machhlimar
Yari Rd
VERSOVA
11
12
4
17
6
7
14
Svenska
Fun Republic
Seven Bungalows
9
Ramada Hotel
15
Mandke
Andheri Industrial Area
Kerkar
18
Ratan Nagar
8
Four Bungalows
ANDHERI WEST
© Inox Spatial
www.inoxspatial.co.in
MAP NOT TO SCALE
Reference
National Highway/ Expressway
Arterial Road
Other Road
Railway Track (With Station)
Hotel
Cinema
Hospital
1
Restaurant
Bus Stand

MAP 6

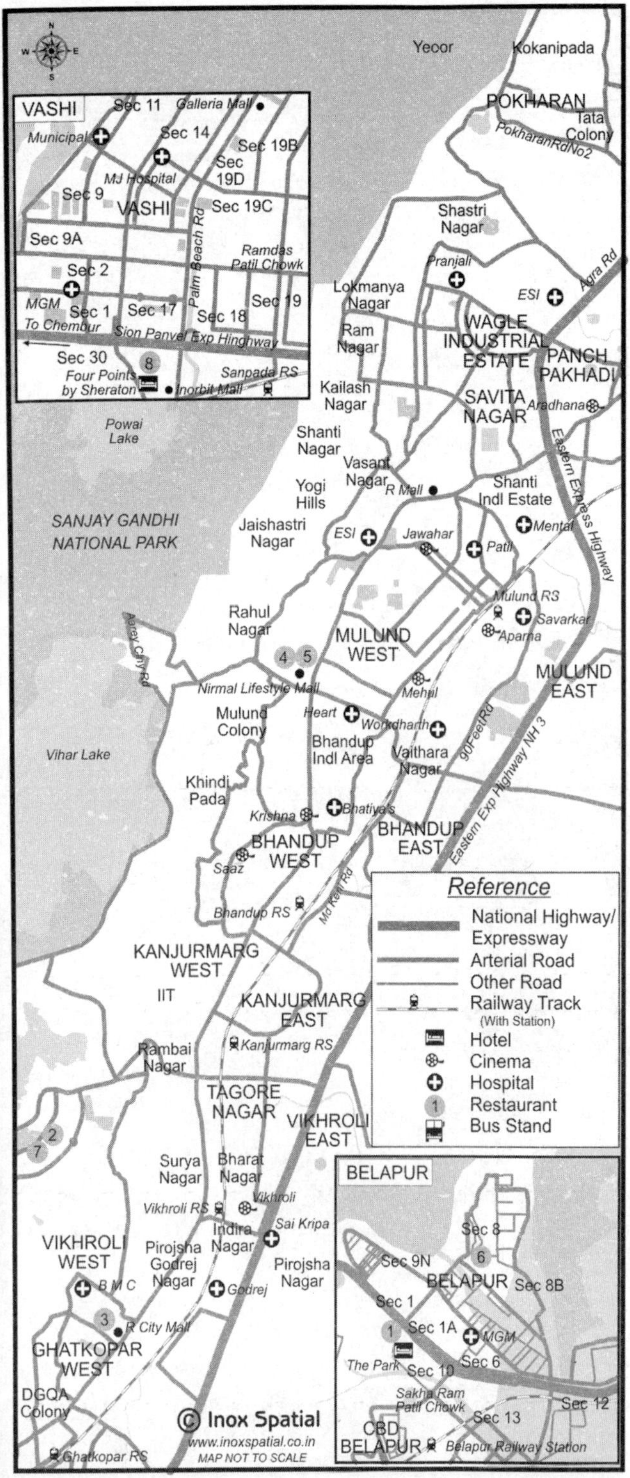
N
S
E
W
Yeoor
Kokanipada
POKHARAN
Tata Colony
PokharanRdNo2
Shastri Nagar
Pranjali
ESI
Agra Rd
Lokmanya Nagar
Ram Nagar
WAGLE INDUSTRIAL ESTATE
PANCH PAKHADI
Kailash Nagar
SAVITA NAGAR
Aradhana
Eastern Express Highway
Shanti Nagar
Vasant Nagar
R Mall
Shanti Indl Estate
Yogi Hills
Jaishastri Nagar
ESI
Jawahar
Patil
Mental
Powai Lake
SANJAY GANDHI NATIONAL PARK
Aarey Chy Rd
Rahul Nagar
MULUND WEST
Mulund RS
Savarkar
Aparna
Nirmal Lifestyle Mall
Mehul
MULUND EAST
Mulund Colony
Heart
Workdharth
Bhandup Indl Area
Vaithara Nagar
90FeetRd
Eastern Exp Highway NH 3
Vihar Lake
Khindi Pada
Krishna
Bhatiya's
BHANDUP WEST
BHANDUP EAST
Saaz
Bhandup RS
Md Kerji Rd
KANJURMARG WEST
IIT
KANJURMARG EAST
Rambai Nagar
Kanjurmarg RS
TAGORE NAGAR
VIKHROLI EAST
Surya Nagar
Bharat Nagar
Vikhroli RS
Vikhroli
Indira Nagar
Sai Kripa
VIKHROLI WEST
Pirojsha Godrej Nagar
Pirojsha Nagar
BMC
Godrej
R City Mall
GHATKOPAR WEST
DGQA Colony
Ghatkopar RS
© Inox Spatial
www.inoxspatial.co.in
MAP NOT TO SCALE
VASHI
Sec 11
Galleria Mall
Municipal
Sec 14
Sec 19B
Sec 19D
MJ Hospital
Sec 9
VASHI
Sec 19C
Palm Beach Rd
Sec 9A
Ramdas Patil Chowk
Sec 2
MGM
Sec 1
Sec 17
Sec 18
Sec 19
To Chembur
Sion Panvel Exp Hinghway
Sec 30
Four Points by Sheraton
Inorbit Mall
Sanpada RS
Reference
National Highway/ Expressway
Arterial Road
Other Road
Railway Track (With Station)
Hotel
Cinema
Hospital
Restaurant
Bus Stand
BELAPUR
Sec 8
Sec 9N
BELAPUR
Sec 8B
Sec 1
Sec 1A
MGM
The Park
Sec 10
Sec 6
Sakha Ram Patil Chowk
Sec 12
Sec 13
CBD BELAPUR
Belapur Railway Station